PENGUIN BOOKS
THE RSS AND THE MAKING OF A DEEP NATION

Dinesh Narayanan is an award-winning journalist based in Delhi. He co-founded and headed the innovative and popular business and tech newsletter The Signal. Previously, he has worked with India's leading publications, including *Economic Times*, *Times of India* and *Hindu Business Line*. He was part of the founding leadership team of *Forbes India* magazine and was its Delhi bureau chief. He cut his teeth as a business journalist reporting on financial markets and gradually shifted to writing on the political economy and occasionally on pure politics. He is deeply interested in understanding the interplay of politics, society and business, and the impact of these on our lives, both as individuals and collectively as a nation.

PRAISE FOR THE BOOK

'The author, Dinesh Narayanan, has written a clear, calm and non-judgemental account of RSS today. It is by far the best book I have read so far on the RSS'—*Hindu Business Line*

'Dinesh Narayanan offers a commendable and well-researched monograph with deep insight, objectivity, clarity and lucidity'—*Open*

'Dinesh Narayanan's *The RSS and the Making of the Deep Nation* steers clear of predictable courses. Not in a hurry to dismiss, eulogise or vilify the RSS, this book captures various facets of the Sangh' —*The Hindu*

'The book offers a dense political canvas, packed with interesting and useful information, intriguing anecdotes, life histories and narratives of critical events, all told captivatingly'—*India Today*

THE
RSS
AND THE MAKING OF
THE DEEP NATION

DINESH
NARAYANAN

PENGUIN BOOKS

An imprint of Penguin Random House

PENGUIN BOOKS

USA | Canada | UK | Ireland | Australia
New Zealand | India | South Africa | China | Singapore

Penguin Books is an imprint of the Penguin Random House group of companies
whose addresses can be found at global.penguinrandomhouse.com

Published by Penguin Random House India Pvt. Ltd
4th Floor, Capital Tower 1, MG Road,
Gurugram 122 002, Haryana, India

First published in Viking by Penguin Random House India 2020
This edition published in Penguin Books 2025

ISBN 9780143474517

Typeset in Adobe Garamond Pro by Manipal Technologies Limited, Manipal

Printed at Repro India Limited

www.penguin.co.in

This is a legitimate digitally printed version of the book and therefore might not
have certain extra finishing on the cover.

To my parents, Narayanan Nair and Krishna,
who, despite their trepidations, always let me be.

Contents

Preface

This book first saw light on 23 March 2020, the day India went into a national lockdown. For the next couple of years, people either stayed indoors or went about stealthily, their masked faces hiding the fear of contact with fellow humans as a virus—unknown to the human body until then, and hence called the novel coronavirus—swept across the world, killing people at will.

Long-established social, economic and political customs and linkages were shattered. It looked like the world would never be the same again. Yet, within four years, it was business as usual. Wars were started and continue to be fought. India's northernmost border too got mired in its worst conflict in decades.

The year 2024 was a landmark one for democracy globally as more than half of the world's population voted to retain or change the regimes they were living in. India too tested the will of nearly a billion of its citizens. A Bharatiya Janata Party (BJP) government led by Prime Minister Narendra Modi had been in power for a decade. It returned in 2019 with the most popular mandate ever received by a political party since the Indian National Congress's record-breaking show in 1984. Yet, a large part of those five years was spent in the shadow of the pandemic. It was peak power for the BJP and, by extension, the Rashtriya Swayamsevak Sangh (RSS), its ideological parent and mentor. The political arm, the BJP, is arguably the RSS's most successful project, turbo-charged in the late noughties on the belief that not only was electoral legitimacy essential for the Sangh Parivar's unhindered functioning and expansion but the Hindu Rashtra of its imagination was unattainable without power.

The RSS has largely crossed out items on its short-term agenda—the Ram Temple is up, Article 370 is gone, the education policy is now tailored as per its wishes, a new penal code is in place and a uniform civil code has been passed in at least one state. The champion of Hindutva even reports *Ghar Wapsi* numbers or the number of those who converted to Hinduism from other faiths, largely Islam, in its annual report.[*] Government officials are now free to come out in the open if they are *swayamsevaks*. A ban had until now ensured that their RSS affiliation remained secret, albeit an open one as hundreds of government officials were actively involved with the Sangh anyway. That includes the judiciary. A Calcutta High Court judge revealed his lifelong association with the RSS in his retirement speech.[†]

Metaphorically, the RSS's expansion and transformation in the Modi years is perhaps best captured by its New Delhi headquarters, Keshav Kunj. The ageing complex built in the 1960s has been replaced by twin towers, each a dozen-storey high and equipped with modern facilities, including meeting rooms, conference halls, library and living quarters. The chief himself has his office and living space near the top.

The BJP's march hit a speed bump in the 2024 Lok Sabha elections when it fell woefully short of its target of 400-plus seats. It

---

[*] 'ABPS - Annual Report 2023-24', Rashtriya Swayamsevak Sangh, 15 March 2024, available at https://www.rss.org/Encyc/2024/3/15/ABPS-Annual-Report-2023-24.html, accessed on 29 October 2024.

[†] Atri Mitra, 'At his farewell, Calcutta HC Judge Chitta Ranjan Dash says he's RSS member, ready to go back', *Indian Express*, 21 May 2024, available at https://indianexpress.com/article/cities/kolkata/at-his-farewell-calcutta-hc-judge-says-hes-rss-member-ready-to-go-back-9341512/, accessed on 29 October 2024.

won a mere 240 seats, down 63 from its 2019 tally. Rival Congress and its regional allies campaigned on the plank that the next RSS agenda was to change the Constitution and deprive sections of the citizenry of their rights and privileges. The BJP's high-octane campaign, where Prime Minister Modi hinted that he was working with divine authority, did not go down well even with the Sangh. To top it off, BJP chief J.P. Nadda also told an interviewer that the party did not need the Sangh's services any more: 'The party has grown and everyone has got their own duties and roles. RSS is a cultural and social organization and we are a political organisation . . . It's not the question of need. It's an ideological front. *Woh ideologically apna kaam karte hain, hum apna*. We are managing our affairs in our own way. And that's what political parties should do.'[*]

It was the culmination of a series of mini-clashes, far away from the public eye, over multiple issues, including economic, environmental and new educational policies. There was also friction over the influence and political relevance of leaders considered personae non gratae by Modi. RSS programmes supported by ministries were cancelled and ministers were instructed that PMO's wishes, not Sangh requests, were priority.[†]

Although the false notes sounded loud in public, it did not slow the Sangh Parivar's ideological spread or work. Not only did it not have much impact, fear of loss of power compelled the two to work together once again in state elections. Strained ties have been mending as no one wants a repeat of 2004 when the Atal Bihari Vajpayee government lost power and the relations between the BJP and RSS hit their nadir.

---

[*] Liz Mathew, 'Nadda on BJP-RSS ties: We have grown, more capable now... the BJP runs itself', *Indian Express*, 22 May 2024, available at https://indianexpress.com/article/political-pulse/nadda-on-bjp-rss-ties-we-have-grown-more-capable-now-the-bjp-runs-itself-9336205/, accessed on 29 October 2024.
[†] The author's conversations with RSS and BJP sources who preferred to remain anonymous.

Unlike Vajpayee, one of Narendra Modi's electoral achievements is that he has managed to make economic hardship less relevant in polls. It is now almost like a corollary to religious polarization. Economic issues such as inflation, wages and equity were the political issues on which communists and socialists built their paradise. The Sangh Parivar had tried to balance economic issues with Hindutva in the 1990s. While V.P. Singh's Mandal politics blunted the sharpening edge of mandir politics, the Parivar evaded irrelevance by joining hands with the communists in opposing multinational corporations and computerization.

Modi, however, hewed another way. One that blended easily with conservative politics all over the world. A free-market-opposing right-wing party is almost an oxymoron. In doing so, he did not toe the Sangh line but dragged the organization on the path he was making. Modi has built a new politico-economic edifice; muscular, personality-oriented, business-friendly and state-supported.

It has led to deep economic polarization and inequality, which is also the case globally. It is not lost on the RSS. In private, many senior RSS leaders say this is fundamentally against what the organization has professed for years. In many ways, Prime Minister Modi is an antithesis to RSS's economic ideology and life philosophy, but in other ways, he is also the ideal swayamsevak, with his feet firmly planted in hardball Hindutva politics.

The first sign of a thaw in relations was Modi acknowledging his ideological roots in a post on X (formerly Twitter), paying compliments to the RSS for its centenary year.[*] Modi also supplied a link to a YouTube video of RSS chief Mohan Bhagwat delivering his customary speech on Vijayadashami, the organization's founding day.

---

[*] 'राष्ट्र सेवा में समर्पित . . .', X (formerly Twitter), available at https://x.com/narendramodi/status/1845049370418479617, accessed on 29 October 2024.

The Vijayadashami speech belied speculation of hidden barbs. In speeches and signed articles after the election, Sangh leaders, including Bhagwat had taken potshots at the government and Modi. That did not happen, however. Bhagwat said he usually delves into the challenges and problems in as much detail as possible in his annual presentation but was limiting himself to only a few this year. That was the result of the coordination meetings of various Sangh arms held in Palakkad earlier.

Bhagwat's speech resonated with the Palakkad discussions on subjects such as border security, southern states and education. The RSS leadership acknowledges that a BJP-led government offers the best opportunities to deepen Hindu nationalism but not necessarily 'swadeshi'. One topic that was discussed extensively but found only a passing mention was agriculture. It believes the policies are not rooted in Indian traditions and local farming community's ethos.

The Sangh sees current economic policies of the government as appeasing corporate, Indian and foreign, interests. In an interview to *The Economist*, foreign minister, Subramanyam Jaishankar, articulated the future of India from the government's point of view: 'So imagine an India with much stronger human resources, with a much better infrastructure, with a much easier, friendlier business club, which has arrangements with a lot of major economies which make possible easier flows and greater confluence. It would be a very different India.'*

There is one section of the RSS that is not at all comfortable with this view. That is largely the old guard, steeped in tradition and community. But there is the larger, younger cohort which is very much in tune with Modi and what it sees as India's image-building in the world.

---

* 'In conversation with Subrahmanyam Jaishankar', *The Economist*, 15 July 2023, available at https://www.economist.com/asia/2023/06/15/in-conversation-with-subrahmanyam-jaishankar, accessed on 29 October 2024.

A Sangh old-timer says: 'The ambition of young *pracharak*s (propagandists) coming out of the RSS system today is not to become Mohan Bhagwat. Their idol is Narendra Modi.'*

Presenting the organization's annual report for 2023–24 to delegates of the Akhil Bharatiya Pratinidhi Sabha, Sangh general secretary Dattatreya Hosabale said, 'Bharat, Hindutva and Sangh are the manifestations of the national selfhood. Tarnishing them amounts to damaging this national self; strengthening them means promoting the national self.'† It is an open statement that, from the Sangh's point of view, there is room for only one idea of India and that is its own. And it will do everything in its power to achieve it.

It has already shown in the Haryana and Maharashtra state elections that the setback in the Lok Sabha elections was temporary. The RSS worked hard‡ in the polls to make sure that BJP candidates romped home. In its centenary year, the organization will shift gears, spreading and deepening its ideological dominance.

Quoting the nationalist monk Vivekananda, RSS's chief of publicity Sunil Ambekar says that there are three stages necessary for the future of India, 'The whole secret lies in organisation, accumulation of power and coordination of will. In the Sangh's life, the first two stages are already true. We are in the third stage and the Sangh is working on the coordination of wills.'§

25 November 2024

---

* Told to the author on condition of anonymity.
† 'ABPS - Annual Report 2023-24', Rashtriya Swayamsevak Sangh, 15 March 2024, available at https://www.rss.org/Encyc/2024/3/15/ABPS-Annual-Report-2023-24.html, accessed on 29 October 2024.
‡ Madhuparna Das, 'Sangh Strategist Who Manoeuvred Mahayuti's Maharashtra Sweep: Meet Atul Limaye', News18, 24 November 2024, available at https://www.news18.com/elections/sangh-strategist-who-manoeuvred-mahayutis-maharashtra-sweep-meet-atul-limaye-9132009.html, accessed on 26 November 2024.
§ Sunil Ambekar, *The RSS: Roadmaps for the 21st Century* (New Delhi: Rupa Publications, 2019), p. 130.

Introduction

On 22 December 2013, Mumbai's historic August Kranti Maidan was packed with thousands of people who had come to listen to a man who had acquired the halo of a political messiah. Hope held sway as for nearly an hour, the man, Gujarat chief minister Narendra Modi, held them in thrall of his oratorical performance.

'Friends, Mumbai is that same land from where in the independence movement, a voice echoed from August Kranti Maidan, an appeal was made: Quit India! That appeal became a mantra in the entire nation and in the end Britishers had to leave India. The voice that started from this land of Mumbai, the mantra of Quit India brought independence to India. Friends, from the same land of Mumbai, once again a cry shall start . . . Congress free India! The land which gave the slogan of Quit India, the same land roars . . . Congress free India!' Modi, who would be prime minister of India five months later, thundered.[1]

Six years after that speech, on 19 December 2019, the vast grounds filled up again. This time it was brimming with rage. Protesters held up signs berating Prime Minister Modi and his deputy Amit Shah for a law that seemed to drive a wedge into the social edifice of the country. The accumulated disappointment of a slowing economy, disappearing jobs and rising social tension had created a pressure cooker that burst open when the Citizenship (Amendment) Bill, 2019, was passed in both houses of Parliament. The law sought to fast-track citizenship for Hindus, Sikhs, Christians, Buddhists, Parsis and Jains were they to face religious persecution in Pakistan, Afghanistan and Bangladesh and seek asylum in India. It, however, omitted Muslims. Shah claimed in Parliament that Muslims cannot face religious persecution in the Islamic states of Pakistan and Afghanistan and the Muslim-majority Bangladesh and hence could not be given refuge in India.

The law by itself, though discriminatory, was not why people were agitated. The home minister had earlier said that the government would also conduct a nationwide survey to prepare a National Register of Citizens (NRC) to identify and segregate illegal immigrants. The new law engendered widespread panic that, in conjunction with the NRC, it could create second-class citizens who might even be sent to detention camps.

Those gathered in Mumbai on the cold December evening were protesting this turn of events. The Mumbai gathering was not the first. The sparks had ignited in Jamia Millia Islamia University in Delhi where students began demonstrating against the government move. It quickly spread to other universities across the country. Soon civil society and even film stars and businessmen joined in even as the home minister, Shah, ordered police to deal firmly with protestors.

The move was perceived to be an integral piece of the grand strategy of the Rashtriya Swayamsevak Sangh (RSS), the parent organization of the Bharatiya Janata Party (BJP) of Modi and Shah, to create a Hindu Rashtra in which Hindus would have primacy. The RSS believes governments had followed a policy of appeasement of Muslims at the cost of Hindus for electoral gains. Modi has often referred[2] to the Central governments until 2014 as Delhi Sultanate, a reference hinting that they were mere extensions of Muslim rulers who established themselves in India in the early thirteenth century. With him occupying the most powerful office in the country, the

Hindu nationalist organization hopes to be able to pursue its agenda without hindrance.

Modi and Shah had kept the faith.

A set of three demands has been the core political objective of the RSS for decades: scrapping Article 370, introducing a Uniform Civil Code (UCC) and building a temple for Lord Ram in Ayodhya.

On 5 August 2019, Home Minister Shah, known as a shrewd strategist, moved a resolution in Parliament to eviscerate Article 370 of the Constitution of India, which gave the Muslim-majority state of Jammu and Kashmir a special status, and bifurcate the state into two Union territories (UTs) of Jammu and Kashmir and Ladakh.[3] Following Parliament approval, President Ram Nath Kovind abrogated provisions of the Article on 7 August.[4] Article 370 was perceived to be a challenge to the territorial integrity of the country and its removal signifies that the political geography of the state is firmly tethered to Delhi.

Criminalization of triple talaq[5] is a step closer to a UCC, the introduction of which would mean cultural consolidation and homogeneous citizenship. The Supreme Court verdict in the Ram Janmabhoomi case greatly legitimized the Hindu Rashtra project, ending a dispute whose origins were, according to the court, 'as old as the idea of India itself'. The judges handed over the site of the erstwhile Babri mosque in Ayodhya to the Hindus, paving the way for a temple to Lord Ram there.[6] The decision, despite acknowledging that the demolition of the Babri mosque was an 'egregious violation of the rule of law', shows an increasing institutionalization of primacy for the majority community's interests. The court, as a consolation for the 'wrong committed', directed the government to give Muslims a five-acre plot elsewhere.

At an informal gathering the next day at the RSS headquarters in Nagpur a top leader said the addendum to the court order was like a *boudhik* or intellectual discourse in RSS camps. The addendum was an unsigned 116-page effort by one of the judges to establish the validity of the Hindu faith and belief that Lord Ram was born where the mosque stood. The land was given to Hindu litigants on the strength of this faith.

The Sangh Parivar had for years determinedly campaigned to establish Ram as the numero uno national hero. With the verdict coming on his watch as prime minister, Modi perhaps redeemed the pledge to the Hindu nation he took every time he stood at attention, right hand held rigidly across the chest, palm facing down in salute to the saffron flag.

The inception of the Hindu nation of RSS's imagination, however, has begun to look like a costly affair.

*

It was the winter of 2007. Narendra Modi had just led the BJP to victory in the Gujarat state assembly elections for a second time, comprehensively trouncing the rival Indian National Congress (INC). The results, however, did not reveal how taut the polls were.

There was bickering within the party. BJP leader Gordhan Zadafia, the junior home minister in Modi's first state cabinet, had rebelled and floated a new outfit called the Mahagujarat Janata Party (MJP) ahead of the elections. The BJP's sister outfits not only kept away from campaigning, some leaders even worked against Modi. In the circumstances, the victory established Modi as the undisputed king in the state's political arena.

As the results came in, a close friend of Modi's heaved a sigh of relief. The friend, a corporate executive, wrote a long letter to Mohan Bhagwat, who was then *sarkaryavah*, or general secretary, of the RSS, the ideological parent of the BJP.

The letter, which was believed to have been copied to a few select leaders of the Sangh as well, despaired for the RSS's attitude towards Modi, then widely known as the Hindu *hriday samrat* (the Emperor of Hindu Hearts). He wrote that Modi was a true RSS *swayamsevak* (volunteer) who had gone through the rigours of organizational training and served it loyally for many years. It was unfortunate, he said, that they were treating him—the most popular leader of his state—with gratuitous disdain. He charged that they were deliberately ostracizing Modi and the approach broke every principle the Sangh stood for.[7]

The letter is said to have arrived at a time of great turmoil in the Sangh Parivar (the RSS family), as the conglomerate of about three dozen socio-political organizations built up by the Hindu nationalist champion RSS is popularly known. The RSS was struggling with shrinking membership and units. Its affiliates were pulling in different directions and the political arm, the BJP, was beset with infighting and intrigue. In a blistering television interview two years before, the RSS *sarsanghchalak*,[8] K.S. Sudarshan, had underplayed the role of BJP legends and former prime minister Atal Bihari Vajpayee and deputy prime minister L.K. Advani in nation-building. Sudarshan chose to lift the Congress party's Indira Gandhi to a pedestal, rating her as the best prime minister the country ever had.

At a public function in Gujarat, he reportedly snubbed Modi, who was seated in the front row. As Sudarshan walked past Modi to the dais, the chief minister stood up with folded hands, but the RSS chief walked on without a glance.[9]

Mohan Bhagwat read the executive's missive with concern. The letter hinted that the rift between the rising star of Hindutva and the RSS leadership was the creation of vested interests within the Sangh. Bhagwat immediately invited the executive to Nagpur for a detailed conversation. In a meeting that went on for hours, the executive further elaborated to Bhagwat how a few leaders within the Sangh and the BJP had created misunderstandings between the RSS top leadership and Modi. He said Modi was as true and committed a volunteer as the RSS could find, someone who had fully internalized its core values and ideology.

Bhagwat appeared moved. He had just received an invitation to launch a book written by Modi although he was undecided about attending. The chief minister wanted him to launch a collection of profiles of people who had influenced and inspired him. Starting with the second sarsanghchalak, M.S. Golwalkar, the book, *Jyotipunj*, included profiles of Modi's mentor Laxmanrao Inamdar, popularly known as Vakil Sahab, and Madhukarrao Bhagwat, Mohan Bhagwat's father. The RSS general secretary travelled to Ahmedabad to release the book,[10] the first function in a long time where Modi had shared the stage with a top RSS official.[11]

Years later, Bhagwat is said to have remarked to a friend that the corporate executive was partly responsible for Modi becoming prime minister of India. Eight decades after the RSS was founded, circumstances and people had come together to bring the levers of power that controlled the destiny of the country within its reach. The RSS believes that, with or without power, steering India's destiny is its founding mission. Bhagwat's statement to the friend was both an acknowledgement as well as an assertion. The statement acknowledged that Modi was the right man for the RSS at that point and he would have been lost because of misunderstandings. The assertion was that the RSS had become influential enough to make a prime minister. Key Modi aides too believe that his chances of becoming prime minister would have been significantly diminished without Bhagwat's and RSS's unstinted support.

*

Mohan Bhagwat and Narendra Modi were born a few days apart; the RSS leader on 11 September 1950, and the prime minister six days later. Both belong to the post-Independence generation of leaders unburdened by the struggle for Independence, the trauma of Partition and the forging of the modern Indian nation. These are historical memories retold to them by an organization born in the tumultuous first half of the twentieth century when the British Empire was just beginning to retreat and national value systems all over the world were being shaped by competing ideological thoughts. They were born when World War II was over, Europe was rebuilding and the icy winds of the Cold War were beginning to rustle.

Their coming together in the common project of recasting the socio-economic and political structure of the country is changing the course of Indian history, pulling it decisively away from liberal socialism and towards a rigid majoritarian nationalism. While Bhagwat brought the RSS's organizational acumen to help the BJP to power, Modi helped situate its nationalist narrative in a modern context of a powerful nation at ease with global currents. It helped that their narrative in some respects aligned with the new wave of fangs-bared nationalism and nativism sweeping across the world, including in the United States and Europe.

The RSS considers itself the committed agent of high Hindu thought that would ultimately baptize the world. 'The World State of our concept will evolve out of a federation of autonomous and self-contained nations under a common centre linking them . . . It is the grand world-unifying thought of Hindus alone that can supply the abiding basis for human brotherhood, that knowledge of the inner spirit which will charge the human mind with the sublime urge to toil for the happiness of mankind, while opening out full and free scope for every small life-specialty. Verily this is the one real practical world-mission if ever there was one,' said M.S. Golwalkar, who led the organization between 1940 and 1973.[12]

Keshav Baliram Hedgewar, a Maharashtrian Brahmin from Nagpur, founded the RSS on the day of Vijaya Dashami[13] in 1925. It was built on the unshakeable belief that India is a Hindu nation that belongs only to the Hindus. Anyone may become its citizen, but the Hindus have a civilizational claim on the geographical entity called India, or Bharat—the name preferred by the Sangh Parivar. The RSS staunchly believes in the cultural unity of not just India but also the subcontinent, including Afghanistan, Pakistan, Bangladesh and Myanmar. It also envisions this large geographical swathe extending from 'Gandhar' (Kandahar) to 'Brahmadesh' (Myanmar) coalescing into a single nation or Akhand Bharat at some point in the future, even if it is centuries from now.

The Sangh has two quests: the first is a Bismarckian dream of creating Akhand Bharat and the second is becoming Vishwa Guru, or world teacher. While Akhand Bharat is a near-impossible proposition from the present vantage, the other, the RSS believes, is within its grasp. That yoga is now accepted and practised across the world and the United Nations now celebrates 21 June as International Day of Yoga is seen as proof of the validity of Indian values and way of life and their global acceptance. As Golwalkar envisioned, the world state of RSS's dreams will evolve out of a federation of autonomous and self-contained nations linked under a common centre. The warp and weft of this global fabric would emerge from Hindu thought. The first step, however, is to convert all Indians to its ideology and build India into a muscular Hindu nation.

The RSS is organized like a military, and much of its ideological framework is derived from nineteenth-century European ideas of nationhood, filtering Indian history and culture through them by Hindu leaders such as Swami Vivekananda, Bal Gangadhar Tilak and V.D. Savarkar. It however rejects the notion of nation state and instead believes in a cultural nation separate from the state. In early RSS literature, some of which it has since discarded, the organization admiringly talks of Russian, German and Japanese nationalism.

The RSS's cultural high ground rests on the belief that India was a nation of advanced knowledge several millennia ago, capable of building sophisticated cities, conducting complex surgeries and unlocking the mysteries of the universe when the rest of the world was still chipping stones to make hunting spears. This advanced civilization, benign and thirsty only for knowledge, was laid to waste by waves of invasions by barbaric hordes that were interested in little more than its gold, land and women. These invasions were topped off by the British who colonized and injected it with a Western sensibility that not only shattered the Hindu nation but also crippled its ability for high thinking. The umbilical cord to the uber-Hindu nation of the past was on the verge of snapping by the time the

British were done with India, destroying its enterprise, discrediting its knowledge and afflicting its mind with cultural dementia. As the poet and philosopher Rabindranath Tagore wryly remarked, '. . . for all our miseries and shortcomings we hold responsible the historical surprises that burst upon us from outside'.[14]

The RSS took upon itself the mission to put together the broken shards, decolonize the Hindu mind, and make the imagined Hindu nation whole again. In resurrecting this nation of its dreams, it wants to unify the people under an umbrella of antediluvian thought, philosophical principles and way of life, while also instilling in them a controlled materialism and muscular nationalism. Social theorist Ashis Nandy described it 'a desperate attempt to capture, within one's own self and culture, traits seen as the reason for the West's success on the word stage'.[15]

Dilip Karambelkar, editor of the Sangh mouthpiece *Saptahik Vivek*, explains that there was no institutional structure in Hindu society required for nationalism to grow. It is fundamentally spiritual and could not develop material tendencies. Hedgewar wanted a materialistic Hindu society and helped create a modern organization resting on the pillars of tradition.[16]

The heart of this kind of response, Nandy says, is to 'decontaminate Hinduism of its folk elements, turn it into a classical Vedantic faith, and then give it additional teeth with the help of Western technology and secular statecraft. Hindus can then take on and ultimately defeat all their external and internal enemies, if necessary by liquidating all forms of ethnic plurality within Hinduism and India, thereby equalling Western Man as a new *ubermenschen*'.[17]

Hedgewar, who was deeply influenced by radical Congressman (and founder of the newspaper *Kesari*) Bal Gangadhar Tilak's ideas of religious and cultural revival, believed that only Hindus had a real stake in the Indian nation and focused his energies on consolidating them under an ideological umbrella of Hindu nationalism. Tilak, the author of *Gita Rahasya*, a commentary on the Bhagavadgita, was described by British journalist Valentine Chirol as the father of

Indian unrest.[18] At the time of the founding of the RSS, the rift between the Hindu and Muslim communities of India had grown wide and deep.

Indian nationalism as a response to colonial rule had largely congealed beneath the broad banner of the INC founded in 1885. But within three decades, other formations such as the Muslim League and the Hindu Mahasabha had also begun to assert themselves. Even though the wish for freedom from colonial yoke was common, each had distinct agendas such as the League's demand for a separate nation for Muslims.

The leaders of these political formations were mostly Western-educated elites and influenced by the socio-political events and ideological pulls and thrusts in European nations such as France, Germany, England and Italy. The seeds of the Pakistan movement were sown, for instance, when Sir Syed Ahmed Khan founded the Muhammadan Anglo-Oriental College, precursor to the Aligarh Muslim University (AMU), in 1877.[19] Maharashtrian politician B.S. Moonje, who led the Hindu Mahasabha from 1927 to 1937, was an admirer of Italian fascist leader Benito Mussolini. Moonje's successor in the Mahasabha and revolutionary Maharashtrian politician V.D. Savarkar, who wrote the first theoretical framework for Hindu nationalism, was deeply influenced by utilitarian theorist John Stuart Mill and Italian nationalist Giuseppe Mazzini. Marxist thought struck root when the Communist Party of India (CPI) was founded in Kanpur in the same year Hedgewar laid the foundation of the RSS.[20] Although many leaders of the INC, including Mahatma Gandhi, Jawaharlal Nehru, Sardar Patel and Subhas Chandra Bose, were Western educated, its nationalism and political strategy after Tilak's death in 1920 were largely shaped by Gandhi's ideas. Trained as a lawyer at University College, London, Gandhi's experiences, experiments and activism later as a brown-skinned lawyer in apartheid South Africa helped him develop the satyagraha method of political action. The new method would place Gandhi as one of the most creative and original political leaders of all time, and the

INC as a unique platform where even conflicting ideas and identities coexisted for a time.

It was in this milieu that the RSS started off as an unknown organization. Its founder Hedgewar would gather a few friends and kids and organize games and drills in the ruins of a mansion called Mohitewada. The necessity of a name emerged when it wanted to expand to other centres than the lone *shakha*[21]in Nagpur's Mahal. Among the names suggested were Doctor Hedgewar Sangh, Hindu Sangh, Maharashtra Sangh and the RSS. The name RSS was hotly contested. Many questioned that if Hedgewar wanted to unite Hindus, how could it be called *rashtriya* (nation). Hedgewar prevailed.

He conceived the Sangh as an independent organization that bowed to no human. It bows to a saffron flag symbolizing the Hindu nation. He presumably saw the benefit of remaining independent of political parties and creating a powerful organization with military discipline, an agile force ready to act on a single command.

Even after founding the RSS, Hedgewar continued to be on the Congress executive council of the Central Provinces. That took him to the Calcutta session of the party in 1928 where he met Subhas Chandra Bose and G.D. (Babarao) Savarkar, V.D. Savarkar's elder brother. Hedgewar was annoyed that Bose would not give up on Hindu–Muslim unity even though he tried to impress upon him that the idea was meaningless. This meeting, where he found himself more in agreement with Savarkar, brought the two Maharashtrians closer and they maintained a close relationship.[22]

Yet, Hedgewar kept RSS politically aloof from V.D. Savarkar's Hindu Mahasabha. Aligning with Savarkar politically would have positioned the RSS as a rival to the Congress, which was a more broad-based platform, and Hedgewar did not want to be antagonistic to the Congress of which he was a member.[23] In earlier years, Hedgewar had enlisted Savarkar to tour shakhas to speak to swayamsevaks about Hindutva. He also liberally sought another Hindu Mahasabha leader and mentor B.S. Moonje's network across the country to help in expanding the Sangh to distant regions such as Lahore and Karachi. He understood that an organization like the RSS could not exist in an ideological vacuum and Savarkar had the ideal larger-than-life image as well as the intellectual prowess to enable it. Hedgewar's biographer, N.H. Palkar, suggests that even though he had similar ideas about Hindu nationhood, 'the logical, lucid and firm exposition of Hindutva in that [Savarkar's] book must have strengthened Doctor's self-confidence. Doctor liked that book immensely and, in those days, and even later he started publicizing the book everywhere.'[24]

It is probable that Hedgewar, who was one of the first to lay his hands on Savarkar's manuscript which expounded Hindutva, started the Sangh on its basis.[25]

The manuscript had been smuggled from Ratnagiri Jail, where Savarkar was interned, to Hedgewar's close friend Vishwanathrao Kelkar in 1923. Hedgewar was also part of the group that started the daily *Swatantrya* under Kelkar's editorship. Published every day, except Mondays, the copy of *Swatantrya* published on 6 November 1924 advertised Savarkar's 'Echoes from the Andamans' on the front page and 'Hindutva' on the last page.[26] After Hedgewar's death in 1940, the baton passed on to Madhav Sadashiv Golwalkar, an ordained monk close to the Ramakrishna order. Hedgewar met him when he was teaching at Banaras Hindu University—the reason why he came to be known as Guruji (teacher).

The teacher was an unusual choice for a successor because he had been in the RSS only for a few years and was unlike other long-time swayamsevaks and Hedgewar's associates in manner and style. He was impatient, short-tempered and spiritually inclined. Weaned on Savarkar's ideas, the RSS had little to do with religion and rituals. Many of its leaders such as Madhukar Dattatreya Deoras were known to be atheists, but Golwalkar was a monk. He had a great advantage though; he was well read and was a forceful speaker in Hindi and English, a valuable asset when the Sangh was preparing to spread its activities to the north and south of the country.

Golwalkar's Sangh expanded rapidly but it grew apart from Savarkar's Hindu Mahasabha which started its own militant wing. At the time, Savarkar was trying to convince the British that the Mahasabha and not the Congress truly represented Indian interests. The RSS soon appeared in the government's cross hairs. In the run-up to the Quit India agitation called by the Congress, the government banned military-style uniforms, marches and training with weapons. Golwalkar kept the RSS away from the Quit India movement.

It was Golwalkar who first articulated the RSS's aspiration of nationhood and the significance of its name clearly. Highly influenced by G.D. Savarkar, Golwalkar proposed the definition of the Hindu Rashtra. His first book, *We or Our Nationhood Defined*, was later disowned by the RSS, but its ideas endured. Every word in the name was carefully chosen, Golwalkar explained. A group of Hindus, Parsis, Muslims, Christians and a few others living in India would not make it a nation. Golwalkar never wavered from the ideas and key definitions as outlined in that first book, though he and the Sangh dropped controversial observations. *We or Our Nationhood Defined* remained the Sangh's guiding document even after the RSS stopped publishing it. Ideologue Dattopant Thengadi and later sarsanghchalak Rajendra Singh have referred to it several times in their speeches, intellectual discourses called *boudhiks* and writings.

RSS rejected the European idea of nation state. 'The requirement for a nation is land. No nation can be conceived in air. The Jews were thrown out of their land by outsiders. They scattered and lived in different parts of the world. They protected their language, religion and books but their existence as a nation was no more. Some years ago, they re-entered their motherland and began reconstructing their life. Now they have the nation of Israel,' Golwalkar said.[27]

He argued that the primary building block of a nation was reverence. If one community reveres a land and another does not, the latter was not part of that nation. A nation was formed of a people who considered a land their mother and themselves its sons.

'The community of this people should have a common system of conduct, same dreams, history, tradition and heroes. Only then will it become a nation. These people should carry the same historical burdens and glory. They should consider other communities that gave them joy as friends and those that invaded them and gave them pain as enemies.'[28]

Golwalkar conceived the land of the Hindus as the subcontinent (similar to Savarkar's definition) stretching from the Himalayas in the north to the Indian Ocean in the south. 'History says that we had built a big empire. The flag of our religion had fluttered in many countries across the world.'[29] This empire later fragmented but the Hindus were a well-developed and efficient nation from ancient times. In this conception, the nation is not a ceaselessly growing organic entity. It is in the perfect and complete form, attained millennia ago. 'These days the word nation often leads to confusion and so, sometimes, we have to specify it as Hindu Rashtra. We have to establish that in this land Hindu means nation and nation means Hindu. That is why the Sangh is called the Rashtriya Swayamsevak Sangh.'[30]

Golwalkar scrupulously kept the Sangh away from agitations and took care to not upset the authorities in any way. His disinterest in politics prompted a large section, including the Bombay province sanghchalak, K.B. Limaye, to leave the organization. The Hindu Mahasabha under Savarkar drifted away from the RSS because of its aloofness and started its own militant wing called Ram Sena. Hedgewar and Moonje worked closely when they were in the Congress. Once Moonje left for the Hindu Mahasabha, differences arose.[31]

Savarkar's dislike for the RSS work grew so much that he commented: 'The epitaph on a Sangh swayamsevak will be: "He was born; he joined RSS; he died."'[32]

Both Hedgewar and Golwalkar perhaps correctly assessed that the Congress would remain the dominant and most broad-based political formation for some time and it would harm the RSS if it aligned with sectarian parties. The RSS saw a surge in membership closer to Independence as Hindus and Muslims became increasingly antagonistic over the demand for Pakistan.

Growing Hindu–Muslim clashes and riots during 1946–47 helped the Sangh almost accomplish what it had set out to do—enjoin the divided Hindu society into battle formation. The Partition of the country in 1947 had made many Hindus in the north of the country restless and reactionary and the RSS benefited from it immensely. Hundreds of its pracharaks fanned out across the country and within a couple of years the RSS was able to start numerous shakhas. Those who had joined the Sangh in large numbers, however, deserted it in 1948 after Jawaharlal Nehru's government banned it on suspicion of its involvement in the assassination of Mahatma Gandhi. The Sangh did not have enough time to 'digest' the hordes that had come to it which would have made it powerful and influential.[33]

British intelligence reports show that the RSS's strength increased quickly in the mid-1940s. A 1946 report called for regular monitoring of private armies, the biggest of which was considered to be the RSS. The all-India strength of the organization in 1941 was 37,362, which rose to 88,265 in 1944. In 1946, it stood at 100,402. The report quoted from a pamphlet distributed among RSS volunteers as saying 'dictatorship was described as the only suitable form of government for India'.[34]

After the ban in 1948, Golwalkar turned the Sangh into an even more introverted organization shunning publicity and making it almost monastic. Golwalkar, however, backed the creation of multiple organizations like a students' union, the Akhil Bharatiya Vidyarthi Parishad (ABVP) in 1948; a political party, the Bharatiya Jana Sangh in 1953; and a global council of Hindus, the Vishwa Hindu Parishad (VHP) in 1964, to spread its activities in conflict-ridden fields. It kept the RSS out of the limelight while the informal arrangements in this conglomerate structure helped it control a diverse set of activities without directly getting involved and staying below the government's radar.

By the time the third sarsanghchalak Madhukar Dattatreya Deoras, popularly known as Balasaheb, took over the reins, the RSS had lost a lot of ground. Though Golwalkar had managed to keep the organization legally unscathed, it was barely keeping its nose out of water. Financially, it was deep in debt due to the 1948 ban and court cases. It paid off its debts only by 1956.[35] Its volunteers were still not accepted in society and shakhas were run almost surreptitiously. Some in the Sangh consider this period as the lost years. Even while Golwalkar was heading the RSS, many of its key initiatives were believed to be the brainchild of Deoras.[36] Golwalkar and he are said to have had serious differences over the organization's development which even led to Deoras keeping away from the Sangh for nearly a decade.[37]

Hedgewar believed that India did not have an evolved Hindu leadership that could direct an independent nation and lead it to an imagined glory. The RSS would be the organization that would build a massive cohort trained in providing leadership in various fields. RSS men were to populate all walks of life, shaping future institutions—political, cultural, religious, social, industrial—in every area. These men were to measure every action against the touchstone of Hindu nationalism, rejecting, subverting, subjugating and, if necessary, destroying everything they suspected could harm the nation. While the core organization itself would remain aloof, people carrying its ideological DNA would go on to become politicians, farmers, teachers, professionals, artists, historians, scientists, soldiers and everything else one could conceive. They would embed themselves in all walks of life, forming something like an artificial neural network in the nation. Eventually, the entire country would respond to its neural stimuli.

The beginning of this total transformation starts at the Sangh shakha. Hedgewar had designed it to mould men of a certain character. The Sangh's daily routine would build an army of volunteers who would create *nitya-siddha shakti*, or innate capability, in Hindu society. If it developed such strength, it would deal with crises and problems on its own. When the shakha network spread to all corners of the country, it would begin a cultural renaissance.[38]

After he took over, Deoras quickly began deploying the Sangh's numerical strength and reach, strategically using it to back political movements and agitations. 'Deoras had seen that a political mind that was distinctly Hindu in character had emerged in the polity. His motto was: *seva* [service], *samrasta* [equitability], *sangharsh* [struggle].'[39]

At a press conference in Delhi in April 1978, Deoras said, 'Under Dr Hedgewar, Sangha [RSS] had a political orientation. Under Guruji the emphasis was on cultural regeneration. In the new situation it will have a new thrust. All our work will have a social content.'[40]

Deoras had seen that by focusing only on organization, the RSS was not really going anywhere. Most of its affiliate organizations were working like sundry others, unable to make any real ideological dent in society. The RSS was seen by people as a Hindu chauvinist organization which operated like a secret society. Deoras figured it was important to engage with communities in ways that was more neutral, secular, narrowly focused and beneficial in building influence. RSS also began encouraging sector-wise organizations such as a doctors' body, lawyers' forum and a consumer protection society. It now has thirty-six affiliate organizations most of which run autonomously. It also has over 1.6 lakh service projects, which range from small scholarship programmes for poor students to speciality hospitals to watershed projects.

While organizations like the Vidya Bharti focused on setting up a network of schools whose core values aligned with the RSS's, others such as the Vanvasi Kalyan Ashram spread through tribal areas, countering Christian missionary activity and organizing forest dwellers and indigenous tribes under the broad Hindu framework.

Yet other institutions such as Samkalp, an organization which helps civil services aspirants with coaching and even accommodation and travel, help populate the governing structure with its own people.

Deoras correctly assessed that with the development of a Hindu political mind, a service-oriented strategy coupled with its organizational strength could bring political dividends. Service projects were typically low-investment, diversified and required little supervision. If a project showed promise of scale, it could be supported at a later stage. If it was limited in scope and scale, it could still be run by the initiative of volunteers yet remain locally beneficial. The important aspect was community building through a network effect.

Political scientist Tariq Thachil's fieldwork has shown the political benefits of service projects. 'This ground-level activism and everyday contact could be converted to electoral returns by patiently earning voter goodwill rather than developing transactional relationships. Service providers converted this goodwill into electoral returns among beneficiaries and some non-beneficiaries through the networks of friends and associates they developed and through their own powers of rumour and suggestion as apolitical residents of high local standing.'[41]

Deoras believed that the Sangh had already lost a lot of time and it should exploit every opportunity to expand its work and reach. He wanted the organization to work relentlessly, whether the situations were favourable or not. Sometimes, the environment had to be changed or created by design.[42]

Political scientist Pralay Kanungo observes, '. . . a sovereign polity had emerged on the foundation of universal franchise and centralized rule had consolidated the national market. Communication network had expanded, and literacy rates had increased. These developments had brought the Indian masses from diverse regions and social backgrounds into direct contact and interdependence. These factors had created an objective situation for the recasting of an all-encompassing, pan-Indian identity. An alternative national definition was needed in such a changed socio-economic-political scenario and neither the Congress nor the left could provide such a definition. Deoras grasped this fluidity and uncertainty in the national political scene and saw the ideal opportunity for the RSS.'[43]

Deoras understood the importance of politics in expanding its influence. His dictum was: The Sangh will do everything; the Sangh will do nothing. Alternatively: The Sangh will do nothing but the swayamsevak will do everything. This seemingly puzzling method becomes plain on analysing the organization's objective—moulding the Indian society to the RSS ideal. The RSS did not want to be just another organization in society. It wanted the *entire* society to abide by its values.

It took decades for the RSS to gain acceptability as it struggled to dissociate itself from the assassination of Gandhi in the public eye. It was seen as a Brahmin supremacist organization that killed Gandhi and differences between Brahmins and non-Brahmins were stark in Maharashtra, the Sangh's home state.[44] This delayed its project by several decades and many trial-and-error experiments had to be done. After Golwalkar handed over charge to Deoras in a letter written from his deathbed in 1973, the RSS got a new direction, and politics and power became an integral part of its strategic planning. Unlike the earlier bottoms-up approach, the top-down strategy would require striking alliances and toning down the rhetoric.

It first found widespread acceptance during the Emergency of 1975–77—the darkest chapter in Indian democracy—which it would later use as a proxy to find legitimacy that eluded it during the freedom struggle. Its deep involvement in building up a campaign ground up to bring down the Indira Gandhi–led Congress government which had become notorious for bad administration and despotism was a demonstration of the role the RSS sees for itself: as a vigilante. It believed that Indira Gandhi's allies were stooges of the Soviet Union.

After the Congress party split in 1969, Gandhi had held on to power with the help of the CPI. The RSS was alarmed at the CPI entrenching itself in the establishment. On its own, the RSS was helpless and needed allies. As Deoras remarked, the Sangh did not have enough strength of its own. While it stayed in the background, organizing and mobilizing, it shrewdly relied on ageing Gandhian Jayaprakash Narayan to spearhead the agitation.

The spectacular success of the anti-Emergency agitation and the consequent formation of the first, though short-lived, non-Congress government of independent India, however, demonstrated that agitational politics could be rewarding for organizational growth. There were valuable learnings. Its student arm, the ABVP, the principal agitational instrument in the early 1970s, had 1.7 lakh students and teachers in 1977. The membership grew to 2.5 lakh in the next five years. The number of shakhas jumped from 10,000 in 1977 to 13,000 in 1979 and the number of swayamsevaks crossed one million.[45]

The RSS maintained good relations with many Congress leaders. It coveted the party because of its broad base, support and representation from all sections and regions of the country, and constantly strived for an ideological control over it. Unfortunately for it, Jawaharlal Nehru's stature and influence kept the party tilted leftward. There were unconfirmed reports that the RSS entered into talks with Congress leaders for a role in the party immediately after Nehru's death. Golwalkar reportedly met with then prime minister, Lal Bahadur Shastri, home minister, Gulzarilal Nanda, education minister, M.C. Chagla and foreign minister, Swaran Singh, and suggested that RSS men be given official responsibility in the Congress.[46] In fact, Indian politics of the three decades after Nehru's death appears to be significantly influenced by the RSS's attempts to loosen the left's ideological grip on the Congress party. During most of that period the left had the upper hand and the RSS constantly tried to wrest away its influence on the party.

Despite efforts, it could not deeply tap the Hindu political consciousness until the 1980s when it began an aggressive mobilization using the VHP. India was still an agrarian country and its politics revolved largely around villages and farmers, especially in north India where caste and community considerations surpassed everything else. Its expansion in the region was largely among the

Hindu refugees from Pakistan and members of the Arya Samaj with which it had close ties.

The RSS still had not made inroads to the hinterland and was limited to urban centres, mainly in the trading community which was then seen as exploitative by the lower classes. The upper caste, feudal Thakurs who wielded tremendous influence in large states like Uttar Pradesh and Bihar, looked down upon the *bania* (trading community) as effeminate and lacking courage. They did not care much for the RSS either; as erstwhile rulers of tiny fiefdoms they considered themselves the real protectors of the Hindus. Individual pracharaks such as Chandikadas Amritrao 'Nana' Deshmukh, Murlidhar Dattatreya 'Bhaurao' Deoras and Moropant Pingle, however, had cultivated good relationships with powerful leaders of the community. Credit for A.B. Vajpayee's victory in his first Lok Sabha election from Balrampur in 1957, in fact, goes to the relationships Deshmukh and Deoras had cultivated among the Thakur community of Uttar Pradesh.

Vajpayee had also contested from Mathura where he lost to the Jat king, Raja Mahendra Pratap Singh, a Gandhian and a Nobel Peace Prize nominee of 1932.[47] The Raja and Maulvi Barkatullah, who was part of the Ghadar Party, had also set up a provisional government of India in Afghanistan in 1915.[48]

Ironically, in 2014, the BJP wanted to hold an event on the Raja's birthday at AMU which was opposed by the then vice chancellor Lieutenant General Zameer Uddin Shah. The Raja was an alumnus of AMU's predecessor the Mohammedan Anglo-Oriental College and the editor of *World Federation* magazine.[49]

In the 1960s and '70s, in Uttar Pradesh, the RSS's efforts to promote diversity within its own organization came a cropper because of caste consciousness. Upper-caste men were loath to take directions from lower-caste pracharaks.[50] Consolidating this divided Hindu society of north India was a humungous task to say the least. An incident in the southern state of Tamil Nadu would present the RSS with a golden opportunity.

In early 1981, newspapers reported that almost an entire village of mostly Dalits in Meenakshipuram converted to Islam. Interestingly, a few months before the incident, the RSS had begun restructuring the VHP. It had moved the then Delhi prant pracharak, Ashok Singhal, who would go on to lead the VHP into the militant force it later became, to the organization.

The conversion set off alarm bells across India. If the RSS saw in Indira Gandhi's early years in power communism's tightening grip on Delhi, it viewed Meenakshipuram as the spectre of an Islamizing India. Hindu–Muslim riots had been occurring frequently in Uttar Pradesh, Bihar, Rajasthan and Gujarat, states where memories of the Partition lingered among the thousands who had migrated from Pakistan. The RSS needed a symbol, something potent and with a national resonance, to rally Hindus around.

It found it in Ayodhya, the birthplace of Lord Ram, the hero of Ramayana, an epic told and retold in practically every Hindu, and often non-Hindu, household from Kashmir to Kanyakumari. The 1980s became a period of a meticulously planned agitation to mobilize the divided Hindu community around Lord Ram, reinventing the mythological king into a symbol of Hindu nationalism. Building a temple at his birthplace where a mosque stood became a project to reclaim the Hindu nation's surrendered mojo.

Meanwhile, in 1989, the Berlin Wall, the forbidding symbol of the iron curtain that divided the world into two ideological poles led by the Soviet Union and the United States, was torn down. In 1990, a coalition of Western powers led by the United States launched a war on Iraq, plunging the region into instability and triggering a volatile future for the world. In 1991, the Soviet Union collapsed, marking the beginning of the end of Russian-style communism that had half the world, including India, in its thrall. The collapse of the Soviet Union created a unipolar world with the US as the unchallenged superpower.

Its political and military power combined with the hegemonic influence of the American dollar on the globe helped create an economic order tailored for big capital and multinational corporations. Around the same time, India, long influenced by socialism, would launch itself into the vortex of global markets.

The years 1990–1992 were defining for independent India when the socio-economic and political landscape of the country was irrevocably changed.

The Ayodhya movement succeeded in consolidating Hindus, but in 1990, the V.P. Singh government introduced quotas for backward communities in government jobs and education. The wily Thakur from Uttar Pradesh's Manda opened a Pandora's box hoping to carve out a backward castes' vote bank for himself on the social justice plank.

The next year, the Narasimha Rao government launched economic reforms, junking the Nehruvian socialist model of development for market-led capitalism. The very next year, a rampaging mob brought down the Babri Masjid, which had been transformed into the symbol of oppression and humiliation for the proponents of Hindutva. While V.P. Singh's initiative and the demolition of the Babri Masjid unleashed forces that created deep fissures in the socio-political edifice, the economic reforms of 1991 sucked somnolent Indians into the 'reality distortion field'[51] of global capitalism in an interconnected world.

The economic reforms brought mixed rewards for the Sangh Parivar. Market freedom empowered and enriched thousands of businessmen, entrepreneurs and professionals, the traditional supporters of the Sangh and its political arm. Reforms also increased urbanization, and improved infrastructure and modern means of communication brought people closer faster. The world had shrunk, and ideas spread faster. As mobility increased, traditional structures such as joint families and village communities broke down. A sense of contentment that had prevailed gave way to new ambition and consumerist aspirations as cable television beamed the glitter and verve of big city life into homes in small cities and rural areas.

It was both an opportunity and a threat as urbanization dissolved long-standing identities (ideal to promote a single national identity) and the individual instead of communities was at centre stage. The RSS, caught unawares, drifted clueless. It saw globalization as dangerous and insidious and multinational corporations as the new colonialists. And the opposition space here was occupied by the left. Opportunistically, the Sangh Parivar joined the battle in partnership with the left.

It was a challenge and opportunity for both the political right and left as discontent and inequality grew preparing fertile grounds for recruitment and indoctrination. The left, which was far more politically entrenched than the right, harvested the early benefits of the initial backlash as its powerful unions and canny leaders converted discontent into political power. But as the markets and big business gradually tightened their grip on policymaking and political institutions, the left's influence declined. Trade unions which often dictated terms to the government were gradually sidelined.

In the first half of the 1980s, the RSS had left the BJP adrift, focusing on the VHP and the Ram Janmabhoomi movement. It was only in the late 1980s that it realigned the BJP, persuading the political outfit to junk its Gandhian socialism for Deendayal Upadhyaya's integral humanism and return to the Parivar furrow. Politically, it was rewarding for the BJP.

The Ram Janmabhoomi movement propelled the first BJP government to power and an RSS swayamsevak, Atal Bihari Vajpayee, became prime minister, the highest executive of the land. The Vajpayee government picked up where the Narasimha Rao government had left off and the RSS behaved as if it was still in opposition. It was a curious situation where the RSS opposed several aspects of the economic policy of the government, and in a sense seemed more aligned to the left than to a government of its own.

While it was jubilant that its own government was in the driving seat, it made a crucial mistake. It tried to reshape the state in its own image. When that did not work, it charged that the state had gone rogue. Vajpayee and his men were behaving less like swayamsevaks and more like 'Congressmen'; allowing multinational corporations a free run, selling state silver to big businesses and keeping the Hindu nationalist agenda—building a temple for Lord Ram in Ayodhya, abolishing Article 370 and introducing a uniform civil code—in cold storage. Worst of all, when four RSS men were kidnapped from Tripura, the government run by its volunteers sat helpless. It acted like a *napunsak* (eunuch),[52] the worst that could happen to an organization that was supposedly producing men of steel.

The RSS was not the only one unhappy with the Vajpayee government. Voters were too. The BJP was defeated in the 2004 elections. The Congress party was re-elected and held on to power for the next decade during most of which the RSS drifted and even suffered the pangs of a shrinking membership and reach. Towards the end of the decade, the organization's very existence was under threat.

The United Progressive Alliance (UPA) government led by the Congress had allegedly discovered organizational links between the RSS and a series of bomb attacks across the country that had killed and injured hundreds of people, mainly Muslims. Infamously classified as Saffron Terror, the Sangh was smack in the middle of investigating agencies' cross hairs. News reports in 2011 suggested its senior leader, Indresh Kumar, could be arrested.[53] Some pracharaks had already been picked up by the police.[54] Sangh leaders believed the government had hatched a plan to implicate even its chief and ban the organization itself. It had to strike back. And it needed a suitable man.

*

The man who would come to the rescue had begun his preparation a long time ago. He was an unusual swayamsevak, one who would both defy and mollify the RSS.

A decade after the Narasimha Rao government decisively reset India's course from socialism to market capitalism, and nearly the same time after the demolition of Babri Masjid, Narendra Modi took charge as chief minister of the western state of Gujarat, famous for its enterprising community of traders, businessmen and industrialists. Over the next fourteen years, Modi, the consummate swayamsevak, emerged as someone who could seamlessly merge business and Hindu cultural supremacy, a formula that had eluded the Parivar.

Modi was not well liked or accepted by RSS leaders and many pracharaks, the real backbone of the organization. They thought he was too independent and individualistic. His unabashed self-promotion was a strict no-no in the RSS which strongly discourages personality cults. But he was adored by its cadres. Modi, like Vajpayee, had an independent mind. However, unlike the poet politician, he was a quintessential swayamsevak. He was every bit a Hindu nationalist and he was willing to work with the RSS if it followed his lead. The Sangh Parivar's quest for the ideal leader ended with him. His rise to the most powerful office in the country was carefully planned and meticulously executed by the RSS. Once the man it wanted was in office, the RSS shifted gears to execute the next stage of its plan: rapidly expand the organization to every nook and corner and wrest control of institutions. Political power would be the agent of change for the RSS as it nears its centenary.

However, it is still not smooth sailing. Several Parivar organizations are at loggerheads with the Modi government. They believe that the Modi government's economic policies fundamentally diverge from the RSS ideals. Other hard-line Hindutva organizations have used the opportunity to use radical tactics against opponents. For instance, Prime Minister Modi had to call out cow vigilantes saying many had made cow protection (a core agenda of the RSS) a business. The RSS had to ensure that VHP's Pravin Togadia, a Modi baiter, was forced out of the organization. Often, the RSS has had to mediate between its organizations to shield Modi from protests and opposition. The opposition has also stepped up its attacks. While some call it a fascist organization, others, like Congress leader Rahul

Gandhi, have likened it to radical Islamic outfits such as the Muslim Brotherhood.

Stung by the growing criticism against it, the RSS decided to do an explainer. It hurriedly organized a three-day lecture series by Mohan Bhagwat himself in Delhi and invited a host of people, including political leaders of all persuasions, diplomats, journalists and intellectuals. The three-day, globally broadcast address was a landmark as Bhagwat presented the Sangh as an inclusive organization which unconditionally respected the Constitution of India, the state and its symbols. He emphasized that it respected even socialism and secularism as they were enshrined in the Constitution.

The sarsanghchalak assured Muslims that without them Hindutva had no existence and even accepted that Lord Ram can be the 'Imam-e-Hind' as the poet Allama Iqbal called him. The RSS went to the extent of removing references to Muslims, Christians and communists as internal enemies of the country in *Bunch of Thoughts*— the collected utterances of the revered second chief Golwalkar and a seminal guide for every swayamsevak. In short, the Bhagwat lectures were an attempt at reorienting the public perception of the Sangh and a bugle call to join the Hindu Rashtra project. One ideologue described the repositioning as a shift from being a socio-political organization to a politico-social one.

Deoras had said that during Hedgewar's time the RSS was political and Golwalkar focused on cultural regeneration. Deoras himself oriented it towards social services. In Mohan Bhagwat's time, it seems the wheel has come full circle. While its goals remain intact, politics is the means of choice for the RSS.

1

Soul-Keepers

In June 2018, the Ministry of Defence and the Prime Minister's Office (PMO) discussed a proposal to train a million young men and women annually to prepare them for the purpose of creating a disciplined nationalist force of youth. Titled the National Youth Empowerment Scheme (N-YES), the year-long training was proposed to be an essential qualification for enrolment in the army and paramilitary services. The scheme was aimed at instilling values of discipline, nationalism and self-esteem in young people, the *Indian Express* reported.[1] The government called the report sensationalizing but did not deny the meeting in the PMO. It said the meeting had discussed strengthening the National Cadet Corps (NCC) and the National Service Scheme (NSS).

Established in 1948, at the instance of then prime minister, Jawaharlal Nehru, and home minister, Sardar Patel, in the wake of the invasion of Kashmir by Pakistan-supported tribesmen, the NCC's stated aim is 'developing character, comradeship, discipline, a secular outlook, the spirit of adventure and ideals of selfless service amongst young citizens . . . and creating a pool of organized, trained and motivated youth with leadership qualities in all walks of life, who will serve the nation regardless of which career they choose'.[2] The NSS was established to provide 'hands on experience to young students in delivering social service'.[3] These organizations' values aligned with those of the RSS although the latter's definition of 'secular outlook' is different. It contends that India is a Hindu nation, and a Hindu by nature and definition can be nothing but secular. Like the NCC, the RSS also considers itself as a reserve force.[4]

The N-YES proposal sounded very close to the RSS's idea of creating a militaristic society. Sarsanghchalak Mohan Bhagwat has claimed that although the RSS was not a military organization, its discipline was like that of the army. While the army may require six to seven months to ready a force, the RSS could raise a trained force of its volunteers in three days.[5]

Organizers of Hindus often rue that they are pusillanimous compared to other communities. V.D. Savarkar, one of the early ideological mentors of the RSS, wrote: 'At the time of the first inroads of the Muhammadans, the fierce unity of faith, that social cohesion and valorous fervour which made them as a body so irresistible, were qualities in which the Hindus proved woefully wanting.'[6]

There is a particularly revealing incident in Narayan Hari Palkar's biography of RSS founder K.B. Hedgewar which illuminates the inspiration and purpose of founding the RSS. On a visit to Pune in 1939, Hedgewar asked volunteers how much time it would take them to mobilize at short notice. Of course, no one had any estimate. The next morning, he asked the city sanghchalak, Vinayakrao Apte, to assemble all volunteers in Pune at Shivaji Mandir grounds in two hours. About 900 volunteers gathered there at the appointed hour. Hedgewar went on to explain the reason for the exercise by recalling an incident from his jail term. One day, the prison alarm went off at lunch hour. Within minutes, all the guards and officials had gathered at the assembly point. Some were half-dressed while others had left their lunch midway. But everyone had picked up their weapons and assembled.

'The significance of this incident became ingrained in my mind. The English are able to rule over this vast country of ours from a distance of over 5000 miles, mainly because they have people at their command who are ever ready to respond whenever a call is given. These are paid servants but we should all be missionaries in the cause of nation ever prepared to respond to the call of the Sangh. Without such preparedness, our country's present downfall can never come to an end,' said Hedgewar.[7]

Hedgewar strongly believed that it was preparedness and discipline that made the British effective. He envisioned a British army–like organization—highly disciplined, motivated and alert—that would assume the mission of safeguarding and governing the nation but would be spread out and embedded across the country. He estimated that the organization would have achieved its mission if it could train 3 per cent of the urban population and 1 per cent of the rural population. This highly trained cohort would provide leadership to the rest of the community. Topped up with a 'nationalist feeling', they could defend the country in any crisis. He had modelled the RSS uniform, training and marching songs with this idea of the British military in mind.

Golwalkar explained the thought behind the targets at a training camp in Jabalpur in 1941. 'It seems some people have not understood the real meaning of Doctorji's percentage. "One and three" does not mean we catch hold of any one or three persons out of a hundred, make them wear uniforms and feel satisfied at having fulfilled the target. When Doctorji talked of one per cent in the rural areas, he meant one capable of leading the remaining ninety-nine. The same applied to the urban areas. A world war is going on, so this is the time to fulfil Doctorji's target as early as possible.'[8]

Over the long term, this volunteer force would be able to influence the country enough to engineer national and community institutions in its ideological framework. This model envisaged replacing the British when the country got independence. At the peak of the Raj a mere handful of British ran the undivided Indian empire. There were only 155,555 British in the country in 1931, according to the census of that year.[9] Of these only 110,137 were men who would have formed the governing cohort, which would have included army officers, policemen, scientists, teachers and missionaries. If it was possible to build an organization whose members could take over the functions these British performed, it would effectively have control of the entire nation. The population of undivided India, including Burma, in 1931 was about 35 crore of which about 4 crore lived in urban centres.[10]

A volunteer strength of 1 per cent of the rural and 3 per cent of urban population, as envisaged by Hedgewar, would have added up to about 4 million in 1931. This primary goal of the RSS remains unchanged. It wants a group of volunteers trained in its ideology to be present in every village and neighbourhood. Mohan Bhagwat uses a story to illustrate what Hedgewar wanted to do with the RSS. When the RSS had about fifty volunteers, Hedgewar was asked what he would do next. He replied he would expand it to 500. What next? It would be 5000. He kept increasing the count but never explained what he would do with them. Finally, he said that the Sangh's objective was just that; create this cohort and leave it to organize Hindu community.[11]

Madhukar Dattatreya 'Balasaheb' Deoras, who trained under founder Hedgewar from the age of eleven and went on to lead the organization after Golwalkar, told volunteers at a camp in Kurukshetra in 1965 that Indians had to develop patriotism the way British developed theirs. 'Thinking of the society and the ever-preparedness to sacrifice everything for the country is also a facet of character. It is said that the Battle of Waterloo was won on the playgrounds of Eaton. It is imperative that we prepare a wholesome environment so that patriotic culture is imbibed through mother's milk, father's instruction, games on the playgrounds and pedagogy in schools. Until such a society is not prepared, special organizations like the Sangh and their unique efforts would be required for the safety and security of the country.'[12]

This identification of itself as a special organization responsible for the country's security is not only self-congratulatory but also an attempt to assume the role of an exclusive arbiter of patriotism.

When it comes to national loyalty, however, even the Maoists—former Prime Minister Manmohan Singh once described them as the biggest internal security threat—have declared that if India is threatened, they would 'stand by the people and rally against the attack'.[13] But the RSS continues to believe and claim that if it were not for its activities and vigil, India would be in grave danger.

The Savarkar brothers—V.D. Savarkar and G.D. Savarkar—played key roles in implanting the ideology of Hindutva and strengthening the fledgling organization. While Hedgewar considered V.D. Savarkar as the ideological guide to the organization, his brother G.D. Savarkar helped in building it. The two brothers seem to have shaped the key definitions that the Sangh would follow for years to come.

In the early days, V.D. Savarkar had accompanied Hedgewar to hundreds of shakhas in Vidarbha to speak to swayamsevaks. Some in the Sangh say that Hedgewar keenly understood Savarkar's appeal as a Maharashtrian revolutionary hero if not a national one. When Savarkar was released from jail and reached Nagpur, Hedgewar is said to have jostled with others at the railway station to get into the compartment so that he could prostrate at his feet. There are even claims that Ganesh Savarkar had composed the original RSS pledge at Hedgewar's request and it was the first time the words 'Hindu Rashtra' were used by an organization.[14]

Ganesh Savarkar also merged his organization, Tarun Hindu Sabha, with the RSS and later got one Sant Panchlegaonkar Maharaj to dissolve his Mukteshwar Dal into the Sangh. The Dal which had drills similar to the RSS had been banned by the government. These mergers increased the number of RSS shakhas in the Central Provinces and Berar.[15]

When Hedgewar died, Ganesh Savarkar wrote to lawyer and Hedgewar's associate Vishwanathrao Kelkar, urging that Golwalkar be made sarsanghchalak and proposing an advisory committee comprising Babasaheb Ghatate, Ramchandra Narayan Padhye, Vishwanathrao Kelkar and others with Abaji Hedgewar (the RSS founder's uncle) as its head. In his book, *Hindu Rashtra: Poorvi, Aataa aani Pudhe* (Hindu Nation: Past, Present and Future), he wrote: 'An organization such as the Sangh cannot remain satisfied with mere numbers of disciplined individuals. The Sangh should gradually find occasions to test its strength. It should create experts in every aspect of the polity so that freedom may be won and maintained. The Sangh followers have taken a pledge to protect "Jati-dharma-samskriti". To make this pledge meaningful and to serve society and gain its support, the Sangh should protect people from riots and foreign aggression.'[16] He is quoted as having told Golwalkar from his deathbed that the Sangh should cultivate experts in economics, education, armed forces, politics, linguistics, intelligence and other fields.[17]

The Sangh considers itself an expert at building organizations and managing events. From the beginning, it has relentlessly focused on the organization, smoothening the rough edges and sharpening the spearheads. It has learnt from others and copied successful models. Fashioned after the British army, it not only borrowed the uniform complete with leather belt and puttees, or leg bindings, but also the marching songs. The route march itself was introduced as a show of strength just like military and paramilitary forces do in areas of trouble to warn citizens. Hedgewar even hired Christian teachers and borrowed English tunes to train the RSS band.[18]

In building and nurturing the paramilitary-style organization, Hedgewar and later Golwalkar made every effort to ring-fence it from any kind of conflicts, mainly legal. It is a cardinal rule in the organization that the organization would be protected at all costs. It is perhaps for this legal insulation that Hedgewar laid down the first principle: the Sangh would not, under its own banner, participate in any activity that could draw the attention of law enforcement. It essentially meant even if a swayamsevak were to get into trouble with the law, the RSS would have nothing to do with it. That most instructions in the Sangh are oral helps maintain this deniability. It is the basis of the oft-repeated contention: '*Sangh kuch nahin karta. Sab kuch samaj karta hai.* Or, *Sangh kuch nahin karta, lekin swayamsevak sab kuch karta hai* (The Sangh does not do anything. Everything is done by the community. Or the Sangh does not do anything, but its volunteers do everything).'

According to Hedgewar's biographer, he himself participated in the Jungle Satyagraha, an agitation launched in the interiors in solidarity with Gandhi's Salt Satyagraha but did not allow the RSS to participate. He said swayamsevaks could participate in their individual capacity. When some Sangh volunteers wanted to participate in Sangh uniform, Hedgewar chided them saying: 'Have you even thought of what could happen to the organization whose work is destined to fundamentally change the country if you are identified with it?'[19] He participated with the idea of going to jail which would have a great pool of nationalist youngsters to recruit from.[20] Similarly, in 1942, despite a large section of the RSS wanting to plunge into the Quit India agitation, Golwalkar refused to budge. Detractors point to the Sangh's non-participation in the freedom movement to run down the nationalist credentials it zealously guards.

The RSS has actively started a campaign to establish that even though the organization itself kept away from the freedom movement its volunteers were fully engaged with it. On Hedgewar's death anniversary on 21 June 2018, the RSS publicity wing released an article by former pracharak Narendra Sehgal. The article claimed that just before World War II began, Hedgewar, Subhas Chandra Bose, Trailokyanath Chakravarty and V.D. Savarkar had a long discussion on young men joining the British army. They also discussed fomenting a revolt in the army and starting the Indian National Army later founded by Bose. The article titled 'Unknown Commander of the Freedom Struggle: Dr Keshav Baliram Hedgewar',[21] which was extracted from a book Sehgal had written, claimed that the RSS founder's contributions were deliberately suppressed by the post-Independence governments.

Although the article gives the impression of a conference of the four leaders, it never happened and Sehgal later claimed that he merely meant that Hedgewar met with the leaders separately at different times.[22] Hedgewar's biographer Palkar mentions a meeting between him and Bose in Calcutta a decade earlier when he was there to attend the Congress session as the member of its Central Provinces' working committee. Palkar notes that Hedgewar disagreed with Bose that Hindu–Muslim unity was possible. He agreed more with Savarkar who was also present at the meeting. This was, however, G.D. Savarkar, popularly known as Babarao, and not the younger one who was known as Tatyarao to friends but was famous as Veer Savarkar.[23] Sehgal also alleged that A.O. Hume, founder of the INC, was a fundamentalist Christian and his objective of founding the party was to undermine the rise of cultural nationalism, Hindutva and other revolutionary activities.

On 10 December 2015, the *Indian Express* published an article by historian Ramachandra Guha[24] which squarely criticized RSS sarsanghchalak Mohan Bhagwat for trying to appropriate B.R. Ambedkar when the organization was viciously opposed to him when he was alive.

'This posthumous appropriation of Ambedkar follows upon the Sangh's similarly cynical appropriation of Gandhi, a reformer whom it opposed when he was alive, but has since sought to claim a kinship with. The RSS was founded in 1925. For many years thereafter, it kept its distance from Gandhi and the national movement. The RSS took part in neither the Salt Satyagraha nor the Quit India movement.'[25]

RSS ideologue M.G. Vaidya replied to Guha's article in a piece in the same newspaper a few days later. Quoting India's second president, Sarvepalli Radhakrishnan, Vaidya said, '"Hinduism is a movement, not a position; a process, not a result; a growing tradition, not a fixed revelation." The RSS, too, moved on, on this principle.'[26]

On the charge of not participating in the key movements during the Independence struggle, he said the average age of RSS volunteers would have been only fifteen or sixteen when the Salt Satyagraha was launched. 'Are they expected to have taken part in that satyagraha?

But the founder of the RSS, K.B. Hedgewar, took part in the forest satyagraha, the equivalent of the Salt Satyagraha, in Vidarbha. He was arrested and sentenced to nine months of rigorous imprisonment.'[27]

On its participation in the Quit India movement, Vaidya said the British had arrested key Congress leaders even before the movement was properly planned and Gandhi did not get enough time to organize the agitation. If he had time he would have 'certainly have contacted the RSS. However, RSS volunteers on their own took part in the agitation. In Chimur, those who were convicted and sentenced to death included one RSS worker. The person who hoisted the tricolour at the government building in Ramtek was an RSS volunteer. While underground, Aruna Asaf Ali got asylum in Hansraj Gupta's house in Delhi. Gupta later became chief of the RSS's Delhi unit. Nana Patil of Satara, who led a fierce anti-British agitation, was underground for many days in the house of Pandit Satwalekar, the sanghchalak of the nearby town.'[28] Vaidya sounded like he was clutching at straws.

The British certainly considered the RSS as a pro-Independence outfit but correctly assessed that it had long-term objectives. This despite the RSS being extremely careful not to rub the law on the wrong side. Its 'good conduct' during the agitation of 1942 kept it out of trouble. Bombay home secretary H.V.R. Iyengar wrote to the Central government that the Bombay government was of the view that no new restrictions on RSS were required apart from the existing one on dress and drill as the Sangh had kept 'itself scrupulously within the law and, in particular, has refrained from taking part in the disturbances that broke out in August 1942'.[29]

Yet, the government kept it under close watch. In October 1942, the chief secretary to Central Provinces and Berar, T.C.S. Jayaratnam, ordered a detailed gathering of information on the RSS from each district after the special branch 'noticed a swing over to a more militant form of programme'.[30] The detailed report that was prepared suggested that the main aim of the Sangh was 'Hindustan for the Hindus', i.e., an India free from the domination by Muslims,

British or any other foreign elements. 'The Sangh rejects the view that this objective can be achieved by non-violent methods.'[31]

The report said the Hindu Mahasabha had recognized the RSS as a national organization in 1932. Secret intra-government communication and police reports sent in from various district headquarters suggest the British believed that the RSS displayed fascist traits and a closeness to Japan and attributed it to the influence of B.S. Moonje. 'The leaders of the Sangh (sometimes called organizers) are entitled "Chalak" (the exact Hindi equivalent of the word Fuehrer),' the report noted. It, however, said the RSS was careful not to upset the government and police and strictly stayed away from the Congress's agitational activities. In some places, it even helped the government undermine the Congress's agitations. It avoided its typical military style drills during its Foundation Day celebrations that year.[32]

British officials gathered much of the data from a 1942 officers' training camp of the RSS held in Pune to which they appear to have got unparalleled access. The report mentioned in detail the intellectual study classes conducted by various leaders. One senior pracharak, Yadavrao Joshi, urged volunteers to give up ideas of individuality. Citing the examples of Japan and Germany, Joshi said that like individuals of those nations, volunteers should totally identify with national ambitions.[33]

The report quoted Golwalkar explaining the RSS work to volunteers: 'This country belonged to Hindus whose forefathers spilt their blood for its sake. The Sangh was meant for the whole of India and therefore termed "national"; but the Hindus alone had so far proved loyal to the country; therefore, they alone were eligible for enrolment in the Sangh. Whoever, forgetting traditions, joins hands with the enemies should be killed even if he were their own brother, because only he who follows and sticks to their principles would be regarded as their real brother. The mental apathy of the Hindus should be removed and a feeling of hatred towards the men of other religions, who were getting high-handed, should be created in them. The Sangh was doing this work.'[34]

Denouncing selfish individualism Golwalkar pointed to France as an example of its ultimate result. He said the Sangh has been started not only for combating Muslim aggression but also for completely extirpating that disease; it was, therefore, necessary to have proper men at the helm whose attention should be focused on achievement of their goal.[35]

Another leader, P.G. Sahasrabuddhe, said that the Sangh followed the principle of dictatorship. Denouncing democratic government as an unsatisfactory form of government, he cited France as a typically bad example. He held up Japan, Germany and Russia as ideal examples of dictatorships. Sahasrabuddhe also impressed upon volunteers the value of propaganda citing Russia and Germany as examples.

Volunteers at the camp were instructed to study the lives of seventeen important personalities. These were Hedgewar, Shivaji, Bal Gangadhar Tilak, V.D. Savarkar, Dayanand Saraswati, Swami Shraddhanand, Lala Lajpat Rai, Agarkar, Swami Ramdas, Swami Vivekananda, Adolf Hitler, Benito Mussolini, Vladimir Lenin, Italian politician and champion of unification Giuseppe Mazzini, Italian military leader and nationalist Giuseppe Garibaldi, Irish politician and later president Eamon de Valera and Chinese leader Chiang Kai-shek.[36]

The suggested reading for volunteers that year included Japan's reorganization; *Unity of Cultures* by Professor D.K. Kelkar; Savarkar's literature; *Hindudom* by Savarkar; Savarkar's lectures; *Literature on Hinduism* by Hindu Bhandar, Nagpur; *History of the Sikhs*; *History of Vijayanagar*; *History of Turks* by Bhave; *History of Congress* by Pattabhi Sitaramayya; *Caution to Hindus* by Savitri Devi; *Danger of Pakistan* by Karandikar; *Harijan Problem* by Professor Mate; *History of Ireland* by Kelkar.[37]

The report noted with interest two incidents that occurred in the Central Provinces. One was in Buldhana where several volunteers, including a cyclist squad, staged an 'attack on a hill'. It ended with a lathi charge. The second was a field day held in Nimar district on

21 June 1942, Hedgewar's death anniversary. The noteworthy feature was that several volunteers of different castes ate their meals from the same dish.[38]

The RSS's zeal for keeping the organization protected until it built what could be called a critical mass of influence in society was matched only by its extreme practicality and ability to adapt to changing situations. A top leader said the RSS has only one sacrosanct principle: 'Hindustan is a Hindu Rashtra and it belongs to Hindus. Everything else can change.' The leader said the idea of Hindu Rashtra is drawn from Vivekananda, Savarkar and Gandhi.[39] This often confuses followers. While they are brought up on liberal doses (though not much of Gandhi, according to multiple sources who have attended RSS camps) of their writings and speeches, those who venture to study each one of them in depth start having questions about the patchwork quilt the Sangh has stitched for them.

According to Vivekananda, what united India as a nation was religion, not race or language. In his mind, in Asia, people of diverse origins and different tongues become one nation if they have the same religion. The people of northern India were divided into four great classes, while in southern India the languages were so entirely different from those of northern India that there was no kinship whatsoever. The people of northern India belong to the Aryan race while those of southern India belong to the same race as ancient Egyptians and the Semites.[40]

When Hedgewar announced to a few friends gathered at his home on Vijaya Dashami day in 1925 that 'we are starting the Sangh today', he did not have a clear structure of operation of the organization to offer them. But he was ready with three principal objectives. The Sangh would focus on developing 'physical, military and political' capabilities in its volunteers.[41]

He modelled shakha activity on gymnasiums popular in the Nagpur of the 1920s. Even the invocation in the early days was a Marathi prayer to Lord Hanuman. These words of Vivekananda perhaps played on his mind: 'My child, what I want is muscles of iron and nerves of steel, inside which dwells a mind of the same material as that of which the thunderbolt is made. Strength, manhood, Kshatra-Virya plus Brahma-Teja. Our beautiful hopeful boys—they have everything, only if they are not slaughtered by the millions at the altar of this brutality they call marriage.'[42]

What Vivekananda articulated to American audiences about India as the world leader of a glorious past laid waste by uncouth invaders resonated with the nationalists at home. He said that not only did India give the world the basis for its religions but also its arts, literature, science, medicine and ethics; even Aesop's fables, Arabian nights and Cinderella.

'And now, what has the world given to India in return for all that? Nothing but nullification [vilification] and curse and contempt. The world waded in her children's life-blood, it reduced India to poverty and her sons and daughters to slavery, and now it adds insult to injury by preaching to her a religion which can only thrive on the destruction of every other religion. But India is not afraid. It does not beg for mercy at the hands of any nation. Our only fault is that we cannot fight to conquer; but we trust in the eternity of truth. India's message to the world is first of all, her blessing; she is returning good for the evil which is done her, and thus she puts into execution this noble idea, which had its origin in India. Lastly, India's message is that calm goodness, patience and gentleness will ultimately triumph. For where are the Greeks, the onetime masters of the earth? They are gone. Where are the Romans, at the tramp of whose cohorts the world trembled? Passed away. Where are the Arabs, who in fifty years had carried their banners from the Atlantic to the Pacific? And where are the Spaniards, the cruel murderers of millions of men? Both races are nearly extinct; but thanks to the morality of her children, the kinder race will never perish, and she will yet see the hour of her triumph,' The *Brooklyn Standard Union* reported on 27 February 1895.[43]

It was a fine exposition of past glory and current national victimhood to an international audience. This pattern continues unchanged in nationalist narratives even today, blaming the dry reservoir of modern discoveries, strong institutions or new ideas to the wayward ways of those who ruled the country after Independence.

At the core of Hindu nationalism is the mortifying image of the effeminate Hindu. The medieval invaders who came through the forbidding Hindu Kush (the name itself is controversial because many believe it means 'Hindu-killer'[44]) mountains thought so. As did the British colonialists. It was this perceived lack of manhood that bothered the Hindu nationalist more than anything else. Wanting peace was seen as a lofty charade to cover up not just lack of courage but weakness. This, they analysed, was not because the Hindu was genetically weak-hearted but because Gautama Buddha intervened in India's history.

'Monasticism is all very good for a few; but when you preach it in such a fashion that every man or woman who has a mind immediately gives up social life . . . who were left to procreate progeny, to continue the race? Only the weaklings. All the strong and vigorous minds went out. And then came national decay by the sheer loss of vigour.'[45]

Like Vivekananda, the Buddhist conditioning of India animated and enraged Savarkar too. He was disgusted by the universalism and non-violence propagated by Buddha's followers. He believed that as long as there was war and conquest, the Hindu nation could not rely on pacifism. He says that the Buddha could have remained unaffected by foreign invaders such as the Huns, but the 'rest of Hindus then could not drink with equanimity this cup of bitterness and political servitude at the hands of those whose barbarous violence could still be soothed by the mealy-mouthed formulas of ahimsa and spiritual brotherhood, and whose steel could still be blunted by the soft palm leaves and rhymed charms'.[46]

Savarkar saw this pacifism as the reason for the victimhood of Hindus and their valorous attempt to preserve their nation. He insisted that the foundations for the Buddhists' work were laid by those who came before them who were much more accomplished.

Savarkar considers Buddhists as part of the Hindu nation but less accomplished than Hindus because of their lack of pragmatism.

'We yield to none in our love, admiration and respect for the Buddha—the Dharma—the Sangha. They are all ours. Their glories are ours and ours their failures. Great was Ashoka, the Devapriya, and greater were the Buddhistic Bhikkus. But achievements as great if not greater and things as holy and more politic and statesmanly had gone before them and indeed enabled them to be what they were. So, we do not think that the political virility or the manly nobility of our race began and ended with the Mauryas alone—or was a consequence of their embracing Buddhism. Buddhism has conquests to claim but they belong to a world far removed from this our matter-of-fact world—where feet of clay do not stand long, and steel could be easily sharpened and trishna—thirst—is too powerful and real to be quenched by painted streams that flow perennially in heavens.'[47]

It is a powerful and provocative statement, one that unambiguously declares that Hindu virility was cauterized by Buddhist pacifism. The pure nobility of Buddhist values perhaps prevented Savarkar from totally discarding them as useless and blaming the times unsuited for them. But he was clear they had no place in the new Hindu India he envisioned. Savarkar believes that while the pacifism and non-violence of the Buddhists disregarded the need for preservation of intellectual and cultural superiority of the Hindu nation, it tugged at the hearts of non-Buddhists egging them to action.

At the dawn of Independence in August 1947, RSS men founded a Hindi monthly *Rashtra Dharm*.[48] Published from Lucknow, its founding editor was Atal Bihari Vajpayee and its general manager was Deendayal Upadhyaya. In the inaugural issue, Upadhyaya wrote a long essay on Indian nationhood titled 'Bharatiya Rashtra Dhara ka Punya Pravah' loosely translated as 'the holy continuum of the Indian nation'. Although similar to Savarkar's thesis, Upadhyaya's essay is less rhetorical. Upadhyaya too identified Gautama Buddha's establishment of Buddhism as a break in the continuum of the

Hindu nation. He describes the centuries following Buddha as the years of conflict and later consensus between the 'centrifugal' forces of Buddhism and the 'centripetal' forces of Hindus.

Upadhyaya says Buddhism emerged in response to the decline of Hindu religion and culture into Brahminical debauchery and chauvinism. A previous correction when the Hindu practice was decaying was brought by 'Bhagawat dharma', which reduced the importance of Vedic rituals, yagnas and worship of deities such as Indra, although it did not sever the connection completely. However, Buddha threw the baby out with the bathwater, Upadhyaya says, when he sought to cut off India from its Vedic roots. He not only stopped ancient rites and rituals, Buddha also preferred Pali over Sanskrit in popularizing his new religion.[49]

According to Upadhyaya, when Buddhism spread to other countries it lost the sense of nation and paved the way for invaders into the country. Buddhism gradually become 'a-Hindu'. 'At this juncture, annihilating Buddhism became a national duty and great men, one after another, set themselves to destroying it. Although foremost among them are Kumarilbhatt [Kumārila Bhaṭṭa]and Shankaracharya, there were many others who took up this national duty.'[50]

Upadhyaya acknowledges that it was in response to the popularity of Buddhism that the Vedic religion started establishing temples and matts. The Puranas and *agama*s (code of rites and rituals) were created to present Vedic ideas in a more popular and accessible manner and yagnas were replaced by ritualistic idol worship. Pilgrimages were started to unify various sects and cults and pilgrim centres—twelve sun temples, eighteen Shiva Jyotirlinga temples, twenty Ganapati temples, twenty-one centres for Shaktas and hundreds of Vaishnava temples—were established across the country. He calls Kumbh Melas mobile national universities and national conventions.[51]

Incidentally, RSS joint general secretary Krishna Gopal said at a public forum in August 2019 that ancient Indians did not worship in temples and did not have idols. These, he said, were inspired by the Greek temples and statues.[52] He also said there were many communities in India and a Hindu identity began to form only when non-Muslims coalesced in opposition to Muslims.

Savarkar had no use for a faith that could not control, if not subjugate, other nations which had an eye on India. In his mind, the only protection was valour and strength born of 'a national self-consciousness'.[53] As Savarkar saw it, the Indian nation was born when Lord Ram killed Ravan and conquered Lanka. He presents it as a conscious nation-building mission by the inhabitants of the Indus Valley.

'At last the great mission which the Sindhus had undertaken of founding a nation and a country, found and reached its geographical limit when the valorous Prince of Ayodhya made a triumphant entry in Ceylon and actually brought the whole land from the Himalayas to the seas under one sovereign sway. The day when the Horse of Victory returned to Ayodhya unchallenged and unchallengeable, the great white umbrella of sovereignty was unfurled over that imperial throne of Ramchandra, the brave, Ramchandra the good, and a loving allegiance was sworn, not only by the princes of Aryan blood but Hanuman, Sugriva, Bibhishana from the south—that day was the real birthday of our Hindu people. It was truly a national day; for Aryans and Anaryans knitting themselves into a people were born as a nation. It summed up and politically crowned the efforts of all the generations that preceded it and it handed down a new and common mission, a common banner, a common cause which all the generations after it had consciously or unconsciously fought and died to defend.'[54]

Upadhyaya too arrives at the same conclusion that it was Lord Ram's victorious Sri Lankan march that united the north and south of the country. This would remain the core of RSS's future programmes and strategies in its ideological warfare. Interestingly, not until the early 1980s did it utilize this political symbol as an instrument of ideological expansion and Hindu consolidation. Building a temple in Ayodhya for Lord Ram was never an integral part of the Hindu-nation discourse throughout the lives of Hedgewar or Golwalkar. One RSS leader pointed out that there is no mention of Ayodhya in the entire twelve volumes of Guruji *samagra* (Golwalkar collection).[55]

Mahatma Gandhi, though politically at the opposite pole to Savarkar, was one of the early proposers of India's historic nationhood and articulated it in *Hind Swaraj* in 1908, fifteen years before the handwritten manuscript of *Essentials of Hindutva* was smuggled out of the Ratnagiri prison where Savarkar was incarcerated.[56] Gandhi wrote that it was the English who created the myth that Indians were not one nation before and that it would require centuries before they became one nation. Gandhi asserted that Indians were one nation before the British arrived. Indians were inspired by one thought and an identical mode of life. The British were able to establish one kingdom precisely because India was one nation. It was the British who divided India.

'I do not wish to suggest that because we were one nation we had no differences, but it is submitted that our leading men travelled throughout India either on foot or in bullock-carts. They learned one another's languages and there was no aloofness between them. What do you think could have been the intention of those far-seeing ancestors of ours who established Setubandha [Rameshwaram] in the South, Jagannath in the East and Hardwar in the North as places of pilgrimage? You will admit they were no fools. They knew that worship of God could have been performed just as well at home. They taught us that those whose hearts were aglow with righteousness had the Ganges in their own homes. But they saw that India was one undivided land so made by nature. They, therefore, argued that it must be one nation. Arguing thus, they established holy places in various parts of India, and fired the people with an idea of nationality in a manner unknown in other parts of the world. And we Indians are one as no two Englishmen are. Only you and I and others who consider ourselves civilized and superior persons imagine that we are many nations.'[57]

Both Savarkar and Gandhi studied European political thought closely but while applying it in the Indian context, they diverged in opposing directions. Savarkar's political philosophy was sculpted in the mould of Italian nationalist revolutionary Giuseppe Mazzini who founded Young Italy, a secret group to promote Italian unification and republicanism. Savarkar even wrote a biography of Mazzini. 'Italy's Ramdas is called Mazzini and India's Mazzini is called Ramdas,' Savarkar said about Mazzini, invoking Maratha king Shivaji's spiritual guru Samarth Ramdas.

Gandhi, equally impressed by Mazzini, gets convinced from the Italian experience that India would benefit from a non-violent struggle. 'Mazzini was a great and good man; Garibaldi was a great warrior. Both are adorable; from their lives we can learn much.'[58] Mazzini says that every man must learn how to rule himself. To Garibaldi, Italy meant only the king but for Mazzini it was every Italian. Garibaldi gave a call and every Italian took to arms. But the gain after Austrian forces withdrew was only nominal and the condition of the people remained the same. 'By patriotism, I mean the welfare of the whole people. And, if I could secure it at the hands of the English, I should bow down my head to them,' Gandhi wrote.[59]

There was, however, another problem, a deeper civilizational one. 'The English are splendidly armed; that does not frighten me, but it is clear that, to pit ourselves against them in arms thousands of Indians must be armed,' he said and also observed a cultural pitfall in it. '. . . to arm India on a large scale is to Europeanise it . . . This means, in short, that India must accept European civilisation, and if that is what we want, the best thing is that we have among us those who are well trained in that civilisation.'[60] Gandhi sought freedom not merely from imperial Britain but the yoke of European civilization.

In a signed article in the *Hindustan Times* on Gandhi's 150th birth anniversary on 2 October 2019, sarsanghchalak Mohan Bhagwat called Hind Swaraj a 'dream picture of Bharat's progress and performance' based on swadeshi. 'We shall take a pledge that we will emulate his sacred, dedicated and transparent life and swa-centric life vision, through which we must inculcate the qualities of dedication and renunciation in our lives to make Bharat the Vishwa Guru,' Bhagwat wrote.[61]

The RSS chief recalled instances of the organization and its founder Hedgewar's contact with Gandhi. Yet, the Mahatma became a part of RSS's daily morning prayer, which recalls its national heroes, only in 1963. A senior RSS leader, who was present when it was debated in Nagpur, recalls that the inclusion was hotly contested and a large section among those gathered opposed it.[62]

An innate sense of cultural harmony undoubtedly ran as an undercurrent through the length and breadth of the subcontinent and its roots no doubt lay in the myriad practices, traditions, history, mythology, culture, and rivers and mountains of the land. India's first prime minister, Jawaharlal Nehru, an internationalist and a committed socialist, perhaps best captured the essence of it in his last will and testament.

My desire to have a handful of my ashes thrown in the Ganga at Allahabad has no religious significance, so far as I am concerned. I have no religious sentiment in the matter. I have been attached to the Ganga and the Jumna rivers in Allahabad ever since my childhood and, as I have grown older, this attachment has also grown. I have watched their varying moods as the seasons changed, and have often thought of the history and myth and tradition and song and story that have become attached to them through the long ages and become part of their flowing waters. The Ganga, especially, is the river of India, beloved of her people, round which are intertwined her racial memories, her hopes and fears, her songs of triumph, her victories and her defeats. She has been a symbol of India's age-long culture and civilization, ever changing, ever flowing, and yet ever the same Ganga. She reminds me of the snow-covered peaks and the deep valleys of the Himalayas, which I have loved so much, and of the rich and vast plains below, where my life and work have been cast. Smiling and dancing in the morning sun—shadows fall: a narrow, slow and graceful stream in winter, and a vast roaring thing during the monsoon, broad-bosomed almost as the sea, and with something of the sea's power to destroy, the Ganga has been to me a symbol and a memory of the past of India, running into the present, and flowing on to the great ocean of the future. And though I have discarded much of past tradition and custom, and am anxious that India should rid herself of all shackles that bind and constrain her and divide her people, and suppress vast numbers of them, and prevent the free development of the body and the spirit; though I seek all this, yet I do not wish to cut myself off from that past completely. I am proud of that great inheritance that has been, and is, ours, and I am conscious that I too, like all of us, am a link in that unbroken chain which goes back to the dawn of history in the immemorial past of India; that chain I would not break, for I treasure it and seek inspiration from it. And, as witness of this desire of mine and as my last homage to India's cultural inheritance, I am making this request that a handful of my ashes be thrown into the Ganga at Allahabad to be carried to the great ocean that washes India's shores.[63]

Nehru's understanding of India and its comparison to the Ganga easily embraced in it all the influences that have merged into the mighty river's perennial flow, an idea also expressed by Upadhyaya.[64]

In fact, one of Nehru's biographers, M.J. Akbar, saw in him the distilled essence of Indian nationalism. Akbar insists Nehru was neither a Gandhian nor a Marxist. He was not orthodox in any way. 'Yet if any name has to be given to his special mix, then it has to be called the ideology of Indian nationalism,' gushed Akbar, who years later became a Union minister from the BJP that reserves a special disdain for Nehru.[65]

Nehru's unconditional belonging to the nation could have been anybody's, irrespective of their caste, religion or ideological belief. The purity of belonging to the cultural inheritance did not have any political purpose nor ambition. The inheritance had to be preserved, enriched and handed down to the next generation with all its glory and awareness. Without a political purpose, however, it was of no use to Savarkar (and perhaps the RSS) who wanted Hindu to be a specific identity, pure and unadulterated by 'alien' cultural contributions.

German political science scholar Siegfried Wolf says Savarkar's use of Hinduism was strategic. In the everyday value system of the majority, Savarkar saw similar threads connecting diverse religious customs and folk traditions going back millennia. 'Savarkar was aware of the potency of religious enthusiasm and claimed that "man cannot remain without religion. Religion is a source of stupendous strength".' Hindutva was to bind the people of the country in a collective identity, as a fundamental pillar of belonging, upholding his 'imagined nation'.[66]

In its strategic form, Hindutva could not coexist with other ideologies. Islam and Christianity could exist within the Hindu framework as mere spiritual pathways to God but not as cultural elements or civilizational contributors that complete the nation. Savarkar argued that even converts, though their ancestors were Hindu, lost their nationhood.

Supporters of Hindutva saw Mahatma Gandhi, a Sanatani Hindu, as a pacifist Muslim appeaser who was stripping the Hindu nation of its manhood the same way Buddha did two millennia ago. The 1916 Lucknow Pact between the Congress party and the Muslim League ratified the representation to minorities in provincial assemblies envisaged in the Morley–Minto reforms but it was seen as a shining example of Hindu–Muslim unity and forbearance even though until then the two parties were rivals. Muhammad Ali Jinnah—who had not yet emerged as the champion of the idea of a separate country for Muslims and become a much-reviled figure for Hindutva supporters and who was then a member of both the Congress and the Muslim League—is widely seen as the agreement's architect. But in the RSS view, Bal Gangadhar Tilak, president of the joint session of Congress and the League, salvaged Hindu interests from the inescapable situation of minority representation pre-decided by the British rulers. The agreement, in its view, was a compromise in hopeless circumstances.

'Everybody was aware of the clear fact that it was not possible for anybody to go beyond the fait accompli Morley-Minto plan, still only such Muslims were chosen for compromise talks as were amenable to Congress nationalism and respected Tilak. The policy of the Gandhi era was exactly the opposite of this. In that era, nationalist Muslims leaders within the Congress were taken for granted and those who were rabidly communal, anti-national and anti-Congress were considered representatives of the Muslims and invited for talks,' Dattopant Thengadi wrote later.[67] Gandhi had supported the Khilafat movement started by Muslims to force the British to recognize the authority of the Ottoman sultan in Turkey as the caliph of Islam. The Ottoman Empire was broken up by the end of World War I and the British paid no heed to Muslims demands. Gandhi saw in the Muslim discontent a strategic opportunity to mobilize their support to strengthen the freedom movement. He believed that the British would not be able to withstand the unity of Hindus and Muslims.

In a letter to Lord Chelmsford, the viceroy and Governor General of India, Gandhi unambiguously made his position clear. 'The Peace Terms and your Excellency's defence of them have given the Mussalmans of India a shock from which it will be difficult for them to recover. The terms violate ministerial pledges and utterly disregard Mussalman sentiment. I consider that as a staunch Hindu wishing to live on terms of the closest of friendship with my Mussalman countrymen, I should be an unworthy son of India if I did not stand by them in their hour of trial,' Gandhi wrote.[68]

Hedgewar disliked the idea of Hindu–Muslim unity and questioned Gandhi about his strategy. He joined issue with Gandhi on his insistence on Hindu–Muslim unity when apart from the two communities, Parsis, Christians and Jews also lived in India. Gandhi replied that it had kindled the spirit of nationalism in Muslims and they were fighting shoulder to shoulder with Hindus in the national agitation. Hedgewar argued that even before the use of the term Hindu–Muslim unity many patriotic Muslims were working under Tilak's leadership. The new terminology, Hedgewar feared, would make Muslims feel superior instead of building unity. 'I don't have any such fears,' Gandhi replied.[69]

To Hedgewar, Gandhi's Ram–Rahim equivalence, in which Rahim had the upper hand, was spurious. Gandhi's Ram was an appeaser and not the masculine conqueror the RSS wanted to project. His way of organizing and leading was not manly enough or suitable for the revival of Hindus who had been persecuted for a thousand years. This victimhood could only be redeemed by a strength that was physical. Like Hindu gods, who are depicted holding out one hand in blessing while also gripping multiple weapons in many other hands, the idea of Mother India is also imbued with physical strength, moral courage and benevolence for its devotees.

Savarkar believed foreign invaders threatened to wipe out the superior Hindu race and their civilization because it had fallen prey to Buddhist pacifism. But true Indians would have none of it. They would draw from an ancient memory in which valour and courage were as central to the civilizational ethos as knowledge and enquiry. 'The leaders of thought and action of our race had to rekindle their sacrificial fire to oppose the sacrilegious one and to reopen the mines of Vedic fields for steel, to get it sharpened on the altar of Kali, "the Terrible", so that Mahakal, "the Spirit of Time", be appeased. Nor were their anticipations belied. The success of the renovated Hindu arms was undisputed and indisputable.'[70]

Savarkar rejected Buddha and his law of righteousness as unsuited for the world which was not yet ready and large-hearted enough. But Buddha is beyond his understanding because his 'ears are trained to the accents and din of this matter-of-fact world'.[71]

Though he conceded that Buddha could be counted as one among the Hindu pantheon alongside Rama and Krishna, even he was the gift *of* the land and not a gift *to* it. Thus, for Savarkar, peace was best kept when the hand held a sword. A nation could not be held together without strength; respect had to be squeezed out. 'As it stands at present the word Hindu has come to be the very banner of our race and the one great feature that above all others contributes to strengthen and uphold our racial unity from Cape to Kashmir, from Attock to Cuttack.'[72]

In Savarkar's formulation of Hindutva, the two primary conditions to be fulfilled by a patriotic citizen of the nation were the land as the 'punyabhu' and 'pitrubhu'—holy land and fatherland. While for all those born here, India would be their fatherland, it would not necessarily be their holy land. The Muslims', Christians' and Jews' holy lands lay in Mecca in Saudi Arabia or Jerusalem or Rome. This definition automatically placed the burden of proving their loyalty to the nation on these people.

> Christian and Mohammedan communities, who were but very recently Hindus and in a majority of cases had been at least in their first generation most unwilling denizens of their new fold, claim though they might have a common Fatherland and an almost pure Hindu blood and parentage with us, cannot be recognized as Hindus; as since their adoption of the new cult they had ceased to own Hindu civilization [Sanskriti] as a whole.[73]

A religious Hindu identity would have been politically challenging because of the diversity of practices, conventions, traditions and even gods. It did not allow itself to be encapsulated in a neat framework like other Abrahamic religions. This drawback is removed in Hindutva which is a more flexible ideological framework akin to a political philosophy. Yet, it chose to not only appropriate elements of Indian religious practices but also claimed an ancient encoding. So it was argued in the Supreme Court in 1995:

> At the outset the appellant submits that Hindutva is not a religion. It is a philosophy like communism or socialism.

The difference is that while communism and socialism are materialistic philosophies intended to secure economic welfare of individuals, Hindutva is a spiritual cum economic philosophy founded and developed from ancient times in this land for securing the all-round happiness of all individuals irrespective of religion of individuals. The stress in this philosophy both on the ruler and the rules is the performance of duty and to conform to a code of conduct. The vast body of proper code of conduct in every sphere of human activity such as personal, social political was called 'Dharma'.[74]

The preservation of culture and pride in intellectual superiority is the dominant theme in the RSS narrative. It links it inextricably to patriotism as Vivekananda had so forcefully presented to his American hosts. This also leads to claims of India being the repository of practically all knowledge known to humankind. It believes the rightful place of the country in the world is of a *Vishwa Guru*, or teacher to the world, but it will achieve it only if Hindus are strong.

This definition of who is a Hindu, though largely accepted by the RSS, is a matter of contention within the organization. A large section believes that Christians and Muslims cannot be considered Hindu, while officially, the RSS has accepted those belonging to the two communities as Hindus precisely because of their blood and parentage. The demand it now makes of followers of other religions is that they pledge their unconditional loyalty to the nation which is often tested in symbols that themselves become a source of conflict. Although not an official policy, Sangh Parivar volunteers often insist that everyone chant 'Vande Mataram' and say 'Bharat Mata ki Jai', more aggressively represented in the slogan: *Bharat mein rahna hai toh Vande Mataram kahna hoga* (You will have to chant Vande Mataram if you want to live in India).[75]

According to the RSS, its practice of Hindutva has three basic values—loyalty to the nation, respect for ancestors and a common culture. The RSS works to 'promote fraternity and that is possible only through unity in diversity'. This expanded Hindutva includes Muslims. 'The day it is said that we don't want Muslims, Hindutva will cease to exist.'[76]

*

In 1987, and then again in 1990, cases were filed against Shiv Sena leader Bal Thackeray, Manohar Joshi and many BJP and Shiv Sena leaders for allegedly breaching election laws when they sought votes in the name of 'Hindu religion and to fight for Hindutva'.

Senior lawyer Rama Jois, who is close to the Sangh Parivar, explained in a submission that Hinduism which comprises within itself the moral values in personal and public life, a deep sense of patriotism, and respect for all religions, was the only remedy to restore the nation's declining health.

In its judgment, the Supreme Court bench, led by Justice J.S. Verma, analysed Hinduism and Hindutva. It said that no precise meaning could be ascribed to the terms 'Hindu', 'Hindutva' and 'Hinduism'. It said the words could not be confined to the narrow limits of religion alone, excluding the content of Indian culture and heritage.

'It is also indicated that the term "Hindutva" is related more to the way of life of the people in the sub-continent. It is difficult to appreciate how in the face of these decisions the term "Hindutva" or "Hinduism" per se, in the abstract, can be assumed to mean and be equated with narrow fundamentalist Hindu religious bigotry . . .' the court said.[77]

It quoted from Maulana Wahiduddin Khan's *Indian Muslims: The Need for a Positive Outlook*:

The strategy worked out to solve the minorities problem was, although differently worded, that of Hindutva or Indianization. This strategy, briefly stated, aims at developing a uniform culture by obliterating the differences between all the cultures coexisting in the country. This was felt to be the way to communal harmony and national unity. It was thought that this would put an end once and for all to the minorities problem.[78]

Bolstering its analysis with Khan's argument, the court said that it indicated that the word 'Hindutva' is used and understood as a synonym of 'Indianization', i.e., development of uniform culture by obliterating the differences between all the cultures coexisting in the country.[79]

The judgment drew a lot of flak from political commentators for it seemed to support Hindutva. But the most important criticism levelled against it was that the judges had entirely ignored Savarkar's seminal text on Hindutva. It was not referred to at all. This was a grave error because even though the court was hearing a petition on the issue of violation of the election laws, Savarkar's book is the foundational work for all modern proponents of Hindutva.

However, Maulana Wahiduddin Khan's analysis that Hindutva strategy envisages creating a uniform culture subsuming diverse subcultures is fairly accurate. In the past, there has been an effort at standardization of Hinduism or Hindu religious practices. This is coupled with the zeal of a section who are quick to take offence and even resort to violence to ostensibly protect the Hindu dharma. Some have even called it Abrahamic Hindutva.[80]

*

From the RSS perspective, having had the experience of various organizations ranging from the militant Anushilan Samiti of Bengal to the pacifist Congress, Hedgewar established the RSS which would be a self-sustaining organization dedicated to only one goal: protecting and nurturing the nation to the pinnacle of glory. It would do that by unifying Hindu society into an irresistible, all-conquering force. The RSS would build an army of swayamsevaks, of every Hindu, who, imbued with the values imparted by the Sangh, would enter various walks of life and engage in activities that would help develop thoughts conducive for the nation to reach the height of glory. 'The Congress was a useful instrument for the achievement of the short-term objective; the Hindu Mahasabha was its refinement; the Sangh was the enduring instrument for the attainment of the final goal.'[81]

According to Ashis Nandy, Hindu nationalist ideologues were not orthodox. They also did not flaunt their orthodoxy unlike Gandhi who proclaimed himself a Sanatani Hindu. They have 'proudly affirmed their links with the nineteenth-century Hindu reform movements, which they see as analogous of a masculine Protestantism, cleaning up a degraded, distorted faith to make it fit the needs of a national state'.[82]

Nandy says the first head of the RSS, Hedgewar, too, could hardly be called a run-of-the-mill believing Hindu. 'An urban, well-educated, modern doctor with poor links to rural India and mainstream Hinduism, Hedgewar, like many pioneers of Hindu nationalism, was an aggressive critic of Hinduism who was exposed to religious and social reform movements, especially the Ramakrishna Mission founded in 1897 by Swami Vivekananda. Hindu nationalism, on this plane, was popular European political theory and political history telescoped into South Asia as a form of toady Hinduism. In retrospect, one realizes why Gandhi insisted that the nineteenth-century religious reform movements had done more harm than good to Hinduism.'[83]

None among his contemporaries have rivalled Hedgewar in organization, and the RSS's longevity and current strength is proof of the effectiveness of its methodology. Mohan Bhagwat has said that the RSS is nothing but a methodology to mould volunteers. The organizational thought process goes: The final goal is illuminated by ideology; in light of the final goal the short-term targets are decided which determine the tactics and broad strategy which provide the logical basis of agitation and current programmes.[84] Yet, in the first decade of building the organization, Hedgewar hardly felt the need for a theoretical framework for the RSS. The Sangh was mostly limited to Marathi-speaking Brahmins. However, its association with Savarkar gave it an ideological grounding. It was only when work began expanding outside the Marathi-speaking regions and he also became aware that he did not have very long to live that Hedgewar felt the need to create a proper structure and a written ideological framework.

Hedgewar's friend, G.D. Savarkar, had written a thesis in Marathi, 'Rāshtramimānsā āni Hindusthānche Rāshtraswarūp' (Elucidation of Nation and the Nature of Hindustan's Nationhood), under the pseudonym Durgātanay. Golwalkar translated it into English in 1938 titled *We or our Nationhood Defined*, most likely on Hedgewar's instructions. Congressman and Hindu Mahasabhaite M.S. Aney wrote the foreword to the book on Hedgewar's request and it was released in 1939 on Varsha Pratipada (the Hindu New Year) in Nagpur. The author Golwalkar was not present as he was in Calcutta. Hedgewar was happy that there was an ideological treatise available to back up the expanding RSS work.[85]

Shreerang Godbole, a former RSS *bhag sanghchalak* in Pune, who has researched the Savarkars' life and work extensively and runs the web site savarkar.org, says that the controversial paragraphs in the book eulogizing Nazi Germany's treatment of Jews as a 'good lesson for us in Hindustan to learn and profit by' were added by Golwalkar and were not part of G.D. Savarkar's original Marathi version.[86]

Godbole acknowledges the contributions of Dayananda Saraswati, Vivekananda, Aurobindo and Lokmanya Tilak in 'laying down the contours' of the Hindutva movement, but he introduces the Savarkar brothers and M.S. Golwalkar as the only three people who definitively explained Hindutva and Hindu nationhood.[87]

The controversial work, which praises Nazi Germany and its ideas for achieving racial purity, would haunt the RSS for generations even though it disowned it a few years after it was published. The most recent disavowal of some of Golwalkar's controversial statements was by Mohan Bhagwat during an unprecedented lecture series in

Delhi in mid-September 2018. Bhagwat said the RSS would rub out some of Golwalkar's old statements and rewrite his books to reflect the new thinking. He was referring to Golwalkar terming Muslims, Christians and communists as internal threats to the nation.[88]

After *We or Our Nationhood Defined* was disowned by the organization, *Bunch of Thoughts*—an edited collection of Golwalkar's speeches and talks published in the mid-1960s—became the essential reference guide for everything related to the RSS. It was essential reading for every volunteer as well as anyone wanting to know about the organization. That has now been replaced by another book—*M.S. Golwalkar: His Vision and Mission.*[89] New editions of *Bunch of Thoughts* would change references to Muslims and Christians from 'internal threats' to 'Islamic fundamentalism' and 'missionary evangelism'. This was to avoid the RSS being labelled anti-Muslim and anti-Christian.[90]

Bhagwat's comments divided the RSS. While nobody openly aired any criticism, several leaders were unhappy that Bhagwat tried to correct the revered Golwalkar. Yet, there were others who were happy that he had sought to return the Sangh to its Hedgewarian origins where nurturing and growing the organization was the most important mission. But the roots of the RSS's ideology may perhaps lie deeper in history, in a book that was once acclaimed by the leading lights of India's freedom struggle.

*

In November 2017, a group of veteran RSS hands held a closed-door workshop called 'Dishabodh' at BJP leader Murli Manohar Joshi's ancestral home in Almora. Joshi himself was present at the workshop which was organized by Mahesh Sharma, a former chairman of the Khadi Board and Village Industries Corporation, who is currently in charge of the RSS's rural outreach programme, Gramoday.[91]

The two-day workshop ended with a declaration to promote dialogue and action for balanced development and bring back policies in line with Upadhyaya's philosophy and an obscure political treatise called *Daishik Shastra*,[92] which was the basis of Upadhyaya's work, *Integral Humanism*.

Golwalkar had discovered the obscure text in his friend and Jaunpur king Yadavendra Dutt Dubey's library in 1958.[93] *Daishik Shastra* was written in Hindi in 1920 by Badrishah Tuldharia, an Almora-based lawyer, and was published in 1921. The political science treatise, Tuldharia wrote in the preface, was compiled from Indian texts that were archaic and ancient. 'It was a science that guards and defends the nation,' he wrote.[94]

Tuldharia sent a portion of the manuscript to Bal Gangadhar Tilak who was so impressed with it that he offered to write a prologue to it. Tilak, however, died before the manuscript was complete and Tuldharia published it as a tribute to him. Mahatma Gandhi, a committed Sanatani, reportedly wanted the book prescribed for students of political science: 'For the first time I had come across an excellent book on oriental politics in Hindi.'[95] Writing in the daily *Navjivan* on 8 February 1923, Gandhi reportedly said that Tuldharia beautifully explains 'the tenets of dharma (that which sustains) and spiritualism in terms of politics. For those who want to read Bhagavad Gita and Upanishads in the language of politics, this book is a must.'[96]

Golwalkar gave the book to Upadhyaya.

The Jan Sangh leader serialized it in the RSS publication *Panchajanya* in 1959. Concluding the series, Upadhyaya wrote: '*Daishik Shastra* is the only book of its kind that presents a lucid explanation of both the hoary and contemporary Bharatiya tenets. Late Shri Badrishah Tuldharia attained the knowledge of hitherto hidden doctrines of *Daishik Shastra* some forty years back through the grace of an ascetic seer Mahatma Shri 108 Sombari Maharaj and later on published the same under the title *Daishik Shastra*.'[97]

The treatise not only explains in detail various principles and methods of governance, it also deals with how to mould citizens and the nation to realize the four purusharthas—dharma (law and duty), *artha* (wealth), *kama* (pleasure and enjoyment) and *moksha* (liberation or salvation)—which are also the central objectives of Upadhyaya's Integral Humanism.[98]

Tuldharia had no idea that his work would inspire an ideology that would become the framework for a political party that would one day control the country's destiny. He had conceived the book in seven sections. In the preface to the original Hindi edition, he says the published work, which lays down broad principles, contains only four. The rest, which deal with policies and practice, remain unpublished and have perhaps been lost.

Considering that the book was published in 1921 by Tilak's friend Narhar Joshi's Chitrashala Press in Pune, and that the founders of the RSS were Tilak's close associates, it is possible that its ideas had influenced or inspired them.

For instance, Tuldharia was impressed by British officials prioritizing national interest over individual interest. He believed that was the tiny European island nation's secret to glory and global dominance.[99] Not only did Hedgewar found the Sangh in the image of the British military, he, and later Deoras, have repeatedly stressed on the patriotism of the British people for whom national interest was paramount.

In the section titled 'Interpretation of Patriotism', Tuldharia theorizes that every community is born with a *chiti* (collective consciousness). 'This chiti resides in every individual of a community in the form of an idea of ultimate bliss. But it does not remain equally pervasive in all the individuals at all the times. During periods of prosperity, chiti resides in all, or a majority of individuals of the community. During adversity, it takes shelter only in the core of the high-born individuals of a pure race.'[100] He calls the 'collectivity of people with one chiti and a specific natural mission' *jati* (community). Although the book rejects the English word nation for 'jati' and calls it community instead, the word that closest expresses the idea appears to be race.[101]

'Natural fighting spirit of an awakened and united community, i.e., its power to defend itself against the onslaughts of any evils is called virat,' Tuldharia writes.[102] He says a great community maintains racial purity, a separate identity from other communities and ensures more virtuosity of its high-born than its low-born.[103]

The book also gives instructions on eugenics to create progeny with the desired characteristics,[104] something the RSS is keenly promoting through its initiative 'kutumba prabodhan' (family enlightenment). It runs a Garbhavigyan Anusandhan Kendra (pregnancy science research centre) in Jamnagar in Gujarat.

The basic ideas of Integral Humanism, which Upadhyaya later developed into the ideological framework for the Jana Sangh, were found in Tuldharia's work. It says unity of belief, tradition, language and state cannot be treated as the basis of Jatitva,[105] which is described as community.

Upadhyaya seems to have taken the fundamental ideas of *Daishik Shastra* to conceptualize Integral Humanism as a combination of Indian and Western ideologies. 'The Western world has made great material progress but in the field of spiritual attainment it has not been able to make much headway. India on the other hand lags far behind in material advancement and so its spiritualism has become a hollow-sounding word. There can be no spiritual salvation without material prosperity. It is necessary, therefore, that we strive for strength and material happiness so that we may be able to build up national health and contribute to the progress of the world, instead of being a burden on it,' Upadhyaya wrote in January 1965.[106]

For this ideal to be translated into practice, he felt, India's programmes had to be grounded in realism.[107] Three months later, Upadhyaya presented the framework of Integral Humanism in four speeches at a special party session in Bombay. The Jana Sangh adopted it as its guiding ideological principle.

A close look at the RSS's organization and functioning show remarkable similarities with Tuldharia's ideas. So much so that often the book reads like an instruction manual which the Sangh followed to the letter. 'Our *Daishik Shastra* considers purification of public opinion as a part of Adhyapan Shastra [science of teaching]. Because the wave of public opinion influences the mental make-up and conduct of people. Even the greatest personalities have to bow before public opinion,' says Mahesh Sharma.[108] It calls 'public opinion' and 'public blaspheme' demons which are the products of the 'educated elite'.[109] 'Nobody's opinions and rationale can earn acceptability only because they emanate from the book-worms. The people's opinion and public logic becomes extremely mean and corrupt when literate fools gain an upper hand amidst the illiterate idiots.'[110] This kind of public opinion and perception needs to be purified, a task left to mendicants and dedicated, celibate missionaries; a description that fits RSS pracharaks and leaders. 'It is the duty of the kings and big business houses to support them fully in their tasks.'[111]

Like the Sangh, Tuldharia also lays down patriotism as the fundamental quality in citizens essential for progress and prosperity. Goddess Lakshmi (of wealth) is propitiated by sacrifice, struggle and supreme patriotism. 'Man is obliged to a country where he has been staying from generations together; whose air-waters have shaped and strengthened his person; where he was created, where his ancestors were born and buried or cremated; where his community has been glorified; whose mere sight unleashes waves of indescribable delight in the heart; which is the very foundation of his existence and that of his community.'[112]

The book says if a person destroys eminent institutions of the country to protect its 'chiti' and 'virat', he cannot be called a traitor. When these two qualities are awakened, the country depends neither on rulers nor administrative systems. 'Nobody would dispute that the Monarchy of Shri Ramachandra was thousand times better than the Democracy of King Ravana.'[113]

Tuldharia also advocates war as a means of 'pruning' communities like a tree of 'undesirable portions'. 'Never should any attempts be made to prevent war . . . the disharmony and disturbances caused by war is not even a hundredth part of that caused by deception and diplomacy.'[114]

These startling principles seem to form the value system on which contemporary politics of the Sangh Parivar is based.

2

The Quest

'Welcome to the governor designate,' the host is said to have exclaimed warmly as Kummanam Rajasekharan, the BJP state president, entered the house in Kerala's Chengannur. It was 25 May 2018. Summer was at its peak and so was the election campaign in the run-up to the Chengannur bypoll necessitated by the death of sitting legislator K.K. Ramachandran Nair of the CPI(M). Rajasekharan was making door-to-door calls in a last-minute dash for his party's candidate P.S. Sridharan Pillai.[1] The unusual welcome surprised him. His host pointed to the television on which the news reported that President Ram Nath Kovind had made two gubernatorial appointments. Kerala state BJP president Kummanam Rajasekharan had been appointed as the governor of Mizoram, and Ganeshi Lal, governor of Odisha.

Rajasekharan did not know. He rang the state leaders of the RSS, his parent organization, who were, coincidentally, gathering in Kochi for a meeting. Neither they nor the national office-bearers of the Sangh seemed to be aware of it.

The RSS state executive council met the next day and decided to take an unprecedented step. It wrote a letter to general secretary Suresh 'Bhaiyaji' Joshi. The message was said to be unequivocal: the BJP had betrayed the Kerala RSS. And Rajasekharan refused to accept the assignment.

That evening, as BJP workers celebrated the government's completion of four years in office, top BJP and RSS leaders were cooped up in party president Amit Shah's house for hours trying to placate Rajasekharan who had flown in the same evening.[2] The BJP leadership is believed to have contended that even though Rajasekharan was an RSS pracharak, he was with the BJP now and the party had the full right to decide his assignment. The Kerala RSS asserted that the BJP may be within its rights so long as the assignment was within the party's fold. This was an independent constitutional position and it had no business appointing its swayamsevak without consulting the RSS. Rajasekharan too remained adamant on his stand.

As the meeting stretched inconclusively beyond midnight, Prime Minister Modi is believed to have spoken with Rajasekharan, who left for Mizoram the next morning, on the telephone. The RSS Kerala unit suspected that two state BJP leaders had been scheming to remove Rajasekharan from the scene as they were losing their clout in the party.[3]

In late 2015, when the BJP wanted a person to lead its state unit, which was rife with infighting, it asked the Sangh to loan Rajasekharan. The Sangh agreed on the sole condition that he would not be shifted for at least two years. As president, Rajasekharan revamped the state BJP unit, and chose many RSS pracharaks to function as party office-bearers down to the district level.[4]

Over nearly a year, the two leaders had quietly managed to convince the party's central leaders of Rajasekharan's inefficiency, the RSS leadership reportedly concluded. According to a senior RSS leader from Kerala, they found evidence for one of the two leaders conspiring against Rajasekharan.[5]

After Rajasekharan was appointed governor, the BJP went into a state of deep crisis as the Sangh remained determined to show that its workers were not to be trifled with.[6] The party's central leadership, which was said to have been ready to announce Rajasekharan's successor, deferred the decision. When the party president visited

Kerala to sort out the issue, RSS state leaders are said to have taken him to task. On his part, the president is believed to have stood his ground that they had no say in the BJP's internal decisions.[7]

In Kerala, most BJP workers are RSS volunteers and it is the biggest province in terms of number of shakhas (around 6845 with a daily attendance of 84,000).[8] Such rebellion is possible only when the pracharak and workers operate within the Sangh framework against an affiliate, not against the parent itself. In early 2017, when its entire Goa unit, led by *vibhag sanghchalak* Subhash Velingkar, rebelled against BJP chief minister and former pracharak Manohar Parrikar, who was seeking re-election, the RSS removed the sanghchalak, effectively cutting off Velingkar and everyone associated with him from the parivar. Velingkar, a Sangh veteran of fifty-four years who is credited with building the organization in the state and who claims to have been Parrikar's mentor, had floated a new party Goa Suraksha Manch to fight elections against the BJP. His plank was making the Konkani language mandatory in schools and stopping government aid to English-medium schools which were mostly run by Christian missionaries.[9]

The Kerala and Goa incidents were aberrations in an otherwise smooth relationship the RSS and BJP had developed in the Bhagwat–Modi era. After Modi completed his hat-trick of victories in the Gujarat state polls in 2012, he emerged as the biggest BJP star and his popularity soared among the ordinary workers of the Sangh Parivar. Meanwhile, Mohan Bhagwat had rid the RSS of its rustiness and brought the BJP under the Sangh's firm grip, even forcing changes in its leadership. Many in the RSS felt he had picked up from where Deoras had left off.

*

Bhagwat was born in Sangli in a Maharashtrian Brahmin family steeped in Sangh values. His paternal grandfather, Narayan 'Nana' Bhagwat, was a Congressman and schoolmate of RSS founder Hedgewar. Mohan was the eldest of three sons and a daughter born to

Narayan 'Nana' Bhagwat's son Madhukarrao and his wife Malatibai. Madhukarrao had worked as a pracharak in Gujarat in the 1940s and then moved back to Nagpur after his eldest child was born. He had graduated in law by then and started practice in Nagpur.[10]

Mohan Bhagwat grew up in Chandrapur in a comfortable home surrounded by fields. He studied in Chandrapur and later in Panjabrao Deshmukh Krishi Vidyapeeth in Akola from where he graduated in veterinary sciences with a gold medal in pathology. He spent most of his time in Nagpur because many subjects of his course were taught in Nagpur University. Bhagwat's life revolved around the RSS and its activities.[11] A senior leader remembers him as a boy running around at a national camp managed by his father.

Bhagwat started a shakha in a government-organized inter-university students camp in 1970. The issue raised a furore and reportedly reached the state assembly where the government denied its existence.[12] Except for his association with the RSS, Bhagwat's childhood and college life were of an average middle-class Indian of the time. He was fond of fashion and singing and performed the Marathi folk art form Bharud. He also acted in and directed plays. Considered a good actor, he won many prizes at competitions. He enrolled for a postgraduate course but dropped out a few months before Emergency was declared.[13]

*

Meanwhile, a future prime minister was growing up in Gujarat where Madhukarrao Bhagwat worked as a pracharak in the 1940s. Narendra Modi was born to Damodardas Mulchand Modi and Heeraben on 17 September 1950. He is the third of six children. The family was of the Ghanchi caste, whose traditional vocation was oil pressing. His father ran a tea stall near the local railway station in addition to the family's traditional caste business of running oil presses.[14]

Modi was enrolled in Bhagavatacharya Narayanacharya High School, a coeducational Gujarati-medium institution in the old part of the town. Though an average student, Modi was good at debates and theatre.[15] Modi's political training began in early childhood. It was a period of tumult as the Maha Gujarat agitation demanding separate statehood was gathering momentum. The States Reorganisation Commission had recommended that Bombay should remain the capital city of both Marathi- and Gujarati-speaking regions.

Modi learnt to shout slogans when he was six years old from a local leader, Rasikbhai Dave. He also disliked the Congress party. 'There is one thing that I remember since then—the strong hatred towards the Congress which was prevalent at that time—became part of me,' Modi told a biographer.[16] He also began attending the local RSS shakha around the same time. In his long association with the RSS, Modi learnt management and organizing skills for which he had a natural bent. Those skills would come handy many years later when he had to organize the Ayodhya Rath Yatra and Ekta Yatra, two cross-country agitational tour programmes that brought electoral dividends for the BJP.

As per traditions of his caste, Modi was married off when he was thirteen years old. His wife, Jashodaben Chimanlal, three years younger to him, lived in the neighbouring town of Brahmanwada. The marriage, however, remained only in memories of the families. Modi left home to wander in the Himalayas when he was eighteen, the age when the final ceremony (*gauna*) of the three-stage marriage was supposed to take place.[17] He returned two years later but once again left for Ahmedabad to help his uncle run a canteen. He did not stay long there either, moving to the RSS state headquarters, Hedgewar Bhawan, as an assistant.[18]

Modi has himself described how the RSS moulded him. 'It was kind of a progressive unfolding. I kept growing, kept speaking, kept understanding more and more, kept on asking new questions every day. It is like no woman can answer the question of when exactly did she learn how to cook. She would have started by cutting and chopping vegetables, at some point she would have helped her mother in doing some other chore, sometime she may have fetched the *atta* [flour], another time she might have just turned the *chappatis* [flatbread] and on other occasions she would have lit the *chulah* [stove]. The process of the Sangh is something very similar—at least it was so in my case.'[19] It was an excellent analogy of how subtly the Sangh conditions and prepares its volunteers.

Both Mohan Bhagwat and Narendra Modi were newly minted RSS pracharaks when Indira Gandhi declared Emergency in 1975. Their paths don't seem to have crossed for many years even though both worked in the same organization. Bhagwat was unexpectedly chosen as general secretary of the RSS in the year 2000. The next year, in a surprise move, Modi was appointed chief minister of Gujarat. For years, however, relations between the RSS and Modi remained frosty. It began to thaw only in the spring of 2008.

It was after many years that the RSS was led by someone as politically minded as Hedgewar and Deoras. Soon the BJP would also get a leader who was an excellent communicator, politically savvy and ruthlessly ambitious. Modi would dominate the BJP the way Indira Gandhi had ruled the Congress.

The RSS–Modi thaw came at a time when it was facing one of its biggest existential threats. The BJP lost the 2009 national elections, the second defeat in a row. After the Congress party–led UPA returned to power with an improved mandate, it began to tighten the screws on the Parivar.

In 2006–07, suspicions of Parivar organizations such as the Bajrang Dal being involved in bomb attacks had started surfacing.[20] By 2008, the police were on the trail of Hindu suspects in bomb attacks on Muslim religious gatherings in Malegaon, Ajmer and Hyderabad, and travellers on the Samjhauta Express to Pakistan. Initially, fringe Hindu organizations such as Abhinav Bharat and Sanatan Sanstha were suspected but later the web threatened to ensnare the RSS itself.

The Central Bureau of Investigation (CBI) arrested Swami Aseemanand or Nabakumar Sarkar, chief of the Vanvasi Kalyan Ashram in the Dangs district of Gujarat, accusing him of planning bomb attacks in Ajmer, Hyderabad and the Samjhauta Express. It also picked up RSS vibhag pracharak of Muzaffarpur, Devendra Gupta, and a couple of other volunteers for their suspected role in some of the bombings. One RSS pracharak, Sunil Joshi, who was alleged to have been the mastermind of the operations, was found murdered in Madhya Pradesh.[21] In 2014, Aseemanand told the *Caravan* magazine in an interview in Ambala Central Jail where he was imprisoned that the plans had sanction from the highest level of the RSS.[22] The charge was categorically denied by the organization as well as Aseemanand.

At a meeting of state police chiefs in August 2010, Home Minister P. Chidambaram urged vigilance against what he termed as saffron terror, a branding that would haunt the Sangh Parivar. 'There is no let-up in the attempts to radicalize young men and women in India. There has been a recent uncovered phenomenon of saffron terrorism that has been implicated in many bomb blasts in the past. My advice to you is that we must remain ever vigilant and continue to build, at both central and state level, our capacities in counter-terrorism,' Chidambaram said.[23]

By 2011, even senior RSS leaders were feeling the heat. In a charge sheet filed in court that year, the National Investigation Agency (NIA), which was formed after a terrorist attack on Mumbai in November 2008, named Indresh Kumar, a national executive council member of the RSS, as one of the co-conspirators in the Hyderabad Mecca Masjid attack of May 2007. RSS leaders feared that the UPA government was determined to jail its leaders and ban the organization by foisting charges of terrorism on it. It suspected a political plot to finish off the organization. The top accused in the case, Devendra Gupta, was convicted in 2018.[24]

'The Sangh was genuinely worried that the UPA would ban the RSS and arrest top leaders. We had clear information about the plan,' said K.C. Kannan, former joint general secretary of the RSS.[25] The RSS felt the return of the UPA regime would finish it off. It could not afford to sit on the sidelines and hope for the BJP to win elections and come to its rescue. It needed to take control.

The RSS found its perfect spearhead in Narendra Modi. A product of the RSS system, Modi had political steel and was an unapologetic adherent of Hindutva. He had proven to be an able administrator who had reinvented himself as a champion of business and economic development. But there was much work to be done. The BJP was a divided house and many leaders had prime ministerial ambitions, main among them was L.K. Advani, once a staunch supporter of the Gujarat strongman but now a thorn in the side. Modi weathered the storm with the unstinted backing of the Sangh, especially Mohan Bhagwat.

At its national executive meeting in June 2013, the BJP selected Narendra Modi as its campaign committee chairman for the Lok Sabha elections. The next day, Advani resigned from all party positions except as the chairman of the National Democratic Alliance (NDA). 'For some time I have been finding it difficult to reconcile either with the current functioning of the party, or the direction in which it is going. I no longer have the feeling that this is the same idealistic party created by Dr Mookerji, Deendayalji, Nanaji and Vajpayeeji whose sole concern was the country, and its people. Most leaders of ours are now concerned just with their personal agendas,' Advani wrote in his resignation letter to party president Rajnath Singh.[26]

More drama ensued on 13 September when the BJP parliamentary board met in Delhi. That evening, Advani got into his car to drive to the meeting but then decided against it. He told Rajnath Singh he wouldn't attend the meeting.[27] While the drama was being played out, a top Sangh official was camped in the Jhandewalan headquarters of the RSS. Giving him company were four former stalwarts of the ABVP who had tirelessly campaigned in the previous few months to blunt opposition to Modi from within party ranks. They egged on the senior RSS leader to intervene to make sure that the announcement of Modi as the BJP's prime ministerial candidate was not delayed. The RSS's wish was conveyed to the BJP president. The board fell in line and announced that the party would fight the 2014 Lok Sabha elections under the leadership of Narendra Modi and he would be prime minister if the party won.[28]

The announcement electrified the party and RSS cadres. Exactly one month later, on 13 October, the sarsanghchalak himself weighed in on the elections. 'We have an immediate though temporary responsibility before us. In democracy, elections may be a matter of politics for contestants but for us common citizens it is an opportunity to perform our mandatory democratic duty. Voters will have an opportunity to elect their representatives in the near future. We have a large number of new and young voters. So as to discharge our responsibility as voters, first and foremost, we have to ensure that our names properly figure on the voters list. 100 per cent polling will make democracy healthier. We have to minutely evaluate the policies of contending political parties as also the character of the candidates while exercising our franchise,' said Bhagwat in his traditional Vijaya Dashami speech in Nagpur.[29] Officially, the RSS did not endorse any party or candidate, but Bhagwat dropped enough hints that it wanted the then dispensation gone.

In a democratic polity, when those who are responsible to ensure the security and progress of the nation lack the necessary competence to face up to the task and even their very intentions are questionable, it becomes incumbent upon the *samaj* to put in its efforts with dedication and valour to overcome the challenges … The economic condition of the nation has an instant and direct bearing on the day-to-day routine and life of the common people. Currently, the common people in our country are reeling under the unbearable weight of unending price rise. Just two years back, loud noises were being made about making our country an economic super-power of the world. But today we are in search of means to arrest the trend of fall in the value of rupee so as to tide over the imminent economic crisis; i.e. fiscal deficit, current account deficit and depleting foreign exchange reserve, and the resultant economic crisis have now become the hot topic of common discourse. Stagnating economic growth, steep rise in foreign debt in comparison to Gross Domestic Product, etc., bear ample testimony to the fact that we are taking our economy in the wrong direction. However, what is more surprising is the refusal of the government to change the course and its continuation with its rigid policies.[30]

On the ground, RSS volunteers were openly canvassing for Modi. One flyer distributed by RSS volunteers in Delhi discussed urban economic concerns such as roads and utilities. It also touched upon terrorism, Pakistan, and 'flying the Tricolour at Lal Chowk' in Srinagar. The reference was to the BJP's Ekta Yatra in 1991 which culminated with the raising of the Indian flag in Srinagar's famous Lal Chowk. The yatra was organized by Modi. The flyer read: 'Do you know who has achieved all of it? One ordinary man in Gujarat.'[31]

RSS volunteers also told Hindus that the BJP would build a Ram Temple in Ayodhya and change the special status of Jammu and Kashmir. At a zonal meeting in Kota, Rajasthan, Bhagwat is said to have declared, '*Ye chunav BJP nahi, Sangh lad raha hai* (It is the Sangh, not the BJP, that is fighting this election.).'[32]

Congress leader Chidambaram called the elections a Mahabharata war of ideologies. Sangh leaders agreed. They called it the Sangh's biggest-ever mobilization after the Emergency.[33]

The result was spectacular. For the first time in its history the BJP came to power with absolute majority, a feat no party had achieved since 1984. The RSS too had reached the peak of its power and influence politically. Its political affiliate was in power without the crutches of a coalition and a dyed-in-the-wool RSS volunteer was the prime minister. It was just a small step towards the ultimate goal.

'We would want the BJP to win all the state elections because only then can significant social, political and cultural changes take place in this country,' Dattatreya Hosabale, RSS joint general secretary told a foreign news agency. 'The 2014 election victory should be seen as the starting point of a long-term mission.'[34]

*

As an organization trying to build a nation, politics is at the core of RSS's strategy. Yet, its relationship with electoral politics has been testy for long. One RSS leader compared electoral politics to a commode—an ugly but unavoidable necessity in the house. One reason for that is the lens through which the RSS views democracy. In its view, democracy only means all opinion is heard but does not necessarily influence the final resolve. It follows this principle scrupulously in its organizational decision making. While an issue is debated thoroughly, once a decision is made, everyone is expected to fall in line. Even if the dissent had valid foundations, it would be canned. Democratic tradition demands that the decision of the majority would be respected but the dissenters would have the right to mobilize and consolidate their view and, if necessary, agitate to overturn the decision. In the RSS, dissent ends with decision.

The RSS wants to unite Hindus and mould enough volunteers to its ideology and beliefs. These volunteers would then occupy leadership positions in various fields, influencing them and helping embed the ideology. The second sarsanghchalak, M.S. Golwalkar, the revered Guruji, during whose thirty-three years at the helm the RSS expanded into an armada-like structure with multiple affiliate organizations, believed that the core organization should only function as an assembly line, churning out good principled men who, in turn, would do the job of nation building. A Union minister and a lifelong RSS volunteer compares the RSS to '…a power station. It constantly generates power. This power is then deployed in various fields where the nation requires it.'[35]

The third sarsanghchalak, Madhukar Dattatreya Deoras, popularly known as Balasaheb, gave the RSS a definite socio-political turn, ending its insularity and pushing it for a deeper involvement with the wider society and its concerns, including political agitations and elections. He strongly believed that social service and political engagement were necessary prerequisites for building the nation of RSS's dreams. Deoras ended the ambivalence towards electoral politics that began after a series of events in 1948 that forced the

RSS, which was until then functioning without a declared structure, to commit to a written constitution.

On 30 January 1948, as Mahatma Gandhi stepped out at Birla House in Delhi for his daily prayer meeting, he was shot dead by Nathuram Godse, a member of the Hindu Mahasabha and former RSS volunteer. The next day, Golwalkar was arrested and the RSS banned.

Golwalkar ordered the RSS to be shut down, but two skilful organizers, Deoras and Eknath Ranade, found ways to keep it functioning. It went underground, springing up in various forms as cultural and sports clubs, continuing its congregations without the usual drill and flag. It suspected that the government, particularly Nehru who strongly believed that the RSS was communal, had merely used the opportunity to destroy it. Its suspicions were rooted in a Congress session in Uttar Pradesh the previous year presided over by J.B. Kripalani, where it passed a resolution urging the government to ban the RSS.[36] This shadow boxing between the Congress and RSS that began in the late 1940s continues to this day. But for the next few years, even after the ban was lifted and its name cleared in court, the RSS withdrew into a shell. Its volunteers were ostracized, and the organization was viewed with deep suspicion.

For instance, the city of Pune was hit with riots and arson. The Brahmin community, which was seen as close to the RSS, was the chief target as people seethed over the assassination of their beloved Mahatma. The then Pune municipal commissioner, S.G. Barve, devised a clever way to stop future incidents. Barve divided the Brahmin and non-Brahmin population of Pune by settling them on either side of Shivaji Road, the arterial road that bifurcates the city. The Brahmins lived predominantly on the west side of the road and the rest on the east. It was common for Brahmins to be stared at angrily and heckled when they ventured to the east side. Children laughed, made fun of them, sometimes even landed a blow or two. There were very few non-Brahmins in the Sangh at the time. The handful that were there also spoke and acted like Brahmins.[37]

In the wake of the murder, the organization was isolated. 'Our experience of isolation in those days was a terrible one. The people were so cowed down that not a single voice of protest was raised against the grave injustice,' Deoras revealed immediately after he took over as chief.[38] Ideologue M.G. Vaidya remembers: 'When we walked on the streets, people would point and say, "Look, there go Gandhi's murderers."'[39]

The Sangh decided it needed a political party to bat for it in Parliament in Delhi and in provincial capitals. However, there was one problem. One of the conditions for lifting the ban on the RSS was that it would stay away from politics. Sardar Patel had given it the option of merging with the Congress, which Golwalkar rejected. During the ban, its central executive council member Eknath Ranade held secret talks with Patel to explore the option of an active political role for the organization. In 1949, the Congress Working Committee voted to admit RSS volunteers into the party but it was overturned a month later with the condition that those who join would have to quit the RSS.[40] This issue of dual membership would haunt the RSS again thirty years later.

Perhaps wary of the organization's love-hate relationship with the Hindu Mahasabha, Patel had insisted that the RSS stay away from politics. Himself a centre-right politician, Patel might have wanted the Sangh cadre to be a counterbalance to the Nehru-led socialists in the party. In the 1946 elections, V.D. Savarkar had announced his support to thirty candidates, including Syama Prasad Mookerjee. On 28 October, he issued a call to all Hindutva supporters in Congress to either join the Hindu Mahasabha or vote for its candidates.[41] To undermine Savarkar, who was getting some attention among Congressmen, the party proactively gave tickets to candidates leaning towards Hindutva. Congress leaders in Nagpur, in turn, went to Golwalkar and asked him to get the Hindu Mahasabha candidate M.N. Ghatate, who was also the RSS Nagpur sanghachalak, to withdraw from the contest. The RSS chief ordered Ghatate to withdraw his candidature in favour of the

Congress candidate. Shantaram Shivram Savarkar, popularly known as Balarao (no relation to the Savarkar brothers although he was V.D. Savarkar's secretary), writes that Golwalkar, unlike Savarkar, believed in 'organisation for the sake of organisation'. He believed freedom could be achieved only when organization was complete. He did not understand that militarization and elections were twin tools to overturn power structures.[42]

After Gandhi's assassination, the government forced the RSS to draw up a written constitution before it agreed to lift the ban. Section 4(c) of the constitution specifically deals with politics. 'The Sangh is aloof from politics and is devoted to social and cultural fields only.' But it also said: 'The swayamsevaks are free, as individuals, to join any party, institution or front, political or otherwise except such parties, institutions or fronts which subscribe to or believe in extra-national loyalties, or resort to violent and/or secret activities to achieve their ends, or which promote or attempt to promote, or have the object of promoting any feeling of enmity or hatred towards any other community or creed or religious denomination.'[43] But then, as a senior leader asked in a private conversation, do most people in the organization even know that the RSS has a constitution?

The Gandhi murder and its consequences expedited the RSS's move towards participation in active politics. Many in the Sangh thought that it would change its character and it was not founded for politics anyway. It then came up with the idea of a party at an arm's length from it, an ingenious way of interpreting the second part of Section 4(c).[44] Several politically minded swayamsevaks were to be lent to the new party. Among them were Atal Bihari Vajpayee, Pandit Deendayal Upadhyaya, Sunder Singh Bhandari, J.P. Mathur, Bhaurao Deoras and Jagannathrao Joshi. There was still one thing lacking: political experience to lead the party.

In 1950, Golwalkar travelled to Calcutta to meet Syama Prasad Mookerjee, who was by then divorced from the Hindu Mahasabha and was looking to start a national political outfit. They met at the house of a volunteer, Bansi Lal Sonee, in the Burrabazar area. Mookerjee had, earlier at a press conference, said that the Hindu Mahasabha was communal because it believed in Hindu Rashtra. Golwalkar said the RSS also believed in the concept though not as strongly as the Hindu Mahasabha. They ended up agreeing that restoration of the Hindu Rashtra was not inconsistent with establishment of a modern democracy.[45]

Mookerjee had joined the Hindu Mahasabha impressed by Savarkar and his political ideas for Hindu consolidation. The Hindu Mahasabha at the time was taking up issues of the Bengali bhadralok and they felt Subhas Chandra Bose in the Congress was not helping their cause in any way.

When he started organizing the Hindus, one of the people who had opposed him was Bose. The Congressman warned him that he would destroy him if he set up a rival political party. It was only after Bose lost to Gandhi's machinations in the party and quit the presidency of the Congress that he made a pact with Mookerjee for the Calcutta corporation elections. The pact broke even before the elections. After the elections, Bose sided with the Muslim League, helping install a Sindhi businessman, A.R. Siddiqui, as mayor.[46]

The idea of a Sangh-backed political party was broached in 1940 itself when Mookerjee met Hedgewar just before the latter's death in Nagpur. In that meeting, Mookerjee suggested that the RSS should enter politics. Hedgewar said it would not participate in the kind of politics prevalent then.[47]

A curious incident occurred just before this confabulation. On 27 December 1939, Savarkar flew the saffron flag at the Deshbandhu Park in Calcutta to inaugurate the Hindu Mahasabha conference, the first attended by delegates from across the country, giving the party a pan-Indian character.[48] Savarkar soon left for Bombay because of bad health. Balarao records an interesting incident from that Mahasabha session.

It was the first time that organization elections were held. Though he was not present, Savarkar asked B.S. Moonje, chairman of the executive council, to conduct the elections. The election to the post of secretary was hotly contested between Indraprakash, Jyotishankar Dikshit and M.S. Golwalkar who was then the RSS general secretary. While Indraprakash won with about eighty votes, Dikshit managed only two. Golwalkar, despite G.D. Savarkar's support and what was then considered the Jugal Kishore Birla group, could get only forty votes. The loss was perhaps too much for Golwalkar who never went back to the Hindu Mahasabha.[49]

Although Balarao Savarkar does not delve into the impact of Golwalkar's loss on the RSS, it is likely that Hedgewar was even more convinced of the pitfalls of aligning with a political party and hence declined Mookerjee's proposal too.

Ideally, the RSS wanted its swayamsevaks to join all political parties; they would be working in different parties during the day and attending shakhas together in the evening 'learning to think and behave that all are patriots having a common meeting ground'.[50]

Stung by the 1948 ban, the Sangh remained a faceless entity, avoiding limelight and building the organization quietly during Golwalkar's thirty-three-year-long tenure as chief. But it tightly controlled, or tried to control, its fledgling affiliates, bolstering the organizations with its own pracharaks while expanding its own network of well-wishers and sympathizers. It led to conflicts, especially with its political arm.

*

After Mookerjee died, a leadership struggle broke out in the Jana Sangh between acting president Mauli Chandra Sharma and the RSS which wanted to take total control of the party, including appointments to key posts and funding. On 3 November 1954, Sharma issued a statement accusing the RSS of interfering in the affairs of the party.

Acute differences of opinion on the question of interference by the RSS in its affairs have been growing for over a year. Many

RSS workers have entered the party since its inception. They were welcomed, as RSS leaders had publicly declared that it was a purely cultural body having nothing to do with politics and that its members were perfectly free to join any political party. In practice, however, it did not prove to be so.[51]

The RSS has a different view about ownership of Jana Sangh. Unlike other political parties, the Jana Sangh was built from the bottom up, according to RSS ideologue Devendra Swarup.[52] The all-India political set-up of the Jana Sangh grew from bottom to top and it was a projection of the RSS organization and ideology.[53] Swarup was a full-timer of the Sangh posted in Allahabad along with Rajendra Singh in the late 1950s and the 1960s. The RSS organized district-wise conventions of educated and politically alert people. Ad hoc committees were created at these meetings. The Jana Sangh came out of the RSS, through RSS initiative. In every district the convention was organized by RSS workers. First district committees were formed, then provincial committees were created and then on 23 October 1951, the all-India committee was formed in Delhi. S.P. Mookerjee was elected president in that meeting in Delhi.

Mauli Chandra Sharma alleged that even Mookerjee was often miffed by the demands of RSS leaders for a decisive role in matters like the appointment of office-bearers, nomination of candidates for elections and matters of policy. 'A vigorous and calculated drive was launched to turn the Jana Sangh into a convenient handle of the RSS. Orders were issued from their headquarters through their emissaries and the Jana Sangh was expected to carry them out.'[54] The party working committee, which met later, refuted the charge and reiterated that it was a dynamic democratic party.

Before the Jana Sangh was started, Mookerjee met Savarkar on 26 August 1952, to discuss the new party. The Hindutva theoretician told him that the philosophy and the programme of the new party were the same as the Hindu Mahasabha. He warned Mookerjee that it would end up like the Congress as 'Muslims would remain Muslims first and Indians never'.[55]

After Mookerjee, who was in touch with the non-Congress liberal streams, died, the Jana Sangh turned towards a severe Hindu nationalism 'becoming more defensive, more provincial, and more responsive to the attitudes of the lower middle classes of the northern towns and cities'.[56]

About twenty years later, another RSS pracharak who was shifted to the Jana Sangh would make a similar allegation about the party's *sangathan mantri* (organizing secretary), who is the RSS's man in the organization. A powerful key decision maker, it is through this person that the RSS enforces its writ while seemingly maintaining a distance and is often the cause of much heartburn. All Sangh Parivar organizations, including the BJP, have an organizing secretary.

In 1973, Balraj Madhok, who was the Bharatiya Jana Sangh secretary handling the northern states, complained that the organizing secretaries wanted to run the party like the Sangh, with total control and brooking no dissent. Madhok wanted the position itself to be abolished.[57]

*

In 1964, the RSS sent Dattopant Thengadi as a Jana Sangh member from Uttar Pradesh to the Rajya Sabha and he remained in the House for twelve years. His main job in Parliament was to network with other party members. A week after he was elected to the Rajya Sabha, Thengadi met Golwalkar in Nagpur who advised him that he no longer needed help from Jana Sangh leaders to meet ministers and officials. Direct interaction with the government would help him in getting the organization's work done.[58]

Golwalkar also wanted him to remain neutral in the House. He predicted that soon there would be a need for opposition unity against the Congress. The Jana Sangh would not be strong enough and would need allies. For that, Thengadi needed to build trust among other political leaders. That would be difficult if he took political positions in Parliament.[59] If he stuck to issues, he would be able to build a network across parties that could be leveraged in future. A decade later Thengadi was the convener of the Lok Sangharsh Samiti, the allied opposition front that fought Indira Gandhi's Emergency. He never got arrested during the Emergency and remained underground throughout.

The Congress under Nehru remained closed to the RSS. Soon after Nehru's death, it had begun efforts to join the Congress party, opening parleys with several leaders to get RSS workers appointed to key positions.[60] Lal Bahadur Shastri had good relations with several RSS leaders. He had helped RSS leader Eknath Ranade in mobilizing support for building a memorial for Vivekananda on a rock island off the coast of Kanyakumari in Tamil Nadu. He had also invited Golwalkar for consultations during the skirmish with Pakistan in 1965.

Soon, however, the Congress party was beset with internal power struggles. Following Lal Bahadur Shastri's sudden death in Tashkent, party president K. Kamaraj installed Indira Gandhi as the prime minister hoping that she would be a puppet, easily manipulated. Instead of a 'dumb doll' as some in the party thought she was, Gandhi turned out to be a wily politician who outwitted the Congress old guard at their own game with help from young socialists in the party and outside support from the CPI. Indira Gandhi's leftward turn alarmed the Sangh, which was a sworn enemy of communism.

*

During the freedom struggle and after, the Congress party had served as a platform for diverse voices from across the political spectrum. This made the Congress a representative party. But this also meant that those leaning to the right and those tilting to the left were engaged in a constant struggle to control its steering wheel. In the early years of Independence, Jawaharlal Nehru, by dint of his personal charisma and popularity both within the country and internationally, managed to keep the wheel firmly in his grip.

As the construction of independent India began, people from the right and the left separated from the Congress to join other political parties or create new outfits to espouse their ideological positions and policies independently. With the split in the Congress, those on the right and the left went their separate ways. While Mookerjee tried to create an umbrella organization of the right, the left and socialists had formed their own set-ups.

The power struggle in the Congress that had begun to simmer after Nehru's death boiled over when Lal Bahadur Shastri died. Indira Gandhi's need for allies in her power games for supremacy in the party and government offered communists the ideal atmosphere to grow roots in the establishment.

Seemingly, the RSS was the Congress's bitter rival, but that perception was not entirely true. There were close contacts between the RSS and the Congress leadership and many in the party were sympathetic to it. An apocryphal story went that when Golwalkar met Jagjivan Ram, who was then Congress president, at a public function, he joked: 'Aap president bane rahiye. Aapse bahut kaam hai humko (You continue to be president. We need you there).'[61] The Indira Gandhi government began to snip the RSS's wings. Then began the RSS's carefully planned campaign to counter the left. What seemed like an attack on Indira Gandhi was in fact a war on communism. As did many previous epoch-defining events in India's history, the sparks first flew in Bihar, the cradle of Indian politics.

In the early 1970s, K.N. Govindacharya was stationed in Patna, the capital of Bihar. Govindacharya, a Tamil Brahmin, had studied in Banaras Hindu University and had become district pracharak in Patna in the late 1960s, rising to vibhag pracharak in 1970. While prant pracharak Madhusudan Gopal Dev stayed away from politics and focused on expanding shakha work, Govindacharya's interest in politics and his position as Patna pracharak brought him in close contact with student leaders.

In 1972, the RSS's student arm, the ABVP, decided to hold a national convention in Patna to help its growth in the state. The convention was to happen in November but ABVP organizers were unable to get it off the ground. Finally, the Sangh stepped in and helped organize the convention.

In December, the ABVP shifted Ram Bahadur Rai, a young activist and skilful mobilizer from Uttar Pradesh, to Patna as all-India secretary in charge of the state. Rai, Govindacharya and former organizing secretary Ravindra Kesari negotiated an unconventional pact with Samajwadi Yuvajan Sangh, a socialist students' organization. Student unions on the right and left of centre had come together. It was the beginning of unlikely political alliances that often brought the right and the left on common platforms.

In Uttar Pradesh and Bihar, the upper and lower castes were aligned with the Congress. The middle castes were predominantly Lohiaite socialists. In Uttar Pradesh, the RSS's base was built among Punjabi traders in the west and central regions, who had migrated from Pakistan after Partition, and some upper-caste landlords of the eastern part of the state. However, most Thakurs and Brahmins, who jockeyed for power in the Congress, did not care much for the Sangh. The tie-up with the socialists also gave the RSS access to leaders of the middle castes such as Yadavs.

In the students' body elections of 1973 at Patna University, Lalu Prasad Yadav and Sushil Modi, who would go on to hold the reins of power in Bihar, became the president and general secretary candidates respectively. Ram Bahadur Rai, who had just been given charge of Bihar ABVP, made Govindacharya relieve Modi, who was then looking after Sangh work in the university, to contest the elections. The rival panel comprised candidates from the upper castes of Rajputs and Bhumihars. Govindacharya and Rai planned a panel, a caste combination of backward classes, bania and forward castes. The panel won.[62]

Meanwhile, a students' agitation was already gathering momentum in Gujarat where Chief Minister Chimanbhai Patel's government had become notorious for corruption. The students' agitation demanding the dismissal of the government was called the Navnirman Andolan (Reconstruction Movement). Echoes of the unrest rang out in Bihar where another Congress government was in power.[63]

Turmoil began with the left parties organizing mass demonstrations. Their call was: '*Pura rashan pura kam, nahin to hoga chakka jam* (Adequate work and full ration or we'll stop the wheels of life).'

In January 1974, following an all-India student leaders' conference in the capital, the Delhi University Students Union (DUSU) decided to hold such conferences in every state. It was held in Bihar in February 1974 in Patna University. The conference, however, did not go well and students split into two camps with the leftists forming the Chhatra Yuva Sangharsh Morcha (CYSM) while the ABVP and non-communist student groups formed the Chhatra Sangharsh Samiti (CSS). Both the groups started organizing activities and mobilizing support. Competition for the political centre stage between the left and right had started in earnest.

The CSS decided to lay siege to the Vidhan Sabha on 18 March 1974. This had been planned at the RSS office. Rai and Govindacharya had anticipated clashes with police, injuries and cases being slapped on activists. They had already met lawyers and prepared for eventualities. At around 10 a.m. on 18 March, Govindacharya took Ram Bahadur Rai on his scooter to the assembly where they met Sushil Modi. Govindacharya stayed back and Rai and Modi went ahead.[64]

Soon students and police clashed. By noon, police started firing at students. Three students died. Retreating students set fire to government buildings, a food warehouse and two newspaper offices.[65] When Govindacharya returned to the RSS office in the afternoon, a swayamsevak who worked in the home ministry had left a telephonic message that a warrant had been issued against him and Rai and the police was planning to pick them up in the evening from the office. An arrest from the RSS office would have been disastrous. Govindacharya went underground.[66]

The next day, they went to meet Gandhian leader Jayaprakash Narayan, popularly known as JP. Extremely annoyed at the students, he said they were all troublemaking monkeys setting fires everywhere. But JP himself had been a student radical when he was studying in Wisconsin, US. He agreed to lead the agitation on two conditions— it should be scrupulously non-violent, and it should not be restricted to Bihar. In a statement the day after, JP said: '…[He could] no longer remain a silent spectator to misgovernment, corruption and the rest, whether in Patna, Delhi or elsewhere. It is not for this that I had fought for freedom.'[67] He reiterated he was going to fight for a 'real people's democracy'.[68]

After that the agitation intensified. On 5 June, JP led a massive street rally ending at the vast Gandhi Maidan in the heart of Patna. At the public meeting, he called for 'total revolution'. With the entry of JP, the Bihar students' agitation was quickly rebranded as the JP movement, instantly giving it the moral high ground and satyagrahi sheen associated with the Gandhian. The branding also gave the Jana Sangh, which could not shake off the reputation of a communal party, legitimacy and adequate cover to mobilize on the ground. A Gandhian associate of JP wrote to him that the leadership of the movement at the grass roots was firmly in the hands of the Jana Sangh. But the swell of anger against the Congress's corruption was so high that even those who stayed away from the Jana Sangh became supporters of the movement.[69]

Govindacharya was in the thick of things. The prant pracharak was out of station and when he returned in the first week of April, he found his vibhag pracharak steering a political protest against the government. Even though he stayed in the background, Govindacharya was deeply involved in the agitation. Complaints about his activities went up to senior leaders.[70] A pracharak was not supposed to be actively involved in politics and agitations. Getting caught was an absolute no-no in the Sangh. It has always been extremely careful about being on the right side of the law.

Balasaheb Deoras, who had just taken over as sarsanghchalak the previous year, was scheduled to visit Bihar. He had already issued a statement that considering what was happening it would be natural for swayamsevaks to participate as they were also suffering, giving Govindacharya's involvement an indirect legitimacy.[71] Officially, however, the Sangh insisted that it had nothing to do with the protests.

Balasaheb sent word to Govindacharya to meet him at a Sangh camp in Siwan in June. Meanwhile, in May, MLAs had started resigning and Bihar's unrest made national headlines. Govindacharya was underground but was in the working committee and planned the everyday strategy and action. It was relayed to the Sangh office from where it was disseminated to others, including JP.[72] The ailing Gandhian was away for surgery in Vellore from 23 April to 5 June. When he returned, he called for total revolution.

Govindacharya reached the Siwan camp before Deoras but could not meet him because the camp in-charge asked him to leave as they had information about an impending police raid on the camp looking for him. He said it would not look good if an RSS camp was raided and that too when the sarsanghchalak was there. He left.[73] Deoras then asked him to join in Nagpur in July where a meeting of prant pracharaks was scheduled. By then the RSS had seen that the agitation was gaining momentum. Senior Sangh leaders such as Nanaji Deshmukh were in touch with JP, and the Sangh was preparing for a larger role for itself. The day after the pracharaks' meeting, Deoras asked Govindacharya to recount everything in detail from the beginning, in chronological order. 'Start from January,' he said. After Govindacharya had done so and brought Deoras up to date on the situation in Bihar, Deoras said: 'Those who should have understood the circumstances did not understand it. Those who did, took decisions they had to take. Govind has not breached discipline.'[74]

Later, at night, Deoras met him once again, alone. He asked what he expected to achieve from the agitation. Govindacharya replied that despite it being twenty-five years since Independence, nothing had changed. 'We want a systemic change.'[75] Deoras bluntly told him it wouldn't happen. The powers wouldn't change. The agitation would have served its purpose if it could become a social deterrent. He then said, 'Now that we have plunged into this agitation; jumped into it without preparation, there would be many troubles. You run the risk of getting arrested. It is possible that I may have to disown you. I might have to say that you were doing it in your personal capacity. Do not get arrested. Whatever happens, we'll see.'[76]

On 4 November, JP was lathi-charged as he was leading a massive rally. Instead of a rapprochement, communication between Indira Gandhi and JP degenerated into a blame game, worsening their relationship. Indira Gandhi tried to reason with him and finally told him that elections were due in 1976 and asked him to test the people's will. JP accepted the challenge and decided to take the agitation national.

On 18 March 1975, the movement's first anniversary began with the police firing on students in Bihar. JP called for all opposition parties to form a united front to fight the Congress. After 1972, Jana Sangh volunteers had ramped up their participation in agitations. Vajpayee went to the extent of saying that the party would not hesitate to encourage people to break laws which kept basic necessities scarce. He sympathized with those who looted fair price shops to feed their families.[77]

The RSS denied its role in the agitations. 'Swayamsevaks too are part of the people. So they too will join the people in reacting to the people's sufferings. But their being with the people does not prove that the Sangh is conducting the agitation,' Deoras said.[78]

On 12 June 1975, Justice Jagmohan Lal Sinha of the Allahabad High Court pronounced his verdict in a case filed by socialist politician Raj Narain who had lost to Indira Gandhi in Rae Bareli in the 1971 elections that Gandhi had fought on the famous slogan 'Garibi Hatao' (Remove Poverty). Justice Sinha acquitted Gandhi on most charges but found her guilty on two counts: the Uttar Pradesh government had built high rostrums to allow her to address election meetings from a 'dominating position'; and her election agent, Yashpal Kapoor, was still a government employee when she started her campaign. The court overturned her election.[79]

Both the charges were frivolous. Journalist Kuldip Nayar commented that 'it was almost like unseating the prime minister for a traffic offence'.[80] But in the charged atmosphere of the mid-1970s, a court verdict against her cemented the public perception of Gandhi and her government as corrupt, unscrupulous and despotic. She suffered another setback on the same day when results of the Gujarat state polls held a couple of days before came in. The Janata Front of the Jan Sangh, Congress(O) and Bharatiya Lok Dal, led by Morarji Desai and backed by JP, won eighty-seven seats against the Congress(I)'s seventy-five in a house of 182. The Janata Front, which was short of majority, was able to form a government only after it allied with Chimanbhai Patel, the same person against whose 'corrupt rule' the students' movement had begun in the first place.[81] Clearly, the movement's original objectives had been forgotten and it had acquired a single target—Indira Gandhi. The cornered Gandhi's reaction was draconian, to say the least, and only served to reiterate her opposition-painted image as a tyrant.

India woke up to a state of emergency on 26 June 1975. Arrests began in the morning. All opposition leaders were jailed. Even those seen as friendly to opposition parties or leaders were picked up. While senior leaders like JP and Morarji Desai were kept at guest houses, the rest were stuffed in whatever prison was available. President's rule was imposed in states such as Tamil Nadu and Gujarat. Censorship was imposed on the media and 253 journalists, including Kuldip Nayar of the *Indian Express* and K.R. Malkani of *Motherland*, were arrested. Literary magazines and journals of opinion were shut down.[82]

The RSS came into its own after the arrests. Its organizational machinery and discipline of cadres were tested to the fullest and it collected honours never won in its history. Some statements appear as if the Sangh almost wished for the arrests; a victimhood to wash away all the taint that had followed it since 1948.

'Talk of another ban on the Sangh had begun right after the first ban was lifted in July 1949. That talk is still going on. Initially we did not take it seriously, but last January-February I thought it necessary to issue statements about it and have done so. The Sangh will not be closed down by putting a couple of thousand swayamsevaks in jail. It is still there. In its work the Sangh does not think whether there will be a ban on it or not. Our determination to carry on Sangh work is unflinching. We have to carry it on fearlessly without bothering about a ban. We should rather think of utilizing a ban, if it ever comes, to our benefit,' Deoras told volunteers in Rohtak ten days before the Emergency was clamped.[83]

All the top RSS leaders in the country were thrown in prison. Those who managed to avoid prison stayed and worked underground. Madhavrao Mulay managed the RSS work in the absence of other leaders even though his health was deteriorating. Mulay's work reminded RSS ideologue Dattopant Thengadi of 'two brave men—Com. Che Guevara, who fell to the enemy's bullet while leading guerrilla warfare in the jungles of Bolivia in spite of illness, and Com. Charu Majumdar, proponent of Naxalism, who had just a cylinder of oxygen at the time of his arrest'.[84] In the afterglow of the anti-Emergency movement, it was not Shivaji or Bhagat Singh that came to the ideologue's mind as heroes but guerrilla warriors of the extreme left. Four decades later, it is unlikely anyone in the Sangh would compare its volunteers to a Naxalite guerrilla or Cuban revolutionary. The Sangh considers anyone even suspected of sympathy for Naxalites as enemies of the nation and Naxalites as terrorists whose rightful place is at the business end of a police bayonet.

Even though, they were in prison, the general atmosphere was of bonhomie as political workers and social activists from across the ideological spectrum mingled freely, forging new friendships and future alliances. The unlikeliest of them all—the RSS and Jamaat-e-Islami Hind—came close; prompting even the imam of Jama Masjid in Delhi to attend an RSS shakha.

By the time the Emergency ended in March 1977, the prisons had forged incongruent groups into a unified opposition ready to take on the autocrat who had dug up the fragile foundations of a fledgling democracy. At the first political rally at Delhi's Ramlila grounds in January 1977, even before the Emergency was officially lifted, people turned out in overwhelming numbers. Atal Bihari Vajpayee, then already a star politician famous for his oratorical flourishes, sent the crowd into raptures with his speech that reportedly began: *Baad muddat ke mile hain, kehne sunne ko bahut hain afsane, khuli hawa mein zara saans to le lein, kab tak rahegi azaadi kaun jaane* (We meet after a long time, there is much to talk about; let's breathe in the fresh air, who knows how long this freedom will last).[85]

The elections routed Indira Gandhi and her Congress party. A government of the Janata Party, truly a rainbow coalition of ideas and ideologies, came to power with Morarji Desai at the helm. The elections after the Emergency was the first time the RSS had actively and openly participated in an electoral campaign. Its volunteer force fanned out across cities and villages canvassing votes for Janata Party candidates. It was also perhaps the biggest mass contact programme the RSS had ever done. Until then it was used to working unnoticed—the very sight of its loose khaki shorts invoking memories of Mahatma Gandhi's assassination. It was the first time that the public was looking at them with admiration—the boys who fought Indira's tyranny and won.

*

Other political organizations boasted of many legends who fought the British Raj. The RSS was bereft of any heroes. There were no legendary freedom movement stories to tell. All that existed was a lingering embarrassment from 1942 when Golwalkar's RSS remained aloof as the entire country plunged into agitation on Gandhi's exhortation to the British: Quit India. It faced intense criticism from within for not supporting the Naval Mutiny of 1946 as well. Many in the Sangh theorize that it was in fact the mutiny and not Gandhi that hastened the British departure from India. But the RSS refused to play any part in it. The Emergency gave the RSS its first martyrs apart from burnishing the organization's reputation as a hero. Almost every leader had a taste of imprisonment. In many places, police brutality amplified the suffering and sacrifice.

Why did the RSS participate in the agitations leading up to the Emergency? Did it plan for a situation like that? Golwalkar is supposed to have anticipated something like it when he told Thengadi that as a parliamentarian he should focus on building relationships across party lines. JP, who had practically retired from politics, had been persuaded by the RSS to lead a movement to reform politics and administration.

Indira Gandhi believed that JP was hostile to her because he was jealous of her father and secretly longed for a ministerial position.[86] JP thought there was a communist conspiracy. He believed that the Indira government was being controlled by the CPI in cahoots with the spymaster of the Soviet KGB. Indira Gandhi's relations with the US had become frosty after Richard Nixon became president in 1969. At the same time, she had warmed up to the Soviet Union. She had signed a friendship treaty with the USSR, and President Leonid Brezhnev and Premier Alexei Kosygin had assured her of Soviet military aid should India go to war with Pakistan.[87]

JP said many Congressmen were 'disguised communists' and enemies of democracy. 'Behind them [Congressmen] is the CPI and behind it is Soviet Russia. Russia has backed Mrs Gandhi to the hilt. Because the farther Mrs Gandhi advances on her present course, the more powerful an influence will Russia have over this country. A time may come when having squeezed the juice out of Mrs Gandhi, the Russians through the CPI and their Trojan horses within the Congress will dump her on the garbage heap of history and install in her place their own man.' JP believed there was a deep Soviet conspiracy to replace democracy with a communist dictatorship that perhaps even Indira Gandhi was unaware of.[88]

The RSS had always maintained that the communists had extraterritorial loyalties and did not have India's interest at heart. The Sangh had been deeply worried about the growing influence of the CPI in the government. It believed the CPI's support to the Congress and left-leaning Congressmen themselves were trying to shackle it. The RSS was alarmed that the Indira Congress at its first All India Congress Committee meeting in Delhi had passed a resolution urging the government to ban the RSS. Around the same time, a Delhi court also banned drills in public places for two months. This, the RSS believed, was the handiwork of the Indira Congress which had been saying that the Sangh was violating its own constitution by participating in politics. Over the next four years when agitations raged in Gujarat and Bihar, the RSS denied having anything to do with the unrest though it said: 'It cannot be denied that the masses have risen in revolt…'[89]

It said the propaganda against it was the handiwork of the Congress and communists, the former because the RSS had 'refused to become a tool in furthering its political ambitions, and the latter because of Sangh's opposition to foreign loyalties and foreign designs'.[90] The RSS and JP had identical fears. It was distressed that the ruling party was not taking nationalist forces like itself into confidence and instead was sidling up to communists. The years leading up to the Emergency were clearly a battle of ideologies and influence over the government.

The RSS believed a plot had been hatched to ban it through an ordinance. Yet it did not blame Indira Gandhi. Addressing a press conference in Lucknow on 31 January 1975, Deoras said:

It seems under the influence of the Communist Party and its lobby within the Congress the government is scheming to throttle democracy, assume dictatorial powers and establish one-party rule. A ban on the Sangh would be a step in that direction, as anti-national forces know that the nationwide and disciplined organization of the Sangh reflects the determination to protect freedom and democracy.[91]

Indira Gandhi believed that JP was being misled by reactionary forces who were perhaps being funded by foreign agencies. Gandhi said that a 'foreign hand' was involved in fomenting trouble against her government. She drew parallels with the coup d'état which was believed to have been engineered by the American CIA that resulted in the overthrow and death of Chile's Marxist president Salvador Allende. Gandhi feared it could happen to her and suspected that the opposition was being encouraged by the Americans.

She was unequivocal in her scorn for the RSS. 'I deplore the type of training that they give to younger people in their shakhas, the violence they preach. But their real weapon is something else— it is the whispering campaign they indulge in,' she said in the Lok Sabha. From among the opposition, she singled out the RSS as following textbook techniques of fascism and accused it of infiltrating government services and administration.[92]

When Syama Prasad Mookerjee started the Jana Sangh, instead of a party of swayamsevaks, he wanted it to be a pluralistic platform with representation from diverse groups. Mookerjee had in mind a federation of parties, including the Hindu Mahasabha, the Socialist Party, the Ram Rajya Parishad, the Forward Bloc, the Revolutionary Socialist Party, the Kisan Sabha, the Soshit Party and the Ganatantra Parishad.[93]

While the Jana Sangh could never become the platform Mookerjee wanted it to be, the post-Emergency Janata Party came close to it. This time the RSS tried its best to remain below the radar to maintain the unity it had helped forge. In 1976, JP called a two-day meeting of leaders of Congress(O), Jana Sangh, Socialist Party and Bharatiya Lok Dal in Bombay. The leaders agreed to merge all their outfits into a single party. The Jana Sangh accepted both secularism and socialism as the governing principle of the new organization which would be called the Janata Party.

After the party won the elections and it was time to choose the prime minister, the contest boiled down to between Morarji Desai and Jagjivan Ram. The Jana Sangh had already promised support to

Jagjivan Ram but at the last minute plumped for Desai, hiding behind Shanti Bhushan's suggestion that the prime ministership should go to someone who had suffered during the Emergency. Jagjivan Ram threw a fit. He felt that high-caste leaders had ganged up to deny him the opportunity. They might have agreed to make him a figurehead president but not the prime minister. When Jagjivan Ram flew into a temper, Atal Bihari Vajpayee wept and put his head in his lap, seeking forgiveness.[94]

The ragtag party was never going to be a cohesive unit. Fissures erupted after socialists led by Madhu Limaye demanded that Janata Party members not have dual membership; of the party and the RSS. The Jana Sangh and RSS vehemently opposed this saying the RSS was a cultural organization that had no interest in politics. The dual membership issue, however, became too contentious and threatened the unity of the party and survival of the government.

As a compromise, Deoras tried to introduce a resolution in the Akhil Bharatiya Pratinidhi Sabha or general body meeting of the RSS in 1978 proposing that people's representatives should not attend shakhas. However, it met with staunch opposition from Dattopant Thengadi and Maharashtra sanghchalak Baba Bhide. Deoras withdrew the resolution.[95] Though the resolution failed to go through the general body and the Janata Party government collapsed soon after, the coalition experiment did provide valuable lessons to the RSS. Most important of all—how to beat the Congress.

Ever since the ban in 1948, the RSS had wanted to dent the brutal domination of the Congress party in Indian politics. It feared that the party had been irrevocably captured by the left and it would always threaten the RSS's existence. The left's overwhelming influence confounded many. 'The "almost complete eclipse" of rightist parties, conservative or otherwise, seemed to be an obvious, yet puzzling feature of Indian political life,' wrote American political scientist H.L. Erdman.[96]

On a visit to Chicago in 1980, Bhaurao Deoras told a group of swayamsevaks that the elections of 1977 had proved that not only the

Congress, but also the prime minister could be defeated. Earlier, the elections of 1967 had proved that the Congress could be vulnerable in the states. Bhaurao considered the 1977 elections as a milestone that built confidence in people that they could change the government. He believed that if a non-Congress government successfully stayed in power for five years, the Congress party would disintegrate.[97]

*

The Deoras brothers keenly understood that sway over the regions north of the Vindhyas was key to control over the country. And the northern parts were more susceptible to emotional manipulation. Nothing exemplifies it more than the docile cow.

No animal in anywhere in the world can claim to have the kind of political power that the cow commands in India, especially in the northern states of the country. It is so revered in states such as Uttar Pradesh and Bihar that the swathe from Bihar to Madhya Pradesh is sometimes referred to as the cow belt. Many communities in the region believe that it is auspicious to feed the first roti made in the morning to a cow.

The cow was the subject of intense debate in the Constituent Assembly which drew up the Constitution of India. Even though there were demands for an explicit ban on cow slaughter to be enshrined in the Constitution itself, it was finally agreed to be included in the Directive Principles of State Policy on economic grounds.

Article 48 on 'Organisation of agriculture and animal husbandry' reads: 'The State shall endeavour to organise agriculture and animal husbandry on modern and scientific lines and shall, in particular, take steps for preserving and improving the breeds, and prohibiting the slaughter, of cows and calves and other milch and draught cattle.'[98]

Exceptions such as West Bengal, Kerala and Goa aside, most other states in the country have since banned cow slaughter. Although the cow has been a revered animal for centuries, the strategic use of the bovine as a political tool continues unabated.

The cow as a Hindu symbol is important to the RSS only for its mobilizational value as explained by Golwalkar. In 1966, RSS volunteers actively coordinated the biggest demonstrations independent India had seen. This was the first time the RSS experimented with political mobilization couched as a socio-religious issue. On 7 November 1966, thousands of people, including women, descended on Delhi in a massive rally on Parliament Street. The crowd fronted by hundreds of naked, ash-smeared Naga mendicants was agitating to abolish cow slaughter, which was also a directive principle in the Constitution.

In the late afternoon, the crowd got violent and went on a rampage in the city, setting fires, destroying vehicles, and raiding ministers' homes. Seven people, including demonstrating Naga sadhus, were killed in police firing near Parliament. Police arrested hundreds of people, including four secretaries of the Sarvadaliya Goraksha Mahabhiyan Samiti, which organized the rally. Others included workers of the RSS, HMS, Arya Samaj and Sanatan Dharma Sabha. Arrested RSS leaders included Vasant Rao Oak, V.P. Joshi and O.P. Tyagi.[99]

The government set up a committee under Justice Sarkar to deliberate on the issue of cow slaughter. Among the members were Ashok Mitra, the Shankaracharya of Puri, RSS chief Golwalkar and National Dairy Development Board chairman Verghese Kurien.

Kurien writes in his biography that while he had an adversarial relationship with the Shankaracharya during the discussions, Golwalkar and he had become friends. In his own words: 'One rather unusual and unexpected development during our regular committee meetings was that during that time, Golwalkar and I became close friends. People were absolutely amazed to see that we had become so close that whenever he saw me walk into the room he would rush to embrace me. He would take me aside and try to pacify me after our meetings, "Why do you keep losing your temper with the Shankaracharya? I agree with you about him. But don't let the man rile you. Just ignore him."' Golwalkar was a very small man—barely five feet—but when he got angry fire spewed out of his eyes. What impressed me most about him was that he was an intensely patriotic Indian. You could argue that he was going about preaching his brand of nationalism in a totally wrong way but nobody could question his sincerity. One day after one of our meetings when he had argued passionately for banning cow slaughter, he came to me and asked, "Kurien, shall I tell you why I'm making an issue of this cow slaughter business?" I said to him, "Yes, please explain to me because otherwise you are a very intelligent man. Why are you doing this?"'[100]

'I started a petition to ban cow slaughter actually to embarrass the government,' he explained to Kurien in private. 'I decided to collect a million signatures for this to submit to the Rashtrapati. I saw that the cow has potential to unify the country—she symbolizes the culture of Bharat. So I tell you what, Kurien, you agree with me to ban cow slaughter on this committee and I promise you, five years from that date, I will have united the country. What I'm trying to tell you is that I'm not a fool, I'm not a fanatic. I'm just cold-blooded about this. I want to use the cow to bring out our Indianness, so please cooperate with me on this.' The campaign took Golwalkar across the country. In one UP village he saw a woman going door to door in the blazing sun canvassing for signatures on the petition. In that moment he realized the potential of the cow as a tool for mobilizing people.[101]

The RSS has perfected this unerring strategy—identify an issue that connects with people, meticulously plan an agitational campaign and implement it methodically.

Ironically, the committee trundled on for twelve years but was wound up when the Morarji Desai government, in which the Jana Sangh was a partner, came to power. It did not submit its report. For the next three and a half decades, the cow mostly remained backstage. It came out up front after the Modi government came to power.

In 2016, several cow protection groups decided to commemorate the fiftieth anniversary of a rally that had ended in riot and police firing. Goraksha Andolan, a cow protection platform founded by

K.N. Govindacharya, planned a rally on New Delhi's Parliament Street, the venue of the past rally. Hundreds of seers and cow protection activists were expected to converge on Delhi for the programme. The RSS's cow protection organization, the Rashtriya Goraksha Mahasangh (RGM), which commemorates the event every year, was also planning to hold a massive programme at the nearby Jawaharlal Nehru Stadium which sarsanghchalak Mohan Bhagwat was expected to attend.

A few months before, just as plans were being finalized, Prime Minister Narendra Modi lashed out at unbridled cow vigilantism. Vigilante cow protection groups had become aggressively active ever since the BJP government had come to power in 2014. They would roam highways and sometimes forcibly enter houses and beat up, sometimes even kill, anyone they suspected of slaughtering cows or eating beef. In September 2015, a Muslim man in Dadri, Uttar Pradesh, was dragged out of his home and beaten to death on suspicion that he stored beef in his refrigerator. In July 2016, four Dalit men were stripped to the waist, tied to an SUV and flogged for skinning a dead cow in Gujarat's Una village.

While he had not responded to earlier incidents, Modi reacted strongly to the brutality in his home state. 'I get so angry at those who are into the Gau-Rakshak business. A Gau-Bhakt [cow devotee] is different, Gau Seva [cow protection] is different. I have seen that some people are into crimes all night and wear the garb of Gau Rakshaks in the day,' Modi said at an interactive session to mark two years of a government initiative. He wanted state governments to prepare a dossier of so-called Gau Rakshaks. 'Approximately 70–80 per cent will be those who indulge in anti-social activities and try to hide their sins by pretending to be Gau Rakshaks. If they are true protectors, they should realise that most cows die because of plastic, not slaughter. They should stop cows from eating plastic.'[102]

The PM's position immediately drew strong reaction from the VHP. Its Ahmedabad unit said in an unsigned statement that thousands of butchers killing one lakh cows every year were not termed 'goondas', but cow protectors like Gita Rambhiya (killed in Ahmedabad years ago) were called 'goondas'. 'This shows your change of heart.'[103] Its Braj region vice president, Sunil Parashar, said Modi would pay for the comments in 2019.

The prime minister's statement made it clear that the government wanted to put a lid on the issue and avoid more negative publicity. The RSS played along. When Goraksha Andolan organizers met with the top brass of the Sangh, they were told that even though the RSS morally backed the event, it would keep away. Eventually, the RGM's event, which was expected to fill a stadium, was scaled down and held in a smaller hall.

Privately, however, the RSS also was seething. At an informal meeting with a few journalists in Delhi, Bhagwat made his displeasure of Modi's statement known.[104] Yet publicly it was more diplomatic. In his annual Vijaya Dashami speech in October 2016, Mohan Bhagwat cautiously endorsed Modi's view stressing the cow's utility value and sacredness. 'Sometimes in some places in these states, the Go-sevaks have to do active campaigns to ensure proper implementation of such laws. But they cannot be compared with those undesirable elements, who raking up the issue of cow-slaughter or spreading unfounded rumours about cow-slaughter, are busy serving their narrow personal or political ends. Nevertheless, the sacred mission of the Go-sevaks would continue and gather momentum.'[105]

What he left out in the speech was although the RSS would continue with its programmes, it would keep them quiet and tone them down so as not to embarrass the Modi government.

Cow protection remains a useful mobilizational instrument in the Sangh Parivar armoury. But the biggest and most successful of them all was another brainchild of the Deoras brothers. After the Janata Party experiment failed, the RSS prepared for its most ambitious socio-political mobilization.

3

The God of Power

The summer of 1983 in India was rather somnolent until it was enlivened by Kapil Dev and his band of intrepid cricketers who beat the West Indies, the reigning kings of the game, to bring home the Cricket World Cup. RSS sarsanghchalak Balasaheb Deoras, a keen follower of cricket, would have been elated. India was on top of the world after all. In a private conversation, a senior RSS leader said Deoras often held forth on the nuances of the game. The leader also enthusiastically reeled off names of Indian cricketers who were swayamsevaks.[1] That summer, however, Deoras was about to take guard in a far more perilous game.

An RSS pracharaks' camp had just ended in Allahabad. Deoras was having a fireside chat with pracharaks when he suddenly asked: '*Suna hai ki Ayodhya mein mandir pe taaley lage hain* (I heard the temple in Ayodhya is locked).' The pracharak in charge of the area stood up and replied in the affirmative. Balasaheb thought for a moment and asked loudly, '*Kab tak rahenge?* (Till when will the locks remain?).' It was classic Deoras. He had just sent out a call to action without really spelling it out. It was over to them now.[2]

It is unlikely that Deoras had not thought about the consequences of his decision. He was extremely careful about using the RSS for campaigns and was conscious of the energy required to run agitations and the resources the organizations would need to deploy. He was certain that whatever be the situation, no campaign was worth affecting the organization's work. It was possible to entrust some people to build public campaigns that would not strain the core RSS, but putting the entire organization at risk was not a gamble he would take. He was particular that the Sangh did not deviate from its ultimate goal of creating a Hindu society that would react reflexively.[3] Those who knew him say he was acutely aware of the political impact the move would have, as well as the risks. The demolition of the Babri Masjid in 1992 ripped apart the delicate fabric of the Indian nation. Deoras was about to sacrifice the relationships and social capital he and his colleagues had built while in jail during the Emergency. The campaign would eventually turn out to be pyrrhic in terms of its social, economic and political costs, not to mention lives lost in riots and conflicts.

On 6 December 1992, hordes of *kar sevak*s (volunteers) climbed atop the domes of the mosque and brought it down within hours. It appeared like a crowd that gradually worked up a frenzy which ultimately broke through the scaffoldings surrounding the structure (there was work going on around it). Whether the precise act of demolition was planned or not, it is certain that the weight of months-long campaign and the charged speeches that were being delivered had the congregation emotionally primed to wreak destruction. The Sangh Parivar's collective leadership had willed the crowd into believing that a historic wrong was being righted and a social architecture was being rearranged.

Girilal Jain, former editor of the *Times of India*, wrote in the RSS publication *Organiser*:

The structure as it stood represented an impasse between what Babur represented and what Ram represents … In fact, in my opinion, no structure symbolized the Indian political order in its ambivalence, ambiguity, indecision and lack of purpose, as this structure. The removal of the structure has ended the impasse and marks a new beginning.[4]

Recalling Jain's article in 2010, on the eve of a high court verdict on the Ayodhya land dispute, columnist Swapan Dasgupta wrote in the *Telegraph* that Ayodhya was not the equivalent of the storming of the Bastille.

> Both the votaries of Hindutva and the beleaguered defenders of the Nehruvian order were united in viewing the demolition as a point of rupture. For the former, the change would herald a Hindu reawakening; for the secularists, it threatened to destroy India's pluralism and transform the country into a *de-facto* confessional State. Both sides of the confrontation, it would now seem, were guilty of hype. India wasn't transformed into a Hindu Pakistan and the Constitutional edifice established in 1950 remained strong and intact. To borrow A.J.P. Taylor's description of the 1848 revolution in Europe, the Babri demolition was a turning point in Indian history when history refused to turn.[5]

The campaign was never intended to be the formula for Hindu revival in the religious sense. It was an experiment—spectacularly successful in hindsight—in consolidating Hindus politically. The purveyors of the strategy could never be sure of its efficacy, but it was worth a try; a Hindu consolidation that went beyond mere political benefits. The campaign was a political exploration and the demolition, a statement of power.

'For some, the temptation of power is supreme,' thus opens the 'Report of the Liberhan Ayodhya Commission of Inquiry'. 'The usual means for acquiring power is through politics. There is always an urge and quest to use politics for acquiring power and for one's own purpose—nothing matters beyond political desirable results, however achieved. In the process of acquisition of power the consequence of the process on the institution, the nation, individual and the society as a whole does not matter. Life itself becomes politicized,' the commission observed in its percipient opening remarks. The commission said that cadres and leaders, both national and local, of the RSS, Bajrang Dal, VHP, BJP and Shiv Sena actively or passively supported the demolition. 'In the process all acts were directed for or to acquire the political power and thereby achieve the politically desirable results,' it said.[6]

In his seminal work, *Crowds and Power*, Nobel laureate Elias Canetti interprets the destruction of representational images as the destruction of a hierarchy which is no longer recognized. 'It is the violation of generally established and universally visible and valid distances.'[7] In the case of Babri, the hierarchy was long gone, but the Sangh Parivar considered the mosque a symbol of a tyrannical legacy enjoyed by Muslims as political privilege even in independent India. That the Babri Masjid was standing was clear evidence of an appeasement that helped tilt the balance in such a way that it frustrated the majoritarian claim on power.

The Sangh Parivar considers the Babri mosque demolition the rightful culmination of four and half centuries of struggle by the Hindus to regain a tiny speck of land believed to be the birthplace of Ram, God and hero of India's most famous and revered epic, the Ramayana. Many Parivar leaders consider the demolition unfortunate but necessary. Uma Bharti, the firebrand BJP leader who is alleged to have egged on the kar sevaks on that fateful day, said in a television interview:

> Let me make one thing very clear. We don't have any regrets about the razing of the Babri masjid. I would have accepted it with pride if I had had myself brought it down. But I did not because I was far from there. Even though we were preparing for the kar seva, none of the leaders who were present there had any idea this would happen.[8]

*

In 1526, the Mongol invader Babur, the great grandson of Timur, defeated Ibrahim Lodi, the ruler of Delhi, in what is now known as the first battle of Panipat. His autobiography, *Baburnama*, says that Daulat Khan Lodi, Ibrahim's estranged cousin, had invited him to invade Delhi, then perhaps the most prized throne east of Constantinople. Though Babur would die four years later, the Mughal dynasty he established would consolidate and rule most of the subcontinent for the next 300.

Current Parivar belief is that Babur ordered the razing of a temple at Lord Ram's birthplace and had a mosque built there. The person in charge of building the mosque was his lieutenant Mir Baqi. There are differences of opinion about the exact date when the mosque was built. Nevertheless, litigation began in 1885 and continues in the Supreme Court even now.

In the judgment on the land dispute in 2010, judges of the Lucknow bench of the Allahabad High Court took care to write a prelude. It began: 'Here is a small piece of land (1500 square yards) where angels fear to tread. It is full of innumerable landmines. We are required to clear it.' The first recordings of the dispute in government documents dates back to 1885 when there were Hindu-Muslim riots in the area. It was noted that Muslims had made a claim on a nearby temple called Hanuman Garhi, asserting that it was a mosque originally. The riot is said to have started at Hanuman Garhi and Muslims were repelled by Hindus. Several Muslims who were killed are said to be buried around the disputed premises.[9]

On the night of 22 December 1949, an idol of baby Ram, or Ram Lalla, appeared mysteriously behind the closed doors of the mosque, directly beneath its central dome. In 2012, journalists Krishna Pokharel and Paul Beckett of the *Wall Street Journal* recreated in narrative detail what happened on the night of 22 December 1949, and the day after, from eyewitness accounts and relatives of the planners.[10] It described how the Faizabad city magistrate, Guru Dutt Singh; district magistrate, K.K. Nayar; and a sadhu, Abhiram Das, all ardent devotees of Lord Ram, hatched a plan to install the idol inside the locked mosque. The trio would hardly have been aware of the enormity of their scheme but what they did would influence the political destiny of independent India like no other event in modern history. It would also begin another series of court cases that are yet to be settled.

*

The region comprising today's Uttar Pradesh and Bihar on the Ganga is arguably the cradle of competitive subcontinental culture and politics. The historic sources of the most enduring socio-political currents of modern India can be traced back to the vast Gangetic plains, sometimes disparagingly referred to as the Cow Belt or Hindi Heartland. These regions identify with the places mentioned in the Ramayana. Even today, people of Mithila, believed to be Sita's home, do not give their daughters in marriage to men of Ayodhya.[11] Modern-day Bihar is also the location of one of the greatest dynasties of India, the Mauryas. Chanakya, the adviser to the first Mauryan king Chandragupta, is credited with writing the *Arthashastra*, a sophisticated treatise on economics and statecraft. Gautama Buddha gave his first sermon in Sarnath near Varanasi, a city so ancient that Mark Twain described it as 'older than history, older than tradition, older even than legend'.

In modern times, Gandhi started the satyagraha political movement in Champaran. Many illustrious freedom fighters came from the state. JP, the force behind the anti-corruption movement leading to the Emergency, was from Sitabdiara in Bihar. Ayodhya, Allahabad and Varanasi in Uttar Pradesh are important centres for powerful Hindu sadhus and sects and the state is also home to orthodox Islamic sects such as the Deobandis and Barelvis. The Islamic seminary, Darul Uloom Deoband, was founded by Muhammad Qasim Nanautavi and Rashid Ahmad Gangohi in 1866, nine years after the 1857 uprising against the British in which they had also participated. It was established to protect the Islamic faith from the onslaught of the Christian missionaries who operated with British patronage.[12] National Security Advisor Ajit Doval once described the Deobandis as nationalists who could even be interlocutors if India wanted to talk to the Taliban in Afghanistan. 'We don't need Pakistanis to act as go-betweens,' Doval said, hinting at the ideological reach of Deobandis.[13]

Uttar Pradesh is also where the movement for a separate Pakistan was born—in the campus of the Aligarh Muslim University founded in 1875 as the Muslim Anglo-Oriental College by Sir Syed Ahmed Khan, a British loyalist and Islamic reformist. For decades, Uttar Pradesh had been roiled by communal tensions and riots. In the 1980s and early 1990s, this cauldron would again boil over with yet another political experiment.

*

The epic Ramayana describes Lord Ram as Ramachandra, firstborn of King Dasharath of the Suryavansh or the clan of the Sun God. He is considered one of the avatars of Vishnu among the holy Hindu trinity of Brahma, Vishnu and Shiva—creator, protector and destroyer respectively of everything in the universe. Ram was the king of Ayodhya, slayer of the expansionist demon king of Lanka, Ravan, and known as the epitome of the Indian male—*maryada purushottam*, or virtuous man—in the sixteenth-century saint-poet Tulsidas's *Ramcharitmanas*, the retelling of poet Valmiki's Sanskrit original in Awadhi. It is the most popular version of the Ramayana in northern India, particularly in the state of Uttar Pradesh. Most Hindus along the Gangetic plain know at least a few verses of *Ramcharitmanas* by heart.

Ram's reign is described as Ram Rajya, the virtuous kingdom of equality and justice that even Mahatma Gandhi longed for in India. Lord Ram was the ideal the RSS had been searching for to position as a purely Hindu national icon who could easily straddle geography, tradition, custom and religion.

'The day when the Horse of Victory returned to Ayodhya unchallenged and unchallengeable, the great white umbrella of sovereignty was unfurled over that imperial throne of Ramchandra, the brave, Ramchandra the good, and a loving allegiance was sworn, not only by the princes of Aryan blood but Hanuman, Sugriva, Bibhishana from the south—that day was the real birthday of our Hindu people. It was truly a national day; for Aryans and Anaryans knitting themselves into a people were born as a nation,' V.D. Savarkar had declared.[14]

Ram had emotional connect cutting across caste and social strata. He was ready for reinvention as the potent symbol of Hindu power. As senior journalist and president of Indira Gandhi National Centre for Arts Ram Bahadur Rai puts it: 'Deoras had finally found the opportunity he was looking for.'[15] The instrument he had chosen was not the BJP, but the VHP which was until a year before just a group of ageing men trying to unite hundreds of sects and cults led by sadhus and godmen, all of whom operated under the umbrella of Hinduism but were often rivals in practice and ritual.

*

Madhukar Dattatreya Deoras, popularly known as Balasaheb Deoras, was the third sarsanghchalak of the RSS. Technically, he was the fourth, counting L.V. Paranjape who was chief for a year when Hedgewar relinquished the position to participate in the Jungle Satyagraha (an inland agitation in support of Mahatma Gandhi's Salt Satyagraha on the coast) of 1930. Hedgewar resumed as chief once he returned from jail.

Deoras joined the Sangh in 1926 when he was just eleven and the RSS was a year old. Trained by Hedgewar, Deoras developed clear ideas about the RSS's work and its future. However, often this vision came into conflict with that of the second and longest-serving sarsanghchalak, M.S. Golwalkar. Deoras instilled in the Sangh the idea that there was nothing so sacrosanct that it could not be broken. The only guiding principle is 'Hindustan is a Hindu Rashtra'. Everything else could change. He pioneered the strategy of the Sangh not limiting itself to shakhas but expanding into all walks of life.[16]

In the late 1970s, Deoras oversaw the establishment of the Vanvasi Kalyan Ashram to expand work in tribal areas, Vidya Bharati to establish schools, Sewa Bharati to oversee charity and community service projects, Kala Bharati and Sanskar Bharati to involve in arts and culture, Grahak Panchayat for consumer protection, Itihas Sankalan Samiti to collate local histories, etc. He was also said to be the principal mover behind establishing the Bharatiya Jana Sangh in 1951 and the ABVP in 1948.

Deoras's idea of an armada-like structure for the Sangh Parivar evolved after the ban in 1948. He based it on the principle: 'The Sangh will not do anything overtly except organizing. Swayamsevaks will do everything else.' He had estimated that if the number of Sangh pracharaks could be expanded to 10,000, the RSS could change the country in ten years.[17]

Golwalkar would often say that even though he was holding the chief's position, the real sarsanghchalak was Deoras, hinting that a lot of decisions were probably influenced by him. Deoras was responsible for training and sending pracharaks across the country. When Sardar Patel's emissary Dwaraka Prasad Mishra, who later became the chief minister of Madhya Pradesh, came to Nagpur to hold talks during the ban on RSS, it was Deoras who spoke on behalf of the Sangh. He told Mishra categorically that Golwalkar would not, contrary to Patel's wishes, pray to Nehru to lift the ban.[18]

After the ban was lifted, Deoras wrote an article titled 'Sangh ka agla kadam' in the Hindi weekly *Yugdharm*, which outlined the RSS's future course of action. In the article, he elaborated on how the Sangh would expand into all walks of life. On seeing the article, sarsanghchalak Golwalkar commented: 'This is great! The next step of the Sangh has been decided and I don't even know about it.' The plan was put to discussion at the next meeting of its provincial heads.[19] When RSS man S.S. Apte, a journalist with UNI who was also the founding general secretary of the VHP, started the newswire Hindustan Samachar in 1948, Deoras handpicked the correspondents. He was also in charge of Sangh's Marathi mouthpiece *Tarun Bharat*.[20]

Even though specifics are not available publicly, some accounts suggest that there were differences between Golwalkar and Deoras on the Sangh's direction. At one point, the differences became acute enough for Deoras to withdraw from the Sangh and retire to Balaghat in Madhya Pradesh to experiment in farming on the vast lands that his family owned. He remained aloof from 1953 to 1960.

One view is that Deoras's heart was in politics, and after the death of Syama Prasad Mookerjee in 1953, he wanted to head the Jana Sangh. He had once told his friend Narayan Baitule: 'RSS has more power than one may imagine. Do not get disheartened. One day I will become the prime minister of this country.'[21]

When Sangh leaders approached him in his self-imposed semi-exile, he refused to talk about it, saying the matter was between him and Golwalkar. However, he told them that he would never allow the Sangh to be split into two. He kept in touch with Nagpur, frequently travelling there and managing the Narkesari Trust, which published *Tarun Bharat*. His involvement in the trust was a demonstration that Golwalkar's disdain for publicity was misplaced. Deoras's motto was 'Organize, agitate and publicize', which was unacceptable in the Sangh at the time. He was prepared to wait for his chance to shape the RSS. Golwalkar finally handed it to him in 1973.[22]

While Golwalkar disliked politics (perhaps because he did not have the acumen for it), Deoras considered politics as a vehicle to bring change. During the first general elections, Golwalkar retired to Tilak's house near Sinhagad where he stayed between 25 December 1951 and 18 January 1952, a whole twenty-five days smack in the middle of the elections that began on 25 October 1951 and went on till 27 March 1952. Meanwhile, Deoras spent his time in Nagpur coordinating election efforts and helping nationalist parties, including the newly formed Bharatiya Jana Sangh.[23]

The personalities of Golwalkar and Deoras were like chalk and cheese. While Golwalkar was a monk and ritualist by nature, Deoras had little patience for rituals, was fond of meat and gave it up only when he was appointed sarsanghchalak. He also had a habit of switching to English when annoyed or giving orders.[24]

*

After the failed experiment of the Janata Party government, Deoras chose VHP as the instrument for his new thrust. Founded in 1964, the VHP was to do social spadework to consolidate Hindus who could be persuaded to back a non-Congress and non-communist political alternative. 'It took the shape of a large non-electoral platform to seek support of Hindus in India and abroad who identified with varied strands of Hindu traditional ideas and wanted to dissociate from the secular makeup of the Indian state as represented by the Congress government. There were also the people who did not want to associate with the RSS or the Jana Sangh at that juncture in politics. An alternative platform which was ostensibly religious seemed the most feasible means by which to organize the support of this constituency, and the result was the formation of the VHP,' Manjari Katju writes in *Vishva Hindu Parishad and Indian Politics*.[25]

The founding of the organization was perhaps expedited because the Pope decided to hold the International Eucharistic Conference in Bombay in November 1964. The announcement in August had come in the background of increased missionary activities in India. About 250 Hindus were expected to be converted to Christianity at the conference. In retaliation, Swami Chinmayananda announced he would convert 500 Christians to Hinduism. Eventually, neither happened.[26]

RSS pracharak S.S. Apte identified the three threats to the Hindu nation—Christianity which owed allegiance to the Pope in Rome, Islam which wanted to convert the world into Pakistan and communism whose loyalties lay with Russia or China. These were the same as identified by Golwalkar. 'The world has been divided into Christian, Islamic and Communist, and these three consider Hindu society to be a very good and very rich food which they feast and grow fat. It is therefore necessary in this age of competition and conflict, to think of organizing the Hindu world to save it from the evil eyes of these three.' Apte pointed to the Naga insurgency in the north-east as an example of Christian missionary–inspired separatism to break up India.[27] The organization was, in fact, founded barely nine months after Nagaland was born as a new state on 1 December 1963.

The RSS had identified the diversity in the Hindu community as its weakness. If they were not brought under one umbrella and goaded to work together on issues such as religious conversion, they could at least agree on a minimum code that could be applied to determine a person as Hindu. This move, which political scientist Jaffrelot terms as strategic mimetism, was designed to counter the unity in the rival religions with a similar structure for Hinduism. This would, most importantly, be useful politically.

At the second World Hindu Conference in Allahabad in January 1979, Deoras said:

> The government thinks that the Hindus have no demands to make as regards even elementary rights, while other religious communities are vociferous and obtain favourable treatment from the same government ... Politicians only think about the next elections and their personal gain. Hindus must now wake up so that, if only by electoral calculation, the politicians would be obliged to respect Hindu sentiments and, as a consequence, re-orientate their policies ... If others submit grievances, they are accepted, but even the most well-founded demands of Hindus are ignored. This is because Muslims and other communities generally vote en bloc, while the Hindus are divided. As soon as the Hindus become united, the government will begin to be concerned with them also ... Consequently, the need of

the hour is to awaken in Hindus[28] the awareness that they are
Hindus.

This mission, he believed, could not be done by a political party.
It required an organization that could work on a sustained basis
without worrying about electoral consequences.

*

The VHP central headquarters is in a cul-de-sac in the R.K. Puram
area of Delhi. It is a run-down building in which old men slowly
shuffle around through dimly lit, musty corridors. It doubles up, like
most Sangh Parivar offices, as home to single men who have worked
for long and are dedicated to the cause.

Champat Rai lives on the second floor in a crammed room.
A double bed is supplemented with bedding on the floor. Various
medicine bottles, books and an electric kettle are arranged on the
floor. A few mementoes—mostly with Lord Ram's image—are
stacked in a shelf and on a top ledge. The only shiny object in the
room is Rai's iPhone 7.

Rai was earlier VHP's general secretary (international) and
now vice president. Like many others, Rai also cut his teeth in the
RSS. He was transferred to the VHP in 1986 as the Parivar ramped
up the Ram Janmabhoomi campaign. From 1989, when the final
thrust began, he was stationed at Ayodhya. He is so involved in the
campaign and the subsequent court cases that he can recall even the
tiniest detail without referring to any document. He draws a rough
but feature-rich sketch of the mosque and the area around it before
1992 showing precise measurements. Rai can recount the centuries-
old history of the conflict in detail. He is also an eyewitness to the
demolition. 'It was God's will,' he says with complete authority.

Rai is one of those quintessential swayamsevaks, cut to perfection
through years of slow sculpting in the shakha. Born into a peasant
family in a small village called Nagina in the Bijnor district of western

Uttar Pradesh, Rai holds a master's degree in physics. He joined the Sangh when he was in high school. The conditioning was deep. 'The Sangh never left me from the first days I started going to the shakha in 1956–57.'

Rai was teaching in a college in Bijnor when Indira Gandhi clamped down Emergency. He was picked up in the first month itself and spent the next nineteen and half months behind bars—first in Bijnor district jail, then in Agra and Bareilly central prisons. 'We held shakha in jail too and did exercises and surya namaskars.'[29]

After the Emergency was lifted, Rai quit his teaching job and became a full-time RSS pracharak, first as district in-charge of Dehradun and then Saharanpur. He became Meerut vibhag pracharak in 1985. A year later, he was sent to the VHP, which by then had become the leading edge of the RSS. That year, on 1 February, a local court had ordered that the locks on the temple in Ayodhya be opened and devotees be allowed inside.[30] The opening of the locks had taken the wind out of the sail of the VHP and associates. Until then they were campaigning to get the temple opened. Now that it had opened, there was not much to do; unless they escalated their demand.

Five years before Rai was shifted to the VHP, the RSS had put its Delhi prant pracharak, Ashok Singhal, in charge of the outfit. On Singhal's eighty-ninth birthday celebrations in Delhi in 2015, RSS chief Mohan Bhagwat recollected the Sangh meeting that effected the change.

Bhagwat first met Ashok Singhal at an RSS camp for district pracharaks in Bangalore. Singhal was the prant pracharak for Delhi and Bhagwat had just been appointed pracharak for Nagpur. Singhal sang and taught songs at the camp. One went: '*Jai jai mera desh mahan. Hindu Hindu ek rahein…*' It was first sung at the Hindu Virat Sammelan in Delhi. The VHP was also a subject of discussion at the pracharaks meeting. It debated what the VHP should be like and what its work should be. Singhal who was the Delhi prant pracharak talked about it in detail. Another pracharak Jai Gopal, who was listening to him commented to Bhagwat: '*Yeh VHP ke baare mein itna bol rahein hain. Lagta hai ye gaye* (He is talking so much about VHP. Looks like he is going away from the Sangh).' By the end of the meeting, it was announced that Ashok Singhal would move to VHP.[31]

Deoras's strategy was beginning to unfold and the VHP was to be the pinch-hitter on the rearranged field.

*

In February 1981, hundreds of Dalit families of a remote village in Tamil Nadu converted to Islam en masse. That incident captured national headlines and came to be known as the Meenakshipuram conversions. Taking cognizance of a *Sunday Standard* report on 12 April 1981, headlined '*A whole village goes Islamic*' and narrating that 180 Hindu Harijan families changed their faith into Islam and another fifty families were likely to embrace it by the end of the month, R.P. Khanna, secretary, Scheduled Castes and Scheduled Tribes Commission, ordered the regional director stationed in Madras to conduct an enquiry.

The report stated that after talking to a cross section of people, including Dalits, caste Hindus and Muslims it found that neither coercion nor foreign money made them embrace Islam. 'Acute poverty, social inequality and persecution by upper-caste Hindus forced some of the Harijans to do so,' it said.

The Harijans could not go to temples and schools freely without any discrimination. The services of barbers and washermen were not available to Harijans. There were separate wells in the localities of Pallans, Arunthathiyars and Thevars. Pallans had their own barbers. Harijans could not get water from the wells in the Thevar locality. There were three tea stalls at Panpoli run by a Moopanar, a Thevar and a Muslim. Harijans could get service at the stall run by the Muslim but not from the other two.

Within days of the conversions, upper-caste Hindus formed an association, Suttuvattara Hindu Samudaya Valarachi Manram, headquartered in Panpoli, to analyse the reasons for the conversions. The society claimed it reconverted thirty-eight Scheduled Caste persons to Hinduism on 6 March. Meanwhile, the VHP had been organizing discourses on Hindu religion. It organized representatives from all over India and abroad to deliver speeches on Hinduism. It even got an American neo-convert to Hinduism to deliver a speech near Meenakshipuram.[32]

On 14 July, it held a Hindu Solidarity Conference in Meenakshipuram bringing many sanyasis and sadhus together on the dais. They declared:

> We, the religious leaders assembled today in Meenakshipuram, solemnly declare that our Vedas and Shastras never mentioned untouchability in any form or in any place whatsoever, but only propounded complete fraternity … We therefore ardently call upon all our Hindu brothers to eradicate all these banes, individually and collectively, and to endeavour to promote equality and fraternity among all sectors of our Hindu people.[33]

A proposed mosque too appears to have become a bone of contention. The Suttuvattara Hindu Samudaya Valarachi Manram complained that a mosque was proposed to be built in the village and wanted it relocated to an alternative site saying it would disturb peace in the village. The local *Indian Express* correspondent told the enquiry officials that a sum of Rs 20,000 was received from abroad to build the mosque.

A government report quoted S. Subramanian, a Scheduled Caste villager, as saying that he was forced to become the vice president of the Suttuvattara Hindu Samudaya Valarachi Manram. He said he would not go to the barber shop as he was afraid of the consequences. He was advised by some of his friends to convert to Islam, but he thought that he had availed himself of many benefits and concessions from the government and that he would be betraying Hinduism if he converted to Islam. He said that the initiative for conversions was from Harijans, and that too, educated and employed ones.

On 9 February, they held a meeting and decided to convert to Islam which was the only course to get away from the word Pallan. They then approached Muslim leaders in Tirunelveli to help them embrace Islam. They had also reported to the director for Scheduled Castes and Scheduled Tribes that for twenty years their elders had been thinking of converting to Islam. They had attempted it thrice before but this was the first time that there were enough numbers and unanimity. It was their belief that at least their children would not be called Pallan and would not be subjected to ill-treatment and harassment.[34]

The RSS's Akhil Bharatiya Karyakari Mandal responded immediately to the conversions. It passed a resolution saying it was deeply concerned with the mass conversions of Meenakshipuram and certain other villages in Tamil Nadu. 'All impartial agencies—press, social institutions, religious and political groups—which have made an on-the-spot study have affirmed the influence of vast amounts of money, coercion and such other illegal and anti-religious methods in the conversion. Even flow of foreign money is strongly suspected,' said the resolution. It said the conversions had a well-planned nature and Muslim proselytizers were exploiting and aggravating untouchability with the lure of so-called equality in Islam (in fact Muslim society too has no less divisions and discriminations) as against the discrimination in the Hindu fold. It warned that such conversions were a threat to national security as it would lead them to be disloyal to the country. 'Experience of past history amply bears out the fact that such conversions do not merely imply a simple change in the way of worship, but destruction of national culture and secessionist tendencies and extra-territorial loyalties and communal animosities and flare-ups as well, which directly strike at the roots of our national integrity and security.'[35]

The RSS had been aware and campaigning on such issues but the conversions surprised the organization. It also shook the rest of the country into realizing the gravity of the situation and helped consolidate the Hindu society, according to an RSS national executive member and head of one of its prominent verticals.

*

The RSS often undertakes nationwide campaigns to increase its reach and influence. After the Emergency, it undertook a massive 'Rashtra Jagran' campaign, aimed at the creation of widespread contacts across the country and expansion of Sangh activities. The Sangh, which enjoyed a strong presence in urban India, had struggled to make inroads into Indian villages. Such programmes continue even today. A senior Sangh leader says the Sardar Patel statue project launched just before the 2014 Lok Sabha elections was a similar one.[36] Announced in 2010, Sardar Vallabhbhai Patel Rashtriya Ekta Trust (SVPRET), a special purpose vehicle set up by the Gujarat government, constructed a 182-metre high statue of Sardar Patel at a cost of over Rs 2000 crore. Called the Statue of Unity, it has come up on Sadhu Island in Kewadia in the Sardar Sarovar lake.[37]

When he was anointed BJP's chief campaign manager in 2013, Narendra Modi announced that the trust would source used iron implements from farmers across the country. The trust would collect 1 kg of iron from each of the six lakh Indian villages. While most people saw a smart nationalistic campaign that would benefit the party and Modi in the Lok Sabha elections, the Sangh saw the project as something designed to get its ideology flowing through villages. The senior RSS leader says the crowds that came to Modi's meetings were not there just to listen to him or drawn by his charisma. The milling thousands chanting Modi's name were seen as a dam-burst of bottled-up emotions that flowed in adoration for the Hindu nationalist leader. It was triggering debate in the media and a national discourse was getting created. It was ideological war with the Congress.

Many of these campaigns fizzle out but the Ram Janmabhoomi agitation paid rich dividends. Keeping a close watch on the tense environment in Ayodhya and Faizabad after the idol of baby Ram was placed inside the mosque, Sardar Patel, who was then home minister, wrote to the Uttar Pradesh chief minister G.B. Pant. Patel was worried that the country had barely settled after the violence following Partition and an incident like this could be like a spark to a powder keg.

> I feel that the controversy has been raised at the most inopportune time both from the point of view of the country at large and of your own province in particular. … So far as Muslims are concerned, they are just settling down to their new loyalties … I realize there is a great deal of sentiment behind the move which has taken place. At the same time, such matters can be resolved peacefully if we take the willing consent of the Muslim community with us. There can be no question of resolving such disputes by force.[38]

While the south was roiled by the conversions and communal disturbances following the Meenakshipuram incident, the north had been burning in communal fires for a while. One of the worst cases of rioting happened in Moradabad, killing an estimated 284 persons.[39] The Provincial Armed Constabulary (PAC), seen to be sympathetic to Hindus, was particularly blamed for the carnage.

A former senior Sangh pracharak who was in western UP at the time says Aligarh was always considered riot prone. 'There were tensions in Moradabad, Bareilly … mostly in western Uttar Pradesh. Some were land related issues, some related to graveyards, some were business related,' he said. He said it was Congress's design to blame the RSS and VHP for everything. It was true that whenever such incidents happened RSS pracharaks and swayamsevaks were involved from the Hindu side. He said the PAC favoured Hindus because the state police always listened to the Congress which was in power in the state. The PAC was occasionally used, and they were not influenced by the local political leadership.[40]

In November 1982, forty-four Muslim MPs, including some from the Congress, submitted a memorandum to the prime minister. 'Communal virus is ever present in our body politic,' it began. 'So, an outbreak of communal violence cannot be prevented. But communal violence can, and must be, controlled within twenty-four hours, if there is political will and if the administration is neutral and effective. All around us we see secular forces yielding ground to the forces of communalism which have penetrated deeply in the political system and in the administration.' The letter took direct aim at the Sangh Parivar. 'The nationwide campaign of vicious propaganda against the Muslim community by the VHP, has corroded the foundations of the secular order and widened the gulf between the Hindus and the Muslims. Today chauvinism is on the offensive with the slogan of "Hinduism in danger". Its object is to generate hatred and distrust against the Muslim community and to force it into cultural assimilation and thus turn secular India into Hindu Rashtra.' The memorandum demanded that violence against minorities be treated as a national issue and on par with violence against scheduled castes and scheduled tribes. The MPs wanted a law similar to the law to protect SCs and STs from atrocities, 'through a Constitutional amendment, if necessary'. It called for a ban on Vishwa Hindu Parishad and RSS. The letter would have set off alarm bells at the RSS headquarters. But what happened next would have raised a giant red flag.

General Shah Nawaz Khan, the octogenarian leader of the Mulk-o-Millat Bachao Tehreek, wrote a letter to Indira Gandhi. Khan was a veteran of the Indian National Army (INA), which fought in World War II. He was tried by the British for treason and sentenced to death even though it was commuted after protests. He joined the Congress in independent India and became a parliamentarian representing Meerut. An Indira loyalist, he had lost to the Jana Sangh in 1967 and 1977. The letter is worth quoting in full.

We, the undersigned bring, with deep pain and anguish, to your notice the unabated violation of the values of secularism and the unmitigated Muslim baiting at the hands of communal chauvinist forces with active connivance and collaboration of sizeable sections of administration and police in various states.

Secular democracy is a precious legacy that we have inherited from our long freedom struggle. This glorious legacy, Madam, is being callously trampled underfoot. Moradabad, Meerut and Baroda are gaping wounds on its body calling for serious flanking and determined action. The active involvement of some sections of the government machinery in these patently anti-Muslim actions, the indifference of a large section of society, the failure of political leadership, and the apparent helplessness of secular forces have caused frustration and dismay all around, particularly among the Muslims who are victims of this ruthless violence.

An atmosphere has been generated through high-pressure propaganda in which even a voice of protest against manifest injustice is difficult to raise, what to speak of demanding justice for the suffering community. The verbal assault that has been launched under the leadership of the RSS and Vishwa Hindu Parishad against the entire Muslim community over a few conversions in Meenakshipuram—unmindful of the fact that the fundamental right of propagation and freedom of faith is being exercised in the form of conversions and reconversions in all directions—is not only flagrant violation of the Constitution but also an indication of the deep inroads that fascist ideas and techniques have made into our social and political life. The pity is that no powerful voice is raised against all this vulgarization and brutalization of human feelings and those that are raised find no response from the ruling circles. On the other hand, there goes on loud, irresponsible and unchecked propaganda about Muslims receiving foreign money to convert India into a Muslim-majority nation. Sometimes even official agencies lend a hand to add to the credibility of such falsehoods…

Madam, you know it very well that Jamiat-Ulama-i-Hind, from its very inception, has constituted an integral flank of the army of Indian freedom fighters, and its founders and early leaders were among those who developed and fostered the ideas of composite nationalism and united endeavour for better life on a secular basis. Naturally, the Jamiat cannot remain a silent spectator to the erosion of those values.

Then came the elections. The Indian National Congress (I) under your leadership issued a manifesto which included the promise to implement all the demands that the Jamiat had been making to strengthen the secular character of Indian society and politics. It promised to create condition in which minorities could act freely and participate in all walks of life, to protect their culture and belief, to curb the activities of communal and divisive forces, to take effective steps to stop communal riots, and to provide full compensation to victims of communal violence.

Specific mention was made of a resolve to create a special force to deal with communal riots.

Madam, we regret to say that none of those promises has been fulfilled. In fact, within a few months of you coming back to power occurred the tragic happening in Moradabad where the festival of Id had been drenched in the blood of innocents by the PAC. Speaking from the Red Fort on 15th August 1980 you had announced that you would see to it that those responsible for Moradabad tragedy would be given exemplary punishment.

What happened? No culprit was apprehended. None was punished. Anti-Muslim tirade continued. The communal elements amongst the general population and within the police got emboldened. The tragedy was repeated in Bihar Sharif, in Meerut, in Baroda, and now in Trivandrum. The poison is going deeper and wider with every passing day.

It is in these circumstances of despair and frustration that we approach you with the following demands:

1. The district authorities and intelligence services should be held responsible for outbreak of communal disturbances. If they fail in controlling disturbances, they should be suspended forthwith and if they are proved guilty they should be strictly dealt with.

2. The intelligence services should be entrusted with the responsibility of tracing out persons suspected of communal riots and special courts should be set up for the disposal of cases and matters relating to communal riots.

3. Those suffering loss of life and property during communal disturbances should be fully compensated or paid at least Rs 100,000 per person dead. Those wounded and those who suffer financial loss should be fully compensated and riot protection compulsory insurance scheme on nominal premium should be enforced.

4. In security forces like PAC and BMP there should be 33 per cent reservation for Muslims and 33 per cent reservation for other minorities. A code of conduct and training programme should be evolved for such forces so that they may be morally and mentally equipped for shouldering their responsibilities in a secular and democratic set up. Till the moulding and restructuring of these security forces is completed, they should not be deployed in riot-affected areas; in such areas central security forces should be posted.

5. Semi-military drills of RSS and other communal organizations, should be banned and the government should arrange for physical training of all children and youth, irrespective of their caste, community and religion.

6. All departments, agencies and organizations of the government should be purged of persons connected with RSS and other such fascist organizations.

7. The clause relating to the Uniform Civil Code should be deleted from the Constitution of the country.
8. Permanent arrangement should be made for the protection of mosques, graveyards, and Auqaf of Muslims, and immediate effective action should be taken to free them from adverse legal possession wherever it has taken place.

We, therefore, urge you to implement these demands, which are your own promises made through the Congress (I) election manifesto of 1980, with immediate effect. In case no satisfactory response is received before 21 February 1983, we shall be constrained to launch a civil disobedience movement in collaboration with other like-minded secular forces.

The threat appears to have worked.

Indira Gandhi replied to Shah Nawaz Khan on 21 January 1983, expressing her concern for minorities and distress at the communal violence and disturbances. Claiming that her election promises were not neglected, she wrote:

The home minister has written to all chief ministers regarding the responsibilities of district authorities and intelligence service. Some states have already introduced compensation schemes for riot victims. State governments have also been advised to prohibit RSS shakhas in public places…

We discourage proliferation of RSS sympathizers in any government organization and have given instructions that shakhas should not be allowed. You will agree that under the rules, it is not easy to dismiss people. In new appointments such attitudes are kept in mind.

If you can cite specific instances of religious places under adverse possession, government will take action under law.

…

Initiative also has to come from the community itself like availing of better educational facilities. But confrontation and spreading of an atmosphere of desperation are likely to be more damaging to the minorities themselves by arousing reaction in other communities.

In Karnataka, the Muslims did not vote for us, with the result that there are now only two Muslim MLAs.

Indira Gandhi set up a committee to look into the grievances of Muslims and also devised a fifteen-point plan to comfort minorities, including more representation in police forces and administration.[41]

*

Even as Indira Gandhi was addressing Muslims' concerns, a Sikh religious leader, Sant Jarnail Singh Bhindranwale, had moved into the Golden Temple in Amritsar with his armed followers and made it his headquarters. Bhindranwale was then spearheading a movement for a separate Khalistan, which incidentally is the most potent separatist movement. It is still smouldering, especially in pockets of the expatriate Sikh community.

Many saw Indira Gandhi's hard-line stand against Akalis as a move to woo Punjabi Hindus both within Punjab as well as in other states. The suspicion was rooted in the way the Congress ran its campaign in the Kashmir and Delhi elections. Parivar leaders suspected she wanted to take advantage of the Hindu backlash. 'Mrs Gandhi's whole strategy has been to pit moderates against extremists,' Vajpayee told the *New York Times*.[42] He said Gandhi was making an open grab for the BJP's constituents.

Incidentally, Deoras had met Sheikh Abdullah, who was then chief minister of Jammu and Kashmir, in 1979 following which his party the National Conference backed a BJP candidate to the election of Jammu mayor. When Congressmen accused Abdullah of supporting Jan Sanghis with an RSS background, he shot back: 'Are Jan Sanghis not Indians? Are they not men?'[43]

In western Uttar Pradesh, towns such as Moradabad, which is known for making brassware, or Aligarh, which is famous for locks, there is a sizeable population of Punjabi businessmen. These Hindu businessmen, a large section of them Partition refugees, have close ties with the RSS and the BJP. However, most of the artisans and skilled workers in these businesses are Muslims. Disputes and conflicts between the owners and workers over wages or other labour issues are common. Sometimes there are skirmishes over land deals. These otherwise business-related conflicts sometimes spin out of control and take a communal colour.

The RSS had deployed its cadres during Partition to protect Hindus and their property. It had also helped refugees set up camps in various parts of the country and helped them with food and shelter. These grateful Hindus became staunch supporters of the Sangh and returned the favour by helping it financially.

The refugees, who had faced many horrors, also carried with them an intense hatred for Muslims. This hatred eventually fuelled conflicts and riots in areas where the refugees settled. As they established businesses and prospered, so did their support for the RSS. According to a Meerut lawyer and former head of the local chapter of a Parivar affiliate, *guru dakshina* (ritual offering to one's teacher; in the RSS's case, to the flag) envelopes have become fatter over the years. The RSS's only official source of income is the guru dakshina, which is presented anonymously at shakhas on the day of Guru Purnima. Considering there was no fixed amount and the principle was each as per his might, the practice was to keep the amounts in sealed envelopes to ensure anonymity. The lawyer said RSS office-bearers often requested a certain amount be given as dakshina.[44]

The RSS was not the only organization weighing in for the Ram Janmabhoomi. Indira Gandhi also knew the political potential of the Hindu holy city. Gandhi, however, was not oblivious of the charge that she was courting Muslims. She had a balancing act in mind, and it involved Ayodhya. She had asked to prepare various plans for the development of Ayodhya. She wanted to develop the city as a pilgrimage centre and was pushing through proposals rapidly. The *Ram ki Purhi* project, languishing for lack of funds, was given the go-ahead. A hotel owned by the tourism department at Ayodhya was modernized and officials were engaged in the process of giving the city a facelift.[45]

In his study published as '*RSS's Tryst With Politics*', Jawaharlal Nehru University (JNU) professor Pralay Kanungo says that Indira Gandhi, who returned to power in 1980, spoke of Hindu hegemony in the Hindi heartland. She adopted a new political approach by making pilgrimages to sacred rivers, shrines and temples across the country. The Congress swept the 1983 elections in Jammu and Kashmir and the Delhi corporation, wiping out a shocked BJP in its own fort of Jammu.

While Gandhi was shifting her strategy, a rebel Congressman was taking up cudgels against Muslims. VHP's Champat Rai remembers Congressman and five-time member of Parliament from Moradabad, Daudayal Khanna, from a Hindu conference, organized by the Sangh and held under the banner of Hindu Jagran Manch in Muzaffarnagar in 1983. The conference's president was Karan Singh, son of the last king of Kashmir, Hari Singh, who acceded to India. Karan Singh, a well-respected leader of the Congress party, had served as a Union minister and was a close friend of Indira Gandhi's. 'We cannot even light a holy lamp at Ram's birthplace in Ayodhya,' Karan Singh, who was a speaker at the conference as well, told the sadhus. 'How shameful a matter is it for 80 per cent of this country's residents who call themselves Hindus?'

Rajendra Singh, who would go on to become the RSS sarsanghchalak, shared the platform with Gulzarilal Nanda, Congressman and former home minister, and Dinesh Tyagi, RSS pracharak and the head of Hindu Jagran Manch in western Uttar Pradesh. Daudayal Khanna is said to have exhorted Hindus to free

Ayodhya, Kashi and Mathura at the conference. The seed of the mass Ayodhya campaign was sown there, according to Champat Rai of the VHP.[46]

The movement got a boost on 4 January 1984 when someone planted a Hanuman pataka (the monkey god Hanuman's pennant) atop the central dome of the Babri mosque. The news spread like wildfire attracting massive crowds. Former prime minister Narasimha Rao believed that to be the moment when the RSS realized the political potential of the issue.[47]

A conference, or Dharm Sansad, of sadhus and sants was held in Delhi later. About 600 of them from all over the country participated in it in Delhi's government-owned conference hall, Vigyan Bhavan, on 7 and 8 April 1984. Although it was organized and directed by the VHP, it remained in the background on specific instructions from Deoras, preferring to let the religious leaders take the lead and limelight.[48]

The gathering issued a code of conduct for individuals, families and society. Its code for the country's statesmen included the demand that three important holy sites—Kashi, Mathura and Ayodhya—be given back to Hindu society. An unregistered trust was formed at the end of the conference in the name of Ram Janmabhoomi Mukti Yagya Samiti. Rai connects the background of Khanna's leaving the Congress and joining the Hindutva fold to the Moradabad riots of 1980.

On the day of Eid that year, a few pigs are said to have run through rows of Eid worshippers in Moradabad, defiling the prayers. It had been a tradition since Independence that when the worshippers returned from the mosque, Hindus there would welcome them with sweets and sherbet. They would set up stalls and invariably the first one was the Congress's. That year, it was manned by Khanna and Moradabad Congress chief Dayanand Gupta. The returning worshippers allegedly beat them up.[49] Gupta is said to have never recovered from the beating and remained bedridden for the rest of his life. An extremely angry Khanna left the Congress.

Newspaper reports of the time corroborate that the incident was caused when some pigs ran into the Idgah while namaz was going on. In fact, communal riots had become frequent in western Uttar Pradesh, especially in Aligarh, Moradabad and Meerut in the late 1970s and early 1980s.

*

The RSS often encourages its volunteers to take up projects and new initiatives. These projects remain individual-driven until the Sangh decides to hold their hand and scale them up. The Ayodhya movement was the brainchild of Moropant Pingle, Nanaji Deshmukh and Bhaurao Deoras who had been preparing the ground for it for a long time. After the baby Ram idol was placed in the Babri mosque, locals used to organize *bhajans* at the site. Interest waned after a while and the bhajans were on the verge of stopping. Deshmukh, who was a pracharak in UP in the 1940s and 1950s, then arranged for the bhajans to continue uninterrupted at the mosque.[50]

After the Meenakshipuram conversions, when the RSS decided to mobilize the Hindu community, it picked up the Ram Janmabhoomi project, for which Pingle and Bhaurao Deoras had prepared the ground. Until then, most in the Sangh were not even aware of it. An RSS resolution of 1959 on the 'issue of temples turned into mosques' is revealing. It laments how tyrannical foreign aggressors destroyed many Hindu temples and built mosques in their place to smite the nationalistic sentiments of Indians.

An intense desire to resurrect these places of worship was ever present at the heart of the freedom movement. It is a matter of great regret that even after the end of British rule, our own government should have remained totally callous to the legitimate rights of the Hindus over such temples.

Out of all such temples, the Kasi Vishwanatha temple occupies a special place of honour because of its unique position as the centre of devotion and faith of all Hindus throughout the country. Lakhs of devotees visit this holy centre every year. The present condition of the temple, however, is such as to severely wound their feelings. The sabha urges the government of Uttar Pradesh to take steps to return this temple to the Hindus, their rights over it having recognized even by the Supreme Court.[51]

Nowhere in the resolution does Ayodhya come up even as a passing reference.

In 1983, the VHP organized a month-long Ekatmata Yatra (unification march). Although the main objective was to raise funds, it was also an experiment in discovering social symbols that resonated most with Hindus on a mass scale. There were multiple processions carrying the image of Mother India and urns filled with water from the Ganga from different parts that winded across the country to converge in Nagpur. The water was bottled and sold to people on the way. The response was encouraging and the contours of Hindutva politics were gradually beginning to take shape.[52]

The brain behind the initiative was Pingle, a Sangh pracharak since 1941. The RSS website describes him as someone mentored by both Hedgewar and Golwalkar and an expert at running big campaigns. He held top positions such as national chief of propaganda, physical training and *boudhik*. Pingle was appointed the convener and controller of Ekatmata Yatra. The next year, the VHP organized Ram–Janki Rath Yatras. Seven chariots were built on Tata 407 trucks. The first one took off from Sitamarhi in Bihar. It was shaped like a temple and Lord Ram and Sita were placed in a mock-up of a prison. In Champat Rai's recollection there was an ocean of people near the Sarayu river when it reached Ayodhya on 7 October.

The crowd kept increasing as people started flowing in from neighbouring villages and the rath slowed down to the pace of the walkers. The Bajrang Dal was also formed around this time as a gaggle of enthusiastic, militant youth. On 14 October, the chariot reached Lucknow and then proceeded to Delhi. It was stopped at

Ghaziabad on 31 October when news arrived that Indira Gandhi was assassinated. The yatra was suspended for a year.

In Narasimha Rao's words: 'The other parties, at least subconsciously, felt in a way cheated in their long-cherished aspiration to come to power just when they had begun to find it within sight and beckoning to them in a couple of months' time before Indiraji's assassination in 1984.'[53]

A year later, on 23 October, Vijaya Dashami, the chariots started rolling again.

*

Meanwhile, a new Congress government was in place in Delhi with the young Rajiv Gandhi as prime minister. After many years of dowdy politics, Rajiv Gandhi was a breath of fresh air. But his reign began with a massacre of thousands of Sikhs in Delhi in revenge of his mother's assassination by her two Sikh bodyguards. In an infamous statement, Gandhi said of the killings, 'But, when a mighty tree falls, it is only natural that the earth around it does shake a little.'[54]

That statement, as well as the killings, was soon forgotten outside Delhi by a nation smitten by Rajiv's smile and his young Italian wife. Gandhi's technocratic team and technological vision promised to free India from trunk calls and Ambassador cars and usher it into the modern age of cable TV and computers. Rajiv Gandhi had acquired the image of Mr Clean and won over even rivals with his courtesy and manners. He would stand up when senior leaders like Vajpayee went to visit him and see them off to the door. Vajpayee once related how Rajiv Gandhi helped him when he was having kidney trouble. Gandhi included Vajpayee in a government delegation to the United Nations (UN) and helped him get treated in New York. 'That is one reason I'm alive today,' Vajpayee said. Ramnath Goenka, owner of the *Indian Express*, told American journalist Jack Anderson, 'Now I can die in peace knowing the country is in good hands.'[55]

However, unlike his mother, who had her finger on the country's pulse, the foreign-educated pilot only had a bird's eye view of India, and was unfamiliar with the ruthless politics of what was sometimes referred to as the 'cow belt' and could not sense the latent communal tensions in the distant villages and small towns of India.

On 23 October 1985, as the Ram-Janki raths started rolling again and slowly wound towards the capital, pressure started building on the political novice. He restarted what his mother could not complete—wooing the Hindus. The Rajiv Gandhi government paved the way for the locks on the mosque to be opened for worship by Hindus. It was like lighting the wick of a long-dormant explosive of catastrophic power.

A report cited a VHP leader confidentially informing that Rajiv Gandhi had indicated in no uncertain terms that the gates of Ram Janmabhoomi should be opened to devotees before Shivratri on 8 March 1986. The Ram Janmabhoomi Mukti Samiti was planning to break open the temple gates that day and a sadhu had vowed to immolate himself if it was not done. The local administration had been prepared in advance. On 1 February, the court verdict was announced at 4.40 p.m. and the lock was broken at 5.19 p.m. A Doordarshan team was on the spot to capture devotees thronging the Janmabhoomi as soon as the gates were opened, indicating that the government had prior knowledge if not a hand in the court order.[56]

After the locks were opened, the VHP lost an issue. But fortunately for it, a rival was born. Within a week, the Babri Masjid Action Committee (BMAC) was formed. Almost immediately, tensions started brewing. In April, the BMAC organized a conference in Faizabad.

When Deoras heard about the Muslim organizations' rally, he called Champat Rai, Onkar Bhave and prant pracharak of western Uttar Pradesh, Om Prakash, for a meeting in Lakhimpur where a Sangh camp was under way. Deoras told them to create such an atmosphere in the country that no one dared to march to Ayodhya.[57]

The VHP immediately organized a Ram Janam Bhumi Mahotsav in Ayodhya. In December, an All India Babri Masjid Conference was held and the Babri Masjid Movement Coordination Committee (BMMCC) was formed with Syed Shahabuddin as convener. The conference called to boycott the Republic Day celebrations but withdrew when it drew flak from many people. It then organized a rally at New Delhi's Boat Club on 30 March 1987, which was the biggest Muslim rally in Delhi thus far.[58]

Deoras's assessment of the moment as a historic opportunity was prescient. In the first few years, the movement was one-sided. Only the Hindu organizations were agitating for it. Though sections of the public supported the idea, it was only the VHP cadres who were organizing campaigns. The opening of the locks changed that. There was a clear opponent with the formation of the BMAC and battle lines were drawn. It was now or never. Government soft-pedalling showed that pressure unsettled Rajiv Gandhi. This was a made-to-order opportunity. This was the moment the Sangh would deploy as much force as possible and push to tilt the balance of power in the Parivar's favour. As the Congress hesitated, the Parivar went all in.

L.K. Advani writes: 'The Congress party, in spite of having a mammoth majority in Parliament, was both unable and unwilling to put the Ayodhya issue in the right perspective before the Muslim community.'[59] Advani categorically said that if the Congress party had consistently supported the Ayodhya movement, the BJP would never have joined the fray.

Advani had become the BJP president the previous May. The party picking up the Ayodhya issue was preceded by an intense debate on the basic ideology and organizational issues of the party. Sometime in 1987, Advani and Vajpayee met Deoras in Cochin. He advised them that the Congress was trying to adopt a Hindutva line but it would not succeed under Rajiv Gandhi. That line, however, would be a natural fit for the BJP and it will be able to get the support of the Hindu society.[60]

Deoras's thinking had clearly changed in the three years that Gandhi had been at the helm. Just after the elections of 1984, in which the BJP was reduced to just two seats in the Lok Sabha, Deoras went to Kerala for a month of Ayurvedic treatment. At a farewell function when he was leaving Kerala, Deoras spoke very highly of Rajiv Gandhi. Nagpur-based businessman Dilip Deodhar, who was close to Deoras and several other Sangh leaders, recalls a conversation with Shrikant Joshi who had just been appointed secretary to Deoras. In the car ride to the airport, Deoras explained the rationale of his speech. 'Growing the BJP is not the RSS's responsibility. We don't look at individuals but support anyone who walks along our thought and ideology,' Deoras was said to have remarked.[61]

Rajiv Gandhi's effort to clean up the system in the initial days was attractive to the RSS, whose then motto was '*swachhata, suraksha* and *samrasta*' (cleanliness, security and equity). It not only meant physical cleanliness but also a clean public life free of corruption. This, it had hoped, Gandhi would provide and so he could be backed. He also seemed to be sympathetic to the RSS's cause and willing to move towards right of centre as his mother had tried to in her last years. In any case, his economic policies were a break from the socialist past. But as Gandhi got increasingly entangled in the Bofors scandal, the RSS began to withdraw.

Deodhar says that Deoras had earlier warned that the Ram temple issue should be handled according to Shiva *neeti* (Shivaji's war strategy of strike and run). He had warned that there was a real danger of the parivar getting badly stuck in the Ayodhya issue and once it did, it would be very difficult to get out.[62]

A month after the BMMCC event, the VHP organized a massive rally in Ayodhya triggering what Narasimha Rao termed a virtual race of rallies. In 1989, the VHP decided to up the ante. On 10 November, a kar seva to begin the construction of the temple at Ayodhya was announced at a meeting of godmen during the Kumbh Mela at Allahabad in February 1989. The Sangh Parivar was putting up its biggest-ever stake—the painfully constructed image, political and social capital and relationships during the Emergency—in the Ayodhya gamble.

Unbeknownst to the larger Sangh Parivar, Deoras was in touch with Rajiv Gandhi. At the time, Congress member of Parliament from Nagpur, Banwarilal Purohit, was slowly becoming vocal about building a Ram temple in Ayodhya. One day, Rajiv Gandhi summoned him and asked him if he knew Deoras and could initiate a dialogue with him. Purohit contacted *Tarun Bharat*'s managing director, Anant Bhide, for help. It was so arranged that Gandhi's emissary, Bhanu Prakash Singh, a cabinet minister in the 1970s and later Goa governor, secretly arrived in Nagpur. He was put up in a hotel near the airport itself. The next morning, he went to the house of an ailing RSS functionary, Babasaheb Talatule, and waited for Deoras. After some time, the RSS chief arrived at Talatule's house in the guise of visiting the ailing swayamsevak and held talks with Singh for more than an hour.

At the meeting, Singh is said to have told Deoras that Gandhi was prepared to allow *shilanyas* (the ceremony of laying the foundation stone for the intended temple on the site of Babri Masjid which had also created a controversy) at Ayodhya provided the RSS backed the Congress party in the forthcoming Lok Sabha elections. Deoras agreed. To reconfirm the deal, then RSS general secretary Rajendra Singh met Home Minister Buta Singh in Delhi.[63]

The government allowed the shilanyas to be performed on 9 November but the Muslim community was furious. There were protests not only in India but throughout the Islamic world, significantly in Saudi Arabia, Iran and Pakistan.

With the BJP raising its sails to catch the wind, the Parivar wanted to make sure the credit did not go to anyone else. After the foundation-stone–laying ceremony, Ashok Singhal said: 'If the Government thinks it has been bulldozed into allowing the foundation-stone laying ceremony, we can bulldoze them further. The awakened Hindus will not stop now.'[64]

After the announcement of the ceremony and kar seva, V.P. Singh, former Congressman who had left to start the Janata Dal, had also sent word to defer it. Singh was trying to negotiate an alliance for the Janata Dal with the BJP for the upcoming Lok Sabha elections.

Deoras called an informal meeting of senior pracharaks, including H.V. Sheshadri, the sarkaryavah, Mohan Bhagwat, who was then kshetra pracharak, and Ashok Singhal. He put V.P. Singh's proposal to vote but also warned them. 'If we decide to go ahead [with the kar seva] there won't be any going back. There will be repercussions. Do not complain later that shakhas have dwindled and work has suffered. Think about it now and decide whether we should go ahead or hold back.' The pracharaks' unanimous decision was to go ahead.[65]

A few weeks later, the parivar held a meeting in the RSS's Jhandewalan office in Delhi. Those present included Parivar leaders Bhaurao Deoras, Rajinder Singh, Ashok Singhal, Kaushal Kishore, Govindacharya and a few others. General Secretary H.V. Sheshadri conducted the meeting. As the meeting was about to conclude, Sheshadri went in to consult Balasaheb Deoras who was resting in an adjacent room. When he came out, Sheshadri announced: 'I, as sarkaryavah of Sangh, am telling you that it is good if shilanyas and alliance both happen. But if only one of the two can happen, shilanyas will be done whether the alliance happens or not.'[66]

RSS leader and author of several books, Ramesh Patange, observes that undertaking to work for the temple construction was the sacred duty of RSS volunteers. That was the top programme on the Sangh agenda. 'Enormous organizational strength was necessary to ensure that the kar seva would take place at the fixed time according to a plan. The entire atmosphere was charged with preparing for the kar seva programme. This programme was of phenomenal significance from the point of Hindu renaissance and emotional reawakening.'[67]

On 4 April 1991, the VHP organized a massive rally at Boat Club, the three-kilometre stretch between India Gate and Rashtrapati Bhavan in Delhi. Deoras told Ashok Singhal to make sure to let it be known that the rally was organized by sadhus and keep the VHP away from the limelight. Champat Rai writes in an article remembering

Deoras that he was the key force behind the Ram Janmabhoomi movement from the beginning till the time the mosque was razed.[68] 'Throughout the movement, the reins of the movement remained with the RSS who used to work out logistics and programmes,' the Liberhan commission noted.[69]

Arguably, no one in Indian politics understood the power of religion and the dangers of mixing religion with politics as much as Mahatma Gandhi. Harnessing the power of multiple faiths for a common political objective with minimal conflict between them was an art Gandhi tried to master but ultimately failed at great peril to the country and self. Gandhi drew energy and inspiration not only from his own faith but also from the Bible and the Quran. This delicate balancing act was not an easy one and even more difficult to emulate.

Advani learnt it the hard way—after opening the Pandora's box. He recounts the experience of his Ram Janmabhoomi rath yatra in his political autobiography *My Country, My Life*. In the very first days after the yatra was kicked off from Somnath temple in Gujarat, it received tremendous response from the public as people waited for hours in villages and tiny hamlets for the rath to arrive. In larger towns and cities, the response was overwhelming. Advani realized that he was secondary and incidental to the campaign. The principal messenger was the chariot itself. People were worshipping it everywhere.

Frankly, I did not expect such an overwhelming response. Looking at my gestures of amazement, Pramod [Mahajan], who was chosen by the party to be my companion throughout the yatra, quipped: 'Advaniji, the response is so big because it is Gujarat. The people here are traditional and religious. Don't think that it would be like this when we enter Maharashtra from Gujarat.' … Pramod was wrong, totally wrong. The response was as big, even bigger, in Maharashtra as well as in all the subsequent states that we travelled through … The rath had thus come to acquire divinity. ... As Gandhiji describes in his book *Hind Swaraj* the village folk were devoid of the influences of city life, commercialism and competitive instincts. Many of them were either illiterate or nominally educated. They had not learnt about Ram by reading; it was as if the knowledge flowed through them, passed on from one generation to the other, or through tales heard in congregations and plays organized at village fairs or on annual festivals like Ram Navami.[70]

Gandhi clearly understood that religion moved people and had profound consequences for politics. It was perhaps not a coincidence that Gandhi's favourite hymn was '*Raghupati Raghav Raja Ram*', dedicated to king Ram. It was an integral part of his daily prayer meetings and public gatherings. 'Ram, Allah and God to me are convertible terms,' Gandhi wrote in *Young India* of 22 January 1925.

Former prime minister Narasimha Rao presents a great example of this dynamic. The VHP ran a campaign (Ekatmata Yatra) carrying *Gangajal* (water from the Ganga) to all corners of the country. It was received well by the people. But Rajiv Gandhi's scheme to clean the holy river for environmental reasons at considerable cost to the government barely evoked any reaction. Rao says, the environment, which almost everyone has been polluting for centuries, is not the same as religion, whose spell of faith has remained indelible on the people's minds for many more centuries. So, while a secular programme, infinitely more useful, could not evoke faith, the mere carrying of Gangajal (even polluted) swayed millions. Narasimha Rao wrote that even the organizers had no clue about the impact the event would have.[71]

This insight was to be crucial for not just the BJP but also for the Sangh Parivar in its future mobilizations. Until then, the Parivar had not experimented with religious symbols, especially not in a political context. Not just that, the organization had difficulty in penetrating rural areas. 'Since its foundation in 1925 ... the RSS has had little success among the peasantry, whose religious beliefs, practices, and sense of community have been less affected by the changes brought on by modernity,' Walter Andersen and Shridhar Damle observed.[72]

The Liberhan Commission which inquired into the events that built up to the demolition of the Babri Masjid in Ayodhya, recorded Advani's statement:

> I would emphasize that in India, political parties are conscious of the fact that there are casteist vote banks—Brahmin vote bank, Dalit vote bank, Thakur vote bank—there are minority vote banks like the Christian vote bank, the Muslim vote bank, and Parsis vote bank. But there is no such thing as the Hindu vote bank and so those who are interested in vote banks appealed either to caste or minority denominations. Between 1949 and 1986, Ayodhya became a matter of public controversy or an issue. Political parties thought it would give political dividends. The turning point was Shah Bano's case … communalism, casteism, religionism, regionalism, etc., are narrower loyalties—I feel that the weakness of the weak political parties for vote bank politics is the principal reason why these loyalties are promoted.[73]

*

In 1991, after Rajiv Gandhi's assassination at Sriperumbudur near Chennai on the campaign trail of the Lok Sabha elections, Narasimha Rao became prime minister. He was the first non-Gandhi-Nehru to head a Congress-led government in more than twenty-five years. According to Sangh sources, Rao had many friends in the RSS. One former pracharak who wrote an article criticizing Rao got a call from sarsanghchalak Rajendra Singh. The sarsanghchalak told him not to criticize Rao as he was a true Hindu.

During his student days, Rao was exiled from Hyderabad for participating in a Congress agitation. He completed his education from Nagpur where he came into close contact with RSS leaders such as the Deoras brothers Bhaurao and Balasaheb, Moropant Pingle and others. He was also in touch with Bhaurao Deoras who was stationed in Delhi. After Bhaurao's death in 1992, Rao was unsure about whom to talk to in the Sangh regarding Hindutva issues, especially the Ram Janmabhoomi agitation. L.K. Advani suggested Rajendra Singh.

Singh writes that he met with Rao several times. He suggested that he convince the Muslim leadership on a collective decision on the issue. It could bring down the BJP's vote share but would benefit the Congress. People not only thought that the Congress was disinterested in the Ayodhya issue but also that it thought like Muslims. Singh presented a plan to Rao.

The Parivar would start building the temple gate first which would be the farthest from the disputed spot. It would take a couple of years and in the meantime Muslims would give up their claim believing that it was a contested place and they would never be able to worship there. Rao appears to have decided to trust him. He perhaps also put faith in Uttar Pradesh chief minister Kalyan Singh's assurances that he would not let anything happen to the structure. Rao later wrote that it was a story of betrayal.

Others, however, saw Rao's complicity in the demolition. At the emergency cabinet meeting convened on the evening the mosque was destroyed, senior Congress leader M.L. Fotedar said, 'Rao was directly responsible for the demolition of the Babri Masjid.'[74] But cabinet members remained listless and quiet. Fotedar, a Kashmiri Brahmin who was brought into the party by none other than Jawaharlal Nehru, considers that moment, when the cabinet remained stoically silent, as identifiably the one when the Congress party's decline began.

*

Sharad Gupta was not on official duty on 6 December 1992. A journalist with the *Times of India* in Lucknow, Gupta had got married on 21 November and was on leave. On the evening of 4 December, he was returning from a trip to Gonda, his in-laws' home in Ayodhya. When he reached Katra on the other side of the Sarayu he was told that the bus he was traveling in would not go any further. Faizabad and Ayodhya were still 8 kilometres away. Gupta managed to ride on the fender of a tempo locally nicknamed Ganeshji for its protruding snout. It trudged across the Sarayu, and when it entered Ayodhya, Gupta noticed that the whole town was teeming with kar sevaks all the way to Faizabad. Gupta found a couple of colleagues at a hotel frequented by journalists. They described to him the preparations for the kar seva and advised him to stay put at home the next day. They said a German photographer had been beaten up and they were looking for BBC journalist Mark Tully. The kar sevaks believed that the BBC and a couple of other foreign radio stations had misreported the events in Ayodhya and they wanted to teach them a lesson.[75] It would be revealed later that the media had been systematically targeted.[76]

Gupta didn't think much of it. He had been witness to the kar seva in 1989 and other similar events before and after. Usually, kar sevaks went to the site, added some sand in a pit and concluded that the kar seva was done. The next morning, he had just stepped out of his home around 10 a.m. when a car with a press sticker screeched to a stop in front of him. Two very excited journalists jumped out and ran to a nearby public phone. Gupta learned that the kar sevaks were breaking down the Babri Masjid. On leave or not, the journalist was not going to miss what was going to be one of the most momentous events in the history of modern India. Gupta's brother-in-law, who was familiar with the narrow lanes of the town, took him on the pillion of his scooter to Parikrama Marg near some mustard fields. The lay of the land there was such that the fields were at a height and the mosque was just ahead of them in low-lying area. From where Gupta stood, the fields were almost at level with the mosque's domes.

The sight was incredible. There was no panic. People were walking about freely. Some people had climbed the dome and were breaking it with pickaxes. A small group of fifteen to twenty policemen were casually resting beneath a tree. There was no other police force.

This is corroborated by then prime minister Narasimha Rao in his book *Ayodhya: 6 December 1992*. On 1 December, during the hearing on a contempt petition related to the Ayodhya dispute in the Supreme Court, the Attorney General gave the judges Intelligence Bureau (IB) reports in a sealed cover. One of the reports said that only one company of the Provincial Armed Constabulary was deployed at the site to maintain law and order. Uttar Pradesh chief minister Kalyan Singh said that two days before the kar seva was to happen, the government had deployed fifteen companies of the PAC and installed metal detectors at several entry points. However, on 5 December, Home Minister S.B. Chavan wrote to the Uttar Pradesh government saying that its security arrangements were inadequate and suggested several measures it should take.[77]

Some months ago, the government had dug trenches around the mosque ostensibly for constructing some facilities for visitors. In July, Gupta wrote in the *Times of India* how about six to eight feet of the mosque's foundation was exposed. The pits were surrounded by pipe scaffoldings and barriers. Now the crowd had pushed down the pipes and the fallen structures doubled up as ladders. Some people pulled out pipes and had begun to tear down the walls. Gupta clambered along the collapsed scaffolding and managed to get inside. There was no one inside and the idols had vanished. He went back to his spot in the mustard fields. It was a good vantage point. Soon, he saw a hole appear in the dome, which kept growing bigger. At around 2 p.m., the dome collapsed. He could hear a woman's voice over the loudspeakers, egging on the crowd: '*Ek dhakka aur do* (Give it one more push).' She then said: '*Abhi khabar mili hai ki Faizabad se paramilitary forces aa rahi hain. Jab tak yeh dhancha zameen pe nahin girta tab tak unko roke rakhna. Kuch bhi kijiye. Jalte tyre phenk dijiye, let jayiye, kuch bhi kijiye lekin unko pahunchne mat dijiye. Raasta block kariye* (We've just got information that paramilitary forces are coming from Faizabad. Do not let them reach until this structure falls. Throw burning tyres or lie down before their vehicles … do whatever it takes to block the way.)'[78]

Around 4 p.m., as he prepared to go home, Gupta saw the second dome coming down. By 6.30 p.m. he got news that the entire structure had been razed. By 8.30 p.m. the Kalyan Singh government was dismissed, and President's rule imposed in the state. For the next couple of days, Gupta kept seeing crowds milling around the town, people carrying pieces of the mosque as souvenirs. He had heard that some mosques were attacked by kar sevaks in Ayodhya but everything was peaceful in Faizabad. Muslims were tense but there was no attack or arson.

In his documentary, *Men in the Tree,* film-maker Lalit Vachani presents three main characters—Sandip Pathey, Purushottam and Sripad Borkar. The trio speak proudly about the RSS's and their own role in the Babri Masjid demolition. 'I was up on the dome,' says Sripad. 'That was a lifetime achievement. We helped make history.' The RSS, according to them, had planned everything to the last detail. 'Nagpur had chosen ten men who could face anything. I was one of them. We worked on the dome with whatever we could lay our hands on—rods, sticks sometimes just rocks. We had only one thing on our minds—demolish the structure,' says Sripad. According to Sandip, the planning and execution were so precise that the details of boys such as age, which train he would travel in, the group leader he would report to … everything was collected. Even those who came independently to Ayodhya on 6 December 1992 had had to report to RSS volunteers and give all their details. 'It wasn't possible for just anyone to go there as a temple volunteer,' says Sandip who was in charge of arrangements in his area. 'The Muslims will come around to our way of thinking. Gradually an environment will build up in which they will realize that Ayodhya, Kashi and Mathura should be handed over to them [Hindus]. Muslims will give up their claims. The biggest strength is organization. When society is not organized even a mouse acts like a tiger. If Muslims want to live in this country,

they must listen to big brother,' says Sripad. Sandip adds: 'If they
[Muslims] don't hand it [Ayodhya] over on their own, whichever
way the Hindu behaves, they must face the consequences.'[79]

Many seniors in the RSS, however, were uneasy with the
organization's involvement in the Ayodhya movement. P. Narayanan,
a pracharak since the 1950s and currently a permanent invitee to the
state executive of the RSS in Kerala, said that Ayodhya was never
ever discussed at Sangh forums or meetings in the early days. 'In the
collected works of Guruji, there is no mention of Ayodhya or Ram
temple even once,' he points out. He said that the RSS' participation
in the Ayodhya movement was a case of the tail wagging the dog. He
said that the single act alienated thousands of people who were Sangh
supporters. 'I remember even Kerala High Court judges participating
in VHP conferences. There was no stigma. Many Muslims and
Christians, similarly, wanted to join the Jana Sangh,' he said.[80] On
the evening of 6 December 1992, V.M. Korath, then editor of the
RSS's Malayalam mouthpiece, *Janmabhoomi*, asked Narayanan, who
was then a correspondent with the daily to write an editorial. He
declined. Narayanan said he could not write an editorial on an issue
he personally opposed.[81]

That the Sangh had political objectives was clear in the way
Deoras skilfully deployed the non-political arm VHP to mobilize
popular support and later fronted the BJP to reap the benefits. The
movement paid electoral dividends. In the Uttar Pradesh elections,
even though the Janata Dal emerged as the biggest bloc winning
206 seats, the BJP won in fifty-seven constituencies. Political
commentators took note.

Advani told Rediff.com in 1997 that Ayodhya was not on the
BJP agenda to begin with. It was only later that it took it up. And
Kashi and Mathura, the other two temples where the Parivar wants
to remove a mosque and a dargah respectively, was also not on its
agenda. Advani said the BJP's decision not to support the Kashi and
Mathura movements was taken on principles. It decided to take up
the Ayodhya issue but not the others because a sessions court had

declared the place a de facto temple by issuing an injunction that the Ram Lalla idols be restored.[82] If the objective was merely the building of the Ram Temple, the RSS would have tried to mobilize support cutting across all sections of the society and political spectrum. It had a successful precedent of a non-political mobilization in the 1960s when Eknath Ranade was entrusted with the responsibility of building a memorial for the nationalist monk Swami Vivekananda.

*

In 1963, Golwalkar sent Ranade, who had quit the position of RSS sarkaryavah some months ago, to take charge of building a memorial to Swami Vivekananda on a rocky islet off the southern tip of the subcontinent in Kanyakumari.[83] It was the birth centenary year of the monk who had delivered a famous speech at the first Parliament of the World's Religions in Chicago on 11 September 1893. A disciple of the mystic Ramakrishna Paramahansa, Vivekananda, as Jyotirmaya Sharma writes, addressed three major concerns of nineteenth-century India—Hindu identity, Hindu nationalism and an equal 'dialogue' between Hinduism and other faiths.[84]

Vivekananda's virile Hindutva coupled with his nationalist fervour influenced Indians across the social, regional and political spectrum. Vivekananda had pronounced India as the punyabhoomi—many years before Savarkar would articulate it in *Essentials of Hindutva*—the land where humanity had attained the highest summits in gentleness, generosity, purity, calmness, introspection and spirituality. The world owed much to the mild Hindu, and the Hindu had lost touch with his tradition because of invasions and conversions. He wanted the nation to be physically strong, of 'men with muscles of iron and nerves of steel', whose manhood was to be forged from the valour of the Kshatriya—*Kshatra-virya*, and the Brahmin's power of intellect—*Brahma-teja*.[85]

The memorial to this nationalist-philosopher-mystic on the rock in Kanyakumari, where he had once meditated, was an important symbol for the Hindu nation of the RSS vision. It was a shrine to Hindu nationalism, and Ranade, a shrewd networker and adept organizer, was sent to Kanyakumari for this pursuit.

Ranade arrived at a time when there were tensions over the ownership of the rock, which was claimed by the large Christian fishermen community for St Xavier. A few local committees that were involved in the Vivekananda memorial had by then evolved into a larger all-India committee with Kerala social reformer Mannath Padmanabhan as its president. Then chief minister of Tamil Nadu, M. Bhaktavatsalam, was against building anything on the rock. Though he was insistent that the rock must be established as Vivekananda Rock and that it had nothing to do with St Xavier as the Christians believed, he had indicated that he would allow only a plaque on the rock. He offered a plot on the shore to build the memorial instead. A few members of this committee had approached Golwalkar to spare someone from the Sangh to canvas at the national level.[86]

Golwalkar sent Ranade because he had worked in Calcutta and written a book on Vivekananda. He knew the leadership of the Ramakrishna Mission well and more crucially, had a good network among Congressmen in Delhi. This was because he had stationed himself in Delhi to clear the Sangh's name when it had been banned in 1948. There, he held secret discussions with Sardar Patel on a political role for the RSS.[87] Above all, he had a reputation in the Sangh: If you want to move the Qutub Minar intact, go to Ranade.

In his recollection, *The Story of the Vivekananda Rock Memorial*, Ranade recounts in detail how he went about building the memorial, using persuasion, guile and leveraging relationships. He spent the next few years working on the project, skilfully cultivating the media, politicians and businessmen to get permissions and funds for the project. He camped in Delhi while Parliament was in session and began frequenting Parliament House every day to canvas support for the proposal. After consulting Congress leader and Union minister Lal Bahadur Shastri, whom he knew, Ranade started a signature campaign to rally support and shrewdly tapped the most influential politicians. He first got Raghunath Singh's signature, an influential MP from Benares who was also the secretary of the Congress Parliamentary Party on a petition addressed to Prime Minister Jawaharlal Nehru. Singh's signature on the top of the page ensured that other Congress MPs signed without question. He collected ninety signatures in the central hall of Parliament within an hour. He also got Ram Manohar Lohia, Vajpayee and leaders from other parties to sign as well.

Next, Ranade contacted communist leader Renu Chakravarti who got him signatures of all her party MPs from Bengal. The next target was Annadurai of the Dravida Munnetra Kazhakam (DMK) whom he met through the party's MP Nedunchezhian. Not only did Ranade get Nedunchezhian's backing for the petition, he also got Annadurai to be a member of the general body of the committee and Nedunchezhian as vice president of the state committee. Annadurai's blessings ensured the backing of all his party MPs. Altogether, Ranade got 323 MPs to back the proposal and sign the petition which would be handed over to Nehru by M.S. Aney, the oldest parliamentarian then. Aney was an old friend of the RSS and had written the foreword to Golwalkar's book, *We or Our Nationhood Defined*.

Ranade approached Lal Bahadur Shastri after securing the signatures. Shastri had earlier promised to intervene with Nehru if he managed to get enough support for the project from other MPs. Now he did, and Nehru issued a statement in response to the petition. 'As far as the Government of India is concerned, we shall very much like to have Swamiji's statue on the rock. But, after all, it is a matter of the Madras government to decide. However, I'm going to Madras soon for unveiling of Swamiji's statue.[88] At that time, I shall speak to the chief minister and see what I can do in the matter.'

While Ranade garnered political support for the project in Parliament, he also collected funds from state governments. Practically every state government contributed to the building of the statue and even the communist government in Kerala, though reluctant when E.M.S. Namboodiripad was the chief minister, released money after Achyuta Menon took over. Tamil Nadu chief minister Bhaktavatsalam, who was vehemently opposed to the project, later became the patron of the Tamil Nadu Committee and sanctioned Rs 4.25 lakh to build jetties. Ranade scrupulously kept politics out of the cause he was espousing and focused on consensus building. In sharp contrast, the Sangh Parivar's approach and language during the Ram Janmabhoomi agitation was aggressive and confrontational. Ranade also mentions that Bhaktavatsalam had made him out to be an agitator who would stop at nothing. In Ranade's view, if he had to agitate to put up a memorial to Swami Vivekananda in this country it would be a disgrace.[89]

It was not as if politics was not involved. Part of Bhaktavatsalam's objections rose from the large section of Christians in Kanyakumari who were traditionally Congress voters. And often there was tension in the district over the rock memorial project. He was worried the issue would become communal and violent.

In 1962, RSS Calicut vibhag pracharak, P. Madhavan, and district pracharak, V.P. Janardanan, selected eight men for a 'mission' in Kanyakumari. In an account published in the *Organiser*, the only surviving member of the team, P.B. Lakshmanan, who was then mukhya shikshak of Vallyil shakha in Calicut, recalled that they organized a boat and took it to Kanyakumari by road. Then RSS prant pracharak, Dathaji Didolkar, had told them that a cross on the rock had to be removed before Vijaya Dashami. Lakshmanan and four others clandestinely reached the rock by boat and removed the cross with powerful drills used in road construction. The next night, another cross was erected which was once again uprooted by the RSS team. The series of events led to tensions between the two communities and the Tamil Nadu government was naturally worried about violence escalating.[90]

It was at this juncture that Ranade entered the picture and took charge of the project. A senior Sangh leader once remarked that the Ram temple in Ayodhya would have been peacefully built long ago if Eknath Ranade had been alive.[91]

But then, building a temple was never really the objective. In the context of the 1980s and '90s, the primary objective of the Ram Janmabhoomi movement was to use it as an emotive issue for political mobilization, consolidation of Hindus and extending the reach of the Sangh into villages. 'The movement was never about building a Ram temple. It was always about consolidating the Hindus.'[92] That goal was spectacularly achieved when a swayamsevak became the prime minister within four years of the mosque coming down. As a former joint general secretary of the RSS said: 'The Sangh never wastes an opportunity. It plans for it minutely and executes it to perfection.'[93]

*

Deoras relinquished his position and appointed Rajendra Singh as sarsanghchalak in 1993. He wanted to quit in 1992 but his colleagues had persuaded him to stay on as they feared the demolition of Babri Masjid and the subsequent ban on the RSS would have been seen as the reason for his leaving.

Even though he was the third sarsanghchalak, it could be said that Deoras had a bigger hand in shaping the Sangh than anyone else. Hedgewar had laid the foundation and built the RSS. Golwalkar steered it through a period of crisis, keeping it safe and away from the public eye, patiently waiting for time to erase the stigma of Gandhi's murder. Deoras initiated the organization's rapid expansion into social work and gave it a political direction through its affiliates. He had realized that the government was hostile to the Sangh, but he also estimated that its networking had created enough goodwill in society. Hence, the expansion of social work. He also insisted that shakhas were the real strength of the organization and they needed to be multiplied. But unlike the introverted, publicity shy swayamsevak of earlier years, Deoras wanted volunteers to be active workers.

With the Ram Janmabhoomi movement and its culmination in the demolition of Babri Masjid, the Sangh had achieved its biggest ever consolidation of Hindus. It had tremendously helped organizational growth, and the BJP and the VHP had acquired a mass base that had no parallel in the world in terms of numbers.

'Ram, the incarnation of God, was exploited by a handful of men for their political power games,' the Liberhan Commission concluded.[94]

4

The Lotus Blooms

Deoras died on 17 June 1996, exactly one month after Atal Bihari Vajpayee became prime minister. In the two decades that he was sarsanghchalak, he had succeeded in making the Sangh Parivar a political force to reckon with. Rajendra Singh and K.S. Sudarshan, who succeeded him, were unable to capitalize on the base he built.

The political agitations of the 1970s had earned the RSS legitimacy and respect but not exclusivity. The spoils had to be shared even with ideological opponents. In Ayodhya it found the ideal fault line although it was replete with risks. Deoras calculated they were worth taking. The strategy would cost it a lot of political and social capital built during and after the Emergency years, but it succeeded in taking a step closer to its ultimate goal by bringing a large number of Hindus, especially in northern India, to its way of thinking. The political and social capital were well spent and in less than a decade it would start reaping rich dividends.

*

It was an announcement that came literally out of the blue. Even the man who made it knew the reaction that would follow. The BJP was holding its *maha adhiveshan* (mega session) at the Mahalakshmi

Racecourse grounds in Mumbai in November 1995. It was called Yashobhoomi. About one lakh delegates had congregated for the conference.

On the second day, 13 November, a massive rally was held at Shivaji Park in Dadar, the venue of many a historic political congregation. 'The timing of the meet was significant ... The mammoth political conference served as a platform to project the BJP as a serious contender for power in the 1996 parliamentary elections,' L.K. Advani later wrote. In his presidential speech, Advani announced: 'We will fight the next elections under the leadership of Shri Atal Bihari Vajpayee and he will be our candidate for Prime Minister. For many years, not only our party workers but also the common people have been chanting the slogan *Agli baari*, Atal Bihari. I am confident that BJP will form the next government under Atalji's premiership.'

The announcement caught everyone by surprise. No non-Congress party had ever announced a prime ministerial candidate before elections. Advani had also not discussed the nomination with Vajpayee who later asked him: '*Kya ghoshana kar di aapne? Kum se kum mujhse to baat karte* (What have you done? At least you could have spoken to me).' Advani replied, '*Kya aap maante agar hum ne aap se poocha hota*? (If I had asked, would you have agreed?)'[1]

Vajpayee's presentation as the future prime minister became a fait accompli not only for the BJP, but also for the RSS. Sarsanghchalak Rajendra Singh met Advani in Orissa soon after the BJP's Mumbai conference. Singh repeated the question Vajpayee asked Advani and said it had created consternation within the Sangh Parivar. While he was personally agreeable with Vajpayee, the organization was not keen.

Advani gave the same answer that he gave Vajpayee. He was certain that Singh would not agree had he consulted him. He had enough reasons to believe that the Sangh would never accept Vajpayee's leadership. In 1991, after the BJP posted its best performance in the Lok Sabha, winning 120 seats, Vajpayee was widely expected to become the leader of the opposition as he was the most senior member. He had earlier served as the legislative party leader of both the Jana Sangh and the BJP. Instead, the RSS surprised everyone by backing Advani for the post.

Advani himself thought it was inappropriate. He sent General Secretary Govindacharya to talk to Rajendra Singh who refused to yield. 'You know the party is in this position because of the temple agitation,' he told Govindacharya. Vajpayee was also an unlikely swayamsevak: a non-vegetarian, who loved his scotch, and who ran an unconventional household.[2]

Advani was more persuasive five years later. He explained his reasoning and analysis of the political situation. Advani appears to have convinced Singh that the BJP was not in a position to come to power on its own, and a 'soft' Vajpayee compared to a 'hardliner' Advani would be more acceptable to other parties to form a coalition government.

Interestingly, Congress leader M.L. Fotedar has claimed that the idea of Vajpayee as prime minister was implanted in Advani's mind by him. Fotedar, who was friends with BJP leader Krishna Lal Sharma, a close ally of Advani, writes in his memoirs, *The Chinar Leaves*, that he told Sharma to convince Advani that the BJP's best chance was to project Vajpayee as the prime ministerial candidate. Fotedar reckoned Vajpayee would be a lesser problem than Advani should the BJP come to power.[3]

The Sangh very reluctantly agreed. It concurred with Advani's political assessment, which was uncannily similar to what Fotedar writes but was aware that it would have to dilute many of its ideological positions. Advani argued that once the BJP was in power, many things would fall in place. The important thing was to form a government. It would give the Parivar access to government files and documents. It would also help establish a relationship with the bureaucracy.

As efforts to build a coalition progressed, the RSS remained uncomfortable. It felt it would have to make too many compromises.

Advani assuaged the leaders and asked them to trust him. Gradually, Advani started becoming 'soft' and a chasm developed between him and the Sangh.

Pramod Mahajan, then a rising star in the BJP and a man known as a consummate deal maker, was in the thick of things, trying to build a coalition. Although Vajpayee was the face of the government, it was Mahajan who helped fix the nuts and bolts of the first NDA coalition.

*

For the RSS, 16 May 1996 was a day of considerable pride. It was the day an RSS swayamsevak was sworn into the most powerful office in the country, seventy-one years after the organization was founded. It did not last a fortnight. Yet it was enough to make the organization acutely aware what the quest for power could mean, the contradictions it would breed and the compromises it would demand. Deoras had clearly indicated that power was an essential requirement for the RSS to achieve what it set out to do.

In the run-up to the 1996 elections, sarsanghchalak Rajendra Singh formally appealed to voters to 'defeat anti-Hindutva elements'. 'Contribute your time and might to the fullest in this popular awakening, which actually is God's work, so that our politics—eclipsed by anti-Hindutva thinking—can come out and shine forth.'[4] On 1 June, the last day of the short-lived government, the cabinet met to recommend dissolution of Parliament and call for fresh elections. It also approved the only other item on the agenda—a counter-guarantee to American multinational Enron Corporation protecting its investment in a power plant on the Maharashtrian coast and ensuring that the company made enough returns from it. If anything hampered the company's functioning, the Central government would compensate it and its partners. Pramod Mahajan and Gopinath Munde, the two Maharashtra stalwarts, were said to be behind the proposal.

The RSS was strongly opposed to Mahajan and Vajpayee's close friend Jaswant Singh becoming ministers when the BJP returned to power two years later. Both had lost their Lok Sabha elections. After their names were sent to the president, Sudarshan, who was then general secretary, intervened late at night saying that those who lost elections did not have the people's trust and should not be made ministers. The names were withdrawn but Vajpayee accommodated Mahajan as an adviser to the prime minister. He later resigned and won a July Rajya Sabha election. Singh too entered the Rajya Sabha and both were inducted into the cabinet in December 1996.

Around the time the BJP came to power at the Centre, the Sangh was planning a major shift in its organizational policy. Deoras was the first sarsanghchalak who gave up his position while still alive. Sarsanghchalaks are appointed for life and there is no way to change unless they themselves decide to relinquish the post. In March 1994, afflicted by advancing age and illness, Deoras announced he was retiring and appointed Rajendra Singh as sarsanghchalak. Singh, who was then sarkaryavah, was the first non-Brahmin RSS chief, and whose mother tongue was not Marathi.

'It was a landmark event. It was established in the Indian political circles and the media that the RSS which was spread across the country was dominated by a handful of Maharashtrian Brahmins. Rajju Bhaiyya's appointment proved that it was just misinformation being spread,' wrote Devendra Swarup.[5]

Considering that the sarsanghchalaks who followed him were both Brahmins and the current chief, Bhagwat, comes from a Maharashtrian Brahmin family close to Nagpur, it is more likely that Deoras chose Singh because he was a Kshatriya from Uttar Pradesh where work on Ram Janmabhoomi, which had become an integral part of the parivar agenda, was incomplete. The battle for hegemony of the Hindi heartland had reached a crucial stage and it would be ideal if a north Indian Hindi speaker headed the RSS. In the post-Ayodhya period, someone like Singh would have been extremely useful, as the Sangh Parivar had undergone the process of making the Sangh a mass organization, which demanded an informal and intimate relationship between the supreme leader and the common volunteer.[6]

Singh was closely involved with the Ram Janmabhoomi movement and was the Sangh's interlocutor with P.V. Narasimha Rao. His appointment was also a way of building relationships with the Thakurs of the state who looked down upon RSS pracharaks as a bunch of people currying favour from banias and who disappeared at the first sign of trouble. Despite their small numbers, the upper-caste Thakurs who owned vast lands and wealth had tremendous influence in Uttar Pradesh and nearby Bihar and Madhya Pradesh. Their feudal legacy continued to influence the politics and social customs of the state, which is one of the most underdeveloped and socially backward in the country. Perhaps because of the long history of conflict with Muslim rulers, the Thakurs consider themselves as natural rivals to Muslims.

Outfits like the Hindu Yuva Vahini, founded by Yogi Adityanath in Uttar Pradesh,[7] and the Karni Sena in Rajasthan are examples of feudal interests continuing to exert their influence not only on politics, but more brazenly, on society. Sections of them, as is evident in news coverage, continue to oppress Dalits[8] and generally regard the RSS's samrasta with contempt. Singh's elevation as sarsanghchalak did little to bring this community to its side. The general decline of the Congress party and fading prospects of power, however, helped attract them to the BJP.

Uttar Pradesh in the 1980s and '90s was going through a churn as Kanshi Ram and Mayawati marshalled the Dalits into a political force to reckon with. What Ambedkar could not do in his lifetime, Kanshi Ram did in his; he built a robust Dalit political movement from the grass roots.

A person who worked with Singh closely says he lacked original ideas but was efficient at running the organization. The legacy of Deoras hung over his rather short term of six years. He was also sympathetic to BJP's interests. While Golwalkar was apolitical, the

Deoras brothers were always thinking from a political perspective. Singh was also politically minded, and the Thakurs of Uttar Pradesh saw him as one of them. He was very impressed by Vajpayee's political sense and tended to heed his opinion. Even Sudarshan said that he was inspired by Vajpayee though he seemed to have changed his view later. During the period of these two, the political arm of the RSS gained an upper hand in the Parivar.[9]

'A stage came after Rajju Bhaiyya [Rajendra Singh] when those in the RSS themselves began to believe that the BJP leaders had become bigger than them,' says Sudhir Pathak, the soft-spoken former editor of *Tarun Bharat*. It was seen most during K.S. Sudarshan's period as sarsanghchalak because Advani was a pracharak much before Sudarshan became one. Advani, four years elder to Sudarshan, was at the peak of his political career even though Sudarshan as RSS chief had to be acknowledged as the guide and mentor of the entire Parivar. It did not help that Sudarshan's ideas, such as an RSS-backed forum for Muslims, often clashed with the RSS's institutional imprimatur.

In the late 1990s, a conversation had started in the Sangh about the age of senior leaders. At one of the meetings of the RSS executive council, a senior leader is said to have walked out saying people as old as himself should not be on the top council. It then informally decided on seventy-five as the retirement age for its leaders.

The year 2000 was a watershed in RSS history. Rajendra Singh, who was frequently falling ill, announced his retirement and handed over charge to K.S. Sudarshan, a telecom engineer and the only person who had served both as the all-India *sharirik pramukh* and *boudhik pramukh* (the chief of physical and intellectual development). Sudarshan was only sixty-nine. Mohan Bhagwat, then just fifty, was made the general secretary. It was a generational change in the seventy-five-year-old Sangh. For the first time, someone born after Independence was leading the organization.

Meanwhile, the first-generation leaders of the BJP were in power. Wielding it were Vajpayee and Advani, two veteran swayamsevaks older than Sudarshan and Bhagwat in both age and experience.

It was an imbalance that would manifest in constant friction between leaders of the two organizations. In the Sangh Parivar, the position of sarsanghchalak is revered, almost divine, irrespective of his age. The convention was to address him as *param poojaniya* (worthy of ultimate worship). Deoras tried to end that practice. He instructed that only former sarsanghchalaks Hedgewar and Golwalkar be addressed with that honorific. He would live with just *mananiya* (respected). The RSS chief is still addressed as param poojaniya when the title sarsanghchalak is used. Deoras was a gifted leader and had clear ideas about the relationships Sangh organizations should have with one another. The Sangh should not go to BJP. The BJP should come to Nagpur. That was the unwritten rule. It was broken when Singh became sarsanghchalak. The Sangh headquarters had practically shifted to the national capital with Singh. He used Keshav Kunj, the Jhandewalan office of the Sangh, as his primary base. So did Sudarshan. The centre of gravity of the RSS shifted from the geographical centre of the country to the hub of political power, New Delhi.

Sudarshan was a micromanager who would not brook even the slightest dilution of the Sangh values even in day-to-day life. A stickler for rules and uniform, the slightest of deviation would provoke the most severe reaction from him. In 1998 when Rajendra Singh wanted to appoint Sudarshan as sarsanghchalak because his health was failing, BJP leaders, including Vajpayee, are believed to have asked him to postpone the decision because they did not get along with him. 'They told [H.V.] Sheshadri who was then RSS general secretary that it would be difficult to run the government even for a day if he is the Sarsanghchalak.'[10]

Sudarshan's whimsical ways were to become public very soon. After Sudarshan became sarsanghchalak, he was to attend an RSS function at a stadium in Delhi. He issued instructions that nobody, including the press and ministers, should be allowed in the function if they did not turn up in the RSS uniform. None of the ministers, including Prime Minister Atal Bihari Vajpayee, Home Minister L.K. Advani and Education Minister Murli Manohar Joshi, all of whom had been swayamsevaks for several decades, attended. Then BJP president Kushabhau Thakre turned up in the uniform but forgot to bring the bamboo staff that completes it. He was asked to go back.[11]

Delhi was Sudarshan's base for most of the time that the NDA government was in power and he frequently criticized the government in public and meddled in ministries. Film-maker Deepa Mehta had a cultural policing experience when she was shooting her film *Water* in Varanasi. Filming was interrupted by RSS and VHP men who burnt down the sets and shouted slogans against her. Mehta was asked to get permission from RSS chief Sudarshan without which the protest would continue. She went to meet him at the RSS headquarters in Delhi one wintry morning.

Sudarshan entered the room wearing a heavy shawl and a saffron balaclava. He walked up to her and quoted a passage from Dante's *Inferno* in perfect Italian, then sat down and told her not to have misconceptions that the RSS was ignorant.

'Why did you make a film like *Fire*? It's not what our culture is about,' he said. Then coming to the topic at hand, he said, 'The Ganga is precious to us.'

'Have you read the script for *Water*?' Mehta asked him.

Sudarshan placed a copy of the script on the table.

'Where did you get that?' she asked because only one script had been submitted outside of the production, and that was to the Ministry of Information and Broadcasting.

Sudarshan said, 'After all, whose ministry is it anyway?'

He then surprised Mehta saying the script was very good and the RSS had only two small objections. One was naming a widow prostitute Janaki, another name for Sita. The other was an old saying that he felt insulted Varanasi. Sudarshan asked Mehta to work with Sheshadri Chari, then editor of the *Organiser*, on correcting her film script and getting it cleared from the Ministry of Information and

Broadcasting. Mehta made the changes and the film released with the RSS's blessings.[12]

Sudarshan's view was that Hindus should be assertive and firm in their belief. It also meant all parivar organizations, including the BJP, should fall in line accordingly. He wanted to spread Hindutva lifestyle everywhere. He felt, by doing so, mindsets would start changing. Even the politics of the country would change. And all of it should happen under the RSS's supervision.

*

In 2004, immediately after the BJP lost the general elections, the RSS top leadership met senior party leaders at Vajpayee's residence. It was a cordial stock-taking meeting. Questions about how the party was disconnected from society and the Sangh itself were asked. The discussion moved on to how the party had drifted away from its ideological moorings that reflected in the economic policies of the government. Questions were raised about Dattopant Thengadi's role. He had called the government *nikammi sarkar* (useless government). The government was even more handicapped because its ideological mentor itself was opposing it.

Columnist Swapan Dasgupta observed:

> Vajpayee, as Prime Minister, sought to enlarge his personal base by reaching out to figures in the erstwhile Congress establishment. He routinely turned down requests from both the RSS and the party. The atmosphere of the Vajpayee court was decidedly anti-RSS. No wonder the Sangh felt slighted, even humiliated. But Vajpayee was Vajpayee, and always a law unto himself.[13]

In the elections, the Sangh had not participated actively. Swayamsevaks had voted for the BJP, but they were not out campaigning. At the stock-taking meeting at Vajpayee's home, Sangh leaders said the government's policies were not aligned with the RSS's ideology. Cornered, Vajpayee is said to have asked: What were the policies where the government drifted away from the Sangh ideology? The leaders pointed out several instances.

Vajpayee then replied that in all the five years, save once when Ashok Singhal had come to meet him over the Ram temple issue, never once had anyone from the Sangh or a representative in the government told him about any difference of opinion. No objections were raised. The former prime minister pointed to one leader and said he was supposed to be the communication bridge between him and the RSS. He was supposed to inform him if anything was amiss. The leader never once told him—not privately or at party meetings or government fora—that he was straying from the Sangh line. He assumed that what he was doing was what the RSS wanted, he is said to have told the group.[14]

On one occasion, Singhal had roundly scolded him for ignoring Ayodhya. During the early days of the government, a meeting was held at Vajpayee's home where Advani, Rajendra Singh, Sudarshan, joint general secretary, Madan Das Devi, who was BJP in-charge in the RSS, and Ashok Singhal were present. 'Ashok Singhal really fired Advani. The feeling was that the Ayodhya land could have been given to the VHP. I was perhaps also a culprit because I was looking at it more passionately,' according to Devi.[15]

The VHP wanted the issue to be taken to its logical conclusion either by an order or legislative fiat. VHP leaders felt it was their government and it was letting them down, but the RSS believed that the NDA should not collapse.

There was one attempt made by some people close to L.K. Advani to solve the Ayodhya issue. The plan was the brainchild of journalist T.V.R. Shenoy who was close friends with Advani, and it was based on support from Shia Muslims. Since the mosque was believed to have been built by Babur's lieutenant Mir Baqi who was a Shia, they could claim the mosque for themselves. And since according to Muslim law a mosque cannot stand over any other religious structure, they would declare it unsuitable for a mosque and hand it over to the Hindus.

Shenoy had travelled to Iran and met a senior Shia cleric who had agreed to come to India and do the handing over. The Shias had put a condition that with the giving up of the Babri Masjid, the Hindus would give up their demand for Kashi and Mathura. The plan was thwarted after VHP leaders refused to give up claim on Kashi and Mathura. Meanwhile, the Kanchi Shankaracharya got involved in the Ram Janmabhoomi issue separately which muddied the waters even more and the plan failed.[16]

At the meeting with RSS leaders at his home, Vajpayee explained that the other parivar organizations such as Bharatiya Mazdoor Sangh (BMS), Bharatiya Kisan Sangh (BKS) and Swadeshi Jagran Manch (SJM) had been strongly opposing many of the government's policies. There always was an understanding that they would help occupy the opposition space. That was their role; to make the opposition irrelevant. Sangh organizations agitated against the government but went only a certain distance when they were asked to step back. On key issues, the government took on board the Sangh views such as in the Doha round of trade negotiations.

Vajpayee's friend and foreign minister Jaswant Singh's closeness with US deputy secretary of state Strobe Talbott was also seen with suspicion by many in the Sangh. *Swadeshi* magazine called Vajpayee a *rashtradrohi* (traitor). Published by the SJM from BJP leader Anant Kumar's house at 30, Prithviraj Road in Delhi, the magazine called the government anti-national. Vajpayee said he was helpless when his own people were calling him traitor. The editor of the magazine, Mahesh Chandra Sharma, later said that it was wrong to call Vajpayee a traitor. 'It [traitor] is a word that should not be used loosely. It was a mistake.'[17]

As the fifty-second anniversary of the country's independence approached, an incident occurred on the north-eastern border that not only hit the RSS directly but also cocked a snook at the BJP's aggressive posturing on national security. On 6 August 1999, insurgents kidnapped four pracharaks from a students' hostel run by Vanvasi Kalyan Ashram at Kanchanchhada in Tripura and took them across the border to a camp in Chittagong in Bangladesh. The RSS blamed the Baptist Church and the National Liberation Front of Tripura (NLFT) for the abductions and put pressure on the Tripura and Vajpayee governments to intervene. Months later, all four pracharaks were found murdered. Mohan Bhagwat, who had just been appointed as the RSS general secretary, lashed out: 'From the day of their abduction, the RSS has been trying hard to get them released. But its desperation was reciprocated by the union and state governments' insensitivity.'[18]

Home Minister Advani felt that charge was unfair on both the state and the Union governments. Then Tripura chief minister Manik Sarkar, who headed a CPI(M) government, had warned Advani more than once about the threat posed by the NLFT and its nexus with the Baptist Church. 'Sarkar, it seemed to me, was genuinely interested in the release of the captives,' Advani wrote in his autobiography.[19]

The kidnapping, which targeted RSS volunteers directly, was the biggest flashpoint between the RSS and the BJP. The Sangh wanted the government to act macho and send troops across the border and bring them back, but both Prime Minister Vajpayee and Home Minister Advani were reluctant to create an international situation.[20] 'Some in the Sangh Parivar felt that I did not put enough efforts to save the lives of the four pracharaks,' Advani writes in his memoirs. 'I must say the government's job became extremely difficult once the kidnapped persons were taken across the border to Bangladesh.'[21]

A national leader of the Sangh who was working in the north-east at the time said the kidnapping had set the RSS work back by a decade in the region. Volunteers were reluctant to venture into remote locations. Besides, the organization felt humiliated that despite being in power it could not protect its own people. The leader said that a senior IPS officer who was a friend of the RSS and posted in the north-east eventually tracked down the murderers one by one and allegedly killed them.[22]

After the electoral loss of 2004, there were three options before the RSS: leave the BJP to its designs, take control and reform the party, or start a new party. Relations between the two organizations had become frosty. In a television interview to *Indian Express* editor Shekhar Gupta in 2005, RSS chief Sudarshan asked: 'What have they [Vajpayee and Advani] done for the country?' He ranked Indira Gandhi as the best prime minister India had had.[23]

Sudarshan felt that there was no point in trying to reform the party. Power corrupts even the best people and he worried that the BJP's power trip was already affecting RSS cadres who were losing interest in Sangh work. 'It was believed that the correction could take place if there was appropriate RSS intervention at all levels. The "retirement" of Vajpayee and Advani was a key component of the RSS strategy. The appointment of Rajnath was supposed to herald a slow organizational takeover which would, in time, lead to the BJP resuming its role as an "ideological" party,'[24] wrote journalist Swapan Dasgupta who was nominated to the Rajya Sabha during the first term of the Modi government.

Other ideas to strengthen the party were also being explored, including ways to insert more RSS volunteers into the party and government. The man who would take up one such assignment was an old RSS hand who also ran a massive business empire.

*

Jai Prakash Agarwal began his business career in 1973 making steel tubes. But he made his fortune selling light. Agarwal's Rs 5,000-crore Surya group now owns one of the most popular lighting brands and also makes steel and PVC pipes, fans and home appliances.

After 1992, when the Sangh Parivar sensed that it was getting closer to capturing power, it started thinking about how to develop trustworthy talent that could help in governance and administration. In 1995, it started training camps for its members of Parliament and legislative assemblies. Agarwal offered his property near Delhi.

Agarwal started Surya Foundation in the early 1990s to train volunteers to help develop backward villages. The foundation set up Surya Sadhna Sthali, a training centre with spartan living quarters at Jhinjholi about 35 kilometres west of Delhi. 'It was simple and austere. JP [Agarwal] liked such army-style life,' according to Govindacharya who helped set up the centre.[25]

The project, funded by Surya group companies, was called Adarsh Gram Yojana (AGY). In 2016–17, for instance, the lighting company Surya Roshni Limited spent Rs 1.28 crore setting up Bal Vikas Kendras (child development centres) in remote villages spread across fifteen states. The project description says 'these centres focus on imparting moral education and values and train them in yoga and meditation to the young school going children and dropouts. They also inculcate the spirit of patriotism in them to develop them into responsible citizens of the country.'[26] The Modi government too loosely adapted the idea into its Saansad Adarsh Gram Yojana. Launched by the prime minister on 11 October 2014, the birth anniversary of freedom fighter and the hero of the anti-Emergency struggle Jayaprakash Narayan, the scheme encouraged MPs to adopt a village in their constituency and turn it into a model of development.

Surya Foundation recruits only RSS volunteers, preferably those who are graduates and have completed the RSS third-year training as well. It advertises for volunteers exclusively in RSS mouthpieces such as *Rashtra Dharm* and *Panchajanya*, seeking young men who grew up imbibing the RSS culture and values.

The applicants go through a rigorous selection procedure beginning with a telephone interview. All the questions and tests are related only to the RSS, its history and personalities. They are quizzed on Hedgewar and Golwalkar's lives. If they have attended advanced camps, they are asked about the procedure for setting up and conducting a shakha, including the various commands used.

Once candidates are shortlisted, they are called for an extensive, five-day test. Candidates who are rejected cannot reapply and the doors to the foundation are permanently shut for them. The five-day tests are again an extensive evaluation of the candidates' knowledge of the Sangh Parivar, its personalities, culture, processes, conventions and concerns. They are required to write essays on subjects close to the RSS such as Kashmir, north-east or tribal issues.

The tests are rounded off with a personal interview which goes deeper into RSS history and mythology. On an average about twenty-five to thirty boys are selected to undergo a three-month training programme. According to those who went through, the training is extremely demanding, and desertions are common. There are endurance modules where trainees have to subsist exclusively on fruits for days together. The toughest one is living only on water for several days. These are interspersed with intellectual classes conducted by Sangh pracharaks and a week-long military training by retired professionals. Once they complete the training most of them are sent out to villages. The trainees are paid a monthly stipend.[27]

The foundation later added a week-long political training module, familiarizing the candidates with the BJP, its structure, relationship with the RSS and its key operations. Later, it also started exclusive political training programmes for select volunteers.

While many trainees are sent to work on the AGY, hundreds of them are also deployed in elections. They are often supplied to the BJP in-charge of each state. Sometimes they are attached to specific candidates. A large cohort of Surya volunteers work exclusively on popularizing the Narendra Modi app, a communication tool specifically developed for promoting Modi.[28]

Once the party is in power, Surya volunteers also get plum postings. They are frequently appointed as personal secretaries or officers on special duty to state and Union ministers, chief ministers, and several in the prime minister's office.[29]

*

While Surya Foundation prepared volunteers for political work, another institution was engaged in building a brigade of nationalist bureaucrats. Samkalp was started in 1986 by Santosh Taneja, a former pracharak. Taneja, who belonged to Dehradun, studied engineering, but instead of working decided to become a full-time RSS worker. He completed the three-year RSS training course in 1969 and was posted in Punjab. He moved to Delhi a few years later and joined the Delhi Development Authority (DDA).

Taneja was highly influenced and inspired by M.N. Buch, the then DDA commissioner. A no-nonsense bureaucrat, Buch had, within a fifteen-month tenure, streamlined processes, started an effective grievances forum for citizens, rewarded hard work and punished corrupt officials in the DDA. Taneja thought the country's administration could be transformed with a few hundred officials like Buch. He discussed the idea with Sangh officials and arrived at a plan to catch them young. He started with a school run by Sangh-affiliate Vidya Bharati in Bhiwani. The plan was to identify talented students and train them from a young age to join the civil services. The initial batch of students were rigorously examined. 'Even their horoscopes were consulted,' Taneja said in an interview at Samkalp's cramped office in the congested Paharganj area of Delhi.[30]

That plan did not take off. It was very difficult to sustain an interest for civil services in young children. But more importantly, the civil services examination and interview are extremely tough. Only a few hundred out of about a million who apply make it every year.

The RSS believes it is the bureaucracy that actually runs the country and until it unravels the left ideology's strong grip on the bureaucracy, political power is of little use. In 1996, a decade after Samkalp was set up, it began to train civil services aspirants, helping them with tests and conducting mock interviews. The next year the first batch of a dozen Samkalp trained candidates made it to the IAS. In 2016, 60 per cent or 646 candidates, including the first and second rank holders, Tina Dabi and Athar Amir, were reportedly trained by Samkalp.[31]

Taneja estimated that there were over 4000 serving officials in various services who believed in the Sangh ideology. With Prime Minister Narendra Modi preferring to delegate power to officials rather than ministers, the prestige and power of 'babudom' has increased and so has the demand for Samkalp among civil services aspirants.

*

In 2004–05, however, fortunes of the Sangh Parivar were at a low ebb. Relations between the RSS and the BJP deteriorated further when Advani visited Muhammad Ali Jinnah's mausoleum in Pakistan in mid-2005 and described him as secular. The RSS was furious. Sanjay Joshi, then general secretary of the party, called Advani while he was still in Pakistan and asked him to report to Jhandewalan as soon as he returned.[32] Advani chose to announce his decision to quit as BJP president to waiting journalists as soon as he landed at Delhi airport.

After he was forced to resign, L.K. Advani left the Chennai national executive with a parting salvo: 'Lately an impression has gained ground that no political or organizational decision can be taken without the consent of the RSS functionaries. This perception, we hold, will do no good either to the party or to the RSS.'[33]

In an internal discussion paper, 'Tasks Ahead: Immediate and Long-term', after the 2004 loss, the BJP acknowledged that many shortcomings had surfaced that were inconsistent with the party's ideals and objectives. 'The need for carrying out corrective measures had become apparent a long time ago. However, the setback that our party suffered in the recently concluded parliamentary elections has made us acutely aware of both the extent of these deficiencies as well as the urgency to remedy them,' it said. Without naming the RSS, the document urged the BJP to consider that it was not functioning in isolation and depended on support from a larger Parivar. 'It is not difficult to know why it has become necessary to make the entire party organization realize that we are an integral part of a larger nationalism-inspired movement, that we are working for a lofty goal of nation-building, and that a BJP worker has no reason to be in the party if he puts his personal interests above his duty to actively work for that goal.'[34]

In 2004 and 2005, the RSS had intense internal discussions about the BJP's condition. The first set of deliberations were held in Haridwar where M.G. Vaidya and others suggested that the RSS should junk the BJP once and for all and float a new political party. Vaidya declared, 'We are Hindutvawadis and our party should follow that line. I will create a party based on Hindutva.'[35]

He found no takers and the RSS decided to back the BJP. Once again, it discussed the party when its national executive met the next year at Chitrakoot. At a press conference on the last day of the meeting, Bhagwat, who was then general secretary, said the state of affairs in the BJP was *asthir* (unsettled) and the party's *gati* (pace) in carrying out ideological and organizational reforms was 'slow'. The RSS was 'waiting and watching' whether the party would adopt the 'right direction' in future. Bhagwat said the party should follow five principles: Hindutva as the ideological foundation of the party; enforcing ethical conduct; evolving a consultative mechanism in the party; collective leadership, not personality-driven; and training cadres.[36]

After Advani quit, former chief minister of Uttar Pradesh, Rajnath Singh, took over as the party president. Singh was seen as a rubber stamp BJP chief carrying out orders from the RSS.[37] He immediately set about repairing relations with the mother ship. In 2006, the BJP amended Article 21 of its constitution to allow full-time workers—a euphemism for RSS pracharaks—to be appointed as organizing secretaries all the way down to the district level. In the Jana Sangh party structure, the organizing secretary wielded real power and practically had veto over every decision mainly because he came from the RSS. BJP broke the legacy on its founding, doing away with the position of organizing secretary.

'The new policy was to establish RSS control over the party at all levels,' Swapan Dasgupta commented. 'The 2006 assembly election in Uttar Pradesh was, for example, entirely managed by pracharaks . . .

The BJP slipped to a poor fourth position but this was explained away in terms of the limited time available to the RSS to make its wisdom felt. There was never any question of the RSS reflecting on the organization's suitability for electoral politics.'[38] Swapan Dasgupta says that as the BJP's leadership crisis festered, the RSS grew more and more reckless in its insistence that only its chosen ones could occupy positions of importance. From being a remote moral ombudsman, the RSS soon transformed itself into a faction in the BJP.

The confusion and disarray in the BJP and the RSS were evident. In April 2005, Sudarshan told Shekhar Gupta, the *Indian Express* editor, on his television show 'Walk the Talk' that Vajpayee and Advani should step aside and let youngsters take over. Sudarshan said that the RSS was unhappy about many government policies and it told Advani to convey the message to Vajpayee. But whether Advani did or did not was unclear. 'We do not think Atalji has done anything great. People are annoyed with him because he never kept the conversation going with affiliate organizations.'[39]

When Gupta asked whom he considered the greatest of Indian leaders, Sudarshan listed Indira Gandhi and Narasimha Rao at the top. He said the greatest quality Indira Gandhi had was that she never allowed anyone to pressure her. She was her own person. When asked about Advani and Vajpayee, he said there was not much they'd done to talk about. It was not the first time that a top RSS leader had praised Indira Gandhi.

RSS ideologue Nanaji Deshmukh, who had worked closely with JP in the agitation against Gandhi and was jailed during the Emergency, called her a colossus and a brave leader in a privately circulated obituary but later published in the 25 November 1984 edition of *Pratipaksh*, the Hindi weekly edited by firebrand socialist and trade union leader George Fernandes. The *Milli Gazette* published an English translation in 2004:

Indira Gandhi ultimately did secure a permanent place at the doorstep of history as a great martyr. With her dynamism borne out of her fearlessness and dexterity, she was able to take the country forward like a colossus for over a decade and was able to build an opinion that she alone understood the realities of the country, that she alone had the ability to run the decadent political system of our corrupt and divided society, and probably that she alone could keep the country united.[40]

The RSS was more worried about the resurgence of the left parties than the shock of the BJP's defeat and the Congress's victory. It was the same worry which guided its tactics in the late 1960s and 1970s. Communism is an ideology it considers a threat to the Indian nation, along with Islam and Christianity. The CPI and CPI(M) together captured fifty-three seats in the Lok Sabha, their best performance in years. This revival of the left concerned the RSS no end. It was so dejected that it even wanted the BJP to consider an alliance with the Congress.

M.G. Vaidya wrote: 'They [the Congress and the BJP] should seriously think whether to have a truck with divisive, narrow-minded, selfish parties or have common programmes on administrative grounds, in the larger interest of the country's unity. If both parties rule the country, this could well be in the interest of the nation.'[41]

The *Organiser* approvingly wrote about the AICC decision to 'aggressively confront and fight the left parties'.[42]

In an editorial on 12 February 2006, it said that the communists should keep their class struggle theories within the confines of the coordination committee. 'But they cannot be allowed to hold the country to ransom in the name of their role in sustaining the rickety regime. That secularism, for which the communists are allegedly making all this fatal sacrifice, is not worth the banner they hold is clear from their own behaviour in the UPA.[43]

It had more advice for the BJP, including a suggestion to ally with Mulayam Singh Yadav's Samajwadi Party.

For the BJP the Karnataka development is a grand new opening ... It will not be a bad idea for the party to scout around for the disenchanted in the UPA and expand the NDA as a larger formation of national will. The AGP in Assam and the Lok Dal in Haryana are its natural allies. The Samajwadi Party in UP is in a frantic search for new alliances. A certain degree of unconventional adventurism is often considered good politics in times of national calamity. And the UPA is nothing less than a national disaster.[44]

On an April morning that year, 2006, BJP leader Pramod Mahajan was shot. He succumbed to his wounds on 3 May. His brother Pravin Mahajan was arrested for the murder. The charismatic leader, with the reputation of a skilled deal maker and fund-raiser, was tipped by many to be the party's next prime ministerial candidate. But destiny had other designs and the BJP fought the 2009 elections under the leadership of its veteran leader L.K. Advani. The party performed worse than in 2004. The sun was inevitably setting over a generation of politicians who grew out of the RSS ideological orchard. Time was ripe for a new generation of leaders with new tactics and ruthless strategies more suited to the age of information to take over.

*

When the Congress-led UPA government was taking yet another left turn in 2004, a state government led by a charismatic pracharak, who broke away from the snail-paced RSS template, was experimenting with a brand of hard-right politics unseen in independent India. His economic model was unabashedly capitalist and big-business friendly even by the standards of reform hustlers. And his politics was so hawkishly Hindutva that even some in the RSS appeared to flinch. His economic development model rested on the bedrock of big industry, new technology and foreign capital.

Narendra Modi became chief minister of Gujarat after bickering in the state unit of the BJP led to the unseating of Keshubhai Patel. Modi took over as chief minister on 7 October 2001, the first full-time RSS pracharak to become the chief executive of a state. He took over with the typical fanfare that has become the trademark of the BJP leader. Over 50,000 people and a galaxy of Union ministers attended the swearing-in ceremony in Gandhinagar, the state capital.[45] The canny politician thought and acted on a scale matched only by his vaulting ambition. What Nanaji Deshmukh said in his obituary of Indira Gandhi applied to Modi so well that it looked like he had taken a leaf out of Gandhi's playbook.

Modi's rise to become chief minister was preceded by some deft political manoeuvring in Delhi where he was stationed as BJP general secretary. A few months before the regime change in Gujarat, the BJP had suffered a series of setbacks. He lobbied hard for the job and is even said to have sowed stories in the media against Patel. A section of the RSS was also unhappy with Modi becoming the chief minister. In fact, one of them, Sanjay Joshi, would be forced out of the party by Modi in a dramatic fashion a few years later.[46]

On the morning of 27 February 2002, a coach of the Sabarmati Express carrying over 2000 kar sevaks returning from a VHP programme, Purnahuti Maha Yagna, in Ayodhya was set on fire at the Godhra railway station. Fifty-nine people, including twenty-seven women and ten children, perished in the blaze. The incident set off communal riots in Gujarat in which over 1100 people were reported dead, a majority of them Muslims.[47]

The riots would remain a blot on Modi's career as the person in charge of the state at the time even though multiple inquiries absolved him of any direct responsibility. People close to him privately whisper that a group within his party and the RSS opposed to him played a key role in making sure he became the lightning rod for criticism even though there were many who were complicit. Widespread criticism from media and civil society, however, steeled him. A person who worked in his office in those days, said he had given explicit instructions to avoid media engagements. He, however, told them to keep a close track of journalists and what they were writing. A large team was specifically set up in the chief minister's office with the sole job of monitoring the media round the clock.[48]

The riots made him *persona non grata* in the West as well. Many countries, including the US, refused to give him a visa for thirteen years. The ban was lifted only when he became prime minister in 2014. The United Kingdom had taken the lead along with the United States Commission on International Religious Freedom, Amnesty International, Asia Watch and other human rights groups in attacking Modi.[49] In time, Modi would reverse all that. He understood that the keys to political power in modern democracies were often tucked away in the vaults of big businesses. He would soon become the darling of businessmen all over the world. If he could not go abroad, they would come to him and walk the red carpet rolled out in Gandhinagar. But before that he had to secure the chief minister's chair.

Even though civil society, media and a large section of the BJP and RSS were against him, the rank and file of the party as well as the Sangh, brought up to be ashamed of the weakness of Hindu society and waiting for new conquests, rallied solidly behind their new Hindu hriday samrat. The result was that the BJP national executive meet in Goa which would have seen Modi's exit, instead saw the entire hall chanting 'Modi, Modi' as the party leadership, including Vajpayee and Advani, who had come determined to sack him, sat aghast. Modi won the day and stayed on, for the next thirteen years.

While Modi's star rose fast, the RSS and BJP's fortunes were somewhat indifferent. Many affiliates of the Sangh Parivar were at loggerheads with the chief minister.

Two years into his term, Modi faced the ire of Parivar member BKS. The farmer's organization, which has a significant membership among Patels, revolted against Modi's efforts to reform the state's bleeding power sector. RSS leader Laljibhai Patel went on a fast outside the state BJP office demanding a rollback after power tariffs were raised. Modi responded by evicting the BKS and some of its leaders from legislators' quarters from where they operated. The government also cut power supply to several BKS leaders' homes for refusing to pay bills. The BKS approached the governor seeking President's Rule to escape Modi's 'Hitler Raj'.[50]

In 2008, VHP chief Ashok Singhal had to intervene with Modi after the government demolished about 200 illegal temples in Gandhinagar and arrested VHP state joint secretary Ashwin Patel for allegedly sending 'defamatory' text messages on Diwali eve. Singhal described the state's actions as similar to eleventh-century Afghan invader Mahmud Ghazni's who had ransacked the Somnath temple.[51]

Modi's style of functioning ticked off his own partymen. In the 2004 Lok Sabha elections, the BJP won fourteen seats in Gujarat compared to Congress's twelve. It was considered a downfall and rebels raised their heads. As many as eighty-five MLAs met state BJP president Rajendrasinh Rana to get Modi removed. A local magazine *Chitralekha* quoted Keshubhai Patel as saying that MLAs were dissatisfied with Modi and that their problems were not adequately resolved. The RSS was split in its opinion but blaming Modi for the poor showing in the election would have meant admitting the cause as the 2002 riots. That it was not willing to do. Sudarshan rejected the notion that the riots were to be blamed for the election results.[52]

In nearly ten of the thirteen years of Modi's reign in Gujarat, he and the Sangh Parivar remained at loggerheads. VHP leader Pravin Togadia and RSS leader Sanjay Joshi were practically exiled from the state. Even those who were not in direct conflict with Modi were sent away. State BJP treasurer Surendra Patel, who, as chairman of the Ahmedabad Urban Development Authority, transformed the city, building a ring road, planning the showpiece Sabarmati river front, and bringing order to chaos, was shunted out to the Rajya Sabha even though his heart was in urban planning.[53]

The RSS's discomfort with Modi was not just his authoritarian ways. It was also his personal style and self-promotion which many in the organization despised. On one occasion during the Emergency, the ABVP was holding a cautious street corner protest meeting in Ahmedabad when Modi passed by. He jumped on to the stage, grabbed the mike and gave a rabble-rousing speech. The audience loved it but senior Sangh leaders berated Modi later for exposing himself and the organization.[54]

Modi's love for Swiss watches, designer spectacles and bespoke garments are also considered flashy and extravagant for the RSS which considers austere living as one of the basic tenets of the Hindu way of life. Interestingly, over the years, Modi's personal style appears to have rubbed off on to the Sangh as well. It is not uncommon to see RSS leaders carrying the latest gadgets and wearing expensive watches now.

The real reason for the distance between the RSS and Modi was, however, power. The RSS state office believed in the supremacy of the Sangh while Modi, holding the constitutional position of chief minister, would have none of it. Rival leaders in the party are said to have worked with the RSS state leadership in undercutting Modi. The chief minister also did not take kindly to Sangh leaders interfering in government matters such as appointments and transfers and cut off their access to the government.[55] This cheesed off the Sangh leaders who ran a campaign against Modi, distancing him further from the RSS.

The turning point came in 2005 when BJP general secretary Sanjay Joshi was caught in a sex-tape scandal. A video which allegedly showed him having sex with an unknown woman was circulated to top BJP leaders. Allegations flew thick that someone was trying to malign Joshi who was reputed to be an efficient organizer and quintessential swayamsevak. L.K. Advani, who was said to have nursing a grouse against Joshi for asking him to step down over favourable remarks he made about Jinnah when he visited Pakistan, joined the chorus to oust Joshi. Joshi resigned from his position as party general secretary. Soon, the RSS also transferred prant pracharak Manmohan Vaidya to Chennai as *saha sampark pramukh.* After the incident, all communications between the Gujarat strongman and the Sangh broke down as many in the Sangh believed that Modi and his coterie was behind fabricating the CD to trap his bête noire. Later, the CD was declared a fake by a government forensic laboratory.

After Rajnath Singh became the BJP president, he inducted Modi to the party's parliamentary board. In a closed-door RSS meeting in Jaipur attended by top BJP leaders as well, party president Rajnath Singh reportedly said that the BJP would return to its roots. In his concluding remarks, RSS chief Sudarshan said the party should shun personality-centric politics and adopt collective leadership. It would ensure that correct decisions are taken and would also mean that responsibility is also collective. There was little doubt that Sudarshan was hinting at Vajpayee and perhaps Modi who had by then gained a reputation of an autocrat. Vajpayee and Advani, however, were not present at the meeting. That year the BJP amended Article 21 of its constitution to allow RSS workers to hold key positions all the way down to the district level.[56]

As elections to the Gujarat assembly approached in 2007, Gordhan Zadafia split from the BJP and formed the Mahagujarat Janata Party. The Sangh Parivar decided to stay distant from everyone, including the BJP. A highly respected senior RSS leader, however, travelled throughout the state urging volunteers to work for Narendra Modi. His efforts paid off and RSS volunteers stepped on to the streets as polls drew near. BJP's seat count came down by ten to 117 but it was still an impressive victory. Anticipation of the next elections begins in India as soon as one poll ends. The 2007 victory cemented Modi's position as BJP's most powerful chief minister but the next big battle for the party was approaching—the 2009 Lok Sabha elections. Preparing for it was the ageing patriarch L.K. Advani.

The Congress party had successfully completed five years at the head of a difficult coalition supported from the outside by the left parties. It had passed important legislations like the Right to

Information Act and one guaranteeing 100 days' work in a year for one person from every rural household. Prime Minister Manmohan Singh had managed to bring the US around in signing a landmark deal allowing India access to the exclusive global nuclear club. But there was no particular sign that the government had done well in the eyes of the people.

It had, apparently. The party bettered its previous tally. It was seen as the increasing faith of the ordinary voter in the Manmohan Singh regime. The victory shocked the RSS. It meant voters were rewarding the leftist turn of the UPA.

Two months before the election loss, the Sangh had effected a generational change. The ageing Sudarshan, afflicted by memory loss, decided to step down and nominate Mohan Bhagwat as the sarsanghchalak. Some Sangh insiders say that Sudarshan was forced to step down because of his embarrassing outbursts and 'Muslim appeasement'. There was much consternation in the RSS about Sudarshan starting the Muslim Rashtriya Manch and hobnobbing with Muslim leaders and clerics.

With the fifty-nine-year-old Bhagwat at the helm, the reins of the organization started by Hedgewar eighty-four years before were firmly back in the hands of a Maharashtrian Brahmin from Nagpur. The centre of gravity had shifted back to Nagpur and Bhagwat intended to keep it that way.

Now Bhagwat wanted to do something about north India's grip on Indian politics. The Sangh's leadership was convinced that caste-oriented, transactional politics shorn of ideology was damaging the country. It believed that parties like the Congress, Trinamool Congress and Samajwadi Party were playing appeasement politics while others such as the Communist Party of India (Marxist) (CPI [M]) were trying to spread anti-national ideology. The first step was to promote relatively young leaders from south of the Vindhyas. The choice finally was another Nagpur Brahmin.

*

Nitin Gadkari was born in Mahal, the neighbourhood where the Sangh was also born. He was practically raised in the RSS. Rising through the Parivar's student organization ABVP and later the BJP's youth wing Yuva Morcha, Gadkari became secretary of BJP's Nagpur unit. In 1985, he contested assembly elections from Nagpur west and lost. Two years later, he was elected to the state legislative council after his mentor Gangadhar Rao Fadnavis died of cancer.[57]

In 1995, when the BJP and Shiv Sena had won the election for the Maharashtra state assembly, the RSS wanted Nitin Gadkari to be inducted into the ministry. But Pramod Mahajan, the architect of the coalition, would have none of it. Mahajan who was promoting his brother-in-law, Gopinath Munde, on the pretext of countering the propaganda that the BJP was a Brahmin–Bania party, insisted that the council of ministers could not accommodate two Brahmins as Chief Minister Manohar Joshi was already there. By then Gadkari was already a state general secretary of the party but he was hobbled by Mahajan's point man, Arvind Shahapurkar, even in Nagpur and Vidarbha.[58] It was not acceptable to the RSS which had watched with discomfort the prodigal pracharak Mahajan growing larger than life.

One morning a private plane landed at the Nagpur airport. The lone passenger L.K. Advani was on his way to Gujarat. R.H. Tupkary, head of intellectual training and RSS–BJP coordinator for Nagpur, had prior information that Advani would be passing through the city. Tupkary was waiting at the airport but Advani did not get off the plane. Finally, Tupkary boarded the plane. He put his request to the BJP president. Advani, at the time the darling of the Sangh Parivar, did not commit anything. But when the next reshuffle happened, Manohar Joshi appointed Gadkari as the PWD minister. Mahajan was not happy. The next time Tupkary ran into him, Mahajan told him that he had made things difficult for him by pushing Gadkari's case with Advani.[59] Gadkari made his name as an able infrastructure builder finding innovative financing schemes and contract structures to attract private builders. The PWD ministry built fifty-five flyovers in Mumbai and the showpiece Mumbai–Pune access-controlled expressway under his watch, earning him the nickname 'pulkari'—bridge-man.[60]

One of the biggest favours Gadkari was supposed to have done the RSS was getting legal hurdles cleared in buying and transferring Hedgewar's house in Nagpur to the Sangh. In 2004, with the Sangh's backing, Gadkari was elevated to Maharashtra BJP president, disregarding Mahajan's pick, Munde.[61]

After the election loss of 2009, Mohan Bhagwat decided it was high time the party was rescued from the cowboy politicians of Delhi and put in the hands of someone with better ideological roots. When Bhagwat was asked by a television interviewer if he saw anyone leading the BJP beyond Arun Jaitley, Venkaiah Naidu, Sushma Swaraj and Narendra Modi, he replied, 'The BJP should look beyond these four. I do not think the party lacks able persons. I feel there are several good leaders in the BJP, who are competent to take over the reins of the organization. There are more than seventy to seventy-five such leaders, who can take up the top job at any moment.'[62]

Towards the end of the year, as speculation in the media was rife that the Sangh wanted Maharashtra BJP chief Nitin Gadkari to be elevated to national president, Venkaiah Naidu, the then national vice president of the party, had a closed-door meeting with Bhagwat in Nagpur. Reports suggested he was clearly told that if the BJP wanted to enjoy the RSS's continued support, it will have to elect a new, young face as its president. As more media reports appeared that the Sangh did not want the 'Delhi quartet' of Jaitley, Naidu, Swaraj and Anant Kumar to become the BJP chief, RSS prachar pramukh Manmohan Vaidya issued a statement saying the organization had good relationships with each one of them and it had neither suggested nor objected to anyone becoming the party chief.[63]

There were three names in the reckoning—Narendra Modi, Manohar Parrikar and Nitin Gadkari. Modi declined saying he did not want a national role just then. A close friend of Modi says he did not want to give up the chief ministership because it offered him constitutional protection in the many cases against him. He was worried that without the cover, the Central government could easily put him in prison.[64] Goa chief minister Manohar Parrikar was disregarded because he had called Advani a 'rancid pickle' a few months before and it had not gone down well within the party. Anyhow, he was also said to be not keen on a national role.[65]

Eventually, the dice rolled in Gadkari's favour and it was widely seen as the BJP following the Sangh's writ. Even though Modi's relations with the RSS had improved by then, Gadkari's elevation is said to have made him wary. He knew that Gadkari was close to Sanjay Joshi and suspected he may promote his fellow Nagpurian and friend in the party. The BJP was recovering from its second consecutive Lok Sabha election loss and needed rejuvenation at the cadre level. Joshi had a formidable reputation for organization building and commanded tremendous respect from the cadre. Besides, Gadkari was a stranger to Delhi and it would be useful to have someone known by your side in a rather alien landscape.

The suspicion kept the chasm between Modi and Gadkari intact. Modi would not engage even though Gadkari tried to communicate with him. In 2011, Gadkari gave Joshi the charge of managing the upcoming Uttar Pradesh assembly elections in 2012. It would be short-lived though. A few weeks later, Narendra Modi skipped the BJP Parliamentary Board meeting in Delhi. He sent word that he was on Navratri fast.

In May, before the BJP national executive meeting in Mumbai, when Gadkari called Modi, the Gujarat strongman is said to have laid down the condition that he would attend only if Joshi was dropped from party positions. Joshi resigned from his party post and prepared to return to Delhi. As the news spread, posters in support of Joshi appeared in Gujarat and Delhi, including at the BJP headquarters. Modi is said to have again called Gadkari and told him to ask Joshi to take a flight to Delhi to avoid show-of-strength spectacles along the route. Gadkari complied and Joshi flew to Delhi.[66]

The episode was a remarkable demonstration of the power imbalance in the BJP leadership structure, the RSS's helplessness and Modi's ruthlessness. According to those who know Modi, he was extremely impressed by Indira Gandhi's political acumen and understood that she drew her strength and legitimacy from the masses. By 2012, Modi had established himself as the foremost political leader in the country, seven percentage points ahead of Rahul Gandhi in nationwide popularity. The gap would widen to thirty-two points in the next two years.[67] Among BJP rank and file and even RSS cadres, he was the unquestioned leader. This rankled the Sangh's pracharak brigade, but they were helpless before his tremendous popularity.

Modi's name was first discussed by RSS leaders as a potential prime ministerial candidate in 2011 in Baroda. At the end of a planned meeting, some leaders stayed back for an informal discussion on the political situation in the country. Most of the two dozen or so present at the meeting opposed Modi. The discussions continued over the next two years in meetings in Chennai, Amravati and Jaipur. Meanwhile, the leaders were continuously being updated of Modi's rising popularity among its grassroots workers.[68]

When the RSS executive council meeting was held in Chennai that year, a top RSS leader of Uttar Pradesh told the national leadership that if Narendra Modi was the prime ministerial candidate, they would deliver forty seats from the state.[69] It came as a shock to the RSS leadership. No one in the history of the Sangh had commanded such adulation. For an organization that abhorred and trenchantly put down personality cults, this was the ultimate insult. Modi had built an aura around him which was so strong that the RSS organization appeared more beholden to him rather than to the wise men of Nagpur. The Sangh Parivar's sense of resignation was palpable in the run-up to the Gujarat elections of 2012 December.

At a provincial meeting in Gujarat, someone reminded Bhagwat about the confusion during the 2007 elections and wanted to know who the Sangh would support. Keshubhai Patel's Gujarat Parivartan

Party was in the fray and Gordhan Zadafia had also merged his Mahagujarat Janata Party into Patel's outfit creating a third front after the BJP and the Congress. Bhagwat is said to have cryptically remarked how they could support those who had decided to go out of the family.[70]

With a thumping victory in the 2012 assembly elections, Modi became one of the few chief ministers to score a hat-trick. He delivered his victory speech in Hindi, not in the native Gujarati, making it abundantly clear that he was ready for the national stage. Modi also gave a clear hint that he would not follow the conventional election narrative. 'We have shown good economics can be good politics. We have also shown good governance can bring electoral dividends,' he said, indicating that his calling card would be development.[71]

Despite years of struggle, economic policy was one area where the Sangh Parivar had been unable to find a strategy that suited its ideological framework which was also unique enough to give it political mileage. Modi had found the perfect solution: the seamless alliance of Hindutva and corporate capitalism.

Sudhir Pathak says that opinion within the organization was divided. 'There were two views—to take only a secularist line, or to have some Hindutva also. The Hindutvawadi group was in favour of Modi. Bhagwat was not taking sides. Advani had shown that the Hindutva line can only take you up to 180 Lok Sabha seats; if you want to carry everyone along, a sober face like Vajpayee was necessary. But then the argument was that in 2004 we saw how far a sober face could take us. So the leaders sort of agreed that in 2014 Hindutva would be the appeal.'[72]

5

Hindu Economics: The Third Way

India was going through an extended period of tumult in 1991. In the general elections two years before, a politically inexperienced Rajiv Gandhi had squandered the massive mandate of 1984 and his Congress party was reduced to merely the largest group in the Lower House of Parliament. Rajiv's finance minister V.P. Singh, who had rebelled against him, had emerged as prime minister at the head of a new formation called the Janata Dal. He was backed by the BJP and the communists, perhaps the last time the right and left came together.

The Sangh Parivar's decade-long Ram Janmabhoomi campaign, now spearheaded by the BJP, was reaching its harvesting stage. There was social and political turmoil across the big north Indian states. V.P. Singh had accepted the Mandal Commission recommendations to offer job quotas to backward castes. The upper castes were up in arms. There were protests across the country and several people immolated themselves amid protests. The enduring image of those protests was of Rajiv Goswami, a student of Delhi University tottering on his feet as flames engulfed him.

The V.P. Singh government fell before it completed a year and was succeeded in November 1990 by another with a breakaway faction of the Janata Dal led by Chandra Shekhar, backed by the

Congress. By the spring of 1991, this government had bit the dust after the Congress withdrew support and was merely in place to oversee elections and carry on bare minimum administrative functions. In the midst of political turmoil, the Indian economy had run aground. And a lame-duck finance minister had to take a call that would change India's destiny.

For over four decades. India had loosely followed the Soviet planning model for its economy. At the time of Independence, there were several ideas that competed for attention. The Congress had designed an economic programme in 1931 and an agrarian plan in 1936. The Congress's Wardha session of 1937 passed a resolution on national planning for economic development. A National Planning Committee was formed with Jawaharlal Nehru as chairman and K.T. Shah as secretary at the Haripura session the next year.[1]

Shriman Narayan Agarwal, the principal of Seksaria College of Commerce in Wardha, prepared a Gandhian Plan. In the foreword, Mahatma Gandhi himself wrote: 'It [the Plan] claims to be a comparative study of the Charkha economics based on non-violence and the industrial economics which to be paying must be based on violence, i.e., exploitation of the non-industrialised countries.' Agarwal envisaged planning based on the indigenous culture and civilization of the nation with the least amount of state control and coercion. That government is best which governed the least. Gandhi did not want Indian villages to catch the 'infection of industrialism'. He wanted self-sufficient village communities in which everyone worked for his or her living on a cooperative basis. There would be no exploitation, and middlemen would be gone.[2]

Other competing strategies included M.N. Roy's People's Plan which was based on rapid expansion of production of basic goods and a focus on agriculture, and Jayaprakash Narayan's Sarvodaya Plan which too was based on Gandhian principles.

The most prominent and famous one of the different plans, however, was known as the Bombay Plan. It was drawn up in 1944 by a group of seven industrialists from Bombay—J.R.D. Tata,

Ghanshyam Das Birla, Purushottamdas Thakurdas, Lala Shri Ram, Ardeshir Dalal, A.D. Shroff and Kasturbhai Lalbhai—and assisted by economist John Mathai. It originated in a document titled 'A Brief Memorandum Outlining a Plan of Economic Development for India' and envisaged heavy public investment in the social and economic infrastructure, in both rural and urban areas.[3]

While Tata and Birla were pioneering businessmen, the others were equally accomplished. Lala Shri Ram who ran the conglomerate Delhi Cloth Mills introduced early reforms such as profit sharing with and managerial participation of employees. Ardeshir Dalal, as resident director of Tata Iron and Steel Company, was the first one to introduce profit sharing bonus for workers. Kasturbhai Lalbhai was influential in establishing the Gujarat University and the Indian Institute of Management, Ahmedabad (IIMA). A.D. Shroff was an unofficial delegate to the Bretton Woods conference, Mathai was a professor of economics and Thakurdas was an adviser to the Indo-British trade agreement.[4]

Reviewing the plan in 1945, economist P.S. Lokanathan said it opened a new chapter in Indian economic history. Vicerory Lord Wavell found in it a 'new approach to the solution of India's intractable political problems'.[5] The industrialists were worried that a future Indian government would be populist and harm prospects of long-term economic development of the country. They wanted to pre-empt it and make the people and future leaders aware of issues of development and distribution. Others didn't think so.

The *Workers' International News* wrote: 'Having been frightened out of their wits by the revolutionary energy of the masses in 1942, now the Indian bourgeoisie attempt to by-pass political power through an economic weapon. This is the background of the famous Bombay Plan put forward by the Indian industrialists.' The CPI's B.T. Ranadive called it a 'blueprint for building capitalism with the aid of the state'.[6] 'We cannot question the sincerity and patriotism of these able and eminent businessmen. Nevertheless, we cannot shut our eyes to the fact that it is essentially a capitalist plan on western lines,' Shriman Narayan Agarwal, author of the Gandhian Plan, commented.[7]

A year before the plan was published, the *New York Times* had remarked: 'The local millionaires deplored what had been happening in the country and pointed out that their object in life being to make money, like most Indian businessmen, they were keeping one foot in the Congress camp, which they expected to see running the country, and another in the British camp which is running it now and gives them fat orders.'[8]

The Rs 10,000-crore (then equivalent to US$30 billion) plan envisaged doubling per capita income in fifteen years and proposed how to fund such an ambition. In that period, agricultural output would rise 130 per cent, industry 500 per cent and services by 200 per cent. It would structurally change the Indian economy; the contribution of agriculture, industry and services to GDP changing from 53 per cent, 17 per cent and 22 per cent respectively at the time, to 40 per cent, 35 per cent and 20 per cent at the end of the plan. The industrialists wanted state ownership and control of key industries and said private enterprise would have to function under tight state direction. They even conceded that every aspect of 'economic life will have to be so rigorously controlled by government that individual liberty and freedom of enterprise will suffer a temporary eclipse'.[9]

The crux of the Bombay Plan was pretty much the core of the planned economic model adopted by the Nehru government although it was never publicly acknowledged. 'Our national aim is a welfare state and a socialist economy. Neither of these can be attained without considerable increase in national income and neither is possible without much greater volume of goods and services and full employment.' Nehru stressed on equitable distribution yet understood the pitfalls of copying the Soviet model blindly. He had a nuanced view of what socialism would be in a country like India. 'If, however, we adopt a policy, in the name of socialism, which actually maintains some fetters or encourages them, then we are moving away from our objectives and preventing the growth of full dynamics. It becomes necessary, therefore, to have a private sector also and to give it full play within its field, provided always that it is coordinated with our planned approach…'[10]

While private enterprises, including foreign firms, were allowed to operate in a limited way, the state was involved, as P.C. Mahalanobis, the architect of post-Independence planning had envisioned, in establishing capital goods manufacturing; industries such as Bharat Heavy Electricals, railway factories and building big dams. Nehru famously called them the 'temples' of modern India.[11] This depended on a high dose of capital as the strategy was based on celebrated economist Joan Robinson's view that it was the rate of investment which governs the rate of saving, and not vice versa.

That's not how it worked out.

The *Eastern Economist*, owned by G.D. Birla, described Mahalanobis as a 'statistician completely devoid of a sense of economic organization', and the Second Plan framework as 'a theoretical shibboleth which if enforced, would in one sweep endanger India's future industrialization'.[12]

Another strong voice that opposed the plan was of economist and liberal B.R. Shenoy who wrote a note of dissent to the Second Nehru–Mahalanobis Five-Year Plan. In the 1955 note, Shenoy points out that the Second Plan 'begins by prescribing the increase in national income which the Plan would set to achieve'. In other words, the plan begins with a certain growth rate and then goes about figuring out how to gather necessary savings. Shenoy says, '…the availability of real resources must be assessed first and the investment plan must match it'. Shenoy also opposed nationalization and control. 'There are great advantages in allowing freedom to the economy, and to the price system in the use and distribution of the needs of production … Controls and allocations are an essential characteristic of communist planning. They do not very well fit in, under planning in a free enterprise market economy.'[13]

When Nehru and Mahalanobis steamed ahead with the five-year plans based on the Soviet model of economic planning, Deendayal

Upadhyaya, the Jana Sangh general secretary, wrote a detailed critique of the government's economic policy in a book, simply titled, *The Two Plans*. Upadhyaya said only Planning Commission member K.C. Neogy, economist B.R. Shenoy and Jana Sangh were counted amongst the heretics who did not faithfully repeat the 'Ramdhun' chanted by the chairman of the Planning Commission. 'Not only in execution, but also in the formulation of policies and fixing upon priorities, a comprehensive and integrated view of all our economic life and body politic has not been taken,' he wrote about the plans.[14]

With minor variations, the first three plans more or less traced the contours of the Bombay Plan, although unacknowledged. The Congress, the left and private entities actively engaged with the question of an economic system for Independent India but there was hardly any meaningful contribution from the right side of the political aisle. Dissenting voices like that of Shenoy were few and barely heard. A decade after Independence, Deendayal Upadhyaya wrote *Bharatiya Arth Niti: Vikas ki ek Disha* (Indian Economic Policy: A New Paradigm of Development), the first economic policy document from a national party that came closest to a conservative voice.

Upadhyaya was the first person in the RSS to write extensively about the Indian economy and try to formulate a broad policy framework for the country. Upadhyaya's thesis known as *Ekatma Manavavad* (Integral Humanism) is mandatory reading for every RSS volunteer.

Upadhyaya was born on 25 September 1916 in his grandfather Chunnilal Shukla's home. Shukla was a station master at Dhankia on the Jaipur–Ajmer railway line. Upadhyaya's father too was a station master at Jalesar Road in Uttar Pradesh. He was brought up by his maternal uncle, Radha Raman Shukla, after his parents died when he was seven. A gold medallist in school, Upadhyaya cleared intermediate education from Pilani and graduation from Kanpur's Sanatan Dharma College.

In Kanpur, RSS pracharak Murlidhar Dattatreya Deoras, popularly known as Bhaurao, who had arrived in Uttar Pradesh to spread the organization's work, recruited Upadhyaya. By 1942, Upadhyaya had become an RSS pracharak and was appointed at Lakhimpur. He climbed the organizational ladder rapidly, becoming the prant saha pracharak in three years. In 1951, Golwalkar shifted Upadhyaya to the RSS-backed political party Jana Sangh started by Syama Prasad Mookerjee. He was chosen as the organizing secretary at the party's first convention held in 1952 in Kanpur, a full month before Mookerjee formally launched the party nationally.

Upadhyaya became the Jana Sangh general secretary after the sudden death of Mookerjee in a Kashmir jail in 1953. He led the party, becoming president in December 1967 until February 1968 when he was found dead on the railway tracks close to Mughalsarai Junction, now renamed after Upadhyaya by the Modi government in his centenary year.

Syama Prasad Mookerjee had thought of Jana Sangh as a 'nationalist alternative to the Congress'. Balraj Madhok, whom Mookerjee entrusted with the job of writing the party's manifesto, recollects that the 'new party will be for a Hindu India, to be a Hindu Rashtra'. Although it was sent to the RSS for approval, the latter did not respond. Mookerjee initially wanted to call it Young India Party but decided on All-India People's Party. In his inaugural speech at the launch of the party in Delhi, Mookerjee said the party stood for a well-planed decentralized national economic plan on the lines of the Sarvodaya scheme [Jayaprakash Narayan's].[15]

Even after Upadhyaya took over, the party did not have any concrete national plan. In 1958, Upadhyaya wrote *Bharatiya Arth Niti: Vikas ki ek Disha*. Although his 'Ekatma Manavavad' was a broad political framework, *Bharatiya Arth Niti* contained economic analysis and specific policy prescriptions. Upadhyaya believed most Indian economists suffered from their Western training and they failed to break out of the framework of Western economic thinkers such as Karl Marx. Industrialization had closely linked the Indian economy with some Western economies, but it was mostly for the benefit of those economies. It had helped the growth of commission agents and traders who had later grown into industrialists. Their fortunes were not dependent on India but tied to the growth of foreigners. Although he doesn't spell it out, Upadhyaya seemed to be taking aim at the industrialists behind the Bombay Plan when he says that 'although they are few in number and their contribution to the national income is small, their influence on the country's economic life was considerable'. He believed their ambition was to replace the foreign occupiers, a sentiment shared by the CPI's Ranadive.[16]

In 1964, when an interviewer asked him if he thought people on the whole had better lives, Upadhyaya said:

> It varies from class to class. The landless labourer is worse off. So is the entire salariat—the fixed income section of the society. The middle peasant is no worse than before. The big peasant is a big gainer. The factory worker does better in the big city than in the small town. The businessman is doing better. So are the senior lawyers, doctors, etc. But you will see, that leaves the majority of people worse off than before. Formerly 'the clerk' or 'the teacher' was a small sahib. Today he is only white-clothed, that's all. He has no savings, no status.[17]

Yet the Jana Sangh was unable to occupy the liberal economic space, partly because C. Rajagopalachari's Swatantra Party was perched there. Minoo Masani, the force behind the party, and Rajagopalachari had positioned the Swatantra Party against Nehru's Licence Raj and pushed for economic freedom and a market-based economy. The Jana Sangh was largely on the same page with the Swatantra Party on many economic policy-related issues.

The Swatantra Party was founded after the Nagpur session of the All-India Congress Committee (AICC) in 1959 passed a resolution on joint cooperative farming and ceiling on landholdings. Masani, who had once described Nehru's five-year plans as the 'source of evil', denounced the AICC resolution in Parliament saying that the farmers of India would fight what was really a move to collectivize

Indian agriculture.[18] Upadhyaya called the Congress's attempt 'an essay in confusion'.[19] He said cooperative farming would intensify unemployment and asked whether this was not a ploy to snatch away farmers' freedom.[20]

But there were sharp differences too.

According to American political scientist H.L. Erdman, most Swatantra leaders and their fellow travellers in the Ganatantra Parishad and Gujarat Kshatriya Mahasabha did not join or align with the Jana Sangh because of its 'de facto' communalism.[21]

That the Swatantra Party leaders found the need for a new party despite the existence of the Jana Sangh showed that unity was difficult, Upadhyaya pointed out. They were on opposing sides when it came to the issue of Kashmir and Pakistan. In fact, efforts to merge the two parties were scuttled because of this divergence. 'Jana Sangh cannot align itself with forces that stand for an ignoble surrender of Indian territory to an aggressor,' Upadhyaya said on the possibility of an electoral alliance between the two.[22]

Political scientist Bruce Graham notes that the Jana Sangh did not have the 'skill and experience to articulate its liberal economic thinking to its supporters looking to it as the champion of cultural nationalism and not expecting economic policies'.[23] This was primarily because of the RSS's stranglehold on the party. The RSS's reluctance to embrace liberal economics would haunt later governments as well.

*

In April 1948, India set out its industrial policy that stressed on 'continuous increase in production and its equitable distribution'.[24] It said the state would play a progressively active role in the development of industries while weapons making, atomic energy and railway transport would be its monopoly.

Eight years later, the government decided to expand the public and cooperative sectors as the roots of Nehruvian socialism dug deeper. 'The adoption of the socialist pattern of society as the national objective, as well as the need for planned and rapid development, require that all industries of basic and strategic importance, or in the nature of public utility services, should be in the public sector. Other industries which are essential and require investment on a scale which only the State, in present circumstances, could provide, have also to be in the public sector. The State has, therefore, to assume direct responsibility for the future development of industries over a wide area,' the industrial resolution of 1956 stated.[25]

The Second Five-Year Plan ended in 1961 and the Third Plan was interrupted by a war with China in 1962 which changed the country's priorities. Stung by the loss to China, Home Minister Y.B. Chavan went on a shopping spree for weapons and war machines. One more war with Pakistan in 1965 coupled with poor growth meant the economy was in dire straits by the time Indira Gandhi took charge in 1966.

Gandhi initially agreed to economic reforms and even went along with an IMF-mandated devaluation of the rupee in 1966. But as her conflict with the group of senior Congress leaders known as the Syndicate intensified, she allied with young socialists in the party. Gandhi circulated a document called 'Stray Thoughts Memorandum' at the AICC session at Bangalore in 1969 proposing abolition of privy purses of erstwhile royals, bank nationalization, introduction of land ceiling and crackdown on monopolies. It was an attempt to paint her opponents in the party as anti-people and pro-rich, and position herself as pro-poor to sidle up to the socialists and leftists who wanted state control of the economy.[26]

Economic growth had fluctuated wildly, the gross domestic product (GDP) dropping from 3.7 per cent in 1961 to 2.9 per cent the following year before rising to 7.4 per cent in 1964. It fell to 2.6 per cent the next year before bouncing back to 7.8 per cent in 1967. From that peak it kept falling until it entered negative territory, the economy shrinking by 5 per cent in 1972.[27]

Industrial investment fell sharply, basic goods production dropped, and shortage of funds hobbled government spending. The influx of about 10 million East Pakistan refugees added to the economy's burden. It was further stretched by the war with Pakistan. Misfortune piled up as rains failed in two consecutive years and a foreign currency shock hit in 1973 when crude oil prices zoomed sending the country into a recession. By mid-1974, inflation was growing at 30 per cent, making food expensive and supply short, fuelling black marketing and hoarding. Industrial unrest gripped the country and an estimated 31 million workdays were lost to strikes, Bombay alone witnessing over 13,000 strikes in a period of nine months. A railway strike, led by the intrepid socialist and trade union leader George Fernandes, which lasted twenty-two days in May 1974 crippled the country. By the early 1970s, the top income tax rate had gone up to an incredible 98.5 per cent. In 1974, the government froze wages by introducing compulsory deposit schemes for the salaried and asked all taxpayers whose annual income was more than Rs 15,000 to deposit 4 to 8 per cent of their income in mandatory deposits.[28]

The Congress split in 1969 after the leadership threw Indira Gandhi out of the party. She won the day in Parliament with the help of the Communist Party of India. Soon, she began nationalizing oil companies and banks that were, until then, owned by private parties. After the post-Emergency government led by Morarji Desai took office, foreign companies such as IBM and Coca-Cola quit the country as it became legally difficult for them to operate in India without local partners. The government also legalized strikes and empowered trade unions.

*

India's post-Independence development strategy had assumed that public savings would generate a pool of funds that could be used for productive investment by state enterprises. Instead, the public sector became a consumer of community savings which was freely available to the government as the new owner of banks. This role reversal was apparent from the early 1970s, and by the early 1980s, the government was borrowing heavily to meet its own expenses as well as finance public sector deficits and investments. Between 1960 and 1975, total state borrowings, including by its enterprises, averaged 4.4 per cent of GDP. It touched 9 per cent by 1989–90. The Central government's internal public debt was over Rs 5 lakh crore by the mid-1990s. Interest payments on these borrowings were nearly Rs 40,000 crore and was nearly 70 per cent of the Centre's fiscal deficit. By the end of the 1990s, the Centre's debt nearly doubled to Rs 9.7 lakh crore.[29]

When Indira Gandhi returned to power in 1980, she took cautious steps away from the controlled economy. The Rajiv Gandhi years saw a quick shake-up of the system. At the Congress Party's centenary session in December 1985 in Bombay, he famously summed up the Indian administration:

> We have Government servants who do not serve but oppress the poor and the helpless, police who do not uphold the law but shield the guilty, tax collectors who do not collect taxes but connive with those who cheat the State and whole legions whose only concern is their private welfare at the cost of society. They have no work, ethic, no feeling for the public cause, no involvement in the future of the nation, no comprehension of national goals, no commitment to the values of modern India. They have only a grasping, mercenary outlook, devoid of competence, integrity and commitment. …
>
> Millions of ordinary Congress workers throughout the country are full of enthusiasm for the Congress policies and programmes. But they are handicapped, for on their backs ride the brokers of power and influence, who dispense patronage to convert a mass movement into a feudal oligarchy. They are self-perpetuating cliques who thrive by invoking the slogans

of caste and religion and by enmeshing the living body of the Congress in their net of avarice.[30]

On a visit to drought-hit Kalahandi in Orissa before the centenary session in 1985, Rajiv Gandhi had remarked that of every rupee spent by the government only 15 paise reached the intended beneficiary.[31]

Despite the massive political mandate and an intent to reform the economy, Rajiv Gandhi was largely unsuccessful. A relative newcomer to politics, he relied on the advice of a group of Western-trained corporate executives turned quasi politicians and bureaucrats such as Arun Nehru, Arun Singh, Mani Shankar Aiyar and Sam Pitroda.

The team tried to shift to a liberal form of development, removing restrictions on industry and freeing technology import. Although Rajiv Gandhi embarked on modernization and economic reforms, his government soon got caught up in a corruption scandal involving purchase of Howitzer guns from Swedish arms maker Bofors AB. But he did unleash a communication revolution in the country by making telecom services cheap and ubiquitous. It laid the foundations of the future information technology services industry in the country. Economic liberalization during those years was piecemeal and halting for various reasons even though the government had decided to move away from socialism. Rajiv Gandhi and his advisers had underestimated the opposition it would have from their own party men; a large section of the party itself was against the policies. Hobbled by his own party and a corruption scandal, governance faltered, and public finances went downhill.

It was this legacy of administration and public finances that Yashwant Sinha, finance minister in the Chandra Shekhar government, inherited. The dire situation was explained by his successor Manmohan Singh a few months later. Internal public debt of the Central government had accumulated to about 55 per cent of GDP. Interest payments alone were about 4 per cent of GDP and almost a fifth of total government expenditure. Foreign exchange reserves, at about Rs 2500 crore, were barely enough to finance imports for a fortnight. In short, India was on the brink of bankruptcy.

One hot day in the summer of 1991, when Sinha had just returned from election campaigning to Patna, he found a finance ministry official waiting for him. He wanted his signature on a file that contained a proposal to mortgage 20 tonnes of gold held with the State Bank of India (SBI) on behalf of the Government of India to the Bank of England for $400 million. It was only the first tranche. More gold, this time from the country's foreign reserves, would have to be pledged to avert the country defaulting on its international commitments. 'I approved the proposal, signed the file, and marked it to the prime minister for his final approval. The deed was done. We were mortgaging our most precious asset, gold, which Indians are sentimental about, to save something even more precious—our honour and prestige,' Sinha wrote.[32]

Soon, a Congress government was back at the centre but with a crucial difference. It was not headed by anyone from the Nehru-Gandhi family or anybody from north India. The prime minister was a low-profile Congressman from Andhra Pradesh, P.V. Narasimha Rao, who was dragged out of semi-retirement and handed the top job.

A few days before Rao took oath as prime minister, Cabinet Secretary Naresh Chandra rang up Rao and said he needed to see something very important—an eight-page memo on the Indian economic crisis. When he gave it to Rao, he asked, 'Do you want me to read this right now? I'm very busy building the cabinet.' Chandra told him the cabinet could wait. When he finished, he asked, 'Is it as bad as this?' Chandra—accompanied by Finance Secretary S.P. Shukla and Chief Economic Adviser Deepak Nayyar—told Rao he could either continue the unsustainable status quo of emergency borrowing or announce that the government planned to liberalize the economy. Chandra told him that if it was the government's new policy there would be less criticism than if it seemed to be dictated by the International Monetary Fund (IMF) and World Bank.[33]

Rao realized that he needed to make some unusual decisions. He chose as finance minister former Reserve Bank of India (RBI) governor and economist, Manmohan Singh—a Sikh with no political background—who was born in 1932 in Gah near what is today Islamabad in Pakistan. Within a matter of weeks, both unremarkable men would be known as the architects of the biggest disruption post-Independence India had seen. But the Congress party had to be convinced first.

When Manmohan Singh presented the draft of the liberalization road map to the prime minister, Rao read the whole draft and told him to add a paragraph on Jawaharlal Nehru, Indira and Rajiv Gandhi's contribution to India's industrial development. It worked.[34]

On 24 July 1991, Finance Minister Manmohan Singh stood up in Parliament to deliver his budget speech. He began with a memory, before going on to describe the precarious condition of the economy, laying down the numbers and sounding a warning:

As I rise, I am overpowered by a strange feeling of loneliness. I miss a handsome, smiling, face listening intently to the budget speech. Shri Rajiv Gandhi is no more. But his dream lives on; his dream of ushering India into the twenty-first century; his dream of a strong, united, technologically sophisticated but humane India. I dedicate this budget to his inspiring memory....

There is no time to lose. Neither the government nor the economy can live beyond its means year after year. The room for manoeuver, to live on borrowed money or time, does not exist anymore ... For improving the management of the economy, the starting point, and indeed the centrepiece of our strategy, should be a credible fiscal adjustment and macro-economic stabilization during the current financial year, to be followed by continued fiscal consolidation thereafter. This process would, inevitably, need at least three years, if not longer, to complete. But there can be no adjustment without pain. The people must be prepared to make necessary sacrifices to preserve our economic independence and restore the health of our economy.[35]

The speech was a classic in balancing acts. There were built-in cushions for anticipated punches, both from the opposition and from within the Congress party as Rao had foreseen.

Singh paid encomiums: 'Thanks to the efforts of Pandit Jawaharlal Nehru, Indira Gandhi and Rajiv Gandhi, we have developed a well-diversified industrial structure. This constitutes a great asset as we begin to implement various structural reforms.' Then, he tagged criticism to praise. 'However, barriers to entry and limits on growth in the size of firms, have often led to a proliferation of licensing and an increase in the degree of monopoly. This has put shackles on segments of Indian industry and made them serve the interests of producers but not pay adequate attention to the interests of consumers.'

In the course of his epoch-altering effort, Singh rewrote the way Indians had perceived wealth, poverty, development and their social interplay. He gave wealth creation respectability and hitherto withheld government sanction. 'We must restore to the creation of wealth its proper place in the development process. For, without it, we cannot remove the stigma of abject poverty, ignorance and disease. But we cannot accept social misery and inequity as unavoidable in the process of creation of wealth.'

Singh went on to describe in detail the adjustments he was making to the government's economic policy. He ended his speech with the now famous flourish:

I do not minimize the difficulties that lie ahead on the long and arduous journey on which we have embarked. But as Victor Hugo once said, 'No power on earth can stop an idea whose time has come.' I suggest to this august House that the emergence of India as a major economic power in the world happens to be one such idea. Let the whole world hear it loud and clear. India is now wide awake. We shall prevail. We shall overcome.[36]

The Congress had started veering off its socialist trajectory a decade before Rao and Singh began reforms. Soon after Indira Gandhi returned as prime minister in 1980, it had become clear that socialism was gradually becoming a mere veneer. In 1984, Finance Minister Pranab Mukherjee announced that India would not use a $1 billion IMF loan, which was the last tranche of a five-year, $5-billion package negotiated after the oil shock of 1979. One of the reasons to terminate the agreement was to pre-empt IMF's conditions. The idea was to make changes in government policy as the IMF would have asked for. It would save the leaders from accusations of capitulating to foreign diktats.

Mukherjee declared it the 'year of productivity', raised production caps in several sectors, and allowed non-resident Indians (NRIs) to invest in Indian firms. By repaying the loan and taking ownership of the reforms, the government avoided too much criticism from the then powerful left, which would have gone for the jugular had the IMF been involved directly. That year, Mukherjee was voted as one of the best five finance ministers in the world by *Euromoney* magazine; an early acknowledgement perhaps that India had agreed to toe the Bretton Woods institutions line.[37]

The Congress party held elections after two decades in 1992 and the new AICC plenary met in Tirupati. In his presidential speech, Narasimha Rao chose to clear the air about the new direction. He said:

In a laissez faire society the underlying assumption is that if each person pursues his own happiness the market will ensure the happiness of all. Communism, in the form in which it has failed, assumed that as the pursuit of the collective individual.

Clearly, we differ from both these assertions. We have to strike a balance between individual and common good. Indeed, there is no contradiction between the two. It is the virtue of democracy that it permits a variety of such pursuits and their fine-tuning from time to time.[38]

Rao redefined self-reliance as the prudence to borrow as per the country's capacity to repay. Rao's skilful centrism was on full display when, acutely aware of conservatives' concerns, he added that it was in 'perfect conformity with Indian tradition and ethos. Therefore, while we are re-defining self-reliance, we are not abandoning the basic principle … There is no way for the Indian economy to remain insulated within its confines any longer. It has to integrate itself with the world economy. The two-way traffic of capital, manpower, technology, etc. will have to be opened up. We have, therefore, to reorient our previous approach to foreign capital.'[39]

*

While Singh and Rao were trying to negotiate the turbulent economic weather in the country, another challenge to developing countries was gathering steam globally.

After the World War II ended, several countries banded together to create an international trade organization to complement the newly formed World Bank and the IMF after the Bretton Woods conference. The pact was called the General Agreement on Tariffs and Trade (GATT). It never took the form of an organization as envisaged but negotiations continued for the next four decades. Together, the institutions were tasked with creating a new global economic order.

In 1986, the biggest negotiations were held in Uruguay and came to be known as the Uruguay round of trade negotiations. That round expanded the scope of the talks to include intellectual property rights and trade in services. In December 1991, Arthur Dunkel, director general of GATT, wrote a proposal compiling the entire negotiations. It was called the Dunkel Draft and would go on to become the foundation document of the World Trade Organization (WTO).[40]

The publication of the Dunkel Draft coincided with Manmohan Singh's radical budget proposals opening up India's economy to foreign participation. The draft was seen as favouring multinational corporations and impinging on the sovereignty of developing countries. It was a terrible deal reflecting an international power structure in which countries such as India had no importance. Commentators called for a policy response that retained a hard-headed nationalism.[41]

The Congress government's new turn raised a storm.

'Liberalization and globalization [is] a case of Satan quoting the Bible,' declared Dattopant Thengadi, the founder of Bharatiya Mazdoor Sangh, Bharatiya Kisan Sangh and the Swadeshi Jagran Manch. 'In its present form, "liberalization" of GATT and the US is downright fraud. Liberalization of Manmohan Singh is sheer gullibility. Liberalization of our air-conditioned radicals is ignorance or hypocrisy. Liberalization is a grave challenge to patriots of all non-American countries,' Thengadi said.[42]

It was amid this political and economic churn that Rao and Singh tried to steer India away from the oppressive industrial permit system, known as the Licence Raj, and socialism towards a more open economic policy where foreigners could have a stake. And it was then that the RSS attempted an ideological intervention in economic policymaking. Until then its forays had been mostly through the BMS, its labour affiliate. Thengadi was practically the lone ideologue who spoke and wrote on economic issues in the Sangh after Deendayal Upadhyaya. Until Thengadi's death in 2004, his perspective on economic policy was barely challenged in the organization.

In fact, speaking to journalists soon after he took over as sarsanghchalak, Deoras hinted that he agreed with the communists on economic ideology. 'Communism may have given us some good things also—no doubt from the economic point of view,' Deoras had said.[43] A few years later, he admitted at a press conference in Delhi that the RSS had never given much thought to economics and it did not have an economic policy.[44]

Late in 1991, Thengadi founded Swadeshi Jagran Manch, an organization dedicated to the cause of indigenization and self-reliance. It was headed by M.G. Bokare, a former vice chancellor of Nagpur University who was much sought after by governments to help in farming policy design. Bokare, a staunch Marxist most of his life, later rejected Marxian economic theory and embraced what he described as Hindu economics, a theory he culled out from Indian scriptures and texts beginning with the Rig Veda. Thengadi described Hindu economics as the interpretation of Pandit Deendayal Upadhyaya's Integral Humanism in the economic field.

In the RSS's view, basic needs must be available to every citizen, but they should limit the amount of material wealth for personal purposes. Golwalkar believed that consumerism was not compatible with the spirit of Hindu culture and the immediate national goal should be self-reliance. He opposed capital-intensive industries and wanted workers to be given ownership of enterprises equivalent to the value of their labour.

Thengadi said that 'Hindu thought' never became popular in the modern context because those well-versed in Hindu scriptures were not acquainted adequately with Western thought. And those proficient in the latter were sufficiently ignorant of the former. Because of intellectual prejudice, scholars could not realize that the 'origins of modern economics could be found in the most ancient book of mankind, the Rig Veda'. The cornerstone of the Hindu economic system is service (not profit), restrained consumption and declining prices.

Bokare believed that Savarkar, the proponent of Hindutva, was a communist in his economic philosophy. His vision of a rationalized Hindu society with large-scale modern industries, planning, national military and public discipline was the closest approximation of planned economy of the Soviet Union. The Hindu economic system, according to him, is one of abundance and cheap prices. Bokare theorized that economic decisions were 'historico-psychological'. The knowledge of the long history of prices impact current decisions and also mould future expectations. Past, present and future were thus rationally synchronized in economic decisions. How would people behave if the Hindu economic system engendered an irreversible historical trend of downward moving prices? In such an economy, paper money would be better than gold as a store of value. 'In Hindu economic system, men will have permanently forgotten gold,' Bokare wrote.

He also found that competition could end wages and result in self-employment for everyone. Competition in boom period creates conditions of overproduction and depression in the market. Workers lose jobs and have no alternative except becoming self-employed. Competition transforms wage-workers into wage-less self-employed who cannot be exploited, nor can they exploit others. 'Thus the disappearance of capitalism and the appearance of decentralised socialism is simultaneously accomplished. It is a peaceful transformation. There is no class war or takeover of the state,' he stated.

Unlike what Karl Marx outlined, Hindu economics 'endorses competition philosophically'. It realizes total decentralization of economic activities of wage-less family enterprises. It continues the flow of science and technology in production because patents would not be allowed in a perfectly competitive economy. Abundance of goods and services becomes the historical trend pushing prices downwards. Yet despite the downward movement of prices there would be no fear of unemployment. All activities are smoothened and synchronized in economic development.

While the issue of finding employment and livelihood will be solved by self-employment, the other factor of production, viz., capital will be supplied by savings and the state. Their own savings will have more value as the economic system will ensure that purchasing power will continue to increase because of the irreversible trend of falling prices. Such savings can be reliably deposited with the state for safety. The state will support the self-employed with interest-free loans. This will also cause the disappearance of banking.[45]

Joint stock companies and stock exchanges have no place in the Hindu economic system even though large enterprises might be required. Then citizens would pool their money and become owner-members of such enterprise which could also borrow interest-free loans from the state. 'All business organisations will be uniform in economic philosophy. They will be free from rent, interest, wages and profit as analytical economic categories.'

Thengadi writes that it was not that elements of Hindu economic philosophy were entirely unknown. Those who wrote about them were ignored because of the 'ideological stability in the western mind and the adherents of each western ideology believing blindly in the inevitability of the ultimate triumph of their own scientific ideology'. In his analysis, the process of disillusionment started after the great stock market crash of October 1987 (known as Black Monday when a market crash was triggered in Hong Kong causing a domino effect across European markets and later the US) and the ushering of Perestroika in the communist world. The psychological status quos were upset. 'The Hindu Economics of Bokare is appearing on the scene at this critical juncture. It boldly pledges to fill up the vacuum and indicate the Third Way which may ultimately be recognised as the Only Way,' Thengadi wrote.[46]

The RSS, though opposed to the ideological tenets of socialism, was inherently comfortable with its social organization patterns which enforced a certain homogeneity and a welfare state. Even in Bokare's thesis, capitalism is eventually replaced by a socialistic pattern but without class struggle.

Its preoccupation with national security notwithstanding, the concept of comprehensive national power, which considers a country's economic might and soft power with equal importance as military capability in assessing its overall strength, was yet to enter the Sangh's institutional thoughts as a strategic concept. Being a closed economy, it did not matter either. An editorial published in the *Organiser* on 29 January 2006, inviting public opinion on the 'role of ideology in polity', commented that coalitions like the NDA which were based on the 'economic promise of prosperity, as against political ideology …cannot be a long-term strategy'.[47] It is evident in the Modi government's economic management where ideological issues seem to enjoy priority even at the cost of policy integrity.

The Akhil Bharatiya Pratinidhi Sabha of the RSS held in 1992, for the first time in its history, passed a resolution that discussed the national economic policy. The resolution expressed concern that '… owing to certain policies unsuitable to our conditions we are today experiencing a deterioration in various spheres of our national life. This clearly points to a basic lapse in the thinking and planning of our political helmsmen: the absence of the spirit of "Swadeshi"'.

The resolution said that the government was being led by international lending agencies and their intention was to corner the natural resources for the resource-intense production processes of developed nations. The policy would expose more and more people to hunger and starvation. It continued:

> It is opening the floodgates for giant multinational corporations and other foreign controlled agencies to stifle such vital spheres of our national life as agriculture, health, education, telecommunications, banking and financial services and affect even the defence, atomic energy and space research. Besides this, our local consumer market is already on the verge of being swamped with foreign articles, threatening all our cottage and small-scale industries.[48]

The resolution explained the objective of the SJM. It was to be the umbrella forum gathering expertise from different fields of economic activity. 'Alerting and mobilizing the popular mind against this harmful drift [are] the crying need of the hour. As such, the ABPS [Akhil Bharatiya Pratinidhi Sabha] welcomes the formation of the SJM by leading thinkers and activists drawn from various fields of national life such as labour, farmers, students, teachers, consumers, cooperatives and others.' The leadership of the SJM was drawn from other Sangh affiliates like labour organization BMS, students' body ABVP, consumer protection outfit Grahak Panchayat and the political arm BJP. Each of these organizations were asked to send two people to SJM.

The next year, the RSS national executive council approved a resolution on the country's economic affairs. Called 'Swadeshi', the resolution expressed concern over 'throwing the door open for foreigners and multinational companies in the name of economic liberalization'. 'It is now patently clear that the International Monetary Fund, the World Bank and the capitalist countries are getting their conditions accepted. The economic imperialism of the West is gaining legitimacy in the name of economic stability, restructuring the economy and globalization.'

The resolution described how the Dunkel Draft was being used to impose the West's economic agenda on developing countries:

> The international forum of General Agreement of Tariffs and Trade, which by its definition, ought to operate only in respect of goods trade and tariffs, is being utilized for a comprehensive control of the economic activity of developing nations by the Western powers ... The Dunkel Draft Text [DDT] is another attempt in the same direction. The so-called proper amendments are sought to be introduced in the Indian patent law and investment measures ... Even though the DDT is as yet not subscribed to, by the government of India, their conditions are already being implemented under the directives of the IMF and WB as a precondition for obtaining loans.[49]

The resolution said the country's sovereignty would be compromised if the Dunkel proposals were to be accepted. It also took aim at multinational corporations (MNCs), calling them dangerous. They would capture the Indian market, rendering Indian companies unviable and resulting in widespread unemployment. Calling for all patriotic countrymen to propagate swadeshi consumer goods, it exhorted them to cooperate fully with the Swadeshi Jagran Manch formed for this purpose.

The ABPS and the Akhil Bharatiya Karyakari Mandal (ABKM) are the two decision making bodies of the RSS. With the two resolutions, the RSS had made unambiguously clear that it opposed the new economic policies of the Congress government.

Commenting on the reforms, Bokare said that they were against the 'ideology of Nehru' in economic development of India. 'The state should honestly inform the people that it is promoting monopoly capitalism in India ... Economic reform philosophically does not connote a change from state planning to monopoly capitalism. Market friendly, competition in economy, market economy as phrases used in official statements and documents is [sic] disinformation.'[50]

It meant that if a government supported by the Sangh Parivar were to come to power, voters could expect a reversal of the policies and they might be replaced with new strategies based on indigenously developed economic thought.

Economic liberalization had brought politics and business closer than ever. Stock market news became mainstream and share brokers such as Harshad Mehta were feted as stars, their fancy cars and luxury apartments making it to magazine covers. The heroes of the new India would be people like Reliance Industries founder Dhirubhai Ambani and Infosys founder N.R. Narayana Murthy. The Sangh's stress on simple living, minimum consumption and a spiritual outlook would militate against the new emerging India which celebrated wealth, aspirations and consumption. To the chagrin of many in the organization, the RSS would find itself travelling in the same coach as its bitter rivals, the Marxists.

Hindu economics would achieve what socialism set out to do: annihilate capitalism and spread social equality:

Hindu economics has a theory of the inevitability of self-employment after the disappearance of capitalism ... all people will become proprietor owners and earn incomes. There will be no proletariat in the economy. If there is no proletariat, there cannot exist capitalist system. An economy without the proletariat is free from exploitation. It consummates the ethos of socialism. Thus theory and programme engender decentralized economy. The theory is universally valid. Hindu economics in this sense is for mankind.[51]

The system that evolved in the 1990s deeply impacted the socio-economic and political fabric of the country. The end result was best described by economist Raghuram Rajan:

There is a darker understanding that preserves the status quo of a super-rich connected elite, an undeserved poor, and a middle-class that feels unable to change the culture of corruption. The middle-class rants on and on about the corruption that permeates the political establishment and officialdom. They dream about the honest incorruptible politician who would come in and clean up the system. Yet they do not see that politicians provide a vital service, that of intermediating between their poorer constituents and an indifferent government. Politicians tell me that much of their time is spent getting services for their constituents that should be a matter of right—a complaint registered in the police station, a pension claim approved by the pension authorities—as well as providing a safety net—some money for a farmer for funeral expenses for his wife or a job as a government peon for the eldest son in a poor family. In return, constituents turn a blind eye to the corruption their politician indulges in. After all, so what if he is a crook, he is their crook.

... No one wants a Don Quixote who will tilt against the system if it means their needs will be ignored while he is attempting systemic change ... In sum, then, instead of redressing the balance between the poor and the rich, between the disconnected and the well connected, between the powerless and the powerful, the Indian state, despite all its socialist rhetoric, often ends up discriminating against the former and in favour of the latter.[52]

These fault lines were barely visible in the early 1990s and it would severely test the RSS's ability to find a transitional economic philosophy to fit in its ideological framework without compromising its social and political positions and alienating its supporters. A Hindu economic system would probably have to wait for a dominant Hindu Rashtra. It required something to counter the new wave of liberalization and globalization. It would be years before Narendra Modi would demonstrate a new framework in Gujarat that seamlessly merged Hindutva with big business. Modi would also show how communication and a certain salesmanship were key to the success of this model. It would fundamentally change the RSS's perspective and prepare it for a new century. Back in the early 1990s, however, it was still struggling to negotiate the socio-economic churn while maintaining the political course.

*

Around the time the RSS was taking a stand against Congress's policy of an open economy and faster integration with global markets, a storm was gathering in Bombay, India's commercial capital and the first stop for anyone wanting to do business in the country. The metropolis and Maharashtra state were business friendly and known for a consumer-oriented culture. Bombay was one of the only two cities in the country where a private company—Tata Power Company—supplied electricity. The other was the West Bengal capital Calcutta where supplier Calcutta Electricity Supply Corporation (CESC) was a private utility. Maharashtra was then, like most other states, ruled by the Congress. The state government in the early 1990s was headed first by Congressman Sudhakarrao Naik and then Sharad Pawar, one of the shrewdest politicians independent India had seen.

An early bird to explore opportunities in India as soon as it opened up was American power behemoth Enron Corporation. It made its pitch in May 1992 when the Union power secretary visited the US to solicit investments in the sector. Within a month of that pitch, Enron signed a memorandum of understanding (MoU) with the Maharashtra State Electricity Board (MSEB) to build a massive power plant near a small fishing village called Dabhol on the Konkan coast. Its partners in the project were American giants General Electric (GEC), which would supply the generators, and Bechtel, which would build the plant.

The project would be the RSS's and SJM's baptism with the travails of dealing with modern businesses. This was the era of giant MNCs where state power and private economic interests were often perfectly aligned. Although India was a sovereign state and a huge, hungry market, those who ran the country were novices at dealing with powerful corporations. For decades, the mere sight of politicians hobnobbing with businessmen raised eyebrows. Except perhaps Mahatma Gandhi, no politician worth his salt was able to carry off proximity to industrialists lightly.

Ravindra Mahajan was running a business consultancy firm when Enron entered India. A trained power engineer, Mahajan instinctively knew that the project was going to be a disaster for the state. Mahajan had earlier worked with Larsen and Toubro (L&T) and GEC. In 1973, he had left his engineer's job at L&T to run the Deendayal Upadhyaya Research Institute in Delhi. He left the Institute when Emergency was imposed and rejoined L&T. He later quit and started a consulting firm. Having worked in the power sector, Mahajan was familiar with the technologies available and costs involved. Sharad Pawar had pitched to the people that as the country opened up, new industries would be established and demand for electricity would increase substantially. The money to set up new power plants would have to come from private investors.

By 1993, Enron had signed a power purchase agreement with MSEB, an exclusive contract under which the state utility will be the sole customer for Dabhol Power Company. It was the first taste for an Indian state in doing business with a multinational on seemingly free market principles. The agreement was confidential and loaded in the company's favour as future events would testify.

Mahajan, who was then the co-convenor of the newly formed Swadeshi Jagran Manch, wrote an article in the Sangh weekly mouthpiece, *Vivek*, criticizing the project. He argued that while state-owned Bharat Heavy Electrical Limited (BHEL) set up thermal power plants at a cost of about Rs 1 crore per megawatt capacity, the Dabhol project would cost about Rs 4.5 crore per megawatt. 'We found a similar project being built in England [Teesside] by Enron that was costing only about a third of what DPC was proposing,' Mahajan said in an interview.

Gradually, opposition to the project began building up and SJM was at the forefront of the agitation. It was the first big issue it had landed, and it was fighting alongside leftist organizations who were also opposed to economic liberalization and entry of multinational corporations. Mahajan's expertise in the power sector took him to left-organized forums even though they were ideologically opposed to the RSS. This was common cause.[53]

The Sangh put its organizational might behind the anti-Enron campaign. At a meeting at Vrindavan to chalk out the RSS's annual agenda, the Mumbai *prant*, or province, listed anti-Enron agitation as its top priority. It was enthusiastically endorsed by the leadership, including then general secretary, H.V. Sheshadri.[54] Mumbai secretary Surendra Thatte was personally leading the protests. Before plunging into the agitation, which had already been started by left parties and independent activists, Thatte met Sheshadri and Thengadi in Delhi. Both gave their blessings to join the anti-Enron campaign. He camped in Guhagarh, a small village near the plant site to organize local communities and lead protests and agitations. Soon, the RSS cadre in Maharashtra became fully invested in the campaign.[55]

The project was estimated to displace 2000 people whose land was acquired. Many of them refused to accept compensation in protest. The project, locals also feared, would pollute fresh water as well as marine life affecting local fishing communities.

The protests were brutally put down and activists were jailed. Thatte was among those who went to jail. A Human Rights Watch investigation said:

> The Dabhol Power Corporation and its parent company, Enron, are complicit in these human rights violations. Enron's local entity, the Dabhol Power Corporation, benefited directly from an official policy of suppressing dissent through misuse of the law, harassment of anti-Enron protest leaders and prominent environmental activists, and police practices ranging from arbitrary to brutal.[56]

It also found categorical evidence that Enron was paying the government directly, specifically to police the protests, and that it was also lending the police its helicopters. Amnesty International found 'suppression of local protests' and said that people who protested against Enron, however peacefully, were liable to 'harassment, arbitrary arrest, preventive detention under the ordinary criminal law and ill-treatment'.[57]

The Houston-based multinational became the stormy petrel in the elections to a coastal state in western India. Globalization had truly come to roost in Indian politics in the elections of 1995 as the allied opposition of the Shiv Sena and BJP turned Enron into the hottest issue of the campaign. There were widespread allegations of possible corruption.

BJP president L.K. Advani called it 'Enron business school' where politicians had been 'educated'.[58] His statement came after Linda F. Powers, Enron's vice president (global finance), testifying before a US Congressional subcommittee on foreign operations, had said the company had spent about $20 million on the education and development process alone. She explained that specialists had worked on issues like electricity sales, fuel supply, environment, site acquisition and permits and approvals.[59]

The Shiv Sena–BJP alliance coasted to power in March 1995. Within two months, the government appointed a cabinet subcommittee headed by deputy chief minister Gopinath Munde to review the Dabhol power project. Munde had, during the election campaign, said, 'We will throw the Enron project in the Arabian sea.' In August, the government scrapped the project, acting on the recommendation of the Munde Committee. Hundreds of activists from the left and right were overjoyed. They had finally won. Or so they thought.

'We will not be dictated by giant powers or power giants,' Advani said. The BJP was already sensing that Enron, and by extension, the Congress government's economic policies could be a potentially rewarding national election issue. *India Today* wrote that the left and the National Front, ever ready to inveigh at Western multinationals, cheered the decision of an ideological camp they otherwise considered untouchable.

For the Sangh Parivar this was an opportunity like the Emergency. It was an issue free from communal tones where a broad political consensus could be built, perhaps even electoral allies gained, to take on the Congress at the national level. Ever since the Ram Janmabhoomi movement had started, the parivar had been accused of playing dangerous communal politics. That could be somewhat balanced and some goodwill regained. Now its government in Maharashtra was showing why it was a party with a difference. Even political rivals grudgingly acknowledged it.

The Munde panel said the previous government committed 'a grave impropriety by resorting to private negotiations' and whatever Enron wanted was 'granted without demur'. Its report critiqued both the process by which the project had been developed and the terms of the deal. It found that the initial memorandum of understanding was rushed and 'one-sided', condemned the absence of competitive bids and lack of transparency in the process, critiqued subsequent changes to the project design as addressing 'only the concerns of Enron', and found that Enron was given undue favours and concessions.[60]

The report also found that the capital costs of the project were inflated, that the rates for the power would be much higher than justified, in part because the contract was based on US dollars (placing the risk of currency fluctuations on the state), that there were outstanding environmental questions, and that the project would adversely affect Maharashtra.

Chief Minister Manohar Joshi said:

> From the speed with which the memorandum of understanding was signed it seemed as if Enron came, it saw, and it conquered. The proposed capital investment in the project is definitely more than it should have been, and there is uncertainty about many components of the power purchase agreement resulting in payment of an unjustified rate which is higher than other comparable projects and therefore the project, in its current form, is not in the interest of the state.[61]

It was believed that the Munde Committee had outsourced most of the work to the SJM. S. Gurumurthy, national co-convener of the forum and Sangh ideologue, had released a report prepared by the outfit. *India Today*'s Sunil Jain said the final Munde Committee report was a toned-down version of the first draft, which was prepared along with Gurumurthy. While the report did not use all the figures in the SJM report, it based its conclusions on them.

The cabinet subcommittee report shared the language and content of the one released by Gurumurthy. The only difference in the text was that the Munde version avoided specifics and tried to sound more reasonable about the cancellation. Gurumurthy charged that state bureaucrats 'deliberately diluted' the draft. The report, quoting a senior BJP member, said Munde had to accept the changes as 'the pressure was too much'.[62]

Within twenty-four hours of the Maharashtra government scrapping the project, the Dabhol Power Company gave it notice for arbitration seeking $300 million compensation. The Maharashtra government countered it by going to court to scrap the agreement alleging fraud and misrepresentation. Chief minister Manohar Joshi, however, indicated that the government may be open to talks.

In November, Enron's high-profile CEO Rebecca Mark visited India to salvage the project. Mark met with Shiv Sena supremo Bal Thackeray, the only man in the state who needed to be on their side. He once famously said in an interview that he held the remote control of the government.[63]

Within a week of the meeting the government constituted a committee to renegotiate the contract. The project was on the road to revival. In January 1996, the Maharashtra government announced that it would accept a revised agreement. The new agreement expanded Phase I of the project from 695 megawatts to 740 megawatts and committed the state to an additional 1320-megawatt Phase II (under the initial agreement, the state was bound only to the Phase I portion). As MSEB was still committed to buying 90 per cent of the plant's output and covering the risk of currency fluctuations, the expansion increased the financial risk to the state under the revised agreement.[64]

That summer, Indian politics took another turn when the first BJP-led government was sworn into office at the centre. It was just what the Shiv Sena–BJP government in Maharashtra needed. The revision of the agreement with Enron meant that a counter-guarantee given by the Central government to the project would become void. India's first government led by a full-time RSS swayamsevak lasted only for thirteen days. But on its last day in office, 27 May 1996, before it stepped out of the door, the cabinet cleared a crucial item on the agenda: Extension of the counter-guarantee given to Enron's Dabhol Power Company by the previous government on 15 September 1994. If the previous assurance was only for the first phase, the Vajpayee government gave a counter-guarantee for the entire project—the 740-MW Phase I and 1320-MW Phase II. It was one of the biggest volte faces the country had seen.[65]

The counter-guarantee reportedly given at the insistence of Pramod Mahajan and Gopinath Munde. Mahajan is said to have convinced the other leaders that not honouring the agreement would affect the country's credibility just when it had embraced globalization. Crucially, foreign investors would shun India, denying the country—which had barely stabilized after the balance of payment crisis of 1991—much-needed capital for growth and development.[66]

The party with a difference whose economic ideology rested on the pillar of swadeshi had begun to succumb to the pressures of modern power politics in which big money and global linkages played a crucial part.

It was a blow from which the SJM never really recovered. Nor did many in the Sangh, like Thatte. The activists on the ground who had opposed the project, however, remained determined. They protested against the BJP government that renegotiated the project. The RSS had, for all practical purposes, pulled the plug on the agitation.

Ravindra Mahajan remembers that whenever they raised the issue with top BJP leaders, they would come up with some lame excuse. The BJP justified the decision saying it was a matter of honouring a contractual obligation and it would affect the country's credibility at a time when it was trying to woo foreign investment. 'It severely dented the credibility of the SJM,' says Mahajan.[67] RSS had no compulsions as the BJP.

Yet, General Secretary Sheshadri gave orders to swayamsevaks to stop agitating against the Enron project. Two senior Sangh pracharaks separately confirmed that Sheshadri had spoken at RSS camps in Maharashtra about Enron and made it clear that the organization was not supporting the campaign any longer.

'Sheshadriji asked me to jump from the seventh floor. I jumped. Now when I've fallen to the third floor, he was asking me to stop. How is that possible?' Thatte said, questioning the RSS's decision. Thatte saw it not only as opportunism but a negation of the fundamental principles on which the RSS stood. 'Doctorji used to say, once you have taken up a work, don't stop until you finish it.' It was also a negation of the principle often repeated in the Sangh that it was far away from politics and power. 'We should not care if our government does not come to power. We are not because of the government but because of our workers. But Sangh acted like Dhritarashtra in the matter,' Thatte lamented, invoking the blind king and father of the Kauravas in the epic Mahabharata.

The Thatte family lives by the values of the Sangh. Photographs of Golwalkar and Hedgewar hang prominently in the living room of his small suburban Mumbai home. His son was all of seventeen when he went to Ayodhya to participate in the Ram Janmabhoomi agitation. But now he was done with the Sangh. He decided to quit despite his friends trying to dissuade him. Senior RSS leader Bal Apte sought to arrange a meeting for him with the then sarsanghchalak Rajendra Singh when he came to Mumbai. Singh refused. He said, 'If it is about Enron, I don't want to meet.'

Thatte was asked to first go slow on the agitation when the election campaign was on. He refused and instead sent his resignation to the prant sanghchalak. Once he quit, he was treated like an outcast. 'We had done so much of groundwork. We camped in Guhagarh and Dabhol for months. Once we jointly agitated with Medha Patkar.' During one of the protests, Thatte was arrested and put in Sangli jail for fifteen days. 'Nobody from the RSS came to visit me. We asked a chartered accountant friend who was also a swayamsevak to meet in jail. A Sangh *adhikari* [official] later asked him to explain why he came to visit me.'[68]

At an Idea Exchange programme with Marathi newspaper *Lok Satta* in September 2012, Mohan Bhagwat faced a question: 'The RSS vehemently opposed Enron but changed its stand when the Sena–BJP combine came to power. [Why?] Bhagwat's reply was evasive. 'I was not there so I will not answer this. But one thing is sure. The basis on which we opposed Enron, if there is a need to do so again, we will.'[69]

The opening up of the economy, however, changed all that.

So far, Thengadi had complete sway over the Sangh's thought process as far as economic policies were concerned. A kshetra pracharak in the north-east in the 1990s who has since given up positions in the Sangh offers a glimpse of the conceptual muddle when he says the RSS could not cope with the post-liberalization changes. He disagreed with Thengadi's position that computerization would kill jobs. Thengadi could never offer a workable swadeshi alternative either. As a result, contradictions abounded. In July 1996, the Keshav Cooperative Bank started functioning in Delhi's Karol Bagh. The bank's website says its establishment was inspired by RSS ideologue Bhaurao Deoras. It proudly states that it offered computerized savings and current accounts from day one which helped it serve its customers better.[70]

The pracharak said that at the time he blindly followed the Sangh because he was a disciplined volunteer and knew only what was taught in the RSS. 'So we too opposed multinationals, automation, FDI [foreign direct investment], etc. We did not have any idea. Neither did stalwarts like Thengadi. They were stuck in their old ways of thinking. Sangh usually opposes everything in the beginning but then starts adopting it itself once it gains traction in the world.' He points to the example of foreign investment which the RSS earlier opposed. 'Now the government is allowing it in even retail and the Sangh is silent.'[71]

In a famous story told and retold by Thengadi's disciples in the Sangh, when Golwalkar was mulling about starting a labour union, he gave the job to Thengadi. He asked him to join a trade union to study how they worked. Following the advice, Thengadi joined the Indian National Trade Union Congress (INTUC). He stayed in the union for a year, before leaving to start the BMS. It was the third affiliate set up by the Sangh in 1955, after the ABVP in 1948 and the Jana Sangh in 1951. After 1991, the quartet of BMS, BKS, ABVP and SJM became the primary instruments of RSS's cut and thrust.

In 1995, the RSS held a review meeting in Nagpur where the political and economic situation in the country was analysed. It was attended by about 100 top leaders and intellectuals of the parivar. Towards the end, the then general secretary H.V. Sheshadri suggested that it was not enough critiquing the reforms and globalization as had been the case through most of the discussions. Sheshadri wanted the parivar to develop an alternative economic path. The job was entrusted to the SJM.

The forum created an action group to prepare a road map for development according to Indian ethos. The group wrote a draft which was first tabled at the BMS national executive held in 1996. Every paragraph of the draft was debated, and corrections and additions made. It was later taken to the ABVP national executive. The SJM central committee had already cleared it. Since it was expected to be the defining document of the RSS's economic policy it was decided that all the mass organizations of the Sangh should discuss and debate it. A day-long meeting was organized in Patna under the leadership of Mohan Bhagwat, who was then based there as kshetra pracharak. Every line of the document was discussed threadbare and amendments made until everyone cleared it.

The final outcome was titled *Bharat ka Abhyuday: Swadeshi Rooprekha* (loosely translated as a swadeshi blueprint for India's rise), and it was meant to be a concept and plan of action for integrated development. It was translated into English and further fine-tuned by the Chennai-based chartered accountant S. Gurumurthy, the Sangh's go-to ideologue for all matters related to the economy and finance. Gurumurthy was then also the national co-convener of the SJM. Both the drafts were released for national debate at the SJM's biennial national conference in Varanasi in 1997.

By the time the SJM held its next national conference towards the end of 1998 at Amritsar, the Vajpayee government had returned to power. When some of those who drafted the plan called for its review, no one seemed to be interested. The painstakingly developed conceptual framework and action plan to rebuild the nation simply disappeared from memory.[72]

The swadeshi plan identified both capitalism and communism as the 'same content in two containers'; both resulting in a drift towards consumerism and exploitation of the environment. 'While capitalism solely rests on market and state as the twin socio-economic delivery systems, socialism primarily rests on the state as the delivery system,' it said. 'In contrast, the swadeshi thought relies on the social institutional order, besides market and state as the economic delivery system … Stated in simple terms, swadeshi rejects materialistic and imperialistic homogenization and aimless transnationalism of the western assumption.'

The draft document had taken up cudgels against globalization and economic liberalization that India had embarked upon in 1991. While Manmohan Singh had seen liberal economy as an idea whose time had come, the Sangh Parivar saw it as an invitation to mercenary multinational corporations. 'Business is war—so a war strategy is needed,' the plan had declared. 'The nation must understand that global commerce is nothing less than a war. It is not just competition for markets, goods and money; it is a socio-political and economic-cultural power game. It is as much a game of deception as any war. In philosophical terms, it is the glorification and legitimization of lust and greed and temporal power,' it added.

It said there was no alternative but to have an 'offensive-cum-defensive' strategy to meet the challenge of globalization, including actively putting up non-tariff barriers. The swadeshi path and action plan suggested focusing on villages and small towns. The three essential ingredients of the plan included relieving people of 'state-dependent mindset and making them self-reliant'; community life as a socio-economic safety net and using 'temples, other places of worship and dharmic institutions' to offer social security.[73]

The BJP-led NDA government however had other ideas. Vajpayee had warned earlier that he would pursue swadeshi economics only if it was possible for him to do so. When he inaugurated the SJM's Swadeshi mela in early 1999, he had said: 'We are all part of the same family. It's good that you have come up with the idea but if I can't execute them, I'll say sorry.'[74]

Signs of dissonance between the parivar and the government were visible within months of its swearing in and clashes were not uncommon. Universal employment is one of the keystones of Deendayal Upadhyaya's economic philosophy. After the Atal Bihari Vajpayee government returned to power in 1998, Mahesh Sharma, who was instrumental in drafting the economic development concept—'Rebuilding the Nation'—two years before, got a request from the PMO to send in policy suggestions. Accordingly, Sharma and Sudheendra Kulkarni drew up a note for the prime minister.[75]

That Independence Day, from the ramparts of the Red Fort in Delhi, Vajpayee announced:

> Removal of unemployment is an important pledge in our National Agenda ... Government has decided that ten crore people should get employment opportunities over the next ten years. This means that every year one crore people should get employment opportunities. A task force will be set up for this purpose and it will present its report soon.[76]

Soon after, Sharma got a call from the Planning Commission seeking his consent to be a member of a task force on job generation. When Sharma received the full list of panel members, he found to his shock that Montek Singh Ahluwalia, a staunch advocate of globalization and liberalization, was heading it. He also saw that Dattopant Thengadi was included as a member.

Sharma got in touch with Thengadi and asked him whether he had given his consent to be a member of a panel headed by Ahluwalia. Thengadi, who had no idea of the task force, wrote an angry letter to Vajpayee. In it, he described Ahluwalia as 'a person who has never lived in a village nor knows anything about the problems faced by the people residing in villages'.[77] The very act of his appointment to the position showed that the government was not serious about finding real solutions to problems that needed to be addressed by the task force, he said.

By mid-1999 the government had fallen and got re-elected with a better mandate in the second national elections in as many years. Later that year the RSS held a *chintan baithak* (a brainstorming session) for taking stock and formulating long-term action plans. On 14 December, at the end of the session, RSS joint general secretary K.S. Sudarshan said the organization was unhappy with the functioning of the BJP-led NDA government. Several people, including BJP president Khushabhau Thakre and prominent leaders such as K.N. Govindacharya, Dattopant Thengadi and Narendra Modi, concurred with the view.

The complaint was that the Vajpayee government was giving in to immediate constraints, including pressures from international agencies, without considering the long-term implications. Sudarshan cited the government's decision of introducing the Insurance Regulatory Authority (IRA) Bill, the ban on sale of common salt and the move to allow 100 per cent foreign investment in the manufacture of cigarettes as issues the RSS did not agree with.[78]

By the end of the year, the BJP had made a commitment to economic reforms, including opening up more to foreign capital. By December, the government introduced a bill allowing foreign investors into the insurance sector.

It would have seemed to the parivar as a deliberate snub considering its swadeshi plan had specifically warned: 'It should be ensured that the Western, and particularly the American, health insurance system which has enslaved the public to the clique of pharmaceutical companies, medical institutions and insurance companies, does not set its foot in India.'[79]

The Vajpayee government continued its economic liberalization policies and the Sangh Parivar its vocal protests. Yashwant Sinha, who was then finance minister, considers himself a staunch swadeshi proponent. He had spoken about swadeshi often from the SJM platform. Before the BJP government came to power, RSS and BJP leaders regularly discussed economic issues. There was convergence on most matters but also divergence of opinion on some. Before he finalized the 1998 budget, Sinha consulted the RSS leadership. They wanted him to present a swadeshi budget. An 8 per cent surcharge on imports introduced in that budget was called a swadeshi measure by the media but Sinha insists that it was merely to raise revenue. Anyhow, the surcharge was reduced to 4 per cent.

It was the first of the budget proposals that Sinha had to reverse. Many others would follow, earning him the nickname 'Rollback Sinha'.[80] Sinha argues that an economically strong and secure India was a sine qua non for swadeshi. His views were, however, not appreciated by proponents of swadeshi and he was seen as a supporter of liberalization, privatization and globalization.

Raising a war cry against the WTO, the IMF, the World Bank and the Union government for anti-labour, anti-farmer and anti-poor policies, the Bharatiya Mazdoor Sangh, trade union wing of the Sangh Parivar, warned the BJP-led NDA government to either correct these policies to protect the sovereignty of the nation and interests of its people, or face the wrath of the masses. The BMS demanded the scrapping of the Enron agreement and reversal of the policy of privatization of PSUs. It demanded a probe into the Enron deal and probes into the privatization of Modern Food Industries and aluminium producer Bharat Aluminium Company Ltd. (BALCO).

Addressing a rally at Ramlila Maidan in Delhi to mark the beginning of a 'mass movement' against the WTO and the 'anti-labour policies' of the Central government, Dattopant Thengadi bitterly criticized the NDA government for its 'anti-national and anti-people policies'. He accused it of betrayal for giving in to the threats of economically powerful nations and in the process sacrificing national interests.

That those leading the government happened to be friends would not deter the BMS from opposing the government, Thengadi said; the BMS only preached and practised the objective policies of responsive cooperation. 'We will oppose the government which opposes the interests of the nation, people and its workers. We oppose multinationals. We will oppose the government which supports multinationals.' To the charge that the Sangh Parivar was bent on unseating its own government, Thengadi said, 'Our rally will not push out the government. The government is pushing itself out. If it goes, it will go because of its wrong policies. Governments have come and gone in the past too.'

Thengadi said they were hoping that the government would resist the threat of sanctions from powerful nations controlling the WTO. This had not happened. Instead of succumbing to such pressures and diktats, the government, he said, should challenge these nations to enforce sanctions. 'We might suffer initially, for about a year and a half at the maximum, and then the economy would prosper again.' His logic was that 'America needs India more than India needs America'; if Vietnam could bring such a powerful country to its knees, India could do it too.[81]

It was perhaps an overestimation of India's position in international power equations and underappreciating the global realpolitik of a unipolar world.

At the BMS's twelfth national convention in Nagpur, Thengadi again attacked the government and Vajpayee viciously. He described Prime Minister Vajpayee as a 'petty politician playing into the hands of his policy advisers with doubtful credentials'. He said previous governments had blindly followed globalization policies on the dictates of the Western powers. It was hoped that the Vajpayee government would be different, but it had belied the expectations of nationalist forces on the economic front. 'We do not see which government is in power. We only look at the policies, if they are compatible with our idea of swadeshi. Our English educated people easily fall for Western propaganda. They start believing that only Western thought and technologies are good.'[82]

These views mirrored those of leftist commentators. Writing on Rediff.com in 1998, Bengal politician and highly regarded Marxist economist, Ashok Mitra, said, '…sooner rather than later, hemmed in on all fronts, the BJP-led government will totally capitulate to the G-8 nations and the World Bank-IMF combine … The videshis will take charge of the economy lock, stock and barrel; with no sign of discomfort, our government will call that a great swadeshi conquest.'[83]

Sarsanghchalak Sudarshan had made the Sangh's position on these issues clear but also said that the BJP being in a coalition had to keep in mind certain sensibilities. Sudarshan was once asked: If India was shining, wasn't it the result of globalization? How would it go along with our swadeshi ideology? Sudarshan explained in detail: 'We have a clear concept of privatization. Business is not the government's business. There is a saying in Gujarat that if the king gets into business, the subjects will end up in poverty. The government should only be in projects related to national security. The rest should be left to the people … We are not opposed to globalization. We are opposed to the entry of multinational companies that destroy our economy.' He believed Indian firms were globally competitive and organizations like the Swadeshi Jagran Manch were fighting for equal treatment for domestic companies. He wanted to stop developed countries' agenda at forums like the WTO.[84]

Despite all the criticism, the Vajpayee government, with little experience of administration, continued with liberalization. Vajpayee rarely responded. He would show the RSS leaders respect but set his own course.[85] Yet, there was little understanding in the Sangh Parivar about the balancing act the government was doing. They had no experience or clear understanding how international capital flowed and global trade worked.

Vajpayee had ordered nuclear tests after he came to power in 1998, inviting international sanctions but collecting high praise from nationalists. The Narasimha Rao government had come on the verge of conducting the tests, but the Americans got wind of it and he shelved it under pressure from the Bill Clinton administration.[86] The tests codenamed Operation Shakti were seen as a show of strength by a resurgent India under a nationalist government, never mind the competing tests by Pakistan and delicate security situation created by the move. Jingoism seeped into economic issues as well, but Vajpayee showed that he understood the importance of robust institutions.

As soon as the government returned to power, one of the first comments by two cabinet ministers was that the new regime wanted a strong rupee. A strong rupee reflected the nation's strength, they said. A shocked Bimal Jalan, then RBI governor, caught the next flight to Delhi and met the prime minister and explained to him how such comments affected market perception and if the government wanted a strong rupee it should convince the markets. Vajpayee immediately called a meeting of his ministers at home and asked Jalan to explain the nuances of international financial markets to the ministers.[87]

The RBI was still perfecting a system of managing the currency. Once when the rupee was plummeting, the RBI attempted to arrest the fall and lost 20 per cent of its reserves in one day. There was no way it could fight the combined might of the market. Gradually, it fine-tuned its strategy. It would never intervene directly, only through SBI or some other bank. It would also not intervene when the exchange rate was going up. It would wait for the market to become nervous and then intervene by selling or buying dollars until it found the targeted level. It never bought or sold at round figures which is where traders expected the bank to step in. It would always buy at fractions. For instance, if the exchange rate was Rs 40 for a dollar and the market expected the RBI target to be Rs 41, it would come in when the rate was Rs 40.7 or 41.1 but never at Rs 41 or 40. It was ingenious and highly effective. Such nuances were lost even on stalwarts of the party who had little idea of how international markets functioned and the impact of global financial flows on the country.[88]

After the nuclear tests, India could have returned to the financial conditions of the late 1980s. Immediately after the tests, a consortium of donors to India suspended aid to the tune of $3 billion. The World Bank held back a loan of $800 million and Overseas Private Investment Corporation that funds private investors paused on its commitments. About 200 government companies, departments and agencies such as the Defence Research and Development Organisation (DRDO), the Department of Atomic Energy (DAE), BHEL, Bharat Earth Movers Ltd (BEML) and the Indian Space Research Organisation (ISRO), could not source technology from international sellers. The sanctions also punished several private firms such as Godrej and Boyce and L&T.[89]

To ride out the sanctions, the Vajpayee government extended olive branches. It gave eleven oil exploration and a majority of thirty-four onshore mineral exploration licences to US companies. India continued to open up its economy but in a calibrated manner. Foreign direct investment (FDI) was allowed in many sectors and the government sold off several of its companies such as telecom carrier Videsh Sanchar Nigam Limited (VSNL) and chemical maker NOCIL.

The economy was again in trouble after the Asian crisis, the Economic Advisory Council (EAC) was expanded with the prime minister himself heading it, and a twelve-member Council for Trade and Industry was appointed. The EAC had heavyweights such as I.G. Patel, former RBI governor, P.N. Dhar, a former secretary in Indira's PMO, and noted economists Arjun Sengupta, Amaresh Bagchi, Ashok Desai, Montek Singh Ahluwalia, Kirit Parekh and G.V. Ramakrishna—along with Vajpayee's principal secretary Brajesh Mishra and secretary in the PMO, N.K. Singh.

At a meeting of the EAC in July 2002, Vajpayee unveiled an economic agenda for 8 per cent growth—featuring plans to provide 10 million job opportunities annually, retarget subsidies and spending, push economic reforms, and better implement policies and improve execution. Through this period, the finance ministry remained dominant in economic policymaking.[90]

The Vajpayee government embarked on one of the most ambitious infrastructure projects undertaken in the country—building a network of highways called the Golden Quadrilateral which connected Delhi, Mumbai, Chennai and Kolkata, and several other industrial towns en route, across thirteen states.

'The Indian government has begun a 15-year project to widen and pave some 40,000 miles of narrow, decrepit national highways, with the first leg, budgeted at $6.25 billion, to be largely complete by next year. It amounts to the most ambitious infrastructure project since independence in 1947 and the British building of the subcontinent's railway network the century before,' the *New York Times* evocatively described the highway construction project. It compared the project with the United States' construction of its national highway system in the 1920s and 1950s which fuelled commerce and development, fed a nation's auto obsession and created suburbs. 'They also displaced communities and helped sap mass transit and deplete inner cities.' The newspaper warned that India would face similar results. 'At its heart, the redone highway is about grafting Western notions of speed and efficiency onto a civilization that has always taken the long view.'[91]

Vajpayee perhaps took the advice of Deendayal Upadhyaya who wanted India to focus on roads instead of railways. Upadhyaya, who was an advocate of decentralization, believed that railways encouraged centralization. He wanted a liberal regime for automobiles and expansion of roads.[92]

Before the Vajpayee government, such an ambitious project was last undertaken by Sher Shah Suri in the sixteenth century when he rebuilt and extended the Mauryan-era Grand Trunk Road linking Kabul to Chittagong. It helped the movement of men and material from beyond the Hindu Kush mountains to the plains of India and the eventual domination of the subcontinent by the Mughals until the eighteenth century when the British brought by sea, European political thought, trading practices and the steam engine.[93]

The Sangh Parivar under-appreciated the delicate balance of the economy at the time. According to a senior Sangh leader, there was mistrust about Vajpayee's cabinet colleagues and powerful bureaucrats such as Brajesh Mishra and N.K. Singh. This was also because the RSS claimed ownership of its swayamsevaks and it could not come to terms with the fact that Vajpayee and company were not acting subservient to it. Although they had a comfortable relationship with Finance Minister Yashwant Sinha, it evaporated rather quickly. They also looked at Jaswant Singh's friendship with US diplomat Strobe Talbott with deep suspicion. It was as if outsiders had hijacked not just their government, but also their swayamsevaks.

Perhaps the Sangh's suspicions were not totally misplaced. In March 2001, *Outlook* magazine ran a cover story alleging that the all-powerful PMO was favouring certain companies and corporate groups: 'It started in 1998 with Singh's ascendancy to the PMO. It has got worse today. Mishra and Singh constitute the powerful arms of the PMO, which has now become an imperial power centre, riding roughshod over the bureaucracy and foisting controversial decisions on various ministries without so much as consulting them.'[94]

The article alleged favouritism in telecom licences and counter-guarantees to power projects. It also said the PMO was pushing for international contracts that could ultimately become an economic burden on the country. In July 2000, K.N. Govindacharya, who was then a BJP general secretary, presided over an SJM meeting in Agra where he called for a second freedom struggle against the government's economic policies.[95]

The RSS did not escape criticism either. In fact, the Sangh was perceived to be siding with big business houses. Sarsanghchalak Sudarshan defended it saying the Sangh did not want foreign companies to listen in on Indians' telephone conversations![96]

It was, however, a period of expansion across the world as exuberant consumption in the US and European economies drove rapid growth in developing economies, especially in Asia, where entire countries offered themselves as production centres for the Western markets to create local jobs and raise incomes. India too enjoyed the boom and new-age entrepreneurs launched scores of start-ups backed by abundantly available private capital. Even state-owned companies like oil giant Oil and Natural Gas Corporation (ONGC) made bold forays buying foreign oilfields and striking billion-dollar deals. Telecom companies Bharat Sanchar Nigam Limited (BSNL) and Mahanagar Telephone Nigam Limited (MTNL) went on a massive expansion, competing hard with private operators such as Airtel, Orange and British Physical Laboratories (BPL). Cut-throat competition benefited the middle class who saw companies falling over one another to offer better products and services at competitive prices. A sense of prosperity pervaded urban India. It was misleading.

At internal meetings of the Sangh, leaders continued to fret and fume. They were unhappy with the BJP's Shining India election campaign.

During the Vajpayee years, India's GDP growth rate fluctuated wildly. It grew 7.5 per cent in 1996 but fell to 4.05 per cent the next year. It steadily rose over the next two years and peaked at 8.8 per cent in 1999 before plummeting to 3.8 per cent in 2000. It languished at that level for a couple of years before recovering to near 8 per cent in 2003 and 2004. Of course, those were the years when Asia was hit by a currency crisis and India was restricted by economic sanctions following nuclear tests.[97]

*

Voters rejected the Vajpayee government in the May 2004 elections. Manmohan Singh, the man who piloted the 1991 reforms, became the prime minister after Congress president Sonia Gandhi, deferring to her 'inner voice', stepped aside to make way for the economist and architect of economic reforms of 1991.

Although the Congress was the largest party in the Lok Sabha, it did not have a majority. It led a coalition of parties which included the DMK and the CPI(M). The United Progressive Alliance government operated on a pre-decided common minimum programme. Even though it was a Congress government supported by the left, many of the programmes it launched would have warmed the cockles of Deendayal Upadhyaya.

In *Bharatiya Arth-Niti: Vikas ki ek Disha*, Upadhyaya elaborates his vision for a domestic economic policy based on Indian conditions and traditions. One of the key pillars of policy in his view is employment guarantee, something P. Chidambaram's budget of 2004–05 introduced in the form of the National Rural Employment Guarantee Act.

Upadhyaya says work for everyone is a parameter of economic democracy as much as a vote for each person is a measure of political democracy. He considers right to work an integral part of democracy and puts the onus on the state to make it happen. If a person doesn't earn a fair proportion of the national income in exchange for work, it is equal to not being employed at all. Minimum wage, equitable distribution and a social security system is an inalienable right of a citizen from his perspective. Upadhyaya advocates full employment instead of trying to reduce unemployment to make the most of India's bulging workforce, 64 per cent of which is underutilized. Male agricultural labourers in villages remain unemployed for ninety-eight days in a year. Even farmers are out of work for about three months. The nature of work for many workers is seasonal, keeping them unemployed for the rest of the year. These workers must be provided with gainful employment.[98]

This was precisely the logic on which the National Rural Employment Guarantee Programme was designed.

The main thrust of Finance Minister P. Chidambaram's budget was providing universal access to quality basic education and health; generating gainful employment in agriculture, manufacturing and services, and promoting investment, all of which Upadhyaya would have approved. It seemed like the Congress government was more in tune with the RSS ideologue than its own pracharaks in power.

*

While the Vajpayee government could not win the approval of the Sangh, another pracharak was making some moves in the western state of Gujarat which would become a template for rulers across the country.

Narendra Modi was friends with many businessmen from his state even during his pracharak days. Delhi-based journalist Sharad Gupta, who frequently met Modi when he was stationed in the capital as the party general secretary, remembers that he always had two mobile phones at a time when the device itself was a rarity. He also frequently changed them. One day, Gupta complemented Modi for acquiring the latest gadgets. Modi replied that those were gifts from Gujarati businessmen. Gupta joked, 'Next time give me your old phone when you change. Even they are the latest.' Pat came the reply, 'You don't know Gujarati businessmen. When they give a new phone, they take back the old one!'[99] Although it was mere banter, Modi's friendship with several Gujarati businessmen was very real. These businessmen stood firmly behind him when he was going through tough times.

Modi at the time also took a dim view of the RSS. Even though he had internalized the ideology, he seemed to disagree with its methods. He felt that the RSS was losing its relevance and did not stand for excellence. Modi believed the RSS was doing mediocre work. Despite the RSS running 20,000 schools and fifty newspapers and journals, none of them had achieved any measure of distinction, and its social work paled when compared with that of Sai Baba, the Radha Soami sect and Swadhaya group. Attendance at RSS shakhas was falling and in Kerala, where it had the maximum number of shakhas, it had no impact and the church and the communists were thriving.[100]

In late 2002, Modi dissolved the state assembly and went in for elections eight months before schedule. After an election campaign charged with Hindutva rhetoric, the BJP won a decisive victory, winning 127 of the 182 seats.

Exactly a year after the riots, the Confederation of Indian Industry (CII) organized a special session in Delhi titled 'Meeting with Narendra Modi, the New Chief Minister of Gujarat' at Modi's request. At the meeting, head of the automobile giant Bajaj, Rahul Bajaj, declared that 2002 was a lost year for Gujarat. 'Why don't we get investment in Kashmir, the north-east, or Uttar Pradesh and Bihar? It is not just the lack of infrastructure, but also the sense of insecurity. I hope this won't happen in Gujarat—all this comes to mind because of the unfortunate events last year,' Bajaj said. 'We would like to know what you believe in, what you stand for, because leadership is important. We are prepared to work with governments of all hues, but we also have our own views on what is good for our society and what works for it.'

When Modi's turn came, he replied icily, 'You and your pseudo-secular friends can come to Gujarat if you want an answer. Talk to my people. Gujarat is the most peaceful state in the country.' Modi continued, turning to Jamshyd Godrej and Bajaj: 'Others have vested interest in maligning Gujarat. What is your interest?'

On his return to Gujarat, Modi engineered a split in CII with a group of Gujarati businessmen, including Gautam Adani of Adani Group, Indravadan Modi of Cadila Pharmaceuticals, Karsan Patel of Nirma Group, and Anil Bakeri of Bakeri Engineers, setting up an organization called the Resurgent Group of Gujarat. It issued a press statement swearing by the pride of Gujaratis and demanded that the Gujarat chapter of the CII withdraw from the industry body. Finally, CII apologized in writing, after Arun Jaitley mediated with the chief minister on its behalf. 'We, in the CII, are very sorry for the hurt and pain you have felt, and I regret very much the misunderstanding that has developed since the 6th of February, the day of our meeting in New Delhi,' the apology read. Three months later, the CII helped Modi organize his first international meeting with investors, in Zurich, under the aegis of the World Economic Forum (WEF).[101]

In 2003, Modi organized a Global Investors' Summit branded Vibrant Gujarat. It would become the chief minister's signature biennial showpiece, copied by other state governments. The first summit, however, was a tepid affair, with less than seventy foreign businessmen attending. No big Indian industrialists participated. Mukesh Ambani skipped the event even though he was announced as participating. MoUs worth about Rs 66,000 crore were signed.

Deputy Prime Minister L.K. Advani attended, though he characterized his presence as coincidence as he was visiting the Somnath temple. He also struck a sour note when he lambasted the heavy security arrangements. 'Do not harass people in the name of security. Heavy security is unfriendly. Celebrations will lose their significance if people cannot participate in them whole-heartedly,' Advani said.[102]

The event was not big enough for Modi's liking. He wanted it to create a buzz, but that had not happened. He let it be known that he wanted none other than Ratan Tata, chairman of the Tata Group at the time, to attend the 2005 edition of the Summit. Modi's best officials were asked to move heaven and earth if need be to get Tata to Gandhinagar, according to a person who was coordinating some of the efforts from the chief minister's office. 'Niira Radia, who was then handling Tata group's external relations, was categorically told that he had to be there,' he said. Finally, Tata agreed.

Modi personally appointed a special protocol officer for Tata and put him up at the state guest house. Later, he greeted Tata with a hug and a broad smile and told him, 'This is where you belong.' Modi is said to have told Tata that he would have heard many things about him that he may not have liked. He had no issues with that, but he should not ignore the business opportunity in Gujarat. It paid off.[103]

A glowing testimonial from Tata appeared on the Vibrant Gujarat website soon after. 'Modi's leadership is exemplary, Gujarat will provide leadership beyond country.' Media magnate and chairman of the Zee Group, Subhash Chandra, called Modi the person who 'redefined politics, performance and principles'.[104]

The real coup that would burnish brand Modi came in 2008 even though he had laid the ground for it in 2007 itself. At the Vibrant Gujarat Summit in 2007, Modi suggested to Ratan Tata that he move the Nano mini-car project, which was facing headwinds in West Bengal, to Gujarat. He promised the most favourable terms.

Tata had by then warmed up to Modi and declared, 'You [as a businessman] are stupid if you are not in Gujarat.'[187] In October 2008, when Tata Motors decided to quit Bengal, Modi jumped at the opportunity, famously texting Ratan Tata, 'Welcome to Gujarat' and then rolled out the red carpet with hefty loans at soft rates and prime land at cheap prices. When the Tatas signed the memorandum of understanding with Gujarat to move the Nano car factory from Singur to Sanand, Modi remarked that to him it was not 'just a project'.[105]

It indeed was not. It was the biggest boost to brand Modi. In the next few years, Modi would position himself as the most dynamic chief minister in India who had transformed his state into an island of prosperity with record growth in agriculture, uninterrupted power supply and an unavoidable destination for businesses investment.

A leader with an RSS arm says there is no doubting Modi's credentials as a patriot and his wish to see India as a powerful nation. While the RSS and Modi concur on the ultimate goal, they have different views on how to achieve it. Modi believes that business runs the world and India needs to strike alliances with big business to become powerful. However, a large section of the RSS sees it as succumbing to Western, especially American, business interests.

They believe Deendayal Upadhyaya for the BJP is more a prop than a guide. At a meeting to chalk out the programmes for Deendayal centenary celebrations, some senior RSS leaders were horrified that BJP president Amit Shah was more interested in renaming the Mughalsarai railway station as Deendayal Upadhyaya station. 'Nobody was talking about *antyodaya* or any such policies to uplift the poor,' a person who attended the meeting said.[106]

A senior Sangh leader who was earlier part of the core group, which takes all the major decisions in the RSS, said he had lost hope that any government will be able to pursue sustainable economic policies suited for Indian conditions as long as they are focused on winning elections.[107]

*

When India threw its doors open to business it also invited in a concomitant problem—a sharp rise in inequality. From the time it became a republic and until 1980, the year Indira Gandhi was re-elected as prime minister, the bottom 50 per cent of the country's earning population captured 28 per cent of total growth, and incomes of this group grew faster than the average, while the top 0.1 per cent's incomes fell. In the next three and half decades, the situation reversed; the top 0.1 per cent of earners cornered 12 per cent of total growth compared to the bottom 50 per cent's share of 11 per cent. The top 0.1 per cent of income earners took away 29 per cent of total growth compared to the middle 40 per cent which got 23 per cent.[108]

On 20 May 2014, on his first day in Parliament as prime minister, Narendra Modi said:

> A government is one which thinks about the poor, listens to the poor and which exists for the poor. Therefore, the new government is dedicated to the poor, millions of youth and mothers and daughters who are striving for their respect and honour. Villagers, farmers, Dalits and the oppressed, this government is for them, for their aspirations and this is our responsibility.
>
> In this election, we stressed on two things—*sabka saath, sabka vikas* (in step with all, development for all). We want everyone's progress and development but it is as important that we take everybody along with us. This election symbolized new hope … I assure you that when we meet in 2019, I will place before you my report card. I will try and achieve the pinnacle of perseverance and hard work … Antyodaya, the service of the

downtrodden, that is what Pandit Deendayal Upadhyaya had stressed. That is why I say that this government is for the poor and deprived.[109]

Modi's capturing the country's most powerful office in the country was in many ways facilitated by the socio-economic changes triggered by the reforms of 1991 and what is known as the Mandal–Kamandal politics, a derogatory reference to quota politics of socialist parties and BJP's Hindu chauvinism. The reforms and the consequent arrival, over the next decade and a half, of modern consumer goods, services and consumption patterns gradually changed the existing socio-economic relationships.

Even though economic reforms started in 1991, the real push came at the turn of the millennium. By then the government had enough foreign exchange reserves and confidence to allow Indians to freely travel overseas for study, business or leisure. Earlier, anyone travelling abroad had to apply to the central bank and wait for days before they got permission and a fistful of foreign exchange. Infosys founder Narayana Murthy had to wait for three years to import a computer and make about fifty trips to Delhi to get the permission.[110]

As the big calendar flip drew closer, English-speaking Indian engineers became hot property in the US and Europe as the Western world got jittery about a bug in computer code that may not recognize the turn of the millennium and set the clock back by two thousand years. Early codes that were written had used a two-digit format for dates; computers would read the year '99' as 1999 but when the clock turned to year 2000, they may read it as year zero. It could cause global catastrophe unless every line of code was rewritten to correct for the anomaly. Indian engineers and software companies were hired en masse by global, especially US, companies, heralding an IT revolution in the country.

This revolution not only expanded the Indian diaspora but also inspired an economic boom in India, suddenly creating millions of jobs and livelihood opportunities. The Vajpayee government's thrust on infrastructure building, privatization of state-owned companies and liberalization of foreign investment norms had come at a time when the global economy was picking up, driven by booming consumption as people spent on personal gadgets, new homes, cars and holidays. Stock and commodity markets were on fire. The insatiable appetite of US and European consumers filled the coffers of exporters from India and China who cranked up production, creating more jobs and attendant services. Business process outsourcing—much of which was young Indians working in call centres attending to foreign customers on behalf of foreign firms—became such a big business that anyone who could speak decent English could get a job with a starting salary in five figures.

The boom filled the Indian government's treasury, providing it with cash to spend on welfare. The United Progressive Alliance government was led by the Congress but was propped up by the left, which forced a leftward lurch in Indian policy, paving the way for job, food, education and information entitlements. Between 2005 and 2007, the Indian economy grew at a scorching pace of nearly 10 per cent.[111]

As private industry flourished and income levels began moving up, the middle class expanded rapidly. McKinsey Global Institute, the research arm of global consultant McKinsey, estimated in 2007 that with the then growth trajectory, Indian income levels would almost triple over the next two decades, and the country would climb from its position as the twelfth largest consumer market to become the world's fifth largest by 2025.

'As Indian incomes rise, the shape of the country's income pyramid will also change dramatically. Over 291 million people will move from desperate poverty to a more sustainable life, and India's middle class will swell by more than ten times from its current size of 50 million to 583 million people. By 2025 over 23 million Indians—more than the population of Australia today—will number among the country's wealthiest citizens,' McKinsey forecast in a study, 'The Bird of Gold: The Rise of India's Consumer Market'.[112]

More and more people moved from villages to towns and cities searching for better livelihood opportunities as agricultural income, on which two-thirds of the country depended on, stagnated. In 1970, wheat procurement price was Rs 76 per quintal. In 2015, wheat procurement rate was Rs 1450 per quintal, an increase of about nineteen times. In the same period, average basic salary plus dearness allowance of Central government employees rose 110 times; school teachers by 280 times; college/university teachers by 150 times; and mid- to upper-tier corporate sector employees by 350 to 1000 times. Meanwhile, school fees and healthcare costs went up 300 times and average house rent in cities rose 350 times.[113]

Between 2005 and 2009, India was feted on the world stage as one of the emerging superpowers. Goldman Sachs wrote the now-famous BRIC (for Brazil, Russia, India and China) research report that predicted India to be the third largest economy in the world after the US and China in less than fifty years. Prime Minister Manmohan Singh sat across from the US president George Bush Jr to negotiate a deal allowing the country a place on the global high table of nuclear powers. It was a long way from just a decade ago when the US was choking India with sanctions for conducting a nuclear test.

The Manmohan Singh government returned to power with a surprisingly better mandate in 2009. Often described as the accidental prime minister, Singh's global reputation had soared so high that US President Barack Obama commented: 'Whenever the Indian Prime Minister speaks, the whole world listens to him.'[114]

However, Singh's stars were on the wane. The next five years were marked by a policy paralysis, corruption scandals and an anti-corruption agitation led by Gandhian Anna Hazare. While the government was besieged by agitators in Delhi, an economic recession had taken root globally following the collapse of investment banks Lehmann Brothers and Bear Stearns in the US. Complex yet unstable financial instruments had built up artificial valuation of poor quality assets which collapsed under their own weight. The contagion spread across the world and all major economies, including India's, were caught in the cold grip of a global recession which forced industrial shutdowns, corporate bankruptcies and widespread job losses.

India's public finances, whose health had helped fund a number of state welfare initiatives of UPA 1, gradually slid into the red again. While the entire country was reeling under the recession, Gujarat led by Narendra Modi was showing excellent growth. Modi made it his calling card as he positioned himself for the top job in the country.

Modi became prime minister with an unprecedented mandate in 2014, triggering celebration in business circles as well as among nationalists who swore by Swadeshi. The mandate for him was seen as the beginning of a new India, which was taking its first sure steps to realize its long-cherished dream of becoming an economic superpower. The widespread image projected by Modi himself and the Sangh Parivar as a whole was that of a wizard with a golden wand.

On 16 May, the day election results came in, the Bombay Stock Exchange's (BSE) 30-share benchmark index shot up 1470 points to hit a record high of 25,375.63 before settling at a new closing peak of 24,121.74 on hopes the new government would fast-track economic reforms.[115]

On 25 September, Deendayal Upadhyaya's birth anniversary, Modi announced 'Make in India', an ambitious plan to attract foreign investors into India. Modi invited foreigners to set up businesses in India. 'We want to present the world the enormous opportunities that India offers as a base for manufacturing, design, research and development,' he said. 'Today, India is perhaps the most open country for FDI.'[116]

Modi's approach to governance was well appreciated by industrialists. It was summed up later by Anand Mahindra at the India Economic Summit organized by the Geneva-based WEF and the CII. Mahindra said: 'The government came across as having new energy. People sensed that there is a new agenda as well as a business-friendly agenda. There is effective leadership from the government and the commercial sector. I leave convinced that there is a very clear road map moving forward.'[117]

Four years later, the environment would remind Mahindra of the days of the Licence Raj, where the role of the government in promoting enterprise was found wanting. Ruing the 'proliferation' of regulation, Mahindra remarked: 'Your job is not to eliminate risk, but to eliminate unwarranted risk. Risk is a very integral element of the capitalist system.'[118]

But in the fall of 2014, industry was high on Modi although murmurs had begun within the Sangh Parivar. Organizations like the BKS, BMS, and SJM complained that they did not have access to the government. Those in the Parivar working on rural affairs felt the government was ignoring villages and the poor for the sake of big business. They took their complaints to senior Sangh leaders who advised them to be patient.[119]

In his Vijaya Dashami speech, sarsanghchalak Mohan Bhagwat said the government's initiatives had raised hope but needed to wait with faith for some time to see how they played out. He said the final test of the efficacy of these policies would be their impact on the life of the last person standing, the one on the last step of the ladder. 'We must remember that self-reliance should be a necessary component of national prosperity and security.'

He also appeared to hint at the growing criticism without naming anyone and seemed to suggest that genuine protests should continue. RSS affiliates had raised the issue of the government's inaccessibility and lack of consultation with stakeholders while formulating economic policy with RSS leaders. They had said members of their organizations would be upset if they did not protest against policies that were against their interests. The Sangh leaders had agreed that their members' interest should be their priority. However, they did not want them to do anything that could destabilize the government.

Bhagwat tried to strike that balance in his speech, appealing to a higher principle of democracy. He said:

The evolution of nations in the world history shows that without active cooperation and participation of people, mere political power cannot bring about the desired change in the society. Therefore, those individuals and organizations who are engaged in giving direction to the society and solving its various problems, must remain active and vigilant. In a democratic system, the governments gain tremendously from their activism, awareness and maturity in the interest of the nation and it also protects the nation from possibility of detracting in the game of power politics.[120]

He advised both organizations and the government to cooperate with each other. 'In a democratic system, it is necessary that these players, the government and administration should keep their dialogue alive; and the government be informed whether the fruits of its policies are reaching the last Bharatiya in the queue or not.'

The peace, with protests remaining muted and contained within the Parivar, would not last as the government steamed ahead urgently to introduce economic reforms. The first major protests erupted in the new year. On 31 December 2014, the government promulgated an ordinance to make land acquisition for projects easier.[121]

The ordinance did away with social impact assessment and diluted the consent requirement of landowners. It created an uproar.

As the controversy raged, US President Barack Obama visited India to hold bilateral talks and attend the annual Republic Day celebrations on 26 January as chief guest. Prime Minister Narendra Modi welcomed him wearing a pinstriped suit. The next day, newspapers reported that the stripes on his suit were actually a monogram—his full name, Narendra Damodardas Modi, artfully woven on in gold stripe. The Savile Row closed-collar suit attracted a lot of derision within the RSS, which prides on simple living and frowns upon self-promotion.

The suit and land acquisition ordinance gave the opposition Congress its first opportunity to attack Modi's economic policies. In the budget session of Parliament, Congress vice-president Rahul Gandhi called his administration 'suit boot ki sarkar' (a government for those wearing suits), a clever jibe that seemed to echo for the next four years.[122]

An issue that plagued the RSS affiliates was that the government was not consulting them. Ministers did not even bother to give appointments to leaders of the affiliates.[123] That changed in the new year. On 5 January, nearly half a million coal workers, including those belonging to BMS, struck work for five days to stop privatization of the coal sector. The strike precipitated a crisis at the country's thermal power stations with coal stocks barely sufficient to run for five days. The government was facing the spectre of large-scale power outages in the country. On the second day, coal minister Piyush Goyal held a six-hour meeting with unions before reaching an agreement that largely appeared like the government had caved in.[124]

It was only the beginning of a long confrontation between the government and RSS-backed organizations. On one side was the Modi government, which wanted to roll out the red carpet for foreign capital, make it easy to do business and promote entrepreneurship, and on the other were the SJM, BMS and BKS which believed in self-reliance, opposed unbridled consumption, and harboured a deep suspicion of foreign investment and multinational companies.

By the time the government was preparing to celebrate its first anniversary in office, the knives were out. 'It is a theory of pain and it is wrong. They [government] are saying let the poor suffer in the short term for future prosperity,' SJM's Ashwani Mahajan said about the land acquisition bill introduced in the Parliament's budget session. 'The ministries are bonded slaves to the finance ministry,' said BMS leader C.K. Saji Narayanan. The government capitulated and sent three of its ministers to hold talks with them.[125]

A few months later, the RSS held a coordination meeting with the BJP and some of its affiliates. Top RSS leaders, including Bhagwat, met with senior cabinet ministers, including Rajnath Singh, Arun Jaitley and Prime Minister Modi. The ministers made presentations and discussed the government's policies and priorities. At the end of the sessions, the RSS said it was satisfied with the government's performance and it was headed in the right direction. However, everyone could not be satisfied, it said. About the criticism that the RSS was acting like a remote control, prachar pramukh Manmohan Vaidya said, 'We have every right to ask ministers, who are also swayamsevaks.'[126]

The friction between parivar organizations and the government intensified as the months wore on, but it never went to the levels seen during the Vajpayee regime. No top Sangh leader ever voiced anything serious against the government. There was no name calling and the prime minister was never brought into public conversations except to praise. Instructions, or advice, as the RSS prefers it, were given behind closed doors and rarely ever made it to the public domain. At the same time, the affiliates were free to attack anyone except the prime minister and the party president.

At a question-and-answer session with Mohan Bhagwat in Kerala in 2014, a taluk sanghchalak asked whether the Sangh doesn't have the responsibility of advising course correction when the driver loses his way. Bhagwat replied, emphasizing that the proper channel to approach the government was not the Sangh:

> We are not onlookers. Neither will we get emotional about issues. The previous NDA government made mistakes. At the time we got emotional and behaved inimically. The question at the time was what are we doing to create coordination. Those positions backfired and the government failed. The government we got after that was worse. We face many large and small issues such as China, Pakistan, Naxalism, conversions, intrusion etc. That is why we should be very careful when we raise our voices against the government and lead agitations. Our protests should not dent the credibility of this government leading to its failure. We should not create space for a worse government to replace this one ....
>
> We trust those on the government now and so we must speak with them in the language of coordination and cooperation. Swayamsevaks are not only in the BJP. Those in organizations like the BMS, Kisan Sangh and ABVP will play their roles. We will not hold back just because there are

swayamsevaks in the government. This is the best government we can get. It would be difficult to imagine what would happen if this experiment fails. Anarchists and Naxalites might become strong. It will lead us to a sort of slavery. We should behave very carefully and have the strength to separate right and wrong. We should be ready to fight wrongs and organizations working in different fields should be ready to agitate [for their issues].[127]

This often led to serious conflicts. In June 2017, five farmers who were part of a protest, were shot dead by security forces in Mandsaur in Madhya Pradesh. Farmer protests had been raging because of low prices for their produce. Madhya Pradesh had been ruled by the BJP's Shivraj Singh Chouhan, who came up through the RSS, for fifteen years. Although Bharatiya Kisan Sangh, the RSS's affiliate for farmers, had not been part of the agitation initially, it joined in later.

After the firing, its vice-president Prabhakar Kelkar lambasted the government. 'What you are seeing is the anger of just a small fraction of farmers. In the past three years, nothing has been done for them, but the Modi government is making profits,' Kelkar said.[128] In another interview, Kelkar said: 'The country is sitting on a volcano. A volcano in the form of farmers' unrest … It can erupt any day … We are not in favour of farm loan waivers. But what makes us angry is the fact that the centre has Rs 15 lakh crore to distribute among fifteen industrialists. In every budget, the centre gives the industries Rs 1–2 lakh crore to address the non-performing assets of industries. So why should not the farmers get that amount?'[129]

Although many in the RSS strongly feel that the Modi government was partial to big business there is nothing much they could do. The farmers' unrest had come months after the Modi government tried an unprecedented monetary policy experiment.

On 8 November 2016, as most people were sitting down for dinner, Prime Minister Modi appeared on national television to make a dramatic announcement. 'I hope you ended the festive season of Diwali with joy and new hope,' Modi began. 'Today, I will be speaking to you about some critical issues and important decisions. Today I want to make a special request to all of you.'

He went on to elaborate about the economic situation that he inherited from the previous government and the steps his administration had taken to improve the condition. Modi painted a bleak picture of how the spectre of corruption had been gnawing at the innards of the country, hollowing it out from within. How a section of society was spreading corruption for their selfish interests. How they had amassed black money. How terrorists were using fake currency to target the country. It was time for decisive action. From that midnight, Rs 500 and Rs 1000 notes would cease to be legal tender.

This surprise attack would help wipe out black money and fake currency in one stroke, the prime minister seemed to imply. Of course, it would cause hardships for a few days, but he believed the citizens of India would do that sacrifice. 'Let me invite you to make your contribution to this grand sacrifice for cleansing our country, just as you cleaned up your surroundings during Diwali. Let us ignore the temporary hardship; let us join this festival of integrity and credibility; let us enable coming generations to live their lives with dignity; let us fight corruption and black money; let us ensure that the nation's wealth benefits the poor,' Modi said.[130]

What followed was nothing like Modi promised or anticipated. Teller machines ran dry for weeks together. Long queues appeared before banks to deposit old currency. Economic activity stalled. The Centre for Monitoring the Indian Economy estimated that 1.5 million jobs were lost in the first four months of 2017.[131] In the first quarter of 2017, GDP growth slumped to a two-year low of 6.1 per cent.[132]

The impact of demonetization continued to reverberate for the next several quarters and economists struggled to assess its actual long-term impact on individual sectors and segments of the economy. Seven months later, the government followed it up with another disruptive measure: the introduction of a countrywide goods and services tax (GST). Although a much-awaited reform and one in the works for many years, its implementation, especially close on the heels of demonetization, caused widespread chaos and hardships.

Whatever the Modi government may achieve or not in its years in power, demonetization would remain a lasting legacy, a manufactured Black Swan event. While the economy continued to remain in the doldrums towards the end of its first term, the government remained in denial. Although in the run-up to the Lok Sabha elections, it talked a bit about economic development, its primary narrative was that of national security.

In its second term, the government struggled to restart the economy. While the banking sector was gripped by a bad-loan crisis, the government's enforcement arms went after industrialists with gusto who were caught in an atmosphere of fear.[133] Investors stayed away and industrial activity ground to a crawl, joblessness increased[134] and GDP growth plummeted.[135] To top it, the government's fiscal numbers came under a cloud.[136]

Meanwhile, the Centre began efforts to dilute fiscal federalism to feed its nationalistic urges. It devised a scheme to cut funds flow to the states and channel it to defence spending.[137] As the Centre struggled for revenues, it put pressure on the Fifteenth Finance Commission to allow it more control over national finances.[138]

The Narendra Modi government had ended the first year of its first term with hope and euphoria, but the first year of its second term was gripped by economic despair and social unrest across the country. The sheen of the India passport[139] was wearing off and the country had slipped ten places in global competitiveness rankings.[140]

Delivering his annual Vijaya Dashami speech in Nagpur, sarsanghchalak Mohan Bhagwat dusted out an old RSS template: 'The prevailing world economic thought is unable to answer many questions. Its standards are also incomplete in many ways; this fact has come before several economists of the world. In that situation, we have to take steps to formulate our own economic vision, policy and system that instil in us capacity to create more and more employment with least consumption of energy that is beneficial for the environment, make us self-reliant in every respect, and create and expand trade relations with the world on the basis of our strength and terms.'[141]

6

Alien Nation

The speeches were meant to wash away fears, misgivings, misunderstandings, misinformation and everything else the RSS thought was sticking to its white wall of reputation. After all, it had just been compared to the Muslim Brotherhood, the fundamentalist Islamic outfit with origins in Egypt. It was the biggest public relations exercise the organization had ever done; inviting even bitter critics such as Congress president Rahul Gandhi, who had made the Muslim Brotherhood comparison, and the CPI(M) secretary Sitaram Yechury (they didn't attend, of course). And the RSS deployed its top asset, sarsanghchalak Mohan Bhagwat himself.

'We say this is a Hindu Rashtra. That does not mean it will not include Muslims. The day it is said that we don't want Muslims, it will not be Hindutva anymore. The day it is said only Vedas will be allowed and not Buddhism, it [the nation] will not remain Hindu,'[1] Bhagwat declared during the unprecedented, globally broadcast, three-day lecture series in Delhi's Vigyan Bhavan. Bhagwat's speech came across as soft and conciliatory with some comments even appearing to be radical departures from his predecessors'.

Bhagwat said that many utterances of former sarsanghchalak Golwalkar would not appear in future editions of his works as they had outlived their relevance. The allusion was to *Bunch of Thoughts* in which Golwalkar describes Muslims, Christians and communists as the biggest internal threats to the nation. Accordingly, the sanitized *Guruji: Vision and Mission* has replaced *Bunch of Thoughts* as the primary guide and text that is mandatory reading for every volunteer.

R. Hari, one of the editors of Golwalkar's *Bunch of Thoughts*, has said that new editions of the book would change reference to Muslims and Christians as 'internal threats' to 'Islamic fundamentalism' and 'missionary evangelism'. Hari explained that the change was necessary as critics dub the RSS as anti-Muslim and anti-Christian.[2] Although many observers, including some old-timers in the Sangh, saw it as the RSS disowning the revered teacher, Bhagwat's statements were the open articulation of a well-thought-out strategy in place for nearly five years.

*

It was a cool morning in Jaipur in March 2013. Delegates or pratinidhis gathered for the annual general body meeting of the RSS were asked to assemble at 6.30 in the morning, two hours earlier than the usual schedule of proceedings. The unexpected change in schedule announced only the previous evening was to ensure that details of the meeting were not leaked out. There was a fairly large press contingent reporting on the general body meeting.

One of the joint general secretaries presented the issue to be debated; Muslims in India and RSS's approach. The RSS leadership had concluded that the population of Muslims in India was very large and a acrimonious existence was neither good for the nation nor for the Hindus. A way had to be found to take them along in national reconstruction without alarming a large section of Hindus indoctrinated for years by its own people to view Muslims as threats. What could be the ways in which the Sangh could establish contact and initiate a dialogue. It had to be done quietly. The Muslim Rashtriya Manch (MRM) was already working publicly in this area. But it was not seen as a successful project.[3]

Later, the delegates were divided into region-wise groups for further discussion. It was then decided that the RSS would begin an outreach to Muslim community leaders. The idea was to listen to the community's grievances and share insecurities of the Hindus and find ways to build confidence in each other. It was also meant to get their buy-in on contentious issues such as Uniform Civil Code and a Ram Temple in Ayodhya.

*

One of the primary reasons for the RSS's formation was the founders' deep insecurity of Muslims' influence in India's socio-political life. The RSS believes that politically Muslims punch much above their weight and an expanding Muslim population is a threat to Hindus. One RSS man who runs a think tank said, 'Muslims are fine as long as their population remains around 10 per cent. Beyond that they start asserting themselves.'[4]

The formation of the Muslim League in 1906 followed by Morley–Minto reforms or the Indian Councils Act of 1909, which allowed communal electorates, gradually began to widen the chasm between Muslims and Hindus. The Congress and the Muslim League reached an agreement in 1916, popularly known as the Lucknow Pact, under which they agreed to more provincial representation to Muslims than their share of population.

Bal Gangadhar Tilak, who had presided over the Pact, passed away in August 1920 and Mahatma Gandhi became the undisputed leader of the Congress. In the run-up to the non-cooperation movement launched in the same month, there were intense debates across the country. Gandhi's support in November 1919 to the Khilafat movement demanding the reinstatement of the Turkish caliph had baffled many Hindu leaders in the Congress. They wondered why Gandhi was supporting a cause that did not have many takers even in Turkey. Gandhi saw it as a glue to unify the two communities against the British in the non-cooperation movement.

It would also cement his position as the pre-eminent leader of the Indian nationalist movement.

In a letter to Lord Chelmsford, the viceroy and Governor General of India, Gandhi unambiguously made his position clear:

> The Peace Terms and your Excellency's defence of them have given the Mussalmans of India a shock from which it will be difficult for them to recover. The terms violate ministerial pledges and utterly disregard Mussalman sentiment. I consider that as a staunch Hindu wishing to live on terms of the closest of friendship with my Mussalman countrymen, I should be an unworthy son of India if I did not stand by them in their hour of trial.[5]

Gandhi's influence on the masses and the temper and tumult of the times were best captured in a letter Tilak's close associate Joseph 'Kaka' Baptista wrote to Mian Mohamed Haji Jan Mohamed Chotani, president of the Central Khilafat Committee. Kaka Baptista was a prominent barrister who established the Indian Home Rule League along with Tilak and Annie Besant. He also became the first mayor of Bombay in 1925. He is believed to have coined the slogan 'Swaraj is my birthright and I shall have it' made famous by Tilak. Former President Pranab Mukherjee referred to it in his speech at the RSS headquarters in Nagpur in June 2018.[6] Baptista wrote:

> I do not believe in Ghandism. He may be a saint. A saint will make a good guide for the kingdom of Heaven, but not for the Empire of India. His influence on the Khilafat committee is too great. I anticipate nothing but Himalayan miscalculations from Gandhi. But he has enormous influence on India and I would not venture to put myself in opposition to him. …
>
> Decide carefully what is to be your *direct object*. Having decided upon the object consider well whether the means adopted are calculated to secure that object. If you reflect well

upon these points and realise the mountains in the way, I have little doubt you will come to the conclusion that Ghandism is sure to prove a miserable failure. I wish you would select your six best men and have a *round table* conference with Messrs. Tilak, Das, Malviya, Lajpat Rai and myself. We may be hopeful to evolve something more hopeful than Ghandism.[7]

Hedgewar saw the 'seeds of a future national calamity in the declaration' (Gandhi's declaration of support to the Khilafat movement) and considered it a 'blank cheque to Muslim leaders'.[8]

The manifesto issued by the Central Khilafat Committee was conscious of the worry of a section of Hindus that the movement had an ulterior aim of bringing India under Islamic rule. So it explicitly stated:

It has been stated that the Hindus have serious misgivings about the ultimate aim. The Musalman signatories therefore desire to state that they have no other aim than to serve their religion and the country of their birth. In serving their religion they wish to keep the *Khilafat* intact. They certainly desire the Muhammadan power all the world over to prosper for the common good of humanity. But they do not desire to oust England and introduce a Muhammadan or any other power to rule over India … The Musalmans of India will fight to the last man in resisting any Musalman power that may have designs upon India.[9]

Baptista was proved right. Although the movement was initially successful in uniting the two communities, it took a wrong turn in Kerala in 1921 where Muslim agitation against the British later turned to anger against Hindu landlords. About 10,000 people, mostly Hindus, reportedly died in conflicts.[10] The RSS was founded four years after the riots known as the Mappila Lahala or Moplah Rebellion. Initially the Sangh was seen as a force that would come to the rescue of Hindus if there were communal riots. Many Hindus admired the army-like discipline and training of the Sangh.

Andersen and Damle have observed that the challenge from Islam in the early 1920s was viewed by many Hindus as a threat to their self-esteem. The proliferation of Hindu sabhas and other Hindu associations were reactions to the growing communal violence, the increasing political articulation of Muslims, the cultural Islamization of the Muslim community and the failure to achieve independence, they say. While these organizations had little effect on British policy, they did advance Hindu unity, while simultaneously generating a heightened sense of Muslim political and cultural consciousness. Such organizations provided Hindus with an opportunity to express their hostility towards the 'oppressors' (the Muslims and the British); and, through them, Hindus may have experienced an increased respect for themselves and their co-religionists for having repudiated the impulse of giving in to their 'oppressors'. It is in this setting of Hinduism in danger that RSS was established.[11]

Some RSS workers often reiterate, inaccurately, that the Sangh was originally founded with the sole objective of fighting the British. Deoras has said that it was only one of the objectives. In the RSS view, the real enemy, the stronger, united and militant foe which threatened the integrity of the country was Islam. Over the years, the RSS's public stance on Muslims changed—even allowing Muslims to have RSS membership—though a large section within the organization strongly believes that Islam should be wiped out of India. While one section of hardliners believe it could be done with radical action, others, including several top leaders favour a more patient strategy of Hinduization.

At the 1970 third year of the three-year officers' training camp of the RSS, a volunteer asked Yadavrao Joshi, then head of Sangh workers across all of south India:

We say RSS is a Hindu organisation. We say we are a Hindu nation, India belongs to Hindus. We also say in the same breath that Muslims and Christians are welcome to follow their faith and that they are welcome to remain as they are so long as they love this country. Why do we have to give this concession? Why don't we be very clear that they have no place if we are a Hindu country?

Joshi replied:

As of now, RSS and Hindu society are not strong enough to say clearly to Muslims and Christians that if you want to live in India, convert to Hinduism. Either convert or perish. But when the Hindu society and RSS will become strong enough we will tell them that if you want to live in India and if you love this country, you accept that some generations earlier you were Hindus and come back to the Hindu fold.[12]

This proposition continues to have importance and validity for the Parivar even today as the *ghar wapsi* (homecoming) campaign shows. After a series of bomb attacks in Mumbai in July 2011, Subramanian Swamy, a fellow traveller of the RSS, wrote an article in the *DNA* newspaper. Swamy, then the president of Janata Party which soon merged with the BJP, wrote:

We need a collective mindset as Hindus to stand against the Islamic terrorist. The Muslims of India can join us if they genuinely feel for the Hindu. That they do I will not believe unless they acknowledge with pride that though they may be Muslims, their ancestors were Hindus. If any Muslim acknowledges his or her Hindu legacy, then we Hindus can accept him or her as a part of the Brihad Hindu Samaj [greater Hindu society] which is Hindustan. India that is Bharat that is Hindustan is a nation of Hindus and others whose ancestors were Hindus. Others, who refuse to acknowledge this, or those foreigners who become Indian citizens by registration,

> can remain in India but should not have voting rights [which
> means they cannot be elected representatives].[13]

Swamy went on to say that the country should be declared a Hindu Rashtra and only those who acknowledge their Hindu ancestry should be allowed to vote. A uniform civil code should be introduced, singing 'Vande Mataram' made compulsory and learning Sanskrit should be mandatory, he suggested.

The place of Muslims in India is a highly debated as well as polarizing subject even within what's termed as the right wing in India. A mixed group of pracharaks and senior volunteers of the Sangh Parivar once paid A.B. Vajpayee a courtesy visit at his official residence. During the conversation, they urged Vajpayee to 'do something about the Muslim problem'. Vajpayee initially kept quiet but when a couple of them continued to belabour the point, he lost his cool. 'Aap batao main kya karoon. Is desh ke 15 karod musalmanon ko samandar mein dal doon? (You tell me what I should do? Should I cast the 15 crore Muslims in the country into the ocean?)'[14]

There is an entire spectrum of opinion within the Sangh too. One section declares that no one in India should be even allowed to practise Islam. They consider several RSS initiatives to be unnecessary concessions made by its leadership to Muslims for political reasons, mainly to help the BJP.

Even as the BJP prepared to conquer Delhi, K.R. Malkani wrote:

> There is no doubt that some people in the Sangh Parivar are
> allergic to Muslims. Apart from the baggage of history—which
> we all carry in varying degrees—the main reason for this was
> the Muslim demand for the partition of India. The RSS had
> been in existence since 1925, but not even one in a thousand
> Hindus had heard of it, until after the [Muslim] League passed
> the Partition Resolution in March 1940. It was a case of action
> and reaction being equal and opposite. As and when India-
> Pakistan problems are sorted out—and a BJP government

can certainly sort them out better and sooner than any other government—the Hindu-Muslim problem also will no doubt sort itself out.[15]

By the mid-1990s, the RSS was well focused on getting its political arm in power. The Babri Masjid had been demolished in 1992 and riots had erupted in many parts of the country. The next year, Mumbai was rocked by serial blasts. Hindu–Muslim relations were at an all-time low.

On 16 April 1994, the RSS founded the Sarv Panth Samadar Manch, or Forum for Equal Respect for all Forms of Worship, at the RSS's Reshimbaug headquarters in Nagpur during a top-level meeting of the labour union Bharatiya Mazdoor Sangh. It was inaugurated by Maulana Wahiduddin Khan before the statue of RSS founder Hedgewar. Jal Gimi, a former vice chancellor of Nagpur University, was appointed the national president.

The forum would touch a raw nerve in the organization.

In 1996, exactly two months after the thirteen-day Vajpayee government fell on 28 May, Sangh affiliate Prajna Bharati organized a seminar in Pune to review the elections and the government's demise. Among those who spoke were K.S. Sudarshan, Murli Manohar Joshi, Dattopant Thengadi, K.R. Malkani, S. Gurumurthy, Devendra Swarup, Muzaffar Hussain, P. Parameswaran and M.G. Vaidya. The seminar also debated taking a more open approach towards Muslims. Some had even suggested adding Jesus and Prophet Muhammad to the pantheon of Hindu gods and goddesses. Speaking at one of the sessions, Shreerang Godbole, then a young endocrinologist and an RSS volunteer for seventeen years, tore into the RSS's attitude towards Muslims.

'The statements of certain Hindu leaders make one feel that there is fundamental ideological confusion among Hindu leaders vis-à-vis Muslims. These statements, particularly as they come from respected Hindu leaders, create and perpetuate misconceptions among Hindu masses about true nature of Islam,' Godbole began.

He said pre-Islamic Arabs and Turks were tolerant people. It was Islam that brutalized them. If Muslims renounce Islam, they would also become tolerant. He said that contrary to the general belief that the Congress uses Muslims as vote banks, it is the Muslims who use political parties. When they saw that the Congress was weak, they dumped it for the third front. They tactically voted to keep the BJP out of power. Godbole said it was 'nonsense' that namaz offered at a disputed site (like Ayodhya) is not acceptable to Allah. He said that both Quran and Hadis exhorted Muslims to destroy idols.

A few days after the seminar, Godbole wrote a letter to Sudarshan, then a joint general secretary. Terming the establishment of the Sarv Panth Samadar Manch a dangerous development, he wrote:

> The concept of Sarva Panth Samadar is even more dangerous than the concept of Sarva Dharma Samabhav mouthed by secularists. With the latter, you are at least allowed equidistance from all religions. With the former, you actually ask me to show equal respect to Sanatana Dharma and Islam. This is not acceptable to me. Instead of indulging in verbal jugglery [Gandhian socialism, pseudo vs true secularism, Sarva Panth Samadar, etc.], Hindu leaders should shed their intellectual inferiority complex and present a true Hindu worldview.[16]

Godbole asked if it includes Islam and Christianity (which seems to be the case), why should it not include Marxism, Nazism and Fascism? 'The Muslim problem is essentially a problem of Islam and its theology—the Quran, Hadis, Sunnah all cultivate an exclusivist, separatist, imperialist political mindset of its adherents. In this respect, Judaism, Christianity, Islam, Marxism, Nazism, Fascism are all similar.'[17]

Godbole, who was until early 2018 a *bhag sanghchalak* (area president) in Pune, is a staunch Savarkarite with even family ties to the freedom fighter and articulator of political Hindutva. He manages websites dedicated to Savarkar and Golwalkar and writes on, as he describes, issues facing Hindu society vis-à-vis Islam and Christianity. Godbole believes there is no way Muslims can ever imbibe the nationalist ethos of their non-Muslim fellow countrymen in a Muslim-minority country.

'Indian Muslims can be Hinduized, not Indianized,' he says. In a paper in a journal published by Ahmedabad-based Bharatiya Vichar Manch, the doctor traced the evolution of the present-day Hindu revivalist movement or Hindutva to nineteenth-century Bengal.[18]

Even if Muslims are Hinduized, they are unlikely to be accepted as part of the nation according to Savarkar's reasoning. The two essential qualifications of one nation one race—of a common fatherland and therefore, common blood—are not the only requirement of Hindutva. Savarkar says:

> The majority of Indian Mohammedans may, if free from the prejudices born of ignorance, come to love our land as their fatherland as the patriotic and noble-minded amongst them have always been doing. The story of their conversions, forcible in millions of cases, is too recent to make them forget, even if they like to do so, that they inherit Hindu blood in their veins. But can we, who here are concerned with investigating into facts as they are and not as they should be, recognize these Mohammedans as Hindus? Many a Mohammedan community in Kashmir and other parts of India as well as the Christians in South India observe our caste rules to such an extent as to marry generally within the pale of their castes alone; yet, it is clear that though their original Hindu blood is thus almost unaffected by an alien adulteration, yet they cannot be called Hindus in the sense in which that term is actually understood, because, we Hindus are bound together not only by the tie of love we bear to a common fatherland and by the common blood that courses through our veins and keeps our hearts throbbing and our affections warm, but also by the tie of the common homage we pay to our great civilization—our Hindu

culture, which could not be better rendered than by the word
Sanskriti suggestive as it is of that language, Sanskrit, which has
been the chosen means of expression and preservation of that
culture, of all that was best and worth preserving in the history
of our race. We are one because we are a nation a race and own
a common Sanskriti.[19]

This one requirement alone, according to Savarkar, disqualifies
communities such as Muslims and Christians from being part of the
Hindu fold. Golwalkar thought otherwise:

It used to be said that a person who has left the Hindu Dharma
once, is gone forever. But this cannot be. He has to be brought
home again. If somebody tries to take away our own people, it
is our first duty to be careful that hereafter nothing of the kind
will happen, and if it does, we must take every step to reclaim
him and bring him home.[20]

Thengadi wanted to rethink the 'Muslim problem' in India.
According to him, the ordinary Muslim was the son of Mother
India, having grown up in the Indian culture and having felt kinship
with Hindus. Thengadi said they were being manipulated by Hindu
political leaders by offering them patronage. Writing in 1991, he
theorized:

A Muslim leadership that can instigate the ordinary Muslim
has not yet emerged. Many of the current Muslim leaders were
legitimized by Hindu politicians. They are their creations not
of the Muslim community. These were not people who had
any support or following in their own community but merely
those who were making statements in the media for cheap
publicity. Many Muslims even came to know of them only
through newspapers.[21]

Thengadi quotes Syed Shahabuddin, former diplomat turned politician and vehement opponent of the Ram Janmabhoomi movement, as writing in the November 1987 issue of *Muslim India*: 'On a per capita basis, Muslims in India nurse more criminality, indeed in big cities the underworld has a high Muslim proportion, specially in smuggling, bootlegging and murder on hire.' This, according to Thengadi, was an issue that needed to be studied scientifically and the responsibility of remedying it rested with the nation and not religion. 'In conclusion, it can be found that India's Muslim problem is created by Hindu politicians and if they change their mindset, the Indian Muslims, like Indonesians, join the national cultural mainstream while maintaining their faith intact.'[22]

In *We or Our Nationhood Defined*, the controversial book written in 1939, Golwalkar says: 'As a matter of fact we have in Hindusthan a triangular fight, we, Hindus, at war at once with the Moslems on the one hand and Britain on the other. The Moslems are not misled. They take themselves to be the conquering invaders and grasp for power.'[23] Thengadi says Golwalkar urged everyone to be 'self-enlightening', or freethinkers. He cites an example of why he could be so authoritative on this subject. Golwalkar completed the manuscript of *We Or Our Nationhood Defined* in 1938.

Hedgewar wanted the book to be reviewed and read widely. He approached journalist Gajanan Triambak Mandkholkar of *Maharashtra* to review the book. When a review did not appear for over two months Hedgewar reminded Mandkholkar who said he had many questions and doubts regarding the subject in the book and wanted to discuss them with the author. Hedgewar arranged for him to meet Golwalkar at his residence for a discussion.[24]

The incident contradicts the RSS's distancing itself from the book leaving it to be considered as a personal project of Golwalkar. Clearly, the book was written with the full knowledge and sanction of founder Hedgewar who then had only a few months to live. That year, Hedgewar had called a chintan baithak in Sindi in Nagpur. That crucial meeting was the first to formalize shakha and organizational structure, uniform and traditions, including the prayer, of the RSS that endure to this day. It is possible that Hedgewar also wanted a written ideological framework for the organization and commissioned Golwalkar to write it.

Ashis Nandy has observed that Savarkar's hatred for Muslims came not from ideas of ritual purity and impurity or caste hierarchy but from his prognosis of communities that could or could not be integrated—assimilated or dissolved—within the framework of a modern Indian state.

This prognosis has remained largely unchanged among advocates of nationalism, especially the Sangh Parivar. Even while allowing, almost as a concession, that Muslims are free to practise their religion in the privacy of their homes, as long as they remain loyal to the country, that loyalty needs to be proven again and again. The proof of that loyalty lies also in accepting Hindu symbols, presented as cultural and non-religious, such as singing 'Vande Mataram' and practising yoga, in public spaces. Even though Savarkar did not conceive the state as a Hindu state, the current narrative emphasizes on moving towards declaring the nation state as Hindu.[25]

That is also the objective behind the Sangh's flagship programme called ghar wapsi. Unlike Islam or Christianity, both actively proselytizing religions, Hinduism did not have an established process of converting a non-Hindu to Hindu. This was first designed by Dayanand Saraswati, founder of the Arya Samaj, in a process called shuddhi (purification). The RSS has adopted the same technique with Muslims, now considered prodigals, to make a repentant return. Their return to the fold is also important because the Sangh suspects Muslims are using their growing population as a strategic weapon to destabilize India.

The debate over the changing demographic structure of the country took a new turn when the socio-economic census of 2001 for the first time counted Indians according to their religion. It found that the Muslim population grew at 36 per cent in the previous decade, faster than Hindus who grew at 20.4 per cent and Christians at 22.6 per cent. Parivar commentators saw alarming signs in the numbers.

'History is witness to the fact that whenever majority has been pushed to a position of minority, that country had to face the curse of partition,' read the introduction to a BJP booklet published after the census data was out. 'Changes in religious demography cost Hindus a third of their territory fifty years ago but the community refuses to learn,' lamented S. Gurumurthy in the same booklet.

Not just the worldwide trend but even India's secular fabric was seen as endangered by the burgeoning Muslim population. Gurumurthy argued that it required a dominant Hindu community. He continued:

Religious demography is the theological manifest of Christianity and Islam and is so natural to them. They invented the critical idea of head count in religion, something which the Hindus never knew and have never understood. Headcount as part of religious faith, from where the idea of religious demography originated, resulted in unbelievable changes in the geography and even history of nations.

If 'secular' polity is the safeguard for Muslims, is this good for them? Obviously, not. For, secularism cannot survive without a dominant Hindu majority. A nominal Hindu majority will not be able to protect secularism. Only a secure Hindu majority will trust secularism, an insecure Hindu majority will abandon it.[26]

In 2003, three researchers, A.P. Joshi, M.D. Srinivas and J.K. Bajaj, at the Chennai-based, RSS-inspired Centre for Policy Studies (CPS) published *Religious Demography of India*, analysing the 100-year trend from 1881 to 1991. Two years later, they updated it to include Census 2001 numbers which were published in 2004.

Sharad Dhole, who would later head one of the most critical projects of the RSS, heard the analysis for the first time at an RSS seminar in 2003 where Bajaj was presenting his research on demographic changes. Bajaj said data showed that there was a distinct possibility that Muslims and Christians together shall become the majority in the Indian region—encompassing Pakistan, Bangladesh and India—early in the second half of the twenty-first century. He forecast that there was a possibility of Indian religionists (mostly Hindus) shrinking to 56 per cent by 2050.[27]

The introduction to the CPS study says:

> Indian religionists have been reduced to a minority in a wide swathe of the territory of Indian Union, stretching from Purnia in Bihar to the easternmost tip of Arunachal Pradesh, and comprising strategically perhaps the most critical region of India. In several parts of this region, Indian religionists do not seem to be welcome anymore.[28]

This research has become the document based on which the Sangh Parivar has evolved its approach and strategy towards Muslims and Christians. Often it finds its way into social media messages warning of an impending demographic imbalance. In his Delhi lectures, Mohan Bhagwat had pointed out that demographic imbalances are created by conversions and infiltration.[29]

*

One day in 1996, much before the CPS found population trends to be alarming, RSS general secretary H.V. Sheshadri was chairing an internal meeting. Sheshadri, who had not slept well, explained that he was recovering from a nightmare. In the dream he was slowly being devoured by a giant, green python. Sheshadri interpreted it as a portent of things to come; a Muslim takeover of India. The answer, he believed, lay in a small town in Rajasthan called Beawar.

The Beawar pariyojana (Beawar project) began in 1973. It was an ambitious plan to bring back 'half Muslims' into the Hindu fold. These were communities that had converted centuries ago to Islam but retained their Hindu way of life; praying in temples and observing rituals. The campaign, however, soon fizzled out as political developments changed priorities.[30]

Rattled by the Meenakshipuram conversions, the VHP restarted the programme in the mid-1980s. It conducted a reconversion campaign in and around Beawar in Rajasthan, which was home to a unique group of people who had accepted Islam but followed Hindu practices. The community of about 300,000 people spread over a few districts of the state was formed of Rajputs who had converted to Islam five centuries ago and claimed ancestry tracing back to Prithviraj Chauhan. Known as Meherat, they prayed in the Islamic way but also worshipped Hindu gods and intermarried with Hindu Rajputs. They revered saints like Tejaji or Baba Ram Deoji (no connection with yoga teacher Ramdev of Patanjali) and either married following Hindu rituals or Islamic nikah depending on individual choices. It was common to find brothers living under the same roof following different religions.

In 1986, the VHP started a concerted campaign to reconvert them into pure Hindus. It claimed it converted 40,000 of them in a single year though conservative estimates put the number closer to 10,000. As the VHP became increasingly involved with the Ram Janmabhoomi campaign, the reconversion activity lost steam. When Sheshadri revived it in 1996, he decided to create a new wing called the Dharm Jagran to focus solely on ghar wapsi. The revival coincided with the publication of a remarkable study.[31]

The Anthropological Survey of India had just completed comprehensive documentation of the country's various communities. Led by its scholarly director general Kumar Suresh Singh, it mapped the cultural, linguistic and biological profile of all communities in the country. The massive project, simply called the People of India, began in 1985 and involved 500 scholars and 3000 researchers.

Investigators spent 26,510 days in the field and interviewed 24,951 key informants, including 4981 women. They conducted interviews in 4592 villages, in almost all districts of the country and in ninety-one cultural regions. The researchers identified, located and studied 4635 communities. 'This has been, for most of us, Bharat Darshan in the truest sense of the word,' Singh wrote in the introduction to the study.[32]

The rigorous research and survey spanning forty-three volumes and 20 million words had some startling revelations. It covered every rite, every custom, every habit of every single community in the country. The study showed about 3600 communities or 78 per cent, including more than half the Muslim communities, drank alcohol. About 15 per cent of Muslims drank regularly while 39 per cent on occasions.[33]

Singh found that there were at least thirty-five communities that observed the tenets of both Islam and Hinduism; 116 communities who shared Hindu and Christian traits; sixteen communities that simultaneously believed in Hinduism, Islam and Sikhism; and ninety-four communities that had traits similar to Christianity and tribal religions. Only one-fifth of the communities were vegetarian. Women traditionally consumed alcohol in many communities. Smoking was common, chewing of tobacco and the use of snuff was also very widespread, and the chewing of betel was common in several communities.

'We are, therefore, largely a drinking, smoking and meat-eating people,' Singh concluded.[34] Singh identified 776 traits to see how they compared across the religious divide. 'Between Hindus and Muslims, the traits matched to the extent of 97 per cent.'[35]

The survey's revelation that instead of becoming Hindu, Islamic or Christian, the country was, in fact, evolving a spectacularly rich, syncretic culture and a liberal ethos vis-à-vis religion, unsettled the RSS which was striving to establish a purely Hindu nation. Yet the data and insights unearthed by the project were a gold mine and led to designing new strategies. The British had undertaken similar studies previously. This was, however, the most comprehensive report—a sociocultural atlas of the country with a very high degree of accuracy—ever prepared in independent India. It was a godsend not only for the RSS but also for the Christian missionaries and Muslim clergy who were looking to expand their flocks. It was now possible to strategize, plan and target their efforts. It was the beginning of a full-fledged war for Indian souls based on data analytics.[36]

RSS leaders point to the Joshua Project, a Christian initiative of Frontier Ventures that describes itself as an apostolic community committed to a common life and vision. 'We are a community of dreamers and doers who deeply desire to see Jesus worshipped in the Earth's darkest corners.'[37] The Joshua Project is a research initiative which collects data to identify and target the ethnic people groups of the world with the fewest followers of Christ. 'Accurate, updated ethnic people group information is critical for understanding and completing the Great Commission. Joshua Project gathers, integrates and shares people group information to encourage pioneer church-planting movements among every ethnic group and to facilitate effective coordination of mission agency efforts.'[38]

It was not only the RSS that saw sinister designs in evangelical Christianity. Some saw it as a strategy for American hegemonic expansion, an opening at the end of the Cold War. Marxist intellectual Vijay Prashad wrote that as the International Monetary Fund forced the state to withdraw from many areas, the US government promoted non-state actors, including evangelical organizations, to do social work around the world. 'It is no accident that the Manila meeting[39] took place in 1989, when the Berlin Wall fell. That same year, US evangelicals held the Global Consultation on World Evangelisation in Singapore and created the Joshua Project,' Prashad wrote in *Frontline*.

The core of the unreached people of the world live in a rectangular-shaped window! Often called 'The Resistant Belt', the window extends from West Africa to East Asia, from

10 north to 40 north of the equator. If we are serious about providing a valid opportunity for every person to experience the truth and saving power of Jesus Christ, we cannot ignore the compelling reality of the 10/40 Window regions and its billions of impoverished souls.[40]

Frontier Ventures, which launched the Joshua Project in 1995, was originally known as the US Center for World Mission and was started in 1976. The project sent alarm bells ringing in the Sangh. It was no coincidence that it started the Dharm Jagran project the very next year. It deputed its provincial pracharak for Rajasthan, Sohan Singh, as the first national chief of the arm. While the VHP began the aggressive agitation for a Ram temple in Ayodhya, Dharm Jagran focused on arresting conversions and bringing back those who converted to other religions. The real goal behind even the Ram Janmabhoomi movement was to unite the Hindu community to oppose Islam, one RSS leader said.

The chief priest of the Ram Janmabhoomi temple, who was murdered soon after the mosque was razed, said in 1990–91 that in the seven preceding years no major political leader of the Ayodhya movement had cared to worship at the temple, except one who had had a *puja* done without herself visiting the temple.[41]

The RSS learnt from Christian data and methodologies how to identify target communities. Several Christian databases publish detailed statistics of communities and religions. The Sangh carefully studied these and statements made by church leaders. The Joshua Project was a key source. It found that often these sources contradicted the Indian census reports and claimed a much higher population of Christians. Census 2011 records the Christian population of India at 2.3 per cent.[42] Some Christian sources, however, put the actual population at as high as 9 per cent.[43] One of the reasons cited for this discrepancy is India's policy on reservation in education and jobs for backward and oppressed classes. While missionary activity is reported to be the most intense among lower castes and tribes, the converted become ineligible for government quota. This often leads them to remain Hindus in official records even though they start practising Christianity. Known as crypto-Christians, this population is reportedly on the rise.

'We checked their [Christians'] own statements and did ground truthing. And actually found it to be true,' says Sharad Dhole.[44]

The RSS believes that converts build a psychological affinity with the people of Western countries and are weaned away from national society. It changes the cultural outlook of the person. 'It is this aspect of Christianity that has today come into conflict with nationalism and has created a strong suspicion in the minds of the national societies,' Shripaty Sastry, a former national head of intellectual training, once said. 'That explains why conversion of a man to Christianity is not just a change in the form of worship but a change in the priority of loyalties. That again explains why Christians are looked upon by many as a potential fifth column.'[45]

The organization intensified its efforts to stop conversions. It claims to annually stop about two lakh Hindus from converting to Christianity and persuades another two lakh to reconvert to Hinduism. 'In Vidarbha, we brought back forty pastors last year,' says Dhole.[46]

Dharm Jagran's strategy is to identify communities that have both Hindus and those who have converted to other religions. For instance, many in the Mala and Madiga communities in Maharashtra have become Christians. Dharm Jagran volunteers do not work among Muslims or Christians but approach those who are Hindus and urge them to bring back those from their communities who have converted. They help build pressure through those who live like Hindus. Such activity often also fuels competition.

When the VHP started its reconversion drive among Meherat Muslims, Islamic organizations, which had struggled to make any headway with the community, jumped into the fray with new vigour. Muslim preachers from outside started visiting the villages more often and construction of mosques got a fillip.[47]

The activities of the RSS, Christian missionaries as well as Islamic preachers are not only widening the chasm between communities, they are also destroying a unique syncretic culture evolved over centuries. The many communities such as the Meos, Meherats or More Salam Rajputs of Gujarat who give their children two names, one Muslim and one Hindu, lose their distinct traditions and rich customs as they are inducted into homogenized groups of narrow identities.[48]

*

Almost ten years after the demolition of Babri Masjid, RSS sarsanghchalak Sudarshan took an initiative to build bridges with Muslim nations. On 2 October 2002, seven envoys from West Asia came to Keshav Kunj, the RSS headquarters in Delhi. It was led by the ambassador of Iraq, Saleh Mukhtar. The others represented Syria, Libya, Sudan, Iran and the United Arab Emirates (UAE). Saudi Arabia was represented by its embassy's first secretary.

They listened to Sudarshan expound on his perspective on global events and Hindu philosophy. Then Sudarshan explained the Sangh ideology and linked it with the Muslim world. He criticized the Indian government's secularism and globalization policies. Later, the Syrian ambassador joked: Sudarshan-ji, how do you serve such tasty (ideological) fare to so many people every day.

The nine years that Sudarshan led the Sangh was the longest period of the RSS trying an outreach programme for Muslims and Christians. It began with an Eid Milan on 24 December 2002. It was attended by Sudarshan, Madan Das Devi, L.K. Advani, Indresh Kumar, Maulana Wahiduddin Khan and Jamil Ilyasi. The idea that the RSS should have an institutionalized mechanism to engage with the Muslim community germinated there. Sudarshan became the champion of the idea that would divide the Sangh.

The name Muslim Rashtriya Manch was formalized at a meeting in Jaipur three years later. The MRM became the flag-bearer of

Hindu–Muslim harmony within the Sangh Parivar. However, it remained an organization that also divided opinion within the Parivar.

The MRM holding Iftar parties during Ramzan has drawn criticism from the Sangh, which has said that the organization was not its affiliate. 'It was organized by the Muslim Rashtriya Manch. The RSS had nothing to do with organizing the event,' Indresh Kumar, patron-in-chief of the MRM, clarified after media reports said the RSS held an Iftar party in July 2015. The MRM had invited diplomats from seventy-one Islamic countries to attend its Iftar held at the Parliament Annexe building in Delhi. Nine ambassadors and twelve deputy chiefs of missions were among the diplomats who attended it. Imran Chaudhry, national co-convener of MRM, said it was a media creation. 'This iftaar party was not organized by the RSS. The Muslim Rashtriya Manch was the organizer,' Chaudhry said. He said the MRM was close to the RSS and acted on plans charted out by it, but it would be wrong to say the RSS organized the Iftar. 'The sole purpose of this iftar was to tell the world that Islam preaches peace and whatever is happening in Syria and other countries in the Middle East is not what Islam preaches.'[49]

In 2016, ahead of an MRM Iftar, RSS Prachar Pramukh Manmohan Vaidya issued a statement saying that the MRM, an organization of and for Muslims, was organizing a mega international Iftar party on 2 July. Muslim intellectuals, representatives from across the country would be participating in this event.

Media reports on RSS conducting iftar party are factually incorrect. RSS is not organizing any such party. MRM organizing iftar party is an independent Muslim organization to create national awareness. RSS shares views of MRM on national issues and supports national awareness programs of MRM as any national cause. Indresh Kumar, senior RSS functionary, keeps contact with MRM. He doesn't hold formal position in MRM.[50]

Indresh Kumar 'keeps contact', however, is an understatement. Even though he does not hold any formal position, no programme or policy of MRM is formulated without his approval. He guides every activity of the organization.

During Ramzan in 2018, Maharashtra MRM convener Mohammad Faruq Sheikh requested RSS Nagpur Mahanagar Sanghchalak Rajesh Loya to host an Iftar party at the Smriti Mandir premises of RSS headquarters. The RSS declined it, saying, 'no parties can be hosted there'. Sheikh was reported saying: 'I thought RSS hosting iftar would send a message of brotherhood at a time the world is talking about growing intolerance in India. What's wrong in that? Last year, we had hosted an iftar party in front of Mominpura's Jama Masjid, in which some RSS, BJP leaders had come.' MRM's national president Mohammad Afzal called the request 'fundamentally flawed'. He said, 'If a Muslim wants to organize [an] iftar party, he cannot ask someone else to host it for him. He has to host it himself. That's why the expectation from the RSS to host it is fundamentally flawed and Sheikh, who enthusiastically pleaded for it, has been told that his expectation was improper.'[51]

So long as Sudarshan was sarsanghchalak, the MRM got a strong push. Muslim leaders frequently visited him and regularly exchanged greetings on one another's festivals. Sangh old-timers say that there was a time when arrangements were made for some Muslims who had come to visit the RSS leader at the Jhandewalan office to offer Namaz. Maulana Kaleem Siddiqui, who publishes the Hindi magazine *Sarva Shanti*, claimed that Sudarshan had even accepted Islam as his religion.[52] People who knew him closely say that he was afflicted by amnesia in his final years. Once, he went missing in Mysore and people searched for him frantically for several hours before they found him.[53]

Sudarshan's zealous attempts to get Muslims on the same side as the RSS created some awkward situations for the organization. On 20 August 2012, Sudarshan, accompanied by his assistant Brijkant and some security personnel, left the RSS office Samidha (also his residence post-retirement) to greet members of the Muslim community. However, the security officers panicked when he said he would go to Tajul Masjid to offer namaz. Finally, state urban administration minister Babulal Gaur dissuaded him from doing so and convinced him to instead meet some Muslim leaders and exchange Eid greetings.

The Jamaat-e-Islami Hind in the 22 September 2012 issue of its mouthpiece, *Dawat*, paid a handsome tribute to Sudarshan saying that Muslims felt sadness after his death when they came to know that Sudarshan wished to offer namaz on the day of Eid but 'was not allowed to do so by his staff and police officers on the pretext of a traffic jam'. The tribute prompted a clarification from Prant Sanghchalak Satish Pimplikar. 'I don't know from where the organization came to know about Sudarshanji's wish to offer namaz. In fact, Sudarshanji, as a sarsanghchalak and even after retirement, maintained cordial relations with people from various communities. If he wished to offer greetings to Muslims on Eid it did not mean he wished to offer namaz.' Pimplikar said as far as Jamaat's condolences were concerned, he appreciated their sentiments but he was unable to understand what the Islamic body 'wanted to achieve by raking up the issue of namaz which could not be established by anyone'.[54] Sudarshan's overtures were seen as eccentricities of a leader whose tenure itself many consider as the lost years of the organization. After Sudarshan's death, the RSS has paid little attention to MRM, focusing on ghar wapsi instead.[55]

*

According to an RSS leader, Bhagwat's position is that he is a leader of a Hindu organization and his job is to unite Hindus. Delivering a lecture in Kolkata in October 2017 on the subject 'Nivedita and Indian Nationalism', Bhagwat recalled an incident.

One of my friends, a learned Muslim asked me why I oppose Sachar committee ... Over the years there has been so many outside influences in Bharat and we assimilated all … we digested all. Some time back we had some indigestion (*beech mein hazma kharab ho gaya*). But it is alright. So many rivers have flowed into Ganga, but Ganga remained Ganga. I told him once they educate themselves and understand the fact, we are ready to withdraw our opposition.[56]

The RSS maintains that Muslims have to accept that they were Hindus generations ago. Otherwise, their loyalty to the nation will always remain suspect. There, the father of Hindutva comes handy.

Staunch Savarkarite Shreerang Godbole says that Indian Muslims can be Hinduized, not Indianized. So the lasting solution to the 'Muslim problem' is ghar wapsi, not MRM. Godbole believes that the MRM project can retard the Sangh's ghar wapsi programme. He considers MRM to be a political project for the BJP and is deeply suspicious of its members. In support of his argument, he presents a letter written by Peace Party leader M.J. Khan who joined the BJP in 2013.

Muslims need to join and engage with the BJP and be seen engaged, voting or no voting. Ideally, voting 10 per cent to BJP will be ideal, as that will create situation of fear and greed. Greed in BJP of getting 20 per cent Muslim votes from 10 per cent by talking good and doing something. Fear among secular brands of losing 10 per cent today and if not going beyond 10 per cent, may lose 20 per cent tomorrow. But, even if no votes, mere engagement itself will help neutralize the communal elements and hardliners, bring the community out of fear that is marketed by secular brands and help the community by treading on new paths, than the beaten one that we have treaded fourteen times in the last sixty-five years and results are for all to see. There may be debate on this, whether Muslims should join BJP or keep distance, as they did all these years. But I am convinced that dialogue and engagement will be good

for the community. More Muslims need to join and engage
to influence decisions not only in secular-branded parties but
also in communal parties, as the Indian state has been giving
chances to both. And it will be good if some Muslims are in all
set of political parties. Hope, I am able to do some good to the
community while in the BJP.[57]

Godbole points out that in the RSS founder's mind, Muslims had
no claim on India. Hedgewar's biographer seems to agree. During
a discussion on riots, a person who had come to meet Hedgewar
said, 'Muslims are traitors and they should be punished accordingly.'
To which Hedgewar replied, 'Muslims are not traitors. Describing
them as traitors would mean that this country is theirs. It would be
appropriate to call them enemies of the nation.'[58] This thought was
taken forward by Golwalkar who described Muslims (together with
Christians and communists) as internal threats.

Lambasting Indresh Kumar for saying that Savarkar represented
the 'hate Muslim' stream in India's freedom struggle, Godbole says
either Indresh Kumar has not read Savarkar's views on Islam or he
is careless with his statements. 'Savarkar never opposed, much less
despised any community merely because of their different identity.
Savarkar was a humanist first and foremost. But this is not the
place to go into that. It is regrettably fashionable for certain Sangh
functionaries to show that the Sangh is distinct from Savarkar.'[59]

While the RSS can take a hard-line stand, the BJP had to be seen
as more accommodating.

'Fifty years ago, Deendayal Upadhyayaji said Muslims should
not be treated as different people. Do not reward them, do not
rebuke them, but empower them. They should not be looked down
nor should be treated as substance for votes, but consider them
your own,' Prime Minister Narendra Modi said at Kozhikode in
September 2016.[60] Yet others swing to the other extreme.

Here's the conundrum that the RSS struggles with. While publicly
it admits that the Indian nation state belongs to Muslims as much as to

Hindus, the idea militates with its core ideological tenet: Hindustan is a Hindu Rashtra or India is a Hindu nation. Accepting that India equally belongs to Muslims is accepting that it is not an exclusive Hindu nation.

According to a person who was earlier heading the Delhi unit of a Parivar affiliate, secular liberals are a bigger problem than Muslims. During a conversation at his office, he said that 'the Hindu has just woken up. Now people are scared. The secular person is our first enemy. I'm a *kattar Hinduvadi*. I say why should someone who speaks against Hindus remain alive. … Now we are boycotting Muslims economically.'

The boycott had already started in Uttar Pradesh and Delhi and was being gradually scaled up. To begin with, Hindu financiers were being persuaded to not fund Muslim traders. Likewise, the person said, they were also canvassing Hindus to not buy from Muslim traders and prevent them from getting jobs. According to him, several resident associations in Delhi are now refusing to allow Muslim workers in their areas. He said workers from other states such as Madhya Pradesh, Chhattisgarh and Odisha were expensive but it was better to pay more than hire Muslims.

As radical Hindus make it difficult for Muslims to live in villages and small towns, they are increasingly getting ghettoized in larger towns and cities. In July 2018, about 100 families from Lisadi in Meerut district in western Uttar Pradesh announced that they were leaving the village en masse following communal tensions. 'For sale' signs appeared on the houses of these families overnight. They read: 'This house is for sale. I am a Muslim. I am selling my house. Here, even small incidents are given communal angle.' The residents alleged that the police was siding with the Hindus. The police, however, dismissed it as a pressure tactic.[61]

Dharm Jagran's Sharad Dhole corroborates that 'beti vyavahar', or marital alliance, is the biggest stumbling block in ghar wapsi. He estimates that it will take another twenty-five years for this to happen. Hindus, for instance, do not marry within the same gotras or clan. After converting to Islam, however, many marry from within the clan. However, every person is aware of who has married whom and from which clan. 'In Gujarat the Rajputs belong to fourteen gotras. That means those who have converted also have fourteen gotras. Since all of them actually know their clans, it is not difficult for them to return to the same one on reconversion.'[62]

While the various arms of the Sangh Parivar worked on the Muslim community on the ground, a Patna-based outfit called the Centre for Policy Analysis (CPA) approached it from a policy perspective. Styled as an independent think tank, it is run by Durga Nand Jha, a long-time RSS volunteer who once headed the economic cell of the Swadeshi Jagran Manch. Jha prepared a report on the Muslim community in consultation with many senior RSS leaders and idealogues.[63]

Sangh Parivar ideologue and president of Ekatma Manavdarshan Anusandhan evam Vikas Pratishthan (Integral Humanism Research and Development Foundation) Mahesh Chandra Sharma, who was also consulted for the report, says he is not in favour of dividing the country into minority and majority. 'It is a polarizing classification,' Sharma said.[64] He said that he attended the consultation in his individual capacity despite being part of the RSS. He insisted that the project was not commissioned by the RSS though even joint general secretary Dattatreya Hosabale had attended consultations.

In October 2018, the CPA published *India Minority Report: An Enquiry into India's Minority Policy and Analysis of Socio-economic Status of Muslim Community of India*. In the works for over three years, the report used government data and surveys to analyse the socio-economic condition of Muslims. The report says that despite the country's partition on religious lines, a large portion of the Muslim population preferred to stay in India, negating the religious division while adhering to cultural and local affinity. 'The sentiment of social and cultural affinity was squandered by the 'majority-minority' approach of the government,' it said. The report says that many religious problems would not have persisted had the establishment of fraternity, not secularism, been the constitutional benchmark.

The CPA publication states that religious issues in India were benchmarked to the value of secularism instead of fraternity which has resulted in them becoming long-drawn-out. The unwillingness of Muslims to yield on issues such as construction of a Ram temple in Ayodhya, and reconstruction of Vishwanath temple in Kashi and Krishna temple in Mathura are seen as proof that the community does not want to mend fences with Hindus. 'By refusing to respect the sentiments of the majority community, the Muslim leadership chose a confrontationist course for the community,' it said about constructing a Ram temple in Ayodhya. This, despite Muslim leaders, even Allama Iqbal, poet and ideological progenitor of Pakistan, acknowledging Ram as Imam-e-Hind, a cue Bhagwat too used in his September 2018 lectures in the capital.

The report advocates the 'philosophy of assimilative diversity' as a means to construct a larger national identity to subsume all others. Concurrent to RSS ideology which stresses national interest above all, the report too says such a philosophy does not 'prohibit any regional or religious group from upholding its distinctiveness to the point it doesn't impede the construction of the national identity'. It posits it as a solution for what it terms assertive diversity in which a community denies diluting its identity indicators to get subsumed in a larger identity. 'This tendency obstructs the community from becoming integrated into the national mainstream [identity].'[65]

The BJP's rise further reduced Muslim participation in the political mainstream. As a party that prioritizes Hindu interests, the BJP fielded only seven Muslim candidates in the 2014 Lok Sabha elections. All of them lost. For the first time in India's electoral history, the ruling party did not have a single Muslim member in the Lok Sabha. Uttar Pradesh, India's largest state by population, 20 per cent of which is Muslims, did not elect a single Muslim to the Lok Sabha.[66]

Unlike what the RSS asserts, patriotism does not reside in a specific national identity. It manifests in its most glorious form in acute distress. Mumbai on the night of 26 November 2008 put it on display. That night, when terrorists ran amok, many ordinary Indians fought them. About ten days later, volunteers in Kerala heard the RSS version. It went:

> Nariman House is situated in a crowded area. People there quickly realised that it had been attacked and terrorists were holed up in the building. The people around that area did not sit inside their homes. They came out in large numbers and started hurling stones through the windows. The terrorists had to withdraw to the inner rooms to escape the barrage of stones and other missiles. Suddenly one of the terrorists came out and sprayed the area with his AK-47. One BJP leader Naresh Goyal who was leading the group was shot. He died later. That enraged the crowd even more.
>
> This rattled the terrorists. They used grenades that they had probably kept for professional forces. It injured many, including one swayamsevak Prabhakar Surve. What surprises and inspires us is the decision of the people to resist. They decided to storm the religious fanatics who were spraying bullets from their AK-47s and raining hell fire from grenades. The NSG commandos walked into this determined common crowd of Hindus. They pacified the crowd and took control of the situation.
>
> The crowd action had reduced the terrorists' arsenal and they could not take strategic position within the building. The conflict in the front helped many others in the building to escape through the back door.[67]

In other, more accurate and detailed accounts of the incident, the resistance was led by Vijay Surve, a member of the Shiv Sena. The person who died did not have any known political affiliations. And the crowd was not of Hindus alone. It had ordinary Muslims and Christians as well. In that moment of crisis their individual identities disappeared, danger forging them into a single defensive unit.[68]

At a memorial function a month later, Surve spoke about the attack and how he and a group of men had managed to hem in the terrorists for a whole day and evacuate several people from nearby buildings before commandos arrived. The crowd reserved the loudest applause for Felix Ambrose who made eight trips to the hospital carrying injured persons. An emotional Surve said, '*Hanif*,[69] *tujh par humein fakr hai. Aur Pakistan waalon, yahan aakar dekho. Yahi hai Hindustan. Yahi hai Mumbai. Yahi hai Colaba. Yahan Hindu, Musalman, Sikh, Isayi aur Parsi sab ek hain, and sab terrorism ke khilaaf ekjut hokar lad rahe hain* (Hanif, we are proud of you. And you, Pakistanis, come here and see. This is India. This is Mumbai. This is Colaba. Hindus, Muslims, Sikhs, Christians and Parsis are all one here and all are united in the struggle against terrorism).'[70]

7

War of Ideologies

On 9 February 2016, some students at Delhi's Jawaharlal Nehru University (JNU) organized an event to protest the hanging of Afzal Guru, who was held guilty of masterminding terrorist attacks on the Indian Parliament in 2001. The meeting was called by some former members of the Democratic Students Union (DSU), an organization that believes in extreme left, Maoist ideology.

Harshit Agarwal, then an MA sociology second-year student at the university and an eyewitness, described the events in detail. He said the former DSU members had termed the hanging as 'judicial killing of Afzal Guru and Maqbool Bhat'. The event was also intended to express solidarity with 'the struggle of Kashmiri people for their democratic right to self-determination'. Many Kashmiri students from inside and outside the campus were to attend the event.

In Agarwal's words, twenty minutes before the meeting was scheduled to start, the ABVP wrote to the administration asking it to withdraw permission to hold the meeting. The administration denied the permission. The DSU then sought help from JNUSU (Jawaharlal Nehru Students' Union) and other left student organizations like SFI (Students Federation of India) and AISA (All India Students Association) to gather in support of their right to democratically and peacefully hold the meeting. DSU, JNUSU and other student organizations decided that they would not let the administration and the ABVP scuttle their hard-earned democratic space, that they would continue the meeting around the dhaba itself and without mics, which the administration denied. However, the ABVP mobilized its cadres and started threatening and intimidating the students and organizers. They started shouting clichéd slogans like '*Ye Kashmir hamara hai, saara ka saara hai!* [Kashmir is ours, all and whole!]' In response, the organizers started shouting, '*Hum kya chaahte? Azaadi!* [What do we desire? Freedom!]' '*Tum kitne Afzal maaroge, har ghar se Afzal niklega!* [How many Afzal's will you kill? There will be an Afzal from every home!]'

According to Agarwal, a group of Kashmiri students had come from outside JNU to attend the meeting and the video reveals that these students had formed a circle in the centre of the gathering. 'And trust me, not one of whom was from JNU! I was present during the event for some time, and I could not recognize a single face from that group as being from JNU. This group of students, who belonged to Kashmir, and had faced the wrath of the AFSPA for decades, were angered to see ABVP disrupt their meeting, and started shouting the slogans against India. In my almost two and a half years of stay in JNU, I have never heard these slogans shouted anywhere. These are nowhere even close to the ideology of any left parties, let alone DSU.'[1]

Three days later, the police arrested Kanhaiya Kumar, president of the JNU Students' Union who had spoken at the event, on charges of sedition. Two others, Umar Khalid and Anirban Bhattacharya, who were also part of the event, were picked up on same charges.

*

About three weeks before the events at JNU, a PhD student at Hyderabad University hanged himself in a hostel room. He left a note.[2]

The letter, concise, dignified and poignant was the last flourish of a short but perturbed life. In one brief sentence—'My birth is my fatal accident'—Vemula described the unfairness to which he had resigned to as someone belonging to a caste considered low in the Hindu social hierarchy. He was not talking only about himself but of a people oppressed for centuries and whose rules of existence were ordained by anyone else but them.

The death shook the country. Vemula belonged to a leftist group, Ambedkar Students Association, which had protested against the hanging of Yakub Memon, who had been found guilty of planning a series of bomb attacks in Mumbai in 1993 ostensibly to avenge the demolition of the Babri Masjid in Ayodhya.

Local leader of the RSS students wing ABVP, Nandanam Susheel Kumar, later alleged that ASA activists had roughed him up. ABVP also complained to the local MP and Union minister Bandaru Dattatreya who passed it on to minister Smriti Irani, in charge of education. Irani wrote to the university vice chancellor, P. Appa Rao, who suspended four ASA activists, including Vemula, and threw them out of the hostel. Vemula and others started a relay hunger strike and on 17 January 2016, he killed himself.

The ABVP's involvement and conflict with the ASA coupled with the ministerial intervention was seen as an assertion of power by a students' union whose parent party was ruling at the centre. Since the Sangh Parivar is perceived by many to be an anti-Dalit, upper-caste-dominated formation, Vemula's suicide was seen as a Dalit driven to desperation by a casteist society and callous political set-up. It was not a happy thought for the RSS which claims itself to be above caste.

A month later, the RSS held its annual *pratinidhi sabha* (general body meeting) at Nagaur. While the pratinidhi sabha is held for three days and is the highest decision-making body of the RSS with about 1500 delegates participating, smaller sessions begin almost a week before. One of these meetings discussed the incidents at JNU and Vemula's suicide.

It was felt that there was a combination of factors working against the Sangh. The left was unable to live with nationalists gaining ground. JNU and Hyderabad University were seen as examples of the left, especially extreme left, academic circles becoming more vehement. One leader present at the meeting described it as a Maoist conspiracy to destroy the cultural integrity of the country. Sarsanghchalak Mohan Bhagwat himself felt that a focused effort was required to take on the left. The RSS saw a confluence of anti-India forces—ultra-left guerrillas backed by Christian missionaries in tribal areas, their intellectual and political supporters in universities, media and Parliament who were exploiting the caste fault lines, and Muslim fundamentalists. Immediately after the incident at JNU, Saha Prachar Pramukh J. Nandakumar was asked to shift his base from Bhopal to Delhi and spearhead the campaign. The Akhil Bharatiya Pratinidhi Sabha formalized his transfer.

The Sangh felt that it lagged in intellectual firepower. 'Even though we had more influence and political power, the intellectual balance was tilted in their [left] favour. Theoretically, they had an upper hand,' according to a senior Sangh leader.[3]

The broad understanding was that the left had become inconsequential in electoral politics, but it continued to be influential in the intellectual space. At a meeting at the RSS Delhi headquarters in Jhandewalan, one Sangh leader analysed the JNU event as urban Naxalism and a deliberate plan to recoup lost ground in the next elections. Even Arvind Kejriwal's electoral success in Delhi eight months after the BJP's national victory was surprising. Kejriwal, a former revenue service officer and later anti-corruption activist, had floated the political outfit Aam Aadmi Party only in 2012 but won sixty-seven of seventy constituencies in Delhi. The lesson for the RSS in his success was that a counter-narrative could be successfully built. According to one person in the media division, the Sangh had hoped to use Kejriwal for its agenda but was unsuccessful.

A large number of RSS volunteers had helped swell the crowds during an anti-corruption agitation started by Arvind Kejriwal and led by ageing Gandhian Anna Hazare. For a brief while, the motley crowd of activists sitting on hunger strike brought back memories of the JP movement. The RSS's involvement was, as is its style, through its volunteers, the organization itself not making any overt commitments or comments. At an informal interaction with journalists in Kolkata in 2011, Bhagwat had said the links between Anna and the RSS went back a long way. 'It was the RSS that highlighted Anna's developmental programmes for villages. We even got Anna to help us in our village development programmes. It was during these interactions that the RSS suggested to him to go in for a movement against corruption,' he said and added that the RSS also asked popular yoga guru Baba Ramdev to join the movement.[4]

Sometime in 2014, Bhagwat went to lunch to his old friend R.H. Tupkary's home. Tupkary, a highly regarded metallurgist who has written several authoritative books on steel-making, retired as the principal of the Visvesvaraya National Institute of Technology at Nagpur. Tupkary remarked to Bhagwat that the Parivar's plank had been stolen by Kejriwal. Tupkary felt that BJP politicians were behaving like Congressmen and were concerned only with enjoying the perks of power. He believed they had drifted away from Sangh values.

'He [Bhagwat] said he has told the BJP leaders the same thing. He told them that they should take note of Kejriwal properly. You should not give tickets to anyone with tainted character. You should offer tickets to only those who are upright, honest … whose image is honest. You should take due care when distributing tickets,' Tupkary recalled. Bhagwat, however, also said that Kejriwal was 'surrounded by Maoists' who could not be trusted.[5]

The RSS saw that the domestic narratives in which the agenda was set by articulate intellectuals were also able to influence international media. Universities, academic circles and media were identified as the left's last bastions that needed to be broken or there was a good chance that they could make a comeback even electorally. The RSS prepared for a focused counterattack. The RSS's *prachar vibhag* would lead the charge.

The Sangh was a publicity-averse organization when Hedgewar and Golwalkar headed it. However, Golwalkar, despite shunning publicity and keeping the Sangh away from the media limelight, let volunteers create trusts to publish journals and newspapers. In 1947, volunteers in Punjab and Delhi created Bharat Prakashan Trust and established an English weekly, *Organiser*. The trust route was repeatedly used to start publications in other languages. In 1970, volunteers also started a news service, Hindustan Samachar, with a network of over 1000 correspondents reporting from twenty-four centres.[6]

Golwalkar's successor Deoras was very clear that the media had a role to play in the Sangh's growth. He frequently engaged with journalists and was forthcoming about the Sangh's objectives and ideology.

In the first few decades after its formation, the RSS relied on word-of-mouth passing of information and the postal network for more formal communication. External communication was non-existent. However, it was meticulous in recording and disseminating speeches and intellectual lectures of its leaders to the cadre. It used an ingenious system of recording important meetings and speeches of leaders. A group of scribes would sit in a horseshoe-shaped row equipped with pencils and paper. When a leader began speaking the first person would write the first line of the speech and tap his pencil on the desk. The next person would begin writing from where the first person stopped. He would write a few words and tap his pencil and the chain would go on. Called the 'tick' system for the sound the pencil tap made, it ensured that not a single word spoken was missed. Several copies of the speech would then be made and distributed.[7]

In 1994, the Sangh set up its prachar vibhag to engage with the wider world. It was first headed by M.G. Vaidya. Independently established trusts started several publications in about ten different languages, including the *Organiser* in English, *Panchajanya* in Hindi and dailies such as *Tarun Bharat* in Marathi, *Swadesh* in Hindi and *Janmabhoomi* in Malayalam. They mostly catered to volunteers and barely reached beyond the organization. The media division was entrusted with engaging with independent newspapers and publications. Until then, except the sarsanghchalak, rarely anyone else in the Sangh gave interviews or held press conferences.

Although the publicity division was set up, for many years its role was limited to overseeing the already established publications and issuing press releases occasionally. Meanwhile, the media world had undergone a rapid change. Cable television penetrated the farthest corners of the country in the 1990s. The explosive growth of telecommunications and the Internet over the next decade revolutionized how news was produced and disseminated. Although the Sangh was a late entrant into the digital game, it caught up quickly.

When Mohan Bhagwat delivered his Vijaya Dashami speech in 2013, a group of volunteers were entrusted with typing out the most relevant lines from his speech. Each point was tweeted on the micro-blogging site Twitter. RSS's tweet storm on that Vijaya Dashami overshadowed cyclone Phailin that had hit the Odisha coast the same day. The prachar vibhag had arrived and one man was largely responsible for it.

*

In 2009, M.G. Vaidya's son, Manmohan Vaidya, who was then the national joint chief of networking based in Chennai and Gujarat prant pracharak for ten years before that, was elevated to the position of Akhil Bharatiya Prachar Pramukh or national chief of publicity. Manmohan Vaidya, a PhD in nuclear chemistry, plays down his role attributing the success instead to teamwork. He also does not like to call himself the chief of publicity or propaganda division. 'It is all-India in-charge of media relations.' According to him, one of his jobs is to counter negative reporting about the Sangh. The other is to bust myths about the Sangh in the media and the media in the Sangh. He also considers it his job to train workers to understand media, interact with it and use it to reach the masses. 'There should be a dialogue,' Vaidya says.

Vaidya held consultations with several volunteers working as journalists, including one on a Shatabdi Express ride between Amritsar and Delhi with Braj Kishore Kuthiala, who later became the vice chancellor of the Makhanlal Chaturvedi University in Bhopal. At the end of it, Vaidya prepared a blueprint for the Sangh to implement over the next few years. Apart from traditional newspapers and magazines, the plan included ramping up presence on television, digital and social media.

Vaidya began by putting together a team of experienced hands. He brought in Jagdish Upasane, an experienced journalist who worked with *India Today* (Hindi), and Dilip Dhanurkar, former resident editor of *Tarun Bharat*, Aurangabad. Jabalpur-based Prashant Pol was brought in to train volunteers and leaders in using the Internet and social media. A software engineer, Ajinkya Kulkarni, who runs a software firm and is simultaneously working on his PhD, joined Vaidya's team in Pune. Umesh Upadhyaya, television journalist and later the media relations executive of Reliance Industries pitched in on using television. Upadhyaya later made a presentation to the Sangh top brass, introducing them to the possibilities of the visual medium. Gradually, Vaidya expanded the team to include about twenty-five members who meet twice annually to plan and brainstorm for innovative ideas. 'It is clear that whoever is in the media, whether they like us or hate us, they will have to come to us. So we should learn to engage them. There is no way out but engage,' says Vaidya.

Vaidya and Upadhyaya determined that there were very few people on television presenting the 'nationalistic view'. There was an urgent need to develop a team of articulate persons to represent the 'nationalistic perspective' in television debates and panel discussions which were dominated by people with leftist views.

In 2010, to prepare volunteers as well as train leaders, Upadhyaya and his team held training sessions in four places—Lucknow, Ahmedabad, Bengaluru and Jaipur. In each of these sessions about thirty people selected from all zones and various arms of the parivar, such as ABVP and VHP, participated. The participants were taught to look professional and sophisticated by controlling their gaze, gestures, speech and wearing TV-friendly clothes.

Around this time, Vaidya suggested expanding the number of people who interacted with the press. Until then, the sarkaryavah used to hold a formal press conference twice every year—once after the national executive met and another after the general body meeting. It was decided that on both these occasions the prant karyavahs or prant sanghachalaks (provincial secretaries or presidents) would also hold press conferences in their respective regions. The local office-bearers would not only brief the press about the resolutions and annual plans decided at the national executive and general body but also talk about local issues as well.

In 2011, the media division held a two-day intensive training session in Indore for all the prant karyavahs and sanghchalaks to interact with the media, especially electronic media. Sarsanghchalak Mohan Bhagwat was present throughout the two days guiding the sessions. The highlight was a mock press conference of Bhagwat. Three journalists were invited to ask questions and the sarsanghchalak demonstrated how to take questions, especially tough ones, and what to answer when faced with loaded queries. After this, press conferences began to be held in about twenty-five places. The training was repeated five years later in Bhopal. Two organizational elections had been held in the intervening years and many office-bearers were changed. The Bhopal workshop was aimed at training the new people.[8]

A similar exercise to train people from across the country on social media was held in Gurgaon in 2015. It was followed up with another workshop in 2016. The media division created subject-wise teams to handle social media operations. An IT chief was appointed for every prant. The attempt was to have at least one person up to the district level. Many of these people work in information technology companies such as Google, IBM and GE. The IT department of the

Sangh works in close coordination with the media division. The IT department also helps in putting up big events such as Rashtroday[9] held in Meerut in February2018 with over 300,000 volunteers participating.

The Sangh's social media involvement is very carefully planned. There are clear instructions to be positive and constructive on the social media wherever the RSS's name is directly involved or the person is identified as an RSS volunteer and to take care to be not seen as divisive or virulent, according to one person in the media division.[10] . It is another matter that unofficially there are a number of trolls that attack the Parivar's opponents and often engage in abusive social media battles on subjects close to the Sangh.[11]

One participant in a social media training camp in Pune in 2017, where about 140 people chosen from all prants attended, said different experts taught them nuances of handling Facebook, Twitter and WhatsApp. They were trained to search URLs to find information and look for stuff people may have said earlier. These help in exposing shifting positions taken by prominent people. They were also taught how to become Wikipedia editors and counter criticism on social media with humour.

In 2013, the media division began engaging with columnists to help them to see 'issues through a nationalistic viewpoint'. It held four seminars—in Kolkata, Delhi, Bengaluru and Ahmedabad—that year and focused on 'Islamic issues and problems', 'Various trends prevailing in Scheduled Castes', 'Emerging scenario in Jammu-Kashmir' and 'Perspective on development of Bharat'. About 220 columnists from across the country participated in the seminars. These interactions also helped develop personal relationships with the Sangh leaders and informal conversations that provided unique insights to journalists. Care was also taken to keep the workshops confidential, especially parts where Sangh involvement in various areas were elaborated. 'During some sessions, we were asked to let it go in one ear and out the other,' according to a swayamsevak-journalist who attended the first workshop in Kolkata in August

2013.[12] A particular session that came with the caution was on the Sangh's work in Jammu and Kashmir.

In Kolkata, Vaidya laid out the objective: help the columnists understand 'nuances of subjects of national importance so that they can project the Hindu nationalist point of view'. They were instructed early on that the seminar was confidential and purely intended as a background.[13]

Shreerang Godbole, who was then a bhag sanghchalak in Pune, explained how the Muslim community was not monolithic but riven by divisions just like Hindus are by caste. He elaborated on how even benign sects such as the Sufis have had a violent past. 'Some of our leaders pay homage to Sufi saints without proper understanding of history,' Godbole told them even as a slide opened, showing L.K. Advani at Ajmer Sharif. This generated laughter in the room, even from sarsanghchalak Mohan Bhagwat. 'The problem is Hindus have started thinking about themselves as minorities. Hindus should have an aggressive, nationalistic stand,' Bhagwat would later tell journalists. Such interactions also paved the way for informal conversations.

During one of the tea breaks, a journalist got chatting with Bhagwat and the conversation veered towards the BJP and Narendra Modi who had weeks before been chosen to lead the BJP's Lok Sabha campaign. 'Modi is the only person who has remained rooted in the RSS ideology,' Bhagwat said. 'We have told them [BJP leaders]— you find good candidates, we will do the rest ...I am telling only you, if we win in 2014, the BJP can be in power for the next twenty-five years. If not, even if all of us try they can't be saved for the next 100 years.'[14]

Such insights about the Sangh's relationships with its various arms are difficult for journalists to find. These forums helped on that count. After the meetings, every prant started keeping a list of columnists categorized according to their subject expertise who could be tapped as per need to publish the nationalistic perspective without it getting involved directly. The media division started preparing and plying the columnists with literature and other material. 'It is not spoon-feeding but merely supplying them content that may help them think differently,' says Vaidya.[15] A list of experts and academicians who could participate in panel discussions and give expert opinions was also drawn up. It gradually decided to let those who speak on behalf of the Sangh on television or write in newspapers to make their association clear as RSS sympathizers or members.

The engagement with the columnists was backed up with top-level interactions with media owners. The Sangh, which until then believed that the media was subsumed by Marxist thought, realized that there were many journalists who were independent or at least not leftists. There were some journalists who had direct relationships with some Sangh leaders. But that was not helping to implement a coordinated strategy.

Top Sangh leaders started visiting offices of television channels and newspapers, especially the English media, to meet such journalists. Sarsanghchalak Mohan Bhagwat privately met with owners of newspapers and television channels and correspondents of leading foreign publications. One large media group's owner-editor was taken to observe an RSS camp where he spent almost a whole day. Later, such excursions were extended to other journalists as well.

The initiative was targeted at building relationships with persons in the media who could act as influencers. It paid off as positive coverage of the Sangh Parivar in mainstream media increased significantly. According to one person in the media division, after one honcho closely interacted with the RSS leadership, his television channel's coverage turned positive overnight. Sangh leaders themselves started writing often in mainstream publications and appearing at prestigious public events. From being publicity shy, RSS moved to the centre of the stage. Vaidya and joint general secretary Dattatreya Hosabale, for instance, spoke at the Jaipur Literary Festival (JLF) and answered audience questions.

A senior person in the media division says one problem that the RSS faced was it did not have enough intellectual institutions like the Centre for Policy Research (CPR) or Centre for the Study of

Developing Societies (CSDS) that could generate studies and papers that were top class in methodology and articulation and favourable to the Sangh agenda. Those who came through the RSS grind were not good for this kind of work and the sympathetic outsiders did not have the DNA of the organization, he said. 'There is a perception about the RSS that it is an organization of crass men which wants to set up a sort of religious monarchy. That needs to change,' said one person in the division. One way is by encouraging academics and students to publish in-depth research on subjects close to the Sangh.

Another RSS arm, the Bharatiya Shikshan Mandal (BSM), set up an institution called Research for Resurgence (RFR) Foundation in Nagpur. The initiative was launched by then education minister Smriti Irani. The event was attended by Union ministers Nitin Gadkari and Prakash Javadekar and Maharashtra chief minister Devendra Fadnavis. Top scientists such as V.K. Saraswat, Narendra Karmarkar and Madhavan Nair too spoke at the event. BSM patron Anirudh Deshpande said the initiative was not intended to resurrect esoteric stuff like the 'Pushpak' aircraft mentioned in the epic Ramayana but to encourage research suitable for the country.[16]

The RFR Foundation later set up a data centre in Nagpur to serve as a digital repository of knowledge for researchers. The BSM would source Indian books, manuscripts and other material, including ancient sources, to aid researchers. Universities where the RSS has influence amended their PhD guidelines, insisting that scholars study and cite from Indian texts and include Indian knowledge traditions in their research.[17]

The RFR Foundation's mission statement is to 'establish global level advanced research centre for varied fields as an integrating platform for scientific community of the world and traditional researchers in all fields of knowledge'.[18] It joined hands with institutions such as the Indian Council of Social Science Research (ICSSR), Jawaharlal Nehru University and Indira Gandhi National Open University (IGNOU) to organize a conference of academic leadership in September 2018 which was inaugurated by Prime

Minister Modi and attended by Education Minister Prakash Javadekar. The conference agreed to make academic research 'more socially oriented, purposeful and applicable by formulating new guidelines'. A key suggestion was to make the 'purpose of research primary than the title'. It also decided to identify '100 subjects of national importance' to conduct research on priority.[19] The initiative seamlessly integrated an RSS agenda into the state-funded apparatus.

People associated with BSM and RFR Foundation now occupy key positions in several universities and nodal institutions regulating research and setting the agenda for higher education. The foundation works with dozens of universities and institutions to change the methods of research. It wants researchers to be not confined by the currently prescribed methodology. Scholars can adopt any number of approaches. They need not register their topic anymore and only need to state the purpose of their research. It signed memoranda of understanding with sixty-four institutions, including sixty universities and IIT, Madras.[20]

Inaugurating the conference, Prime Minister Modi said, 'Education should not be confined to just teaching in classrooms. There is one common point in the education vision of Dr B.R. Ambedkar, Dr Ram Manohar Lohia and Pandit Deendayal Upadhyaya—character building. Character is more important than knowledge for a person. Without character, a knowledgeable person becomes more dangerous to society than a wild animal.'[21]

*

The RSS had quickly grasped the changing landscape of communications technology and invested heavily to adapt itself. It knew that unlike in the past, expanding communication channels would be key to its growth and relevance. To its pleasant surprise, it found that social media's total informality and anonymity was tailor-made for it. Within a few years, it had built up a well-oiled machine. Within five years, the RSS transformed from an introvert backroom organization to a publicly chest-thumping nationalist one. This formidable information machine was cranked up to full steam in mid-2016 after the death of Rohit Vemula and the incidents at JNU.

In an introduction to Lok Manthan, a programme organized by the Madhya Pradesh government in Bhopal in mid-November 2016, J. Nandakumar said: 'There are divisive forces working overtime to debilitate the Nation. We've to be aware of those dangerous trends growing in our society. Mainly, two segments are active in the disintegrating exercise. First one is the continuing effect of the colonization that derailed our crucial intellectual system.'

Nandakumar identified the colonial legacy in education as the first reason and called for devising a 'modus operandi to decolonize the Indian minds'. The second, he said, was the 'divisive ideology and activities of the forces, the votaries of the outdated class struggle theology'.

Holding the left in the crosshairs, he said:

> They are well versed in unearthing our differences and constructing fault lines between the so-called classes. It is not a difficult task to point out the outward differences among men. Colour, body structure, dress, language, place of stay and birth cannot be same. But these Marxian theologians, posing themselves as great intellectuals, are trying to derive sadistic pleasure by raking up these flimsy and trivial matters. They are trying to create chaos and confusion in the society through an ideology that is defective in theory and dangerous in practice. Further, they have no love lost for Bharat. For them, Bharat is not a single nation, but a conglomeration of many different nationalities … And the part played by the Indian Communists during the Chinese aggression against Bharat in 1962, is still vivid in our memory.[22]

Presenting the annual report of organizational activities at Nagaur in March 2016, RSS general secretary Suresh Joshi called the incidents at JNU and Hyderabad University a conspiracy to destabilize the country. He said that the acceptance of the nationalist discourse had been gaining steadily and the resultant unease among the anti-national and antisocial forces had come to light through certain recent incidents. The anti-national activities at the Bhaaganagar (the RSS's name for Hyderabad) University and the JNU had, according to him, thoroughly exposed their conspiracy.

> In the last few months, reports about anti-national and subversive activities in certain universities, has become a matter of concern. When renowned and premier universities, which are expected to groom patriotic citizens by imparting them the lessons of unity and integrity generate people who raise the slogan calling for breaking of and destroying the nation, this naturally becomes a matter of concern for the patriotic people. When they find certain political parties supporting such antinational elements, their concern grows further.
>
> In the name of freedom of expression, how the slogans calling for the breaking up of and destruction of the nation, can be tolerated, and how the guilty, who had hatched the conspiracy to blow up the national Parliament, can be honoured as martyrs? Doing so it, itself will be treated as an antinational act. Those who do such things have no faith in our Constitution, judiciary, Parliament, etc. These subversive elements have made these universities the centres of their activities for long.[23]

For the RSS, communism is one of the biggest three threats to the Hindu nation, the other two being Islam and Christianity. Ideologue Deendayal Upadhyaya once termed the communists as weeds. Months before his premature death, Upadhyaya told workers at Thrissur in Kerala in 1967:

> Until Sardar Patel threw them out of the Congress, Communists like EMS and AKG continued in that party [Congress]. In 1948,

they tried armed revolution in Kerala, Bengal and Andhra but Patel suppressed them all and banned them. It was Nehru who removed the ban and gave them legitimacy when he invited them to travel with Bulganin and Khrushchev. It is said that Nehru promised the Soviet leaders that he would allow Indian Communists to work unhindered if they promised to shun violence and work like a regular political party. We do not want to oppose the Communists on everything. We would merely want to remove all obstacles while doing positive politics. It is like a farmer roots out weeds from his fields.[24]

*

The RSS and CPI(M) in Kerala, particularly in the northern district Kannur, have been locked in a deadly battle for decades that has claimed scores of lives from both sides. Kerala is socio-politically unique because it has human development and living standards similar to many developed countries. It also is perhaps the only place in the world where communism, Islam, Hindutva and Christianity (the RSS sees Islam and Christianity not only as religions but also as political ideologies) are well matched in terms of economic and political influence.[25]

Conflicts started right from the early 1940s when the RSS started taking roots in the southern sliver of a state that had, as of July 2019, 5300 daily shakhas,[26] more than any other prant or province in RSS terminology. RSS's organizational division of the country differs from Indian administrative divisions. Some states such as Uttar Pradesh have multiple prants, while some others such as Goa and a part of Maharashtra together become western Maharashtra prant. As was the norm then, a Maharashtrian, Neelkanth Yashwant Telang, was sent as the first pracharak to Trivandrum in February 1942. Telang stayed only for eight months and was followed by two others who also stayed only for a short while. The Sangh can be said to have really started after

Manohar Dev took charge in 1944–45 in the capital of the then Travancore state.

However, it had better success in Malabar, which was then part of the Madras Presidency, where Dattopant Thengadi had arrived as a pracharak in March 1942, around the same time that Telang came to Trivandrum. Thengadi came with an introduction letter from a leading lawyer of the Madras High Court, V. Rajagopalachari. It helped him make contact with the upper crust of Calicut's Hindu society, including lawyer P.K.M. Raja, a scion of the Zamorin royal family. Raja also became the sanghchalak.

In what would today be called a ghar wapsi, a prominent Muslim family in Calicut (now called Kozhikode) converted to Hinduism and, interestingly, started following the Brahmin way of life. The converted brothers, Ramasimhan and Dayasimhan, were murdered by local Muslims. While Ramasimhan remained a bachelor, Dayasimhan married an upper-caste Namboodiri girl, the alliance arranged by RSS man Valyunni Thirumulppad who was also Thengadi's local guardian.[27]

Violent skirmishes between the CPI(M) and the RSS started after the Sangh's political arm, Jana Sangh, started active work in the state. Jana Sangh, which was until then considered a north Indian party, held its national convention in Calicut in 1967. The event served as an announcement of the arrival of the newest contender on the block for political space in the state. The series of killings in north Kerala started in April 1968 with CPI(M) trade union leader, P.P. Sulaiman, who was hacked to death on his way home from the Birla-owned Mavoor Gwalior Rayons' factory in Calicut. The attackers were alleged to be RSS men.

The Kannur killings began exactly a year later when Jana Sangh worker Vadikkal Ramakrishnan died after he was allegedly assaulted by CPI(M) workers in April 1969. Pinarayi Vijayan, who became chief minister of Kerala in 2016, and party state secretary, Kodiyeri Balakrishnan, were the prime accused in the case. While RSS leaders say that the attack on Ramakrishnan was premeditated, news reports of the time suggest it was due to axe injuries sustained during a fight between the two groups. The CPI(M) believes there were economic interests at play.[28]

*

Kannur district headquarters of the CPI(M) is a double-storeyed signature of Kerala architecture style in a leafy plot of a quiet neighbourhood in the heart of the city. If local RSS volunteers are to be believed, this has always been the neural centre of violence in the district. The overlord of this domain between 2010 and 2019 was P. Jayarajan, the longest-serving district secretary of the party in Kannur. Jayarajan and several other CPI(M) workers were jailed after the murder of Kathiroor Manoj, Kannur district sharirik pramukh of the RSS, on 1 September 2014, a week before Onam, Kerala's most popular and egalitarian festival. The CBI filed a charge sheet against Jayarajan in 2017.[29]

The prologue to the murder happened on 25 August 1999, the day of the state's most popular festival, Onam. On that day, a group of RSS workers, led by Manoj, allegedly stormed Jayarajan's house just as he was sitting down for lunch, and assaulted him. A severely injured Jayarajan escaped with his life but lost movement in his left hand.[30]

Jayarajan says the RSS wanted to break the growth of communism among workers of Mangalore Ganesh Beedi in Kannur. The owners of this enterprise were Mangalore-based businessmen. 'The RSS itself acknowledges that the company was a nursery for communism where groups of sixty to seventy workers read newspapers collectively and engaged in political discussions.'[31]

Communist leader A.K. Gopalan had been campaigning for a comprehensive law for beedi workers and finally managed to ensure that the Central government passed the Beedi and Cigar Workers' Conditions of Employment Act in 1966. The legislation sought to formalize the employer–employee relationship in the industry and introduced provident fund, gratuity, maternity benefits and medical allowance for employees. However, it was left to the states to form their own regulations. While state governments ignored the Central law, the EMS government that came to power after the 1967 assembly elections passed a state law the very next year. It led to court cases and the employers declaring that the communist menace had created an industrial climate that was not conducive to normal functioning.

On 15 October 1968, Mangalore Ganesh Beedi, the biggest company in the state, closed down all operations in Kerala. The owners made it clear that the workers had to opt for 'outwork system' in which the company would supply leaves and tobacco and workers would roll beedis at home. They would be paid by the count. This plan served the dual purpose of breaking workers' unity and weakening them financially. The move affected about 12,000 workers in the late 1960s in the undivided Kannur district that included today's Kasaragod. These workers also doubled up as CPI(M) cadre and worked among the people.

In the CPI(M) version, Vadikkal Ramakrishnan was a henchman for Mangalore Ganesh Beedi who was used to enforce the outwork system while an article in the *Organiser* said 'the cold-blooded murder was without any sort of provocation'.[32]

The violence continued through the 1970s and early 1980s interspersed with periods of tenuous peace. In 1978, chief instructor Chandran of the RSS's Panunda branch was killed in an assault while the volunteers were engaged in their daily drill. R. Hari writes in the Malayalam booklet *Sangha Charitravali* (History of RSS) that it was the first time a 'Sanghstan' (the spot where RSS volunteers raise the saffron flag and conduct drills) was attacked.[33]

Choorayi Chandran, a former teacher at Thalassery's Brennan College, says that at the time the CPI(M) overestimated the RSS's strength. The area where Vadikkal Ramakrishnan was killed is called Chettimukku, home to non-Malayali business communities like Prabhu, Kini, Konkani, Chetties and Pais. 'We had the impression that all these people were RSS members even though most of them were Congress. We had a slogan then: *Manjakkodiyum sanyasikalum paikkale mechu nadakkatte* (Let the yellow [read saffron] flag and sanyasis shepherd cows). Today, no partyman [CPI(M) workers] will dare to raise that slogan.'

Chandran alleges that the RSS started attacking beedi workers and began acting like rowdies hired by businessmen to oppress workers. In Kannur, the RSS acquired a reputation of being anti-workers, not anti-Muslims. The attacks were all on CPI(M) workers who were Hindus. The mistake CPI(M) made was of retaliating. Had they not, people would have isolated the RSS. It, however, brought the party some unexpected dividends. Minorities started voting for it. For instance, Muslim youth started joining SFI in Brennan College. That encouraged the CPI(M) to continue the violence and position itself as the force that could take on the RSS.[34]

After the Emergency, RSS ideologue P. Parameswaran took over as director of Deendayal Research Institute in New Delhi. In 1980, when a CPI(M) government led by E.K. Nayanar came to power in Kerala, Parameswaran reached out to E.M.S. Namboodiripad, the then CPI(M) general secretary with a suggestion to hold a dialogue between the party and RSS to end the violence. EMS suggested talking with Nayanar who was scheduled to be in Delhi soon and a date was fixed. The then RSS national baudhik pramukh or national chief of intellectual training, R. Hari, and Kerala prant pracharak, K. Bhaskar Rao, were also invited to be part of the discussion. However, events took a different turn.

On the day the discussions were to take place at Kerala House in Delhi, V. Muraleedharan, a member of the RSS-affiliated students' wing ABVP who later became the BJP state chief, was arrested in connection with CPI(M)–RSS clashes in Thalasserry. ABVP workers of Delhi laid siege to Kerala House where Nayanar was staying under the mistaken impression that it was K.G. Venugopal, the then Kerala state organizing secretary and Sangh pracharak, who was arrested. Parameswaran, worried about the talks getting derailed, telephoned Nayanar. The chief minister reportedly said, 'So what, Parameswaran? They are after all boys. You come with your colleagues; let us have the dialogue.'

The jovial Nayanar appears to have won the day and a pact was reached to formally continue parleys at a neutral venue—a swayamsevak businessman's house in Kochi. Politburo member P. Ramamoorthy, Kerala home minister T.K. Ramakrishnan and senior leader M.M. Lawrence represented the CPI(M), while Dattopant Thengadi, R. Hari and senior pracharak P. Madhavan participated from the Sangh. A lot of care appears to have gone into the meeting. Hari and Lawrence were classmates in school and shared a good rapport. Thengadi had arranged for *paan,* knowing Ramamoorthy was fond of it. Discussions continued for the whole day and several proposals to end the violence were thrashed out, including meetings of top leaders whenever tensions arose.[35]

'The party informed every unit that we should not obstruct the work of other outfits. We should not attack shakhas. We are a democracy and everyone has the right to spread their work. It was as explicitly stated as that and strictly followed. The peace held for some time,' according to Chandran, then a member of CPI(M)'s Dharmadam local committee. Chandran left CPI(M) in 1986 to join his mentor and Kannur strongman M.V. Raghavan who rebelled and left the party to form the Communist Marxist Party or CMP.[36]

The peace not only appears to have held long enough but there is some indication that the RSS may have covertly helped the CPI(M) come back to power in 1987 when E.K. Nayanar became chief minister for the second time.

On 13 December 1987, Deoras spoke at the Hindu Sammelan organized at Ramlila Maidan in Delhi. In his speech, he spoke about Hindu reawakening in Kerala. Deoras said parties had had to compromise with either Christians or Muslims to form governments in the state. But the RSS had built a strong presence with shakhas in excess of 4000 and it had been successful in creating unity among Hindus. 'For the first time the communists said the Muslim League and the "Christian" Congress are communal parties and it would not make any electoral compromises. They reaped the benefits and won the election.' Deoras emphasized that the communists could come to power because of the Hindu awakening.[37]

Chandran says things started changing after the VHP started its Ram Janmabhoomi campaign in the wake of the Meenakshipuram conversions, and the strategy the CPI(M) adopted as a response was all wrong. He recalls a local committee meeting where a leader, who is now at the top rung of the party, said that minorities are ignoring the party and we should take on the RSS to get their respect. 'I spoke against the move and insisted that violence was not our party's culture. The leader said, "There appears to be such an opinion in the party but our decision stands." That was a big foul from our part,' Chandran says using an analogy from football, the only game that is played in Kannur with fervour more intense than politics.[38]

Even though there were occasional peace talks later, mostly initiated by local administration officials or police, there was nothing comprehensive, and violence between the two opponents erupted frequently. The next major peace effort came almost twenty years later.

Meanwhile, tit-for-tat attacks kept claiming the lives of scores of young men from both sides. When Nandakumar first started his pracharak life in Kannur he faced stiff resistance from CPI(M) workers. He still remembers the day party workers disrupted his shakha.[39] After five Sangh volunteers and two CPI(M) workers died in violent clashes in March 2008, the US embassy in Delhi commented in a confidential memo:

The RSS/BJP altercation with the CPM shows the deep and abiding hostility between the two sides. The Kannur violence coming on top of violence in Nandigram and Munnar in recent months shows the propensity of the CPM to use violence and brutal tactics to protect its turf. It may have found its match, however, in the willingness of the RSS to go toe-to-toe with it.[40]

Though the violence in Kannur was endemic, it never really caught the attention of the national media which is mostly dictated from the newsrooms in Delhi. Nandakumar wanted to change that.

In August 2016, Nandakumar launched an anti-communist campaign called Redtrocity, the catchy branding splicing together the red colour of communist parties with atrocity. The ground was already prepared for a media blitzkrieg. Writing in *Outlook* in April 2016, journalist Advaita Kala, who regularly spoke for RSS victims on social media and Redtrocity events, made a facetious connection between JNU and Kannur in Kerala in a short piece that did not mention even one victim from the rival side.

> Last month, in the same week that Kanhaiya Kumar became a symbol of free speech, a younger man from the RSS, Sujith, was dragged out of his home and hacked to death in front of his parents and mentally challenged brother. As his frantic cries sliced through another dark night, Kanhaiya's speech was being played on loop and the CPI(M) raised his right to free speech in Parliament. You may, therefore, be excused for not having heard of Sujith either—not when he lived, especially not when he died. Sujith's death was taken away from him, much like his life … the clarion call for civil rights in Delhi is amplified, the human rights violations in Kerala muted. Ghettoizing murder helps explain it better, especially when the losing side holds an ideology that is abhorrent to the powers that control the discourse.[41]

The first Redtrocity event[42] was a seminar at the Constitution Club in Delhi where one speaker was Sadanandan Master, a schoolteacher whose legs were chopped off in a violent attack allegedly by CPI(M) workers in 1994. Master was a member of the SFI, the students wing of the CPI(M), in his college days but later moved to the RSS. In what was seen by many as retaliation, an SFI leader, K.V. Sudheesh, was hacked to death before his elderly parents the very next day.

Another speaker at the seminar was N. Sarasu, the retired principal of the prestigious Government Victoria College in Palakkad. She was given a mock funeral on 31 March 2016, the day of her retirement, by unknown students. *The Hindu* reported that a symbolic 'grave' appeared in front of the main building of the college on 31 March and the inscriptions on it said that the grave was dug for Ms Sarasu, who was retiring after twenty-three years of service. A wreath was placed on the grave, which was decorated with yellow and pink flowers. A death note was found next to it with scathing allegations against Ms Sarasu, whose actions as principal had allegedly provoked not only SFI activists but also some teachers of the pro-CPI(M) service organization.[43]

Breaking into tears, Sarasu alleged at the seminar that she had been targeted and isolated by her colleagues and students for her initiatives to reform the quality of education and attempts to enforce discipline among students as well as teachers. The RSS students wing ABVP took up her cause later.

*

A new CPI(M)-led government was sworn into office in May 2016. The tri-cornered elections were fought fiercely because it was the first time that the BJP had made a serious electoral play in the state. In previous elections, the BJP was just an 'also-ran' despite the strong RSS presence. It had never won a single seat in the state even though it regularly put up candidates.

Often, the RSS had even forsaken the BJP to favour the Congress party. In the 2001 assembly elections, it advised the BJP that instead of contesting all the seats, it strategically contest about forty seats and tacitly support the Congress in the rest. The BJP, however, did not pay heed to the advice and put up candidates in almost all seats. A miffed RSS then decided to support the Congress to defeat the CPI(M).[44]

Former joint general secretary of the RSS, K.C. Kannan, who gave up all official positions in 2014 to start a family and help run his wife's condiments business, ruefully admits that the RSS work is incomplete in the state because it has not been able to convert it into political power even though the Sangh has had the largest number of shakhas in the state of Kerala for years.[45] The main reason is that the biggest 'Hindu party' in Kerala is the CPI(M) in terms of community-wise support. Hindus are a little under 55 per cent of the population followed by over 26 per cent Muslims and 18 per cent Christians as per Census 2011. Large sections of the Ezhava community, which forms a little under a fourth of all Hindus, have traditionally supported the CPI(M). The party also counts on support from a fair number of economically lower-middle-class but socially upper-caste Nairs, and Scheduled Castes.

In 2016, the BJP tied up with the newly formed Bharat Dharma Jana Sena (BDJS), a party established by Tushar Vellapally, son of Vellapally Natesan, general secretary of the Sree Narayana Dharma Paripalana Yogam (SNDP), the largest organization of the Ezhava community. It was the culmination of an effort started by VHP leader Ashok Singhal in 2010 when he first broached teaming up with SNDP politically, according to a senior RSS leader in Kerala. The BJP hoped to capitalize on the SNDP's clout in the community to wean away voters from CPI(M). That did not happen and the CPI(M) won the legislative assembly.

*

One warm summer night in 2016, two men met at the Kannur guest house. One was a *kriya yogi* and the other, P. Jayarajan, a man who, his rivals say, wields the power to decide whether a person in the district lived or not. The yogi, M, is an unusual person.

M, as he is popularly known, was born Mumtaz Ali Khan into a Pathan family in Thiruvananthapuram. Mumtaz started having spiritual experiences when he was a young boy and at nineteen left home. He roamed the country meeting mystics and finally finding a kriya yoga master in the Himalayas with whom he wandered the snowy mountains for three years, according to his rather eccentric autobiography *Apprenticed to a Himalayan Master*. His master had renamed him Madhu. A person from the Jaisalmer royal family shortened it to 'M'.[46]

M returned to the plains, first taking up a job at *Organiser* and later working with Jiddu Krishnamurti in Chennai. He finally set up the Satsang Foundation which runs an ashram and school in Madanapalle on the Andhra–Karnataka border. Unlike many spiritual leaders with long beards and flowing robes, M is usually clean shaven and is often seen in trousers and shirts.

When the left government came to power in Kerala, M had just completed a year-long peace walk from Kanyakumari to Kashmir, winding through all the big states. Flagged off by RSS general secretary Suresh Joshi in Kanyakumari, the walk attracted civil society leaders and politicians in all states irrespective of party affiliations as it passed by. In 2014, M had also led an hour-long yoga camp for CPI(M) workers in Kannur where Pinarayi Vijayan was present.[47]

M decided to use his good relationships with both CPI(M) and RSS leaders to initiate a dialogue. He knew the key person for peace from the CPI(M) was Jayarajan, the all-powerful Kannur district secretary. In the party's scheme of things, district secretaries are extremely powerful and have great freedom to decide on what happens in their domains.

That summer night, M wanted to know from Jayarajan himself if Kannur could hope for peace. Jayarajan started off by recounting everything RSS has been doing historically. M cut him short: 'Perceptions differ. The RSS has a different view. But views don't matter now. History is history.' M wanted to talk about new beginnings. Jayarajan extended his limp hand and said: 'Believe me when I say this. Unlike what many would have told you, I'm not a beast. I don't have any personal grudge against anyone and I'm not seeking revenge for what was done to me.' That was what M wanted to hear. He had already done the background work.[48]

A few weeks before, M had broached the subject of peace talks to Chief Minister Vijayan mentioning that he knew RSS leaders well and if he would be interested. 'Will they listen?' Vijayan had asked. Incidentally, that is exactly what the RSS leaders in Kerala later said about the CPI(M). Kerala state secretary P. Gopalan Kutty's (popularly known as 'Master') first response to M's proposal was: 'We know about you and your spiritual standing. But will the communists agree?'[49]

M then met Suresh Joshi at the RSS's Kochi office. Joshi responded positively to the proposal. M wanted to consult the sarsanghchalak too. A meeting was arranged on the sidelines of a function at Vigyan Bhavan in Delhi. There he had asked Mohan Bhagwat to suggest names who could act as point persons. Bhagwat gave him four names.[50]

With all the key players on the same page, M booked a suite at a luxury hotel in Thiruvananthapuram. RSS state secretary Gopalan Kutty Master, vibhag prachar pramukh Valsan Thillenkeri, *Janmabhoomi* managing director M. Radhakrishnan and former prant pracharak S. Sethumadhavan arrived early. CPI(M) state secretary Kodiyeri Balakrishnan arrived next. Later in the night, Kerala chief minister Pinarayi Vijayan walked in, alone. He had arrived at the hotel without any police escort. The top-secret meeting would have been stillborn if news leaked. Both parties kept their word.[51]

As the talks began, one of the RSS leaders let loose a tirade on the atrocities by the party. Vijayan sat quietly, occasionally casting a glance at M. After a few minutes, M interjected and urged him to patiently listen to what Vijayan had to say. Vijayan said quietly, 'I've not come here to wash past linen. I'm interested in ending this violence.'[52]

It broke the ice. They resolved to set up mechanisms for regular meetings and talks at all levels. For the first time in over three decades, the CPI(M) and RSS's top leaders, one of them also the executive head of the state, had together decided to break the cycle of killings that had consumed too many lives. They owed it to the numerous orphans and widows of Kannur.[53]

Vijayan suggested that they hold a meeting in Kannur, the epicentre of the conflict in the presence of the chief actors. Gopalan Kutty says the talks were held in a cordial atmosphere unlike on earlier occasions when such meetings often turned accusatory and abusive. They took precautions to ensure the talks were not derailed this time. Vijayan said he would go ahead and announce that the CPI(M) and the RSS have reached an agreement to bury the hatchet. This would check any attempts to derail the pact.

However, one week later, an RSS worker was attacked in Kannur. Gopalan Kutty immediately called Vijayan, and the chief minister responded promptly. Kutty thought the chief minister was genuine in his attempts at peacemaking.

Both parties then set up communication links at every level. CPI(M) leaders say they didn't even know who the RSS workers were and who oversaw the area because they worked discreetly. Names and telephone numbers of persons were exchanged to make contact and it was agreed that both parties would rush their leaders to the spot in case of an incident.

Even as the talks were on and confidence-building mechanisms were being put in place, the RSS continued to build pressure nationally through its Redtrocity campaign. In December 2016, Pinarayi Vijayan had to abandon a function organized by Malayali organizations in Bhopal after Sangh Parivar activists threatened to disrupt it and showed placards saying, 'Kerala CM P. Vijayan Go Back.'[54]

The two sides accuse one another of planning and executing the murders with the full knowledge and participation of the respective leaderships. They admit that retaliatory strikes have happened. But both deny any of those were premeditated, planned or with the knowledge of leaders. They prefer to see the incidents as angry reaction of near and dear ones. The RSS's main grouse is that the CPI(M) was not allowing it to function in many places. It also said the police should act independently. It accused that violence shot up whenever the CPI(M) was in power.

'Even when we are talking about peace, we feel that there is a section that is working against it,' says Vijayan.[55] The CPI(M) says that the RSS has focused on certain centres in Kerala to establish their influence though it has been unsuccessful. The state police, in a reply under the Right to Information (RTI) Act to one Gangadhar Patil in Bengaluru in November 2016, released statistics of what it considers political murders in Kerala.[56] The data showed that the two sides were evenly matched, with the CPI(M) losing thirty workers and the Sangh Parivar thirty-one between 2000 and 2016. The total number of political murders was 170 during the period.

While RSS leaders acknowledge that weeding out the left, lock, stock and ideology, is a priority, Chief Minister Pinarayi Vijayan says the RSS wants to annexe Kerala through force. Sometimes it brings volunteers from outside. They use money power and muscle power. Even in places that the RSS labels as CPI(M) villages, there is RSS presence. It may not be strong but still it is present unlike their claim that the CPI(M) doesn't let them work. Vijayan says the RSS training itself is such that it encourages criminal tendencies. 'In one criminal case we found that a shakha-going school student was involved.'[57]

The chief minister, who has been the chief driving force of the dialogue with the Sangh, doesn't blame everyone in the organization. He says there are people in the RSS who genuinely want peace but those who don't are more influential in the Sangh's decision-making process. On the charge that his own party is at the forefront of violence and murderous attacks, he doesn't rule out the possibility of involvement of some party members but insists that the party or its leadership has never planned to attack anyone. He also says that he has instructed police to conduct unbiased investigations.

*

Valsan Thillenkeri is considered by many as P. Jayarajan's counterpart in the RSS, a man who can match left aggression with equal force.

The CPI(M) believes Valsan plans all the violence from the RSS side just as the RSS considers Jayarajan as the mastermind behind every killing of Parivar workers.

Valsan is a short man with a handlebar moustache and watchful yet easy demeanour. He is the principal of Pragathi College, a private institution run under the auspices of Sangh affiliate Vidya Bharati. Sitting on the top-floor yoga hall of the college on a hot summer day, Valsan talks softly about the many RSS and BJP workers brutally hacked to death. He remembers the peace talks clearly, including the dates on which each measured step was taken. It is not very different from listening to Vijayan or Jayarajan. The explanations and the accusations are the same. Only the roles are reversed.

Valsan doesn't deny the possibility of retaliations from the RSS's side but says it is mostly cadres who, having lost friends and family and consumed by grief, might have retaliated. He denies that the RSS ever planned any attack. He says the RSS has only one demand: freedom to expand its work unhindered. Valsan says violence increases whenever the CPI(M) comes to power. That is because they use the police to their advantage. Police should be independent but it rarely is, he alleges.[58]

Despite the talks, attacks on both sides have continued. However, both sides also say that the talks were not futile. The intensity and frequency of the violence have reduced. They say it is very difficult to control cadres, who have been brought up on a steady diet of violence and who have lost friends and family, from exacting revenge every time an incident occurs.

Although the talks this time appear to have helped somewhat, peace is unlikely to hold for too long as Kerala remains the RSS's unfinished agenda. Its political arm, the BJP, has managed to convincingly defeat the CPI(M) in Tripura, once considered an unconquerable fort. Kerala is the only remaining bastion of communism.

However, the tiny state is a different ball game because issues that are important and emotional in the northern parts of the country rarely have any resonance in Kerala. For instance, cow slaughter cannot be made an issue in the state where beef is freely consumed by all communities. There are many RSS volunteers who do not have any problem consuming the meat. Kummanam Rajasekharan, former RSS pracharak and former Kerala BJP president, had once said that he had no issues with people eating beef. He, however, supported cow protection not for emotional reasons but for its economic utility.[59]

*

The Redtrocity campaign perhaps was the RSS media wing's most successful campaign so far and it managed to take the fight right into the rival camp. Social media warriors from both sides were fully engaged but the RSS had an advantage in the mainstream media. Its relentless campaign forced national newspapers and television channels to write and broadcast the conflict in the tiny state to the rest of the country. What until then remained a local issue became a prime-time debating topic on many television channels. The RSS is determined to uproot the CPI(M) from Kerala but the communists are ready to dig in for as long as it takes. And the RSS wants to do it its own way rather than depend on the BJP.

It received another chance in September 2018. The Supreme Court ordered that the doors of the popular temple of Sabarimala, situated atop a hill in the thickly forested Western Ghats in Kerala, be opened to women of all ages.[60] The temple to the celibate deity Ayyappa traditionally did not allow women between the ages of ten and fifty (roughly the menstruating age) to enter the shrine.

Two years before, at its annual general body meeting, general secretary Bhaiyyaji Joshi had clearly articulated the Sangh's stand on temple entry for women. He had made the organization's stand clear when temple entry activist Trupti Desai was agitating for entry for women at Shani Shingnapur in Maharashtra:

Because of some unfair traditions, at certain places there has been a lack of consensus on the question of temple entry. Wherever such problems exist, attempts should be made to bring about a change of mind through proper discussions. It has to be borne in mind that such sensitive issues should not be politicized, and should be resolved only through discussion and dialogue, and not through agitations.[61]

In a television interview ahead of a Supreme Court hearing on Sabarimala, Joshi reiterated that court order must be accepted and such traditions cannot continue in modern times.[62] He also told a television channel in Kerala that only a few temples out of thousands do not allow women entry. 'We believe it [entry ban] should not exist even as an exception.'[63]

Immediately after the court order, the state government led by Pinarayi Vijayan vowed to make all the arrangements for women's entry into the shrine. However, protests erupted within hours. At the forefront was the Nair Service Society, a non-political community organization of upper-caste Nairs. What caught everyone by surprise was women of the community hitting the streets in hordes. A few days later, R. Sanjayan, deputy director of the Sangh-inspired institution Bharatiya Vichara Kendram, wrote an article in *Janmabhoomi*, the Sangh's Malayalam mouthpiece. Titled 'Sabarimala: Unnecessary Controversies Irrelevant', the article strongly backed the court order.

Sanjayan said that some people were trying to confuse Hindus based on the court order, and it should not be allowed. Urging the state government to make arrangements for the likely increase in women devotees to the temple, he said discrimination had no scriptural support and more women devotees at the temple would only increase its prestige, not diminish its purity. Sanjayan added that it was difficult to disagree with the court's argument that the ban on women in Sabarimala is not an essential element of religious faith and that the Constitution, though it guarantees religious freedom, cannot contradict other fundamental rights.[64]

When the protests continued, the RSS and BJP sensed an undercurrent of resentment against the Vijayan government, especially among the upper-caste Nairs. It sensed a political opportunity in the Sabarimala muddle and decided to fish in troubled waters. Soon, RSS and BJP leaders were seen organizing protests across the state. On 5 October 2018, five days after the judgment, Joshi issued a statement deferring to the protestors. '…it is an issue of a local temple tradition and faith to which sentiments of millions of devotees, including women, are attached. These sentiments of the devotees cannot be ignored while considering the judgement,' it said. 'Unfortunately, the Kerala government has taken steps to implement the judgement with immediate effect without taking the sentiments of the devotees into consideration. There is an obvious reaction to the same by the devotees, especially women, who are protesting against the forceful breaking of the tradition. While the Supreme Court Judgement should be respected, Rashtriya Swayamsevak Sangh calls upon all the stakeholders, including spiritual and community leaders to come together to analyse and address the issue availing judicial options also.'[65]

In the weeks that followed, the state government dug in its heels, invoking the progressive social tradition of Kerala and its renaissance spirit of welcoming change and embracing modernity. RSS and BJP leaders took to the streets against the state government's attempt to implement the Supreme Court's order.

'Sabarimala is a golden opportunity for us. It is a puzzle and we cannot foresee how it will be solved,' BJP president Sreedharan Pillai was heard telling youth wing volunteers in a leaked video. He went on to claim that BJP leaders planned agitations and disruptions and that he had planned strategy with Sabarimala temple priests and other stakeholders.[66]

The agitations, blockades, protest marches and strikes continued throughout the last weeks of 2018 and early 2019 when the temple opened for its pilgrimage season of two lunar months. But the Pinarayi government remained unmoved from its stand.

Whether the Sabarimala volte-face helped the BJP make political inroads in Kerala, as the RSS had hoped when it diluted its long-standing principled position for a more populist alternative, will be known only in 2021 when the state goes to elections. It remains the last communist bastion in the country. BJP breached the CPI(M)'s Tripura fort in early 2018 when it beat politburo member and three-time chief minister Manik Sarkar's bid for re-election. However, it was more a decimation of the Congress party in the state than the destruction of the CPI(M) which retained a 42.2 per cent vote share, a 6 per cent slide from the previous election. The Congress party's vote share eroded from 36.5 per cent in 2013 to a meagre 1.5 per cent five years later while the BJP's swelled from 1.8 per cent to 43.6 per cent.[67]

Within days of Manik Sarkar being voted out of power, a statue of Russian revolutionary leader Lenin in Belonia town in South Tripura was pulled down.[68] A few days later, the Marx-Engels Sarani leading up to the chief minister's residence was renamed Shyama Prasad Mookerjee Road.[69] The Sangh Parivar had begun peeling off the symbols of its strongest ideological rival in earnest. It was a demonstration of its credo in the Mohan Bhagwat era: political power would be the sledgehammer with which the RSS would enforce change.

8

A Nation Within

On 22 June 2005, then US ambassador, David C. Mulford, sent a confidential cable to Washington titled 'Socioeconomic Future of Indian Dalits Remains Bleak'. The cable was a status note on the condition of Dalits in the country.

Ram Nath Kovind, current president of India but then a BJP MP from Uttar Pradesh, who was interviewed by American diplomats, told them that open discrimination against Dalits had reduced dramatically in the preceding decade. However, he also predicted that caste-based discrimination would exist for at least the next fifty to hundred years in India. Kovind suggested that since the Hindu religion condones caste, it would take longer for the Indian government to end caste discrimination than the US administration to eradicate racial discrimination in their country. The true basis of discrimination was economic in nature rather than caste-based, as the haves discriminate against the have-nots and use the caste system to perpetuate differences between economic groups. Comparing the caste system to the trade guilds in feudal Europe (in that certain groups performed specific jobs), Kovind said under the caste system persons acquire their trade at birth, while the guilds allowed job mobility. Caste factors were used to protect jobs and livelihoods more than anything else.[1]

While Kovind was right that caste discrimination would remain for a long time, his reading of the nature of that discrimination was grossly inadequate as events have frequently borne out.

In late March 2018, Pradeep Rathod, twenty-one, was allegedly murdered in Timbi village in Bhavnagar district of Gujarat. Police reportedly found that Rathod, a Dalit, was killed because he was riding a horse, which did not go down well with the upper-caste people of the village.[2] A Dalit man was beaten up by a group of 'unidentified' men with lathis, and forced to say 'Jai Shri Ram', 'Maa Kaali ki Jai' and 'Bholenath ki Jai', allegedly for tearing posters of Hindu gods outside the houses of his own community members in Muzaffarnagar's Purqazi area and sticking B.R. Ambedkar's pictures instead. The beating, which was caught on camera, showed the Dalit man wearing a helmet begging for mercy.[3] In early October 2017, ANI reported that a young Dalit person was thrashed in Limbodarai village in Gandhinagar in Gujarat because he was sporting a moustache. In the video, twenty-four-year-old Piyush Parmar claims that upper-caste men thrashed him and his cousin because they did not like a moustache on a lower-caste person.[4]

A simple Google search merely saying 'Dalit youth' throws up page after page of such accounts of atrocities, sometimes for merely eating food in the presence of upper-caste men or sitting on a chair. While north Indian states such as Uttar Pradesh and Rajasthan feature regularly, Gujarat from the west also comes up. From the south, Andhra Pradesh and Tamil Nadu hit the headlines frequently for attacks on Dalits.

In mid-2016, men who claimed to be cow vigilantes, tied four Dalits to an SUV and flogged them for several hours in Una village near the famous Gir National Park, home to the Asiatic lion, in Gujarat. They were accused of killing and skinning cows. The incident caused a national uproar. A senior leader of the RSS said that the organization was sufficiently shaken by the incident. 'We held a *samrasta* meeting the very next month in the district. The

RSS also decided to intensify its samrasta efforts in the wake of the incident,' he said.[5]

Uttar Pradesh, Bihar, Rajasthan and Andhra Pradesh lead the table of crime against Scheduled Castes, according to the National Crime Records Bureau. Eight out of ten accused for atrocities against Dalits and tribals are never convicted. Anecdotal evidence suggest that crimes against, oppression and unfair treatment of Dalits have been increasing over the years. On the one hand, the RSS is trying to woo them towards the Sangh Parivar but on the other, upper-caste Hindus only see an unfair playing field for themselves vis-à-vis Dalits in terms of acquiring jobs and getting placements in educational institutions.

The RSS faces a complex array of issues when approaching Dalits. Founded by Maharashtrian Brahmins, the organization's leadership has historically been skewed towards upper castes, although, owing to its foundational military ethic, it practised an egalitarianism rare in organizations. Like armies, its *esprit de corps* was restricted to the organization and it did not bother itself with the intense discrimination in the world in which it operated. Unlike social organizations whose aim was reform, the RSS saw itself as a protector and consolidator of Hindus and the Hindu nation. Even social service became a part of the Sangh's core activity only when Deoras used it as a tool to expand the organization's reach and influence.

At an internal RSS meeting in Kerala in 2014, Mohan Bhagwat, who was touring the state, faced a question from a taluk sanghchalak. 'It appears caste consciousness is increasing even as the Hindu society progresses. Many incidents in Kerala and elsewhere point to that. Do you think the Sangh can stop such thinking?' Bhagwat replied, 'The Sangh should not get into eradicating or opposing caste. Caste is a system (though now perverted) that exists in the society. It would remain until the society believes in it. When it becomes disagreeable, society itself will reject it. The society should think about it. Not just the Sangh.'

It was a peculiar answer that reveals a dilemma: It is accused of casteism if it portrays caste as a useful social system gone awry. If it rejects it, it risks upsetting its own well-wishers and supporters. Either position also comes with a political cost that the Sangh is not prepared to pay.

'We are not supporting it because if we do then those who are anti-caste will become anti-Sangh. We are not opposing it because if we do then those who support it will stand against us. We are neither supporters nor opposers. That the age-old caste system is now decrepit is a fact but it does not have an alternative. But it is not the Sangh's job to find one,' Bhagwat said. The only way out then is to take the high ground away from the turbulent waters. 'Our job is to create a Hindu society that is not casteist by nature. Affection and respect should grow to eliminate casteism. Differences and discrimination in society should go and a brotherhood of Hindus should develop among all sections.'[6]

This position is slightly different from the one Balasaheb Deoras, months after he became the sarsanghchalak, took in the mid-1970s. Deoras wanted the 'caste system to die'. Efforts to push the organization towards eliminating caste, despite Deoras's best labours, never really bore fruit because it largely reflected the views prevalent among Hindus. And, as Bhagwat said, the RSS is not yet prepared to take a tough reformist stand that could be perceived to be against a section of Hindus, specifically, anti-upper-castes. It is also mindful of BJP voters and does not want to rock the boat for the party. One statement suggesting a review of India's reservation policy by Bhagwat in the run-up to the Bihar elections is believed to be the reason the party got drubbed in the state.

Quota politics gradually started heating up in the late 1970s when Bihar proposed reservation for backward communities in government jobs and education. It came to a boil after the V.P. Singh government implemented the Mandal Commission recommendations. The second Backward Class Commission was set up by the Janata Party government headed by Morarji Desai on

New Year's Day 1979. Its chairman was B.P. Mandal, a former chief minister of Bihar for a brief period, whose name became synonymous with the Commission's report. By the time the Commission submitted its report on 31 December 1980, the Morarji government had fallen and Indira Gandhi was back in power. She put it in deep freeze. Perhaps if the Morarji government had survived, it may have done the same thing or perhaps followed the Bihar model which was much less disruptive.

In 1978, Karpoori Thakur, chief minister of Bihar's then Janata Party government, which had representation of all major castes, suddenly announced 26 per cent reservation for backward castes in government jobs. Thakur had not even consulted his cabinet. Predictably, the upper castes were agitated. The then Janata Party president, Chandra Shekhar, set up a committee, which had Thakur and some of his ministers, to look into the issue. Lawyer Shanti Bhushan, who was then the Union law minister in the Morarji government, was the convener of the panel.

Bhushan told Thakur that it was important to keep the upper castes in confidence. He would not be able to implement it without their support. Thakur pointed out a constitutional problem: upper castes were not allowed to have a quota. Bhushan suggested a formula that circumvented the constitutional hurdle; keep 3 per cent reservation for women irrespective of caste within the 26 per cent. Since upper-caste women were more educated and had better social mobility, the entire quota would almost exclusively go to them. He also suggested another 3 per cent jobs be reserved using income as a criterion. This 3 per cent could also be cornered exclusively by upper caste families for the same reason that they could compete better against the other castes even if they were poor.[7]

The formula would be well within the Constitution and assuage upper castes as they would have a 6 per cent quota. The backward castes would get 20 per cent. Bhushan recommended splitting up the 20 per cent into quotas for most backward and less backward castes. This was to prevent more powerful communities such as Yadavs and Kurmis from cornering the bulk of the quota. The compromise formula worked for all, and the Bihar government introduced the reservation system.

However, 1990 was different. The political cauldron in Delhi was boiling over and the Ram Janmabhoomi movement was fast approaching its pyrrhic finale.

The Sangh Parivar, particularly the VHP and a resurgent BJP, which had junked Gandhian socialism as its guiding principle for Integral Humanism, were at their belligerent best. The then BJP president L.K. Advani was about to embark on his most ambitious political journey on a truck modelled as a chariot to agitate for a temple in Ayodhya. The Ram Janmabhoomi movement had stirred up Hindu emotions like never before. A year before, the VHP had got a Dalit volunteer from Bihar to lay the foundation stone of the Ram temple to underline the movement's casteless, pan-Hindu character. The RSS's efforts to unite Hindus seemed to be paying off. And the BJP had slid into position with a resolution endorsing construction of a Ram temple in Ayodhya at its national convention in Palanpur in June 1989.[8]

Amid the turmoil, V.P. Singh announced in August 1990 that his government would implement the Mandal Commission recommendation introducing 27 per cent reservation in Central government jobs and college admissions. BJP leaders could not oppose it as not only was it supporting the government, it had also promised the implementation of the Commission's recommendation in its election manifesto. Singh's move blew open the centuries-old divisions in Hindu society that had been temporarily forgotten in the carefully calibrated frenzy of the temple movement.

The burning symbol of the protests etched forever in public memory was a student of Deshbandhu College, Rajeev Goswami, who set himself on fire in front of his college in Delhi to protest the government's move. Advani and BJP MP Madan Lal Khurana visited Safdarjang Hospital to see the parents of Rajeev Goswami but students hooted them away. Advani faced the heat of the protests even during his rath yatra when his chariot was pelted with stones by Mandal protesters.[9]

The implementation of the Mandal Commission report was a setback to the RSS's efforts to consolidate Hindus. The chasm between upper and lower castes widened. Even though Deoras had tried to push the organization towards an active outreach to lower castes and Dalits, the organization had not internalized the idea. And the issue was so pregnant with politics that it became too hot to even mention publicly.

*

In August 2017, when Pragya Pravah, the intellectual arm of the RSS, organized a conclave ('Decolonizing the Indian Mind') of Sangh intellectuals at Gandhi Smriti at Rajghat, one of the first points that cropped up in discussions was about the RSS position and government policy on caste and reservations. When one person urged the Sangh that reservation should be based on the level of deprivation rather than caste, sarsanghchalak Bhagwat reportedly said half in jest, 'Humne agar aarakshan ka "aa" bhi bol diya to controversy ho jayegi. Is liye hum chup hi rahenge is vishay par (Even if I utter the "aa" of aarakshan [reservation], there will be a controversy. So we will keep quiet on the subject).'[10]

The Sangh's public utterances on caste and quota, quite clearly, are determined by the political situation in the country even though it is steadfast on the opinion that reservation should be based on economic backwardness. There is also a Dalit consolidation experimenting politically by teaming up with Muslims in many places. Gujarat Dalit leader and member of the state assembly, Jignesh Mevani, openly called for a Dalit–Muslim consolidation to 'uproot the fascist forces ruling the country for the last four years'.[11]

The Supreme Court in March 2018 indicated that it was keen to interpret the stringent Scheduled Castes and Scheduled Tribes (Prevention of Atrocities) Act a bit more liberally allowing bail for those arrested under the law.[12] It was immediately seen as a dilution of an Act which was rarely implemented in its spirit.

On 2 April, Dalits held countrywide protests, stalling road and rail traffic and taking out rallies against the 'attempt to dilute the Act'.[13] In western Uttar Pradesh, two people reportedly died, and several were injured as the protests turned violent. A year before, Saharanpur in western Uttar Pradesh had been rocked by violence when upper-caste Thakurs took out a procession through a Dalit neighbourhood while celebrating Rajput king Maharana Pratap's birthday. It was later alleged that the Thakurs beat up several Dalits and burnt about 100 homes as the procession turned violent.

Dalits saw it as rising upper-caste hooliganism because Thakur Ajay Singh Bisht had just become chief minister after the BJP swept state elections in March 2017. Yogi Adityanath, as Bisht is popularly known, is also the head priest of Gorakhpur's Gorakhnath Matt, a monastery of the Nath sect of celibate monks who practise kriya yoga. His caste by birth is Thakur who were the erstwhile landowning feudal lords in states like Uttar Pradesh, Madhya Pradesh and Bihar. Yogi emerged as a firebrand Hindu leader over the past two decades, winning elections from Gorakhpur and setting up an organization called the Hindu Yuva Vahini comprising militant Thakur youth beholden to him. The organization has considerable clout in eastern Uttar Pradesh where even the administration is said to bow to its aggression.

Uttar Pradesh, one of the most divided states in terms of caste, religion and class, has been the epicentre of the Sangh Parivar's political project beginning with the anti-cow-slaughter agitation of the 1960s and later the Ram Janmabhoomi movement. No other state generates as much passion for Ram Janmabhoomi as much as Uttar Pradesh and Bihar. In most southern states, and even in a state like Gujarat, it's a moribund issue with the young generation weaned on a liberal dose of modern consumerism and American-style capitalism that celebrates wealth and power. 'I was an active participant in the Ram Janmabhoomi movement. But my children don't care about it.

They are more interested in Porsches and fancy mobile phones,' a former state leader of the RSS in Ahmedabad said.[14]

Yogi's rise to the chief minister's office had created apprehensions in Dalits that the state would be run over by Thakurs. The May 2017 violence in Saharanpur appeared to cement the belief. It prompted the Dalits, middle-caste Yadavs and Muslims to join in a political alliance. It is what the RSS feared the most. Both communities combined are numerically strong and can be electorally potent. Socially, it also sees this combination a threat to Hindu unity and hence the Hindu nation. The framing of the conflict is deeply problematic for the RSS.

A group of Dalit workers of the Bahujan Samaj Party (BSP) in a slum in Agra explained how this was not just caste war but also an ideological battle. 'This is a fight between the ideologies of Hedgewar and Ambedkar,' said one of them, a production manager at a shoe factory.[15]

This is one battle the RSS does not want to lose. It wants Ambedkar on its side, but on its own terms. The then RSS chief of media relations, Manmohan Vaidya, said even Ambedkar had not intended reservations to continue for perpetuity.[16] It has been trying hard to appropriate the Dalit leader but has met with patchy success. Its outreach to Dalits always stumbles on its perception among them as a Brahmin organization. The Dalit communities' mistrust of the Parivar has forced the Sangh to tread more carefully.

Speaking at a conference on 'Nationalism and Ethical Practices in Business' at the BSE, Bhagwat said politics reflects society and caste in politics was a reflection of that.

Samaj mein ethical practices ki jitni aadat hai, utni politics mein reflect hoti hai . . . Udaharan ke liye, jaat-paat ki rajneeti mujhe nahi karna, aisa main sochke bhi jata hoon lekin samaj toh jaat-paat par vote deta hai, toh mujhe karni hi

padti hai. Mujhe wahan tikna hai, tabhi toh main parivartan
laoonga . . . (The ethical practices of society are reflected in
the politics of the country. For example, I don't want to resort
to caste politics, but I am compelled to do it because society
votes based on caste. If I stay in power, only then can I change
the system.[17]

It was a significant statement; the clear public articulation that
political power is the necessary and chief instrument for change.
As a former pracharak commented, 'The RSS was a socio-political
organization. Now it is a politico-social organization.'[18]

*

This RSS's stand on caste is a departure from its pre-Mandal one
articulated by Deoras who was clear that the Sangh was duty-
bound to help get rid of the caste system. He knew the RSS was
already late and decided to take it head-on as soon as he took over as
sarsanghchalak. In a landmark speech delivered in Pune, he attacked
the varna system and caste.

Circumstances have changed so much that even to say that
Varna Vyavastha and caste system, which could serve as a
necessary basis for the proper functioning of the society, exist is
ridiculous. Perversion and confusion pervade the atmosphere.
Castes no doubt exist, but they have nothing to do with the
preservation of the social fabric.[19]

Deoras had just become the sarsanghchalak the previous year after
the death of Golwalkar. In the initial years, the RSS had not actively
engaged with the issue of social discrimination. Golwalkar was a
supporter of the fourfold caste (varna) system. He justified it saying
that the system, at the time of origin and in early practice, did not

have untouchability. It was a mere segregation of people according to their vocation and a person's caste was not determined by birth but by aptitude. But it did not matter to Deoras. He was clear caste had no place in modern India.

He said the caste system had to die and the people had to think how to guide it along the correct path of termination. He called untouchability a terrible folly and said that 'it must, of necessity, be thrown out lock, stock and barrel. There are no two opinions about it.' Paraphrasing Abraham Lincoln on slavery, Deoras said, 'If untouchability is not wrong, then nothing in the world is wrong!'[20] Deoras had radical ideas on addressing the Hindu social systems and the way the organization approached them, but his fellow travellers were not yet ready and he withdrew them.[21]

In 1969, Golwalkar gave an interview to the Marathi publication *Navakal* in which he discussed the fourfold varna system. He suggested that a religious leader, a shankaracharya, should garland and embrace a Dalit and declare the end of untouchability. His views created a storm. Critics picked on Golwalkar, questioning the legitimacy of a religious leader in issuing a *diktat*. Those within the Sangh were so insulated from what was happening outside that even the few Dalits in the organization had no idea what Golwalkar was talking about. Ramesh Patange deals with the question quite extensively in his book, *Manu, Sangh and I*.

The autobiographical book also indicates how the typical RSS volunteer lived in a bubble that not only insulated him from varied experiences and ideas but also kept him ignorant of social realities unless he took an effort to investigate himself. It was more blissful ignorance than enlightened awareness of caste-based discrimination.

Patange, who has been associated with the Sangh forum Samajik Samrasta Manch from its inception and has been the editor of its bulletin *Samajik Samrasta Patrika*, rues that even though he had been going to Sangh shakhas from his childhood, he was unaware of the work of Mahatma Phule or B.R. Ambedkar. Patange, says the RSS's galaxy of heroes consisted of warrior kings like

Shivaji and Rana Pratap, Guru Nanak, and Subhas Chandra Bose, all battle veterans. 'There was total darkness in this respect [about Phule and Ambedkar] in my student days . . . My incomprehensibility of Guruji's interview on Chaturvarnya, and of the storm raised in its wake, was due to my own unawareness of social issues.'

The Sangh believed caste issues would be resolved once it succeeded in transforming the entire society. It had underestimated the deep roots of caste and the power of politics to sharpen or smoothen differences. Deoras understood this and knew that RSS must ponder over ways to overcome caste divisions to create a religion of nationalism. Without such a consolidation, the Hindus would be fewer in number and hence weaker. However, his colleagues were not as perceptive as would be clear later.

The Sangh was sure that caste would fade into irrelevance as the influence of its ideology rose. However, it had grossly misread the tea leaves. Caste was going to be the most important determinant of identity politics, especially in the politically influential north Indian states. The Congress party was adept at the game. The Jana Sangh and later the BJP took some time to learn the ropes. Once it did, the BJP played the game better than anyone else. Once its own political arm started playing the caste game, the Sangh made compromises too.

Patange says he was aware of Phule from school textbooks and had heard of Ambedkar but was unaware of the intellectual content of their revolt and revolutionary impact of their work. The extent of ignorance of a volunteer about the issue and his distance from the society in which he functions is clear from this incident Patange mentions. They lived in a happy bubble the RSS had created for them.

'Is untouchability still prevalent in our villages?' Patange asks pracharak and Emergency prison-mate Balasaheb Dixit after first reading about Dr Ambedkar's life. Dixit explained to him how meticulously untouchability was observed with separate teacups for upper and lower castes kept in restaurants as well as other practices.

'I asked him, then what was the Sangh doing for untouchables. Did we make special efforts to bring them to the Shakhas? Does the Sangh do anything to change the society's attitude to them? We were really not doing anything to eradicate this social evil.' Patange was the secretary of a Sangh division at the time and it bothered him that the problem had not been referred to at all in the Sangh.

Patange, a tailor's son, grew up in one of the slums of Bombay. Yet he found very few from the large fishermen community of the city in RSS shakhas. The number of Dalits was negligible. Mahatma Phule and Ambedkar started finding a place in Sangh programmes only after the Emergency, and Patange took the lead in talking about them.

> I can give an instance of how limited was the social awareness of the Sangh worker. In 1978, the Maharashtra Assembly passed a resolution approving the change in the name of the Marathwada University. The approval produced sharp and bitter reactions in Marathwada. Dalit localities were set on fire. The issue of changing the name of the University soon turned into an issue about the very identity of Dalits. In those days, I used to read about these reactions in newspapers, but they did not produce any specific response. I would not be very wrong if I said that I had not realized the social significance of the issue. The Sangh had also not taken any particular stand on it.[22]

The Sangh's ambivalence continued until it came up before Deoras who said, 'I think the change in the name should be endorsed. Those who oppose it are not right in their thinking.' Some workers in Marathwada, however, did not think that way. They were of the view that the Sangh should keep away from the controversy, for the time being. They prevailed. Later events would show how the Sangh seems to take quick and definite decisions on such issues when there is an opportunity or challenge. At other times, they take a long time to find traction.

The commonly used word for equality is *samata*. However, when the RSS wanted to launch the Forum for Social Equality, it chose to call it Samajik Samrasta Manch. The reason was branding. The RSS believed that the movement for equality (*samata*) was exclusively leftist. 'If we started our movement with their shibboleth, people will not realize the uniqueness of our movement. Moreover, the leftists will start claiming that "the Sangh is borrowing their words because the Sangh philosophy does not have room for equality",' Dattopant Thengadi explained. He wanted to give the concept of equality a distinct RSS branding; some sort of equality-plus. 'We want Samrasta which alone can bring equality on a durable footing,' he said.

The Samajik Samrasta Manch was launched on 14 April 1983 at Pune. Yet, Phule and Ambedkar remained strangers to an average volunteer who continued to view Dalits with suspicion. Patange writes that the reason for the animus was the policy of reservation, the language of revolt in Dalit literature, the tenor of speeches of leaders in the Ambedkar movement and their hostility towards Hindutva. Phule and Ambedkar were also absent from the writings of Hindutva followers. The Samajik Samrasta Manch started projecting the Phule–Ambedkar philosophy in a different context. The slow adoption of the Dalit icons into the Sangh pantheon had begun.

Yet, it was like swallowing bitter medicine. When Patange published a booklet called *Samajik Samrasta, Dr Hedgewar and Dr Ambedkar* in 1988, he faced flak from swayamsevaks in Vidarbha, the RSS's birthplace. The cover had both Hedgewar and Ambedkar and Hedgewar was without his customary cap. On returning from a tour of Vidarbha, Patange's colleague Sukhdev Navale informed him that people in Vidarbha were greatly annoyed by the book. 'They feel you are doing all this to please Dalits. They asked me, "Who is this Patange? What does he think about himself?" You may be in trouble, Ramesh,' Navale told him.[23]

The meeting of the RSS's Akhil Bharatiya Pratnidhi Sabha of March 1981 was held in the background of unrest in Gujarat over a new reservation policy. That year, a new Congress government headed by Madhav Sinh Solanki came to power in the state. Solanki, a 'lower-caste' kshatriya, had the support of over 100 MLAs who were from the Scheduled Castes and Tribes or from the backward castes. The government introduced reservation at the postgraduate level in medical colleges for SC and ST candidates and also those from socially and educationally backward castes or class, which had about eighty-two communities, including some Muslim, in it.

The upper castes were up in arms calling the quotas unfair and demanded that only merit be considered for faculty appointments and college seats. Even though merit appeared to be a progressive argument, it was being used as a weapon to defend moribund Hindu hierarchy and maintain socio-economic status quo.[24]

For the first time, the ABPS had a resolution on reservation to debate. It was introduced at the instance of Deoras himself. The debate was heated and went on for a long time and majority of the delegates were against it.

The final draft read:

> The ABPS feels deeply perturbed over the explosive situation in Gujarat and elsewhere arising out of the issue of reservations. As one believing in the indivisible unity of the entire Hindu society including Harijans and tribals, the RSS has consistently been endeavouring to arouse this inherent spirit of oneness. The RSS considers it necessary that reservation be continued for the present with a view to bringing all these brethren of ours who have remained backward in educational, social and economic fields over the centuries at par with the rest of society.

The resolution said the quota policy had become a political tool and suggested setting up a committee of non-partisan social thinkers to study problems arising out of reservations and suggest steps to uplift Harijans and tribals. Reiterating that reservations cannot be permanent, it called for concessions for other economically backward sections as well.

The Sangh position remains unchanged in nearly four decades. A few months after he took over as sarsanghchalak, Mohan Bhagwat was asked his opinion on quotas. He replied that the issue had become politicized and the only way was to hand over the matter of reservations to a non-political body which should work with the goal of eradicating discrimination completely so that there was no reason or necessity for quotas.[25]

In the second half of 2015, Gujarat was again gripped by an anti-reservation agitation by Patidars, a numerically strong peasant community. The agitation was extraordinary in its organization and silent marches. As the agitation caught national attention, Mohan Bhagwat pitched in.

In an interview to the *Organiser* on Deendayal Upadhayaya's hundredth anniversary, Bhagwat was asked: 'You said integrity and honesty are the main parameters. Do you see any such policy initiative, undertaken or suggestive, which is in tune with integral humanism?'

The sarsanghchalak's reply was intriguing, both for its timing and tenuous connection to the subject at hand.

Reservation for backward classes is the right example in this regard. If we would have implemented this policy as envisaged by the constitution makers instead of doing politics over it, then present situation would not have arrived. Since inception it has been politicized. We believe, form a committee of people genuinely concerned for the interest of the whole nation and committed for social equality, including some representatives from the society, they should decide which categories require reservation and for how long. The non-political committee like autonomous commissions should be the implementation authority; political authorities should supervise them for honesty and integrity.[26]

The statement was quoted widely, and it was interpreted to mean that the Sangh wanted reservations to go. Although the Sangh later clarified that it strongly supported reservation for backward social groups, the damage to the BJP was done. It lost the Bihar assembly elections. Yet it was clear that the RSS's fundamental position on reservation was unchanged. In another context, Deoras had remarked, 'Those who demand reservation only on basis of caste are suffering from casteism, and those who demand reservation only on the basis of financial condition are ignoring the unfortunate, thousand-year-old history of our country.'[27]

Despite all its efforts, RSS leaders, most of whom belong to upper castes, consider reservations as an unnecessary appeasement of Dalits that ignores merit and promotes mediocrity if not ignorance. They favour reservation to the economically backward irrespective of caste or religion.

In 1981, when the resolution justifying reservations was introduced, workers from Gujarat vigorously opposed it. Every word was put under the lens. 'Many representatives opined that the Resolution was hasty, and likely to evoke adverse reaction in a large section of the people. Swayamsevaks from Gujarat understandably were naturally were unhappy. I was intently listening to the discussions. In view of so much opposition from workers, I was worried and felt the resolution would not go through. But it did,' writes Patange.[28]

Deoras appeared to be calm. After the debate was over, the meeting broke for tea. When the meeting resumed, he said, 'I have heard the discussion in the meeting. I have understood that many amongst us are not in favour of the resolution. I request you all to imagine yourself in the place of those for whom the reservations are meant. Try to enter their minds and see the present condition of those of our brethren, who have been neglected for hundreds of years. Understand their feelings. Then only take your decision.'

The resolution was passed, and the Sangh had officially endorsed reservations, albeit, with a lot of reservation. A senior leader, who was present at the meeting, says the resolution would never have passed if

Deoras had not made it clear that he wanted it. 'No one in the RSS would go against the sarsanghchalak's wishes, especially in public,' he says.[29]

Incidentally, the RSS resolution was adopted within a few weeks of mass conversion of Dalits to Islam in Meenakshipuram in Tamil Nadu.

Patange mentions an incident that shows how despite spending many years in the Sangh, swayamsevaks are unable to internalize the composite Hindu identity the RSS wants to cultivate.

One Balasaheb Gaikwad from Ahmednagar, belonging to the Mahar community, had converted to Christianity but wanted to return to the Hindu fold. The Hindutvavadis, who had a latent anger towards Ambedkar for converting Mahars to Buddhism, were happy that one of them was coming back and perhaps many others would follow.

The Sangh, however, faced a peculiar problem. Conversion does not end untouchability. Instead of being a Christian Mahar, he would be a Hindu Mahar. So, they decided to make him a Buddhist. Gaikwad would have none of it. A senior swayamsevak confronted Patange on why he was pushing Gaikwad to Buddhism. In Patange's words:

In Maharashtra, the number of Hindu Mahars is negligible. Most of them have embraced Buddhism. If Gaikwad were to be reconverted, where would he find a place in the Hindu social structure? Buddhists would not only not accept him but regard him as an enemy of Dr Ambedkar's thought. The Hindu society will not immediately accept a convert. The Hindutva protagonists, who were eager to bring Gaikwad back to the Hindu fold, did not feel themselves concerned with these social questions. They yearned for publicity for themselves, and for the credit of the conversion.[30]

'You attend *prabhat* [morning] shakha daily, isn't it?' I asked. 'Yes,' he replied. He did not understand the thrust of my question. 'Then you are conversant with the *Ekatmata Mantra* [unity hymn] which we recite in the morning shakha. A line in that hymn describing the criteria of Hindu says, "*Bhudhdhastatha arhant, boudhdha jainaha.*" You know it, I suppose.' 'Yes, I recite it,' he answered. 'It means Jains, Buddhists, Sikhs, Vedics, Vaishnavs all are one, all are Hindus. We also hear in the Sangh that Jainism, Buddhism, Sikhism are not alien religions. They are all branches of the Sanatana Dharma. If someone becomes a Jain or a Buddhist or a Sikh, he does not become a non-Hindu,' I said. I further told him that even if Gaikwad became a Buddhist, he, by our tenets, would be deemed Hindu. Slowly he understood what I was saying. Still, he asked, 'Hindu or Buddhist if it is only a nominal difference why not allow him to be a Hindu? At least that will not create any confusion.'[31]

A hierarchy clearly exists in which a Buddhist is not really considered at par with a Hindu even in the giant umbrella of Hindutva. Also, interestingly, the sense of equality *the Ekatmata Mantra* tries to project is visible to Patange, who knows the Dalit experience, but not to the upper-caste person.

Despite attending scores of boudhiks and camps, Hindu and Hindutva mean different things even to those in the Sangh. Nine decades of constant drumming notwithstanding, the Sangh is unable to contain multiple deep-rooted identities within its carefully constructed ideological framework or assuage communitarian insecurities.

*

The issue of changing the name of Marathwada University to Ambedkar University had been hanging fire since 1978. Even Deoras had supported the name change. Yet, the Sangh put it on the back burner until the early 1990s. Patange's account is revealing.

At a meeting in Jalna, a volunteer asked general secretary H.V. Sheshadri to spell out the Sangh standpoint on the *naamaantar*, or name-change issue. Sheshadri replied in clear and unambiguous terms, 'The Sangh is not opposed to the change in the name of the university. The *naamaantar* should be made, and the Marathwada University should be named after Dr B.R. Ambedkar.'[32]

That night, a meeting of all workers was held at Jalna. District karyavahs, pracharaks and activists from various RSS arms attended the marathon meeting. In the meeting, some argued that 'the *naamaantar* was an imposition; it is a demand from leaders from Pune and Bombay; it is an appeasement of Dalits, politically, we will be finished'. The objections were forcefully presented. The counter-arguments were 'the *naamaantar* is a must for social reasons, the Ambedkarite people should develop confidence in us and supporting *naamaantar* is a way to win their trust; we should give a rejoinder to the Shiv Sena's arguments: support to the *naamaantar* will not lead to political damage.' These arguments were also vigorously put forward. The debate ended with the RSS supporting the name change.

According to Patange, 'Designated as the Manuists in the progressive parlance, the RSS had taken one more step forward.' Although, it looked like in a socio-political contest, politics won the day, or night. The incident shows that despite its claims of being apolitical, the RSS was highly conscious of perception and sensitive to the political impact of its decisions.

Under Deoras, the Sangh had shed its inhibitions cultivated assiduously in the Golwalkar era and had gradually began to face outside. It was most pronounced in the outreach to communities within the Hindu fold long rejected by their own brethren as outcastes. 'Just as it was necessary to tell the people that the Sangh programmes belong to all Hindus, it was also necessary for the Sangh, to be perceived that way. This was extremely difficult for the Sangh. But the process had begun.'[33]

*

There are many ways to champion a cause. The difficult way is to assiduously build a movement, gradually converting opponents through debate and persuasion. The easier one is to embrace an existing champion as one's own. It is a tough task when the champion is someone you had opposed once. That is the case with the RSS's embracing of Ambedkar.

By no stretch of imagination can Dr B.R. Ambedkar be seen as having any sympathy for the Hindutva cause. Yet, the Sangh is now pulling out all stops to accommodate even that uncompromising critic of the Hindu society and religion. Just after Ambedkar had announced that he would convert to Buddhism in December 1956, Golwalkar wrote an article in the *Panchajanya*'s November edition[9] Contending that religious transformation is possible at an individual level, he asked:

> Is such mass conversion ever possible in any true religion? Every individual going in for conversion should first be able to evaluate the spiritual, moral and practical ideals of his original religion or faith and also the one he is going to embrace. Such a conversion involves a basic change in his perception of all the social spheres as well. Is such a fundamental and comprehensive change possible in mass conversions?[34]

The question not only failed to empathize with the social position of Dalits, it completely missed the point.

As an upper-caste Brahmin, Golwalkar's understanding and experience of Hinduism was of the privileged high order, delving in Sanskrit texts and happy meanderings in the high philosophies of the Upanishads and Vedas. The Dalit on the other hand lived and died in misery with no experience of or contact with that high culture. Ambedkar digs out passage after passage from the revered *Manusmriti*, historically considered the inviolable law by many, if not all, upper-caste Hindus, to show the ignominy and misery of the Dalit existence as it was preordained by the society. So much so that the Shudras' second name had to denote servitude and the first name had to be something 'contemptible'.[35]

The Dalit's memory as a part of the Hindu social order was of beatings and humiliations, of the object that others were too disgusted to touch. They prayed to the same deities, but their prayers would have mostly been a lament on their existence in constant pain and indignity. They were aware that converting would not change any of that but knew they were throwing away the yoke that held them captive to an inheritance of misery. As Ambedkar asked pointedly: does Hinduism recognize their worth as human beings? 'The wrongs to which the untouchables are subjected by the Hindus are acts which are sanctioned by the Hindu religion.'[36] Ashis Nandy points out that although Ambedkar rejected Islam and Christianity as possible refuges, he chose an austere form of Buddhism that was akin to them rather than the more popular Theravada which is closer to Hinduism.

Perhaps no one has described caste in a modern context better than Ambedkar:

> The atomistic conception of individuals in a society so greatly popularized—I was about to say vulgarized—in political orations is the greatest humbug. To say that individuals make up society is trivial; society is always composed of classes. It may be an exaggeration to assert the theory of class-conflict, but the existence of definite classes in a society is a fact. Their basis may differ. They may be economic or intellectual or social, but an individual in a society is always a member of a class. This is a universal fact and early Hindu society could not have been an exception to this rule, and, as a matter of fact, we know it was not . . . A caste is an enclosed class.[37]

Some castigated Ambedkar as a British stooge who actively conspired with them to undermine the Congress, Mahatma Gandhi and the freedom movement. In his acerbic work, *Worshipping False Gods*, former BJP minister Arun Shourie says Ambedkar saying that society, nation and country are just words is similar to what Christian missionaries have been preaching to Indians for a hundred years.[38]

Although the RSS has tried to keep social discrimination out of the organization, the upper-caste origins of those in leadership positions and the lack of leaders with the lived experience of discrimination made it almost impossible for it to internalize it. As Shourie's book shows, even the learned in the organization tried to underplay the Dalit cause. It is a common foible of those from privileged backgrounds who, even if well meaning, are incapable of fully appreciating the memory and experience of those oppressed. Their responses are formulaic and theoretic.

*

There is a new term the Sangh wants to popularize—assimilative diversity.[39] It is a cleverly vague term used to choose whom to include and whom to exclude. While the Muslim and Christian carry the responsibility of assimilation on their own shoulders, Buddhists, Jains, Sikhs and animist tribes are already included in the overarching definition of the cultural Hindu. The upper-caste tradition and cultural experience, however, are far removed from those of other castes.

The theoretical framework of the RSS's nationalist narrative built around ancient cultural roots and tradition, therefore, comes off at the seams when it interacts with India's social structure. Reforming traditions and cultural practices enmeshed in the warp and weft of the social structure without tearing the fabric is a delicate task made even more difficult by the upper-caste overhang in the Parivar.

Sarsanghchalak Mohan Bhagwat blames the 'ancient Brahminical system' and acknowledges that the upper castes must be prepared to face and bear anger to atone for the centuries of discrimination. That is easier said as events over the years have shown. Bhagwat explained the Sangh's method by relating an incident. An RSS volunteer was asked that if Lord Ram was a Hindu icon, did he support his slaying of Shambuka too? In the Ramayana, Rama cuts off the head of the low-born Shambuka for doing penance which only Brahmins and Kshatriyas are permitted to do. According to Bhagwat, 'This is a tricky question for a Hindu. It creates the dilemma of denouncing Prabhu Ram or supporting the killing of Shambuka.' The volunteer's answer was not only clever but also a perfect example of the RSS method. He said that by asking the question, the questioner (who presumably was a sceptic) accepts the historical existence of Lord Ram. After establishing that as a 'fact' in his favour, the volunteer obfuscated the issue itself.

> Now whether Ram really killed Shambuka, this is a debatable issue as many believe that this whole chapter is added in Uttar-Ramayana [later part]. The Ram we worship only killed the unjust and devil king. Slaying of Shambuka is not a matter of respect for us with reference to Prabhu Ram and if it is ever proved that Ram was responsible for the killing of Shambuka, we will denounce that.[40]

While the volunteer accepted that the existence of Ram could be proven by the mere asking of a question, he made the veracity of the event itself a matter of belief and any negative fallout contingent on evidence of the killing. This then is at the heart of the matter; the implication will remain false until proven otherwise. Interestingly, it is a device even the Supreme Court appears to have employed while allowing the Hindu claim over Ram Janmabhoomi.[41]

Although social reform movements have played a significant part in Dalit emancipation in many parts of the country, the biggest levellers have been urbanization, industrialization and English education—three megatrends of the past couple of centuries that broke down spatial boundaries, increased personal intercommunity interactions and helped upward mobility. The RSS ideology does not sit comfortably with the trends but political power and communication technology offer it an opportunity to take control and shape the customs and traditions that are replacing old ones; recast them into more widely acceptable norms and simplifying the practice of being Hindu enough to fit modern lifestyles.

The RSS believes the differences will disappear once all Indians are united by the religion of nationalism. However, like all religions and ideologies, its symbols and rituals are defined by the high priests of nationalism and the self-appointed arbiters measure and certify individuals' loyalty as Shourie did with Ambedkar.

Ashwamedha: Final Mile on the Political Horse

Nationalism is a slippery word, elusive and easily manipulated. In the RSS view, however, nationalism and patriotism are one and the same. In his essay 'Notes on Nationalism', George Orwell cautions against confusing nationalism with patriotism which is 'devotion to a particular place and a particular way of life, which one believes to be the best in the world but has no wish to force on other people'. Nationalism, Orwell says, is inseparable from the desire for power. 'The abiding purpose of every nationalist is to secure more power and more prestige, not for himself but for the nation or other unit in which he has chosen to sink his own individuality.'[1]

The erasure of the self is a defining feature of the RSS. It not only encourages submission but also demands total fealty from its volunteers irrespective of the position or office they occupy.

Two discussions and their denouement stood out at the Akhil Bharatiya Pratinidhi Sabha of the RSS in Gwalior in March 2019. The general elections were near, and the Sangh was girding up its loins to put its entire organizational might behind the BJP, and more importantly, Narendra Modi. The RSS had concluded that the Parivar needed a few more years to remould the Indian state's institutional architecture in its ideology.

Several RSS leaders are said to have expressed their reservations about Modi. It is believed that some had personal dislikes while others believed that his stardom was not in keeping with the organizational ethos. After all, Modi was a swayamsevak. One person commented, without naming Modi, that he was worried for the nation because personality cults could be harmful to its interests.[2] Sarsanghchalak Mohan Bhagwat is said to have taken the comment head-on and made the RSS's position crystal-clear. Modi was not only a swayamsevak and a pracharak, he was an ideal person to carry out the task cut out for him with single-minded determination and honesty. As a politician and administrator, he was carrying out his role perfectly. It was not possible for him to explain all his decisions as prime minister of the country but there could be no doubt that whatever he did would be in the national interest, he said. As for bringing harm to the nation, the questioner needn't worry. The RSS was on guard, Bhagwat reportedly said, firmly putting a lid on the discussion.

The second debate was more complicated and concerned a matter of great sensitivity: entry of women into the hill temple of Sabarimala in Kerala. The general body had proposed to introduce a resolution on gender equality based on the Sabarimala issue. In conclaves leading up to the general body meeting where final drafts of resolutions are presented for approval, delegates of Bharatiya Stree Shakti (BSS), a relatively young organization, complained that nobody had asked for their opinion before the RSS finalized its stand on the issue. It became a fait accompli for them and they had to defend it. They regarded it as an imposition.

Gender equality is a relatively new issue for the RSS which is exclusively male. Not that the RSS had not faced it before. The first time the question of excluding women from organizational activities was raised was in 1936 when Laxmibai Kelkar asked Hedgewar why he was restricting the RSS to men. Although the founder acknowledged that women had a role to play in nation building, he was reluctant to include them in the organization. He saw them playing a supporting part rather than on the front lines. He, however, suggested they start a separate organization if they wished and were willing to run it on their own.

Kelkar founded the Rashtra Sevika Samiti, the women's arm of the RSS, with an identical acronym, on Vijaya Dashami day in 1936 in Wardha. Although the Sevika Samiti was founded ten years after the RSS, it never expanded the same way as the men's outfit. Its membership was meagre and activities minimal.[3]

The Bharatiya Stree Shakti was formed in May 1988 with the stated aim of promoting gender equality in society. It held its third national convention in Nagpur in January 2018 on completion of three decades. 'We are of the firm belief that irrespective of gender disparities both men and women should strive to eradicate the exploitation of women which is the result of the patriarchal social structure and create a society where gender equality and gender justice prevails,' its president, K.S. Jayasree, wrote in the preface to the souvenir celebrating the organization's thirtieth anniversary. BSS worked on issues such as national policy on women, smart cities, surrogacy bill and various laws affecting women, family and society, to look at them from an Indian perspective.[4]

In the same month, another seminar by RSS's intellectual arm Prajna Pravah on women's issues explained the Indian perspective. The introduction to the seminar noted that Western feminism came to the *Third World* in three waves—the first bringing with it focus on suffrage and political rights; the second came with issues of workplace, sexuality, family and reproductive rights; and the third looked at the micro-politics of gender.

'In India, contemporary feminists have been manipulated through marketing and mainstream media and sold a clichéd lifestyle as politics and political opposition. Thus, while it is feminist to consume the latest clothes and addictive substances that the market offers, these remain lifestyle choices rather than opposition to patriarchy,' the introductory note said. According to it, women's assertiveness in India is linked to the traditions of goddess worship and 'Shakti' as the embodiment of female power. 'This, is the reason why, unlike the west, in India, men too have historically participated in the women's rights movement . . . Because of the tradition of goddess worship, Indian men are socially adjusted to the idea of women in positions of power,' it said rather naively. It broadly identified the main problems faced by Indian women as 'patriarchy and related hurdles and questions of Identity—Who am I?'[5]

Stree Shakti looks for answers to modern gender issues in Indian philosophies and traditions. It wants to find indigenous models of Stree Shakti and policy recommendations for Indian women. But often it finds itself trapped in larger organizational requirements and in opposition to other organizations within the Parivar. One senior Stree Shakti leader took objection to some initiatives and practices within the organizational conglomerate. 'Why should you refer to women only as mothers and sisters? Why should even Bharat Mata be depicted in the way she is shown now? That is stereotyping women,' she said. There are differences even within the organization on how women should behave, dress and carry themselves. At one Stree Shakti meeting in Delhi, women from Maharashtra were surprised when their colleagues from the north disapproved of them not wearing dupattas (scarves) over their salwar-kameez.[6]

At the general body meeting at Gwalior there were long debates on presenting the resolution as a gender equality issue. Bhagwat intervened to say that the practice of not allowing women into the temple was restricted to one place of worship because of local traditions. It should not be seen as a gender equality issue.

Ultimately, the resolution that was approved was nothing but a rant against the CPI(M) government in Kerala. As one RSS man commented wryly, 'The Sangh had no objection to allowing women entry into Sabarimala. Its only objection, it seemed, was it was being done by a communist government.'[7]

The resolution said:

Entire Hindu society has been facing an unfortunate situation where the ruling Left Front Government in Kerala is trampling upon the sentiments of Hindu society under the pretext of implementing the verdict of the Constitution bench of the Honourable Supreme Court allowing women of all ages to enter the holy Sabarimala temple.[8]

The RSS's view on Sabarimala was shaped by ideologue R. Hari, a former national chief of intellectual training. 'The uniqueness of Hindu culture is the freedom it accords the Comrade to wait in the car while his wife visits the Pazhani temple. It is Talibanization when you insist otherwise,' says Hari who has written extensively on reforming anachronistic rituals and traditions.[4] In his Malayalam book *Mattuvin Chattangale* (Change the Norms), Hari argues in detail why women should be allowed inside the Sabarimala temple.[9] The essay quoting texts and traditions had more or less become the RSS's official line on the issue.

The Supreme Court judgment allowing women to enter the Sabarimala temple and the public reaction changed all that and painted the organization into a corner. RSS leaders were at the forefront of aggressive protests. Television visuals showed some creating a ruckus on the sacred steps of the temple itself.

A top leader at the Gwalior ABPS is said to have commented that there were strategic reasons for the organization to take the call (on Sabarimala). He said it was not necessary that leaders and cadres approach issues in identical ways. Even if leaders took a soft stand, the cadre faced with ground realities could be rough and aggressive.

Its ambivalence in the run-up to the state elections not only upset its women volunteers, it also spoiled the BJP's closest chance so far to win a Lok Sabha seat from Kerala, which remains a distant chimera for the most efficient political apparatus that India has seen in three decades. To add insult to injury, Hindu discontent on account of Sabarimala filled the Congress party's sails, helping it sweep the state.

*

Although Kerala remained unconquered, the BJP, riding a groundswell of jingoism, consolidated and expanded its presence in the rest of the country and increased acceptability among various communities and castes. The party demolished the opposition in 2019, cementing the reputations of Narendra Modi and Amit Shah as the most effective duo to fight national elections. The RSS's role in these victories was not small. It rallied its troops and plunged into electoral politics as it had never done before.

In many places, senior RSS pracharaks were directly overseeing BJP candidates' campaigns.[10] The organization complemented its groundwork with social media campaigns too, helping BJP fight rivals in states such as Rajasthan and Madhya Pradesh where the party had suffered electoral setbacks in assembly polls.[11] Its most crucial contribution, however, was as the BJP's ear to the ground, constantly updating leaders of the people's mood and response to issues.

With the authoritative BJP victory, the RSS project of wresting the political initiative from the Congress and other regional formations is more or less complete. The Congress party is a shadow of its old self. Others such as the Samajwadi Party and Bahujan Samaj Party in Uttar Pradesh, the Rashtriya Janata Dal in Bihar and the CPI(M) in Bengal are fading into relative irrelevance.

Soon after the government took charge, Mohan Bhagwat told Sangh workers in Kanpur that the organization would play the role of an adviser to the government whenever it faltered. He said any democratically elected dispensation should be wary of 'misuse of power'.[12]

Swapan Dasgupta had observed after the BJP's 2009 electoral defeat:

> The RSS has always nurtured a deep disdain for politics. The founders of the movement, and particularly M.S. Golwalkar, viewed politics as naturally divisive and a distraction from the RSS' central project of nation-building. While the RSS

leadership thought it important to influence political thinking, it was always wary of excessive involvement. The full-timers of the RSS were, in particular, always advised to maintain a healthy detachment from partisan politics.

. . . It is hard to put a finger on exactly when this delicate arrangement [of RSS leaders' ability to persuade rather than control BJP] began to be disturbed. After the BJP's spectacular surge in 1991 and its success in forming state governments, some local RSS bigwigs developed an undue interest in political power. Pressures from lay swayamsevaks on the local RSS translated into RSS pressure on the BJP leadership. The most glaring example of this was the manner in which Jaswant Singh's appointment as finance minister was scotched in 1998 at the behest of a RSS notable who, it was widely believed, was acting at the behest of corporate interests. Throughout their tenure in government, both Vajpayee and Advani used to complain bitterly at the attempted micro-management by the RSS leadership. The RSS, it was clear, was hell bent on enlarging the *Lakshman rekha* of the relationship. The RSS was initially prone to leveraging its volunteer army for securing political returns.[13]

Over the years, not only has the distance reduced, a good number of lawmakers from the BJP trace their roots back to the RSS. Key party positions in state units are increasingly managed by former RSS pracharaks. RSS has clearly become one of the routes to political power. Interestingly, now that the ruling political establishment is dominated by RSS volunteers who include Narendra Modi and Amit Shah, the party is functionally more independent than ever of the RSS.

It was evident when the RSS took the lead in rekindling the Ram Janmabhoomi movement. Unlike the 1980s and 1990s when the RSS stayed in the background, it was at the forefront in 2018. Sarsanghchalak Bhagwat himself sparked off the debate when he demanded a law to build the temple.[14] In his customary Vijaya Dashami speech, Bhagwat said that delay in building the temple was unnecessarily testing the patience of society.[15]

The VHP began what it called the 'final' battle to build a temple for Lord Ram in Ayodhya. It announced on 5 October 2018 that it was beginning a campaign to pressure the government to enact a law to build the temple. 'It was decided in the Udupi Dharma Sansad [in November 2017] to give time to the Supreme Court. The Court has shied away from its duty by letting the case drag for a long time. Now we are demanding a law,' Alok Kumar, working president, VHP, announced. 'This is the final battle.'[16]

In late November 2018, it held a massive rally in Ayodhya in which BJP ally Shiv Sena too joined.[17] The Parivar followed it up with a *dharam sansad* and another huge gathering at Ramlila grounds in Delhi in December.[18]

Over the next few months, RSS and VHP leaders made public statements and organized events to drum up support for the movement. The VHP had planned to corner lawmakers in their constituencies but that didn't take off, seemingly because the BJP quietly let it know that it would be taking things too far. While many in the party also agreed that a limited-scale agitation may be good for the upcoming elections, Modi remained mum. A person close to the party leadership said the movement was finally canned because Modi did not give his assent.[19] Besides, terror struck on 14 February 2019. That afternoon, forty Central Reserve Police Force (CRPF) soldiers, who were part of a convoy on the Srinagar–Jammu highway in Pulwama district in Kashmir, were killed when a suicide bomber rammed an explosives-laden car into their truck. Pakistan-based outfit Jaish-e-Muhammad claimed responsibility for the attack.[20]

India retaliated a few days later with airstrikes on terror camps in Pakistan's Balakot area. In an aerial skirmish the next day, India and Pakistan shot down one another's fighters. While Pakistan never acknowledged that one of its planes was shot down, an Indian pilot,

Abhinandan Varthaman, was captured and released after a few days by Pakistani defence forces.[21]

The dramatic events of February and March ignited a furious nationalism which was also fuelled by the BJP's formidable communications machinery. Destroying all opposition and demolishing rational perspectives, the Modi-led BJP won 303 seats in the Lok Sabha, twenty-one seats more than in 2014. In its second coming, the Modi government displayed its ideological loyalty.

The victory cemented the BJP's position as the flagship of the Sangh Parivar and Modi and Amit Shah its unrivalled leaders. In private conversations, RSS leaders admit that Modi is more popular with its cadres than its own leaders. The unmistakable hint from the BJP leadership has been that the Sangh is better off keeping away from politics. It is not as if the BJP and its leaders are no longer following the Sangh philosophy or advice. Ideologically, the party and the parivar reflect the Sangh more than ever in its history. At the same time, some RSS leaders who tried to influence political decisions and appointments have been clearly told by the BJP leadership that it was not their place to decide what was in the best interests of the party. They remain totally committed to it, the agenda remains set and consultations regular, but the course is firmly set by the political leadership.[22]

'Bharatiya Janata Party, Bharat Sarkar and Sangh are three different entities. Sangh doesn't interfere in it. Our swayamsevaks are there, so if we say or do something, they certainly think about it,' Mohan Bhagwat said at a public event called Gyanotsav in Delhi on 18 August 2019. 'It is possible they would agree with us or they can also say that "you are our sarsanghchalak but we don't agree with you". They are responsible for the consequences of their actions. We can't save them. Their blessings and sins are their own.'

Notes

Introduction

1. https://www.narendramodi.in/full-speech-shri-narendra-modi-at-maha-garjana-rally-in-mumbai-2810 (accessed on 19 December 2019)
2. https://www.narendramodi.in/cm-to-address-people-across-26-places-using-3d-projection-technology-4892 (Accessed on 19 December 2019)
3. https://www.youtube.com/watch?v=x9DE4t-qpt0 (accessed on 8 August 2019).
4. https://www.thehindu.com/news/national/explained-presidents-order-scraps-its-predecessor-and-amends-article-370/article28826722.ece (accessed on 8 August 2019).
5. https://www.indiatoday.in/india/story/triple-talaq-bill-passed-by-parliament-bjp-calls-it-victory-of-gender-justice-congress-says-historic-mistake-1575395-2019-07-31 (accessed on 8 August 2019)
6. Case number 010866-010867 / 2010 M. Siddiq (D) THR. LRS. Vs Mahant Suresh Das https://main.sci.gov.in/judgments (accessed on 20 November 2019)
7. Based on the author's multiple interviews with two people close to Mohan Bhagwat and Narendra Modi.
8. In the RSS structure, the sarkaryavah is the executive chief of the organization. The sarsanghchalak does not have any executive power or role and is considered the guide and philosopher. However, he is revered and respected and rarely is a major decision made without his knowledge or advice. He is *param poojaniya*, or the one worthy of ultimate worship. The sarsanghchalak has been alternatively called the RSS chief in some instances in this book for ease of reference.
9. Based on the author's multiple Interviews with a person close to Narendra Modi. Also, please refer to K.S. Sudarshan's comments

after Narendra Modi assumed the charge of Gujarat chief minister in 2007, https://www.outlookindia.com/newswire/story/whoever-wins-should-do-good-work-says-rss-chief/530104 (accessed on 30 May 2019).

10. Mohan Bhagwat speaking at the release of *Jyotipunj* authored by Narendra Modi https://www.youtube.com/watch?v=COF5muJ-h5g (accessed on 1 June 2019).

11. Based on the author's interviews with two people close to Narendra Modi and Mohan Bhagwat.

12. Dattopant Thengadi, *Third Way* (Sahitya Sindhu Prakashana, Bangalore, 2017), p. 254.

13. According to Hindu mythology, on this day, Lord Ram killed the Lankan king Ravan who had kidnapped his wife Sita. In large parts of India, especially in the east and north-east, another story takes precedence. It is believed that Goddess Durga slew the demon Mahishasura on this day. It is generally regarded as the victory of good over evil and restoration of dharma.

14. http://tagoreweb.in/Render/ShowContent. aspx?ct=Essays&bi=72EE92F5-BE50-40D7-8E6E-0F7410664DA3&ti=72EE92F5-BE50-4A47-2E6E-0F7410664DA3&ch=1 (accessed on 19 February 2019)

15. Ashis Nandy, *Time Warps: The Insistent Politics of Silent and Evasive Pasts*, Permanent Black, Delhi, 2002. p. 77.

16. Author's interview with Dilip Karambelkar at his Mumbai office in March 2018.

17. Ashis Nandy, *Time Warps: The Insistent Politics of Silent and Evasive Pasts*, Permanent Black, Delhi, 2002. p. 78.

18. https://archive.org/details/SrimadBhagavadGitaRahasya-BgTilak-Volumes1And2/page/n13 (accessed on 20 July 2019)

19. https://www.amu.ac.in/amuhistory.jsp (accessed on 20 July 2019)

20. https://www.communistparty.in/about (accessed on 3 May 2019). The CPI(M), however, considers Abani Mukherji and M.N. Roy to have founded the Communist Party of India on 17 October 1920, in Tashkent.

21. The smallest and primary building block of the RSS organization, shakha attendance is mandatory for the beginner as well as the veteran swayamsevak, all the way up to the sarsanghchalak. Held every day, it is an intense one-hour session comprising drills and discussion with ritualistic raising and lowering of the saffron flag.

22. Narayan Hari Palkar, *Dr Hedgewar (Charitra)*, Published by Dr Surendranath Mittal, Prayag Varsh Pratipada Vikram, 2019 (1962), p. 199.

23. Walter K. Andersen, Shridhar D. Damle, *The Brotherhood in Saffron: The Rashtriya Swayamsevak Sangh and Hindu Revivalism* (Westview Press, USA, 1987), p. 40.

24. Narayan Hari Palkar, *Dr Hedgewar (Charitra)*, Published by Dr Surendranath Mittal, Prayag Varsh Pratipada Vikram, 2019 (1962), p. 199.

25. Ibid., p. 128.

26. *Ibid.,* p. 130.

27. M.S. Golwalkar, *Rashtra* (Hindi), Foreword by Dattopant Thengadi (Janki Prakashan, New Delhi, 1991), p. 239.

28. Ibid., p, 240.

29. Ibid., p. 241.

30. Ibid., p. 240.

31. K.R. Malkani, *The RSS Story* (Impex India, 1980), p. 115.

32. Ibid.

33. Balasaheb Deoras, *Rashtriya Swayamsevak Sangh: Lakshya aur Karya* (Lokhit Prakashan, Lucknow, fifth edition, 2008), p. 68.

34. 'Volunteer Organisations, Private Armies—Decision to Call for Monthly Reports from the Province', In the Articles of National Archives digitized records. File number HOME_POLITICAL_I_1946_NA_F-28-5.

35. Walter K. Andersen, Shridhar D. Damle, *The Brotherhood in Saffron*, p. 113.

36. Based on the author's interviews with multiple Sangh leaders.

37. Baburao Chauthaiwale. *Mere Dekhe hue Deoras* (Bharatiya Vichar Sadhana, Nagpur), p. 41.

38. Balasaheb Deoras, *Rashtriya Swayamsevak Sangh*, p. 38.

39. Author's interview with Dilip Karambelkar, editor, *Saptahik Vivek*.

40. Suchitra Kulkarni, *RSS-BJP Symbiosis: On the Cusp of Culture and Politics* (Prabhat Prakashan, New Delhi, 2017).

41. Tariq Thachil, *Elite Parties, Poor Voters: How Social Services Win Votes in India* (Cambridge University Press, New York, 2014), p. 264.

42. Balasaheb Deoras, *Rashtriya Swayamsevak Sangh*, p. 63.

43. Pralay Kanungo, *RSS's Tryst with Politics* (Manohar, Delhi, 2002) p. 180–81.

44. Balasaheb Deoras, *Rashtriya Swayamsevak Sangh*, p. 68.

45. Christophe Jaffrelot (ed.), *The Sangh Parivar: A Reader* (Oxford University Press, New Delhi, 2005), p. 4.

46. 'RSS attempt to enter Congress', *The Patriot*, 20 August 1964, P.K. Malaviya private papers. National Archives portal, http://www.abhilekh-patal.in/jspui/handle/123456789/2690330?searchWord=Golwalkar&backquery=[location=&

query=Golwalkar&originalquery=&rpp=50&sort_by=dc.date.
accessioned_dt&order=desc] (accessed on 26 October2018).

47.   https://www.nobelprize.org/nomination/redirector/?redir=archive/
       show.php&id=6519 (accessed on 16 November 2018).

48.   https://www.thehindu.com/features/friday-review/history-and-
       culture/seminar-at-the-aligarh-muslim-university-highlighted-the-
       contribution-of-its-alumni-including-that-of-raja-mahendra-pratap-
       in-indias-freedom-struggle/article6830815.ece

49.   https://www.indiatoday.in/india/story/amu-scraps-mahendra-
       pratap-birthday-event-on-campus-vice-chancellor-warns-of-massive-
       unrest-228947-2014-11-28 (accessed on 16 November 2018).

50.   Author's interview with K.N. Govindacharya, former RSS pracharak
       and BJP general secretary.

51.   A phrase used by Apple founder Steve Jobs's colleague to describe
       Jobs's persuasive charisma.

52.   An RSS joint general secretary's description in a conversation with the
       author in 2014.

53.   https://www.indiatoday.in/india/north/story/rss-leader-indresh-
       under-scanner-for-terror-links-78727-2010-07-15   (accessed   on
       30 April 2019).

54.   https://www.indiatoday.in/india/north/story/rss-leader-indresh-
       under-scanner-for-terror-links-78727-2010-07-15   (accessed   on
       30 April 2019).

Chapter 1: Soul-Keepers

1.   https://indianexpress.com/article/india/to-instil-discipline-nationalism-
      government-discusses-military-training-plan-for-disciplined-10-lakh-
      force-of-youth-5262501/ (accessed on 6 November 2018)

2.   http://nccindia.nic.in/en/genesis (accessed on 6 November 2018).

3.   https://nss.gov.in/about-us-0 (accessed on 6 November 2018).

4.   Ibid.

5.   https://indianexpress.com/article/india/rss-chief-says-can-raise-force-
      in-days-army-needs-months-hindutva-bjp-5060182/   (accessed   on
      6 November 2018).

6.   Jyotirmaya Sharma, *Hindutva: Exploring the Idea of Hindu Nationalism*
      (HarperCollins *Publishers* India, 2015), p. 152.

7.   Narayan Hari Palkar, *Dr Hedgewar (Charitra)* published by
      Dr Surendranath Mittal (Prayag Varsh Pratipada Vikram, 2019
      [1962]), pp. 374–75.

8. Dattopant Thengadi, *Nationalist Pursuit*, English rendering by MK alias Bhausaheb Paranjpe and Sudhakar Raje (Sahitya Sindhu Prakashan, Bangalore, 1992), p. 44.

9. https://archive.org/stream/CensusOfIndia1931/Census%20of%20 India%201931#page/n437/mode/1up (accessed on 9 October 2018).

10. http://censusindia.gov.in/Census_And_You/old_report/ Census_1931n.aspx (accessed on 9 October 2018).

11. http://rss.org//Encyc/2018/9/18/Bharat-of-Future-An-RSS-perspective.html (accessed on 9 October 2018).

12. Balasaheb Deoras, *Rashtriya Swayamsevak Sangh: Lakshya aur Karya* (Lokhit Prakashan, Lucknow, 5th ed., 2008), p. 12.

13. https://www.hindustantimes.com/india/if-taliban-attack-india-we-ll-fight-them-say-maoists/story-kb47VKnhrvUIcAtj3noqoI.html (accessed on 29 October 2018).

14. http://savarkar.org/en/pdfs/babarao-savarkar-v003.pdf (accessed on 26 September 2018).

15. Ibid.

16. Ibid.

17. Ibid.

18. Narayan Hari Palkar, *Dr Hedgewar (Charitra)*, p. 200.

19. Ibid., p. 224.

20. Ibid.

21. Article by Narender Sehgal emailed to author by Indraprastha Vishwa Samvad Kendra on 19 June 2018.

22. Author's telephonic conversation with Narendra Sehgal on 23 August 2019.

23. Narayan Hari Palkar, *Dr Hedgewar (Charitra)*, p. 199.

24. https://indianexpress.com/article/opinion/columns/bhagwats-ambedkar/ (accessed on 7 May 2019).

25. Ibid.

26. https://indianexpress.com/article/opinion/columns/ misunderstanding-the-rss/ (accessed on 7 May 2019).

27. Ibid.

28. Ibid.

29. Bipan Chandra, *Communalism in Modern India* (Har Anand Publications, Delhi, 2008), p. 141.

30. https://indianexpress.com/article/opinion/columns/ misunderstanding-the-rss/ (accessed on 7 May 2019).

31. 'Rashtriya Swayam Sewak Sangh, Organization and Development, Each District of C.P. and Berar at the end of the year 1942', National

Archives digitized record, File Number 28/3/43 (accessed on 10 October 2018).

32. Ibid.

33. 'Notes on the organization aims, etc. of the Rashtriya Swayamsevak Sangh', Home department document on National Archives portal. File number HOME_POLITICAL_I_1942_NA_F-28-8 (accessed on 10 October 2018).

34. Ibid.

35. Ibid.

36. Ibid.

37. Ibid.

38. Ibid.

39. Author's interview with the senior leader in February 2018.

40. Report of Lecture in Oakland on 19 March 1900; *Vivekananda: Complete Works*, Vol. VIII, https://www.ramakrishnavivekananda. info/vivekananda/volume_8/notes_of_class_talks_and_lectures/the_ people_of_india.htm (accessed on 7 May 2019).

41. V.R. Karandikar, *Teen Sarsanghachalak* (Marathi), Hindi translation by Mohan Bande (Snehal Prakashan, Pune, 2001), p. 6.

42. http://www.ramakrishnavivekananda.info/vivekananda/volume_5/ epistles_first_series/068_alasinga.htm (accessed on 8 August 2019).

43. 'India's Gift to the World', *The Brooklyn Standard Union, 27* February 1895; *Vivekananda: Complete Works, Vol. II;* Reports in American Newspapers, http://www.ramakrishnavivekananda.info/vivekananda/ volume_2/reports_in_american_newspapers/indias_gift_to_the_ world.htm (accessed on 26 September 2018).

44. http://koenraadelst.blogspot.com/2010/10/meaning-of-hindu-kush. html (accessed on 30 October 2018).

45. http://www.ramakrishnavivekananda.info/vivekananda/volume_3/ buddhistic_india.htm (accessed on 26 September 2018).

46. V.D. Savarkar, *Essentials of Hindutva*, downloaded from http:// savarkar.org/en/encyc/2017/5/23/Essentials-of-Hindutva.html (accessed on 1 June 2019).

47. Ibid.

48. RSS denies it runs any publication. A senior leader told the author that publications are started and run by people inspired by the RSS.

49. Deendayal Upadhyaya, '*Bharatiya Rashtra Dhara ka Punya Pravah*', *Rashtra Dharm*, Shravani Poornima, Vikram Samvat 2004 [August 1947].

50. Ibid.

51. Ibid.

52. RSS joint general secretary Krishna Gopal's lecture on *Hindutva* at Malviya Smriti Bhawan, New Delhi, on 28 August 2019.
53. V.D. Savarkar, *Essentials of Hindutva*, downloaded from http://savarkar.org/en/encyc/2017/5/23/Essentials-of-Hindutva.html (accessed on 1 June 2019).
54. Ibid.
55. Based on my interview with a RSS leader in February 2018.
56. For more on the origins of *Hindutva*, refer to the insightful paper '*A Hindu Conservative Negotiates Modernity. Chandranath Basu (1844–1910) and Reflections on the Self and Culture in Colonial Bengal*', by historian Amiya P. Sen. In the second half of the nineteenth century, Bengal was witness to a raging debate on Hinduism, lives of Hindus, reform and modernity. While educationist and social theorist Bhudeb Mukhopadhyay argued that community took precedence over the political nation and went on to write a code for daily living, Bankimchandra Chattopadhyay argued that modern Hindu's hopes lay in suitably imitating the ways of the English. Chandranath Basu, an English translator in the employment of the British in Calcutta, invented the term *Hindutva* in his 1892 work *Hindutva: Hindur Prakrita Itihaas* (Hindutva: the authentic history of the Hindus). Sen writes that the substance of Basu's writings overturn the idea suggested by Chattopadhyay. 'He argued that meaningful change began with the self itself and not with the social or political environment in which it was historically located.' Sen says 'Chandranath almost unfailingly evaluated social ideas and practices in the comparative scale of civilizations and his conclusions, predictably enough, proudly acclaimed the "superiority" of Hindu life as against the European.'
57. Mahatma Gandhi, *Hind Swaraj or Indian Home Rule*, p. 63. https://www.gandhiheritageportal.org/ghp_booksection_detail/LTM4ODYtMTE=#page/82/mode/2up (accessed on 8 August 2019).
58. Ibid.
59. Ibid.
60. Ibid.
61. https://www.hindustantimes.com/india-news/mahatma-gandhi-150th-birth-anniversary-emulating-the-mahatma-s-vision/story-Nm343TPpvMXF6UzjldQ2yL.html (accessed on 25 November 2019).
62. Author's interview in 2018 with a former RSS ideologue who was witness to the debate on including Mahatma Gandhi's name in the morning prayers now known as Ekatmata Stotra.

63. M.J. Akbar, *Nehru: The Making of India* (Roli Books, New Delhi, 2005), p. 584.

64. Deendayal Upadhyaya, 'Bharatiya Rashtra Dhara ka Punya Pravah'.

65. M.J. Akbar, *Nehru: The Making of India*, p. 579.

66. Siegfried O. Wolf, 'Vinayak Damodar Savarkar's Strategic Agnosticism: A Compilation of his Socio-Political Philosophy and Worldview', Working Paper No 51, (Heidelberg Papers in South Asian and Comparative Politics, 2010).

67. Dattopant Thengadi, *Nationalist Pursuit*, p. 23.

68. M.K. Gandhi's letter of 22 June 1920 to Viceroy Chelmsford, National Archives of India, HOME_POLITICAL_A_1920_NOV_19-31 (accessed 22 July 2019).

69. Narayan Hari Palkar, *Dr Hedgewar (Charitra)*, p. 88.

70. V.D. Savarkar, *Essentials of Hindutva*, downloaded from http://savarkar.org/en/encyc/2017/5/23/Essentials-of-Hindutva.html (accessed on 1 June 2019).

71. Dattopant Thengadi, *Nationalist Pursuit*, p. 23.

72. V.D. Savarkar, *Essentials of Hindutva*, downloaded from http://savarkar.org/en/encyc/2017/5/23/Essentials-of-Hindutva.html (accessed on 1 June 2019).

73. Ibid.

74. Rama Jois, *Supreme Court Judgement on Hindutva: A Way of Life* (Suruchi Prakashan, New Delhi, 2013), p. 8.

75. https://www.hindustantimes.com/delhi-news/du-protest-live-abvp-set-for-another-march-gurmehar-says-saddened-by-politics/story-6bu9Nk5dbXBPK9CSo39lBO.html (accessed on 7 May 2019).

76. http://rss.org//Encyc/2018/9/19/Bharat-of-Future-An-RSS-Perspective-day-2-mohanji-bhagwaat.html (accessed on 25 November 2018).

77. Supreme Court Judgment, http://www.sci.gov.in/jonew/judis/10197.pdf (accessed on 14 May 2018).

78. Ibid.

79. Ibid.

80. Tufail Ahmed, https://www.firstpost.com/india/abrahamic-hindutva-the-religious-fundamentalism-that-is-a-threat-to-indias-tolerant-and-pluralist-civilisational-order-2-3825669.html (accessed on 4 August 2018).

81. Dattopant Thengadi, *Nationalist Pursuit*, p. 38.

82. Ashis Nandy, 'The Demonic and the Seductive in Religious Nationalism: Vinayak Damodar Savarkar and the Rites of Exorcism in Secularizing South Asia', http://archiv.ub.uni-heidelberg.de/volltextserver/9086/1/HPSACP_NANDY.pdf (accessed on 10 October 2019).

83. Ibid.

84. Dattopant Thengadi, *Saptakram* (Suruchi Prakashan, New Delhi, 1985), p. 5.

85. Narayan Hari Palkar, *Dr Hedgewar (Charitra)*, p. 366.

86. Author's multiple interviews with Shreerang Godbole in Pune in 2018.

87. M.S. Golwalkar, *Rashtra* (Hindi), Foreword by Dattopant Thengadi (Janki Prakashan, New Delhi, 1991), pp. 103–04.

88. http://rss.org//Encyc/2018/9/20/Bharat-of-Future-An-RSS-Perspective-Day-3.html (accessed on 1 June 2019).

89. Walter K. Andersen and Shridhar D. Damle, *The RSS: A View to the Inside* (Penguin Viking, New Delhi, 2018), p. 329.

90. Author's interview with Mahesh Sharma in 2018.

91. Ibid.

92. Ibid.

93. Badrishah Tuldharia, *Daishik Shastra* (English: Bharatiya Polity and Political Science), translated by Ashok Bhandari (Vishwavidyalaya Prakashan, Varanasi, 2003), p. x.

94. *Ibid.*, p. v.

95. Tuldharia's son-in-law Giriraj Shah in the preface to the English translation of *Daishik Shastra*, p. v. This could not be verified independently.

96. *Ibid.*, p. vi.

97. Badrishah Tuldharia, *Daishik Shastra* (English: Bharatiya Polity and Political Science), p. 115.

98. Badrishah Tuldharia, *Daishik Shastra* (Hindi) (Punarutthan Trust, Ahmedabad, 2007), p. 16.

99. Badrishah Tuldharia, *Daishik Shastra* (English: Bharatiya Polity and Political Science), p. 26.

100. Ibid.

101. Ibid., p. 27.

102. Ibid., pp., 26, 30.

103. Ibid., p. 160.

104. https://www.news18.com/news/india/do-you-want-your-baby-to-have-aryabhatas-brain-or-rana-prataps-build-rss-garbhvigyan-kendra-has-a-recipe-1667553.html (accessed on 7 December 2018).

105. Deendayal Upadhyaya, *Principles and Policies*. Draft adopted at the Jana Sangh national executive held at Vijayawada, 23–25 January 1965.

106. Ibid.

107. Ibid.

108. Author's interview with Mahesh Sharma in 2018.

109. Badrishah Tuldharia, *Daishik Shastra* (English: Bharatiya Polity and Political Science), p. 184.
110. Ibid.
111. *Ibid.,* p. 195.
112. *Ibid.,* p. 33.
113. *Ibid.,* pp. 188–89.
114. Ibid.

Chapter 2: The Quest

1.   Interviews with Kummanam Rajasekharan and with Rajasekharan himself.
2.   Author's conversations with two Kerala RSS leaders and Kummanam Rajasekharan.
3.   Author's interview with three people, including two RSS state executive members.
4.   Author's interview with sources privy to the discussions.
5.   Author's interview with a senior RSS leader in Kerala.
6.   https://www.telegraphindia.com/india/medical-scam-rocks-kerala-bjp/cid/15211140 (accessed on 5 December 2018).
7.   Author's conversations with multiple people involved with the matter in the state and Amit Shah's team.
8.   https://timesofindia.indiatimes.com/city/kozhikode/rss-added-8000-new-members-in-kerala-last-year-state-chief/articleshow/63322319.cms (accessed on 2 July 2018).
9.   Author's interview with Subhash Velingkar in January 2017.
10. Dinesh Narayanan, 'RSS 3.0', *The Caravan*, May 2014 http://www.caravanmagazine.in/reportage/rss-30 (accessed on 30 May 2018).
11. Ibid.
12. Ibid.
13. Author's interview with Mohan Bhagwat's brother Ravi Bhagwat at Chandrapur in late 2013.
14. https://caravanmagazine.in/reportage/emperor-uncrowned-narendra-modi-profile (accessed on 27 October 2018).
15. Ibid.
16. Nilanjan Mukhopadhyay, *Narendra Modi: The Man, the Times* (Tranquebar Press, Delhi, 2013), pp. 30–31.
17. https://caravanmagazine.in/reportage/emperor-uncrowned-narendra-modi-profile (accessed on 27 October 2018).
18. Ibid.
19. Nilanjan Mukhopadhyay, *Narendra Modi: The Man, the Times*, pp. 30–31.

20. https://old.himalmag.com/component/content/article/1340-saffron-terror.html (accessed on 8 September 2018).

21. Charge sheet in FIR No. 2 dated 6 April 2011, filed before the honourable IV additional metropolitan sessions judge in the special court for NIA cases, Hyderabad, Andhra Pradesh. *State vs Devendra Gupta and Others.*

22. ttps://caravanmagazine.in/reportage/believer (accessed on 5 September 2019).

23. https://www.ndtv.com/india-news/saffron-terrorism-a-new-phenomenon-says-home-minister-chidambaram-428832 (accessed on 8 September 2018).

24. https://economictimes.indiatimes.com/news/politics-and-nation/devendra-gupta-convicted-in-ajmer-freed-in-hyderabad-mecca-masjid-blasts-case/articleshow/63792761.cms (accessed on 24 July 2019).

25. Author's interview with K.C. Kannan, former joint general secretary of the RSS, in January 2018.

26. https://www.news18.com/news/politics/full-text-of-lk-advanis-resignation-letter-614958.html (accessed on 8 September 2018).

27. https://www.news18.com/news/politics/advani-modi-live-638522.html (accessed on 8 September 2018).

28. Author's interview with a person present at Jhandewalan with the senior RSS leader.

29. http://rss.org//Encyc/2014/1/30/mohan-bhagwat-vijayadashami-speech.html (accessed on 24 September 2018).

30. Ibid.

31. http://www.caravanmagazine.in/reportage/rss-30 (accessed on 8 September 2018).

32. Author's interview with a veteran RSS functionary in Rajasthan who was present at the meeting.

33. http://www.caravanmagazine.in/reportage/rss-30 (accessed on 8 September 2018).

34. https://www.reuters.com/article/us-india-rss-specialreport/special-report-battling-for-indias-soul-state-by-state-idUSKCN0S700A20151013 (accessed on 8 September 2018).

35. Author's informal conversation with the Union minister in January 2019.

36. Deoras on16 December 1973. *Onward March*, a booklet based on Deoras's interaction with journalists in Bangalore (Prakashan Vibhag, Rashtriya Swayamsevak Sangh, 1974), p. 19.

37. S.H. Deshpande, *Sanghaatle Divas ani itar lekh* (Marathi) (Suparn Prakashan, Pune, 1983) p. 2.

38. Deoras on 16 December 1973. *Onward March*, pp. 20–21.

39. Author's interview with M.G. Vaidya in Nagpur in November 2013.

40. Tathagata Roy, *Syama Prasad Mookerjee: Life and Times* (Penguin Random House, New Delhi, 2018) pp. 296–97.

41. Balarao Savarkar, *Swatantryaveer Savarkar, Akhand Hindustan Ladha Parv, (January 1941 to August 15, 1947)*, Veer Savarkar Prakashan, Mumbai, 1975, p. 342.

42. Ibid.

43. Arun Anand, *Know About RSS* (Prabhat Prakashan, Delhi, 2016), p. 122.

44. Interview with Tathagata Roy, author and governor of Tripura governor, May 2018.

45. Tathagata Roy, *Syama Prasad Mookerjee: Life and Times*, pp. 299–300.

46. Ibid., pp. 82–83.

47. Narayan Hari Palkar, *Dr Hedgewar (Charitra)* published by Dr Surendranath Mittal (Prayag Varsh Pratipada Vikram, 2019, (1962), p. 416.

48. Tathagata Roy, *Syama Prasad Mookerjee*, p. 82.

49. Balarao Savarkar, *Swatantryaveer Savarkar, Hindu Mahasabhaparv, Bhag 1 (June 1937 to December 1940)*, Veer Savarkar Prakashan, Mumbai, 1975, p. 284–97.

50. Deoras on 16 December 1973, *Onward March*, p. 21.

51. Bruce Graham, 'The Leadership and Organization of the Jana Sangh 1951 to 1967', in Christophe Jaffrelot (ed.), *The Sangh Parivar: A Reader*, ((Oxford University Press, New Delhi, 2005), p. 234.

52. Author's interview with Devendra Swarup in 2014.

53. Dinesh Narayanan, 'RSS 3.0', *Caravan*, http://www.caravanmagazine.in/reportage/rss-30 (accessed on 31 May 2018).

54. Bruce Graham, 'The Leadership and Organization of the Jana Sangh 1951 to 1967', p. 235.

55. Dhananjay Keer, *Veer Savarkar* (Popular Prakashan, Bombay, 1966), p. 448.

56. Bruce Graham, 'The Leadership and Organization of the Jana Sangh 1951 to 1967', p. 237.

57. Ibid.

58. Thengadi related this story to former ABVP worker, Gopakumar; author's interview with Gopakumar in mid-2018. He now works for Third World Network on issues related to international trade and healthcare.

59. Author's interview with Gopakumar in mid-2018.
60. 'RSS attempt to enter Congress', *The Patriot*, 20 August 1964; P.K. Malaviya private papers, National Archives portal (accessed on 26 October 2018).
61. Author's conversation with a former RSS pracharak and general secretary of the BJP, in 2018.
62. Author's interview with K.N. Govindacharya, former pracharak and general secretary of the BJP, in 2018.
63. Ramachandra Guha, *India after Gandhi* (Picador, London, 2008), p. 477.
64. Author's interview with K.N. Govindacharya, former pracharak and general secretary of the BJP, in 2018.
65. Ramachandra Guha, *India after Gandhi*, p. 478.
66. Author's interview with K.N. Govindacharya, former pracharak and general secretary of the BJP, in 2018.
67. As told to the author by K.N. Govindacharya.
68. Ramachandra Guha, *India after Gandhi*, p. 479.
69. Ibid.
70. Author's interview with K.N. Govindacharya, former pracharak and general secretary of the BJP, in 2018.
71. Ibid.
72. Ibid.
73. Ibid.
74. Ibid.
75. Ibid.
76. Ibid.
77. Walter K. Andersen and Shridhar D. Damle, *The Brotherhood in Saffron*, p. 186.
78. P.G. Sahasrabuddhe and Manik Chandra Vajpayee, *The People vs Emergency: A Saga of Struggle* (Suruchi Prakashan, New Delhi, 1991), p. 28.
79. Ramachandra Guha, *India after Gandhi*, pp. 488–89.
80. Bipan Chandra, *In the Name of Democracy* (Penguin Books, New Delhi, 2003), p. 65.
81. Ibid.
82. Ramachandra Guha, *India after Gandhi*, p. 502.
83. P.G. Sahasrabuddhe and Manik Chandra Vajpayee, *The People vs Emergency: A Saga of Struggle*, pp. 28–29.
84. Ibid., p. 30.
85. Tavleen Singh, *Durbar* (Hachette India, 2012), p. 60.
86. Bipan Chandra, *In the Name of Democracy*, p. 58.

87. https://www.nationalheraldindia.com/opinion/1971-when-indira-gandhi-outwitted-nixon (accessed on 1 September 2018).

88. Jayaprakash Narayan, 'Prison Diary', https://archive.org/details/in.ernet.dli.2015.103060/page/n21 (accessed on 24 July 2019).

89. *RSS Resolves 1950-2007* (Suruchi Prakashan, New Delhi, 2007), p. 66. This is a compilation of RSS resolutions in the period.

90. Jayaprakash Narayan, 'Prison Diary', https://archive.org/details/in.ernet.dli.2015.103060/page/n21 (accessed on 24 July 2019).

91. P.G. Sahasrabuddhe and Manik Chandra Vajpayee, *The People vs Emergency: A Saga of Struggle* (Suruchi Prakashan, New Delhi, 1991), p. 60.

92. Bipan Chandra, *In the Name of Democracy*, p. 78.

93. Tathagata Roy, *Syama Prasad Mookerjee: Life and Times*, p. 302.

94. Shanti Bhushan, *Courting Destiny* (Penguin Books India, New Delhi, 2008), p. 148.

95. Author's interview with K.N. Govindacharya, former pracharak and general secretary of the BJP, in 2018.

96. H.L. Erdman, *The Swatantra Party and Indian Conservatism* (Cambridge University Press, New York, 1967), p. 11.

97. Author's 2018 interview with Sridhar Damle, co-author of *Brotherhood in Saffron and RSS: A View to the Inside*, who was present at the Chicago meeting.

98. https://indianexpress.com/article/explained/directive-principle-not-right-how-cow-protection-became-part-of-constitution-4683383/ (accessed on 21 February 2019).

99. *The Times of India*, New Delhi edition, 8 November 1966.

100. Verghese Kurien, *I Too Had a Dream* (Roli Books, New Delhi, 2005), p. 184.

101. Ibid.

102. https://www.ndtv.com/india-news/pm-modi-hits-out-at-cow-vigilantes-says-most-cows-die-after-eating-plastic-1441079 (accessed on 30 May 2018).

103. http://indianexpress.com/article/india/india-news-india/youll-pay-for-it-in-2019-polls-vhp-warns-modi-2960667/ (accessed on 30 May 2018).

104. Author's interview with two journalists who attended the meeting in 2018.

105. http://rss.org//Encyc/2016/10/11/vijayadashami2016eng.html (accessed on 30 May 2018).

Chapter 3: The God of Power

1. Author's conversation with the leader in 2018

2.   Author's interview with Champat Rai, former Vishwa Hindu Parishad (VHP) international general secretary and current vice president

3.   *Rashtriya Swayamsevak Sangh: Lakshya aur Karya* (Lokhit Prakashan, Lucknow, 2008), pp. 16–17.

4.   Girilal Jain, *Organiser*, 31 January 1993.

5.   Swapan Dasgupta, *The Telegraph*, 17 September 2010, http://swapan-dasgupta.blogspot.com/2010/09/twenty-years-too-late.html

6.   Report of the Liberhan Ayodhya Commission of Inquiry, Chapter 1, para 1.1 and 1.2, https://mha.gov.in/about-us/commissions-committees/liberhan-ayodhya-commission (accessed on 12 May 2019).

7.   Elias Canetti, *Crowds and Power* (Penguin Books, London, 1981), p. 20.

8.   Rajiv Shukla, 'Ru-Ba-Ru with Uma Bharti', October 2008, Zee Television http://rajeevshukla.com/VideoLib.aspx?i=95 (accessed on 11 May 2019).

9.   In the High Court of Judicature at Allahabad (Lucknow Bench). Other original suit no 1 of 1989, judgment reserved on 26 July 2010, judgment delivered on 30 September 2010.

10. Krishna Pokharel and Paul Beckett, 'Ayodhya: The Battle for India's Soul', *Wall Street Journal* https://blogs.wsj.com/indiarealtime/2012/12/03/ayodhya-the-battle-for-indias-soul/ (accessed on 11 May 2019).

11. http://www.manushi-india.org/yes_to_sita_no_to_ram.htm (accessed on 5 September 2019)

12. http://www.darululoom-deoband.com/ (accessed on 11 May 2019).

13. Ajit Doval, Nani Palkhivala Memorial Lecture at Sastra University, 21 February 2014, https://www.youtube.com/watch?v=v4RaCJrT51w&t=6s (accessed 11 May 2019).

14. V.D. Savarkar, *Essentials of Hindutva*, http://savarkar.org/en/encyc/2017/5/23/Essentials-of-Hindutva.html (accessed on 1 June 2019).

15. Author's conversation with Ram Bahadur Rai, president, Indira Gandhi National Centre for Arts, in 2017.

16. Ram Bahadur Rai, *Hamare Balasaheb Deoras*, Ram Bahadur Rai and Rajiv Gupta (eds), (Prabhat Paperbacks, New Delhi, 2017), p. 14.

17. V.R. Karandikar, *Teen Sarsanghachalak*, translated from Marathi to Hindi by Mohan Bande (Snehal Prakashan, Pune, 2001), pp. 472, 475.

18. Ibid., p. 552.

19. Ram Bahadur Rai, *Hamare Balasaheb Deoras*, p. 16.

20. V.R. Karandikar, *Teen Sarsanghchalak*, p. 553.
21. Sanjeev Kelkar, *Lost Years of the RSS* (Sage Publications, New Delhi, 2011), pp. 100–01.
22. Ibid.
23. Ram Bahadur Rai, *Hamare Balasaheb Deoras*, pp. 16–17.
24. Ibid.
25. Manjari Katju, *Vishva Hindu Parishad and Indian Politics*, Orient Longman, Hyderabad, 2003. p. 2
26. Christophe Jaffrelot, 'The Vishva Hindu Parishad: Structures and Strategies', Christophe Jaffrelot (ed.), *The Sangh Parivar: A Reader* (Oxford University Press, London, 2005), p. 319.
27. Apte quoted in ibid., p. 320.
28. Ibid. p. 326.
29. Author's interview with VHP vice president Champat Rai in 2017.
30. Cited by Justice S.U. Khan, the High Court of Judicature at Allahabad (Lucknow Bench). Other original suit no 1 of 1989, judgement reserved on 26 July 2010, judgement delivered on 30 September 2010.
31. https://www.youtube.com/watch?v=imHog_QgAP8 (accessed on 29 May 2018).
32. A.G. Noorani, *The Muslims of India: A Documentary Record* (Oxford University Press, New Delhi, 2011), ebook, p. 226, 228–29.
33. Christophe Jaffrelot, *The Hindu Nationalist Movement and Indian Politics 1925 to the 1990s* (Penguin Books, New Delhi, 1996), p. 349.
34. A.G. Noorani, *The Muslims of India: A Documentary Record*, pp. 228–29.
35. *RSS Resolves 1950-2007* (Suruchi Prakashan, New Delhi, 2007), p. 101.
36. Author's interview with the senior Sangh leader in early 2014.
37. https://timesofindia.indiatimes.com/city/ahmedabad/Statue-of-Unity-36-new-offices-across-India-for-collecting-iron/articleshow/24306198.cms?referral=PM (accessed on 16 August 2019).
38. A.G. Noorani, *The Muslims of India: A Documentary Record*, pp. 291–92.
39. https://www.indiatoday.in/magazine/nation/story/19801130-communal-riots-and-violence-become-the-byword-in-moradabad-821637-2014-01-03 (accessed on 16 August 2019).
40. Author's interview with a former senior Sangh pracharak from UP in 2017.
41. A.G. Noorani, *The Muslims of India: A Documentary Record*, pp. 238–39, 245, 247, 249.

42. Ibid., p. 255.

43. K.R. Malkani, *The RSS Story* (Impex India, New Delhi, 1980), p. 107.

44. Author's interview with the lawyer, former Meerut chief of Bajrang Dal.

45. P.V. Narasimha Rao, *Ayodhya: 6 December 1992* (Penguin Viking, 2006), p. 31.

46. Author's interview with Champat Rai.

47. P.V. Narasimha Rao, *Ayodhya: 6 December 1992*, p. 23.

48. Report of the Liberhan Ayodhya Commission of Inquiry, Chapter 6, para 58.4, https://mha.gov.in/about-us/commissions-committees/liberhan-ayodhya-commission (accessed on 12 May 2019).

49. Author's interview with Champat Rai.

50. Author's interview with Sridhar Damle, co-author of *Brotherhood in Saffron: The Rashtriya Swayamsevak Sangh and Hindu Revivalism*, and who knew Pingle and Deoras closely, in 2018.

51. Collection of RSS resolutions, *RSS Resolves 1950-2007*, p. 15.

52. Walter K. Andersen and Shridhar D. Damle, *The Brotherhood in Saffron*, p. 135.

53. P.V. Narasimha Rao, *Ayodhya: 6 December 1992*, p. 31

54. Manoj Mitta and H.S. Phoolka, *When a Tree Shook Delhi: the 1984 Carnage and its Aftermath* (Roli Books, New Delhi, 2007) p. 3.

55. N.P. Ullekh, *The Untold Vajpayee: Politician and Paradox* (Penguin Random House, 2017), pp. 135–36.

56. A.G. Noorani, *The Muslims of India*, p. 260.

57. Author's interview with Champat Rai.

58. P.V. Narasimha Rao, *Ayodhya: 6 December 1992*, p. 39.

59. L.K. Advani, *My Country My Life* (Rupa and Co., New Delhi, 2008), p. 366.

60. Ram Bahadur Rai, *Hamare Balasaheb Deoras*, p. 39.

61. Author's interview with Dilip Deodhar, an RSS volunteer and businessman who has closely interacted with several senior Sangh leaders, especially Deoras, over more than five decades. He often appears on television as a self-appointed RSS spokesperson.

62. Ibid.

63. Author's interview in 2014 with a person instrumental in arranging the meetings.

64. Pankaj Pachauri, *India Today*, 15 December 1989, https://www.indiatoday.in/magazine/special-report/story/19891215-ramjanmabhoomi-babri-masjid-row-govt-faces-a-tough-challenge-816834-1989-12-15 (accessed 12 May 2019).

65. Author's interview with Champat Rai.

66. Author's interview with a leader of the RSS and the BJP leader present at the meeting.

67. Ramesh Patange, 'Manu, Sangh and I', digital version of English translation of the Marathi original, *Me, Manu ani Sangh*, available at http://www.hvk.org/specialreports/mms/ch3.html (accessed on 12 May 2019).

68. Champat Rai, *Hamare Balasaheb Deoras*, p. 454.

69. Report of the Liberhan Ayodhya Commission of Inquiry, Chapter 6, para 61.32, https://mha.gov.in/about-us/commissions-committees/liberhan-ayodhya-commission (accessed on 12 May 2019).

70. L.K. Advani, *My Country My Life*, pp. 375–76.

71. P.V. Narasimha Rao, *Ayodhya: 6 December 1992*, pp. 30–31.

72. Walter K. Andersen, Shridhar D. Damle, *The Brotherhood in Saffron*, p. 248.

73. Report of the Liberhan Ayodhya Commission of Inquiry, Chapter 4 Sequence of Events, p. 67, https://mha.gov.in/about-us/commissions-committees/liberhan-ayodhya-commission (accessed on 10 May 2019).

74. M.L. Fotedar, *The Chinar Leaves: A Political Memoir* (HarperCollins *Publishers* India, Noida, 2015), p. 277.

75. Author's interview with journalist Sharad Gupta in 2018. Gupta had covered the events leading up to the demolition of the Babri Masjid. He was also an eyewitness to the demolition.

76. For a detailed discussion on the attack on the media during the demolition of the Babri Masjid, see report of the Liberhan Ayodhya Commission of Inquiry, Chapter 13, https://mha.gov.in/about-us/commissions-committees/liberhan-ayodhya-commission (accessed on 12 May 2019).

77. P.V. Narasimha Rao, *Ayodhya: 6 December 1992*, pp. 123, 129–30, 247–48.

78. Author's interview with journalist Sharad Gupta in 2018.

79. Lalit Vachani, *The Men in the Tree* (2002), Compact discs distributed by Magic Lantern Movies LLP. Quotes are author's translation from Hindi.

80. Author's interview with P. Narayanan, permanent invitee to RSS executive council, Kerala, in 2018.

81. V.M. Korath, *Ormayude Nilaavu* (Tapassya, Calicut, 2006), p. 283.

82. https://m.rediff.com/%0D%0Anews/1998/jan/12varsha.htm (accessed on 12 May 2019).

83. Eknath Ranade, *The Story of the Vivekananda Rock Memorial*, as told by Eknath Ranade (Vivekananda Kendra Prakashan Trust, Madras, 1995), p. 13.

84. Jyotirmaya Sharma, *Hindutva: Exploring the Idea of Hindu Nationalism* (HarperCollins *Publishers* India, 2015), p. 91.

85. Ibid., pp. 118–19.

86. Eknath Ranade, *The Story of the Vivekananda Rock Memorial*, pp. 3–4, 10.

87. Tathagata Roy, *Syama Prasad Mookerjee: Life and Times* (Penguin Random House, 2018), p. 297.

88. Another statue of Swami Vivekananda in Madras city.

89. Eknath Ranade, *The Story of the Vivekananda Rock Memorial*, pp. vii, 18–24, 50, 70.

90. 'A saga in nutshell', http://www.organiser.org/Encyc/2013/1/19/A-grand-project-to-commemorate-Swami-Vivekananda;-executed-Magnificently.aspx?NB=&lang=4&m1=&m2=&p1=&p2=&p3=&p4=&PageType=N

91. Author's conversation with the senior leader.

92. Author's interview with a national Sangh leader in 2018.

93. Author's interview with a former joint general secretary of the RSS in January 2018.

94. Report of the Liberhan Ayodhya Commission of Inquiry, Chapter 6, para 61.34. https://mha.gov.in/about-us/commissions-committees/liberhan-ayodhya-commission (accessed on 12 May 2019).

Chapter 4: The Lotus Blooms

1. L.K. Advani, *My Country My Life* (Rupa and Co, New Delhi, 2008), p. 472–73.

2. N.P. Ullekh, *The Untold Vajpayee: Politician and Paradox* (Penguin Random House, New Delhi, 2017), pp. 147–48 .

3. M.L. Fotedar, *The Chinar Leaves: A Political Memoir*, HarperCollins *Publishers India*, Noida, 2015. p. 286.

4. Pralay Kanungo, *RSS's Tryst with Politics*, Manohar, New Delhi, 2002. p. 229.

5. Devendra Swarup, *Hamare Rajju Bhaiyya*, Devendra Swarup and Brij Kishore Sharma (eds) (Prabhat Paperbacks, New Delhi, 2017), p. vi.

6. Pralay Kanungo, *RSS's Tryst with Politics*, Manohar, New Delhi, 2002. p. 224.

7. https://thewire.in/video/watch-17-years-of-hindu-yuva-vahini-yogi-adityanath (accessed on 3 June 2019).

8. https://www.youthkiawaaz.com/2018/04/bharat-bandh-rajasthan-sc-st-act-karni-sena/ (accessed on 3 June 2019).

9. From author's conversations with a senior RSS leader who worked closely with the Deoras brothers and Rajendra Singh.

10. Dinesh Narayanan, 'RSS 3.0', *The Caravan*, May 2014 http://www.caravanmagazine.in/reportage/rss-30 (accessed on 30 May 2018).

11. Ibid.

12. Devyani Saltzman, *Shooting Water: A Mother-Daughter Journey and the Making of a Film* (Penguin Books, New Delhi, 2006), pp. 76–77.

13. http://swapan-dasgupta.blogspot.com/2005/

14. Author's interview in 2018 with the head of an RSS institution who is intimately aware of the details of the meeting.

15. Dinesh Narayanan, 'RSS 3.0', *The Caravan*, May 2014 http://www.caravanmagazine.in/reportage/rss-30 (accessed on 30 May 2018).

16. Author's interview in 2014 with T.V.R. Shenoy.

17. Author's interview in 2018 with Mahesh Chandra Sharma, the then editor of the magazine.

18. https://timesofindia.indiatimes.com/india/Abducted-RSS-men-killed-in-Tripura/articleshow/472452524.cms (Accessed on 13 May 2019).

19. L.K. Advani, *My Country My Life*, p. 730.

20. Author's interview in 2014 with a senior leader of the Sangh who was in charge of the north-east at the time.

21. L.K. Advani, *My Country My Life*, p. 730.

22. Author's interview in 2014 with a senior leader of the Sangh who was in charge of Tripura at the time.

23. Walk the Talk with Shekhar Gupta aired on NDTV on 17 April 2005, https://www.ndtv.com/video/shows/walk-the-talk/k-s-sudarshan-part-i-7080 (accessed on 13 May 2019).

24. http://www.india-seminar.com/2010/605/605_swapan_dasgupta.htm (accessed on 28 July 2019).

25. Author's interview in February 2019 with K.N. Govindacharya who was BJP general secretary in the 1990s.

26. https://csrbox.org/India_CSR_Project_Adarsh-Gram-Yojna-Haryana_6446 (accessed on 3 December 2018).

27. Author's interview with a volunteer who underwent training at Surya Foundation, became a trainer and has worked on various Surya projects in different parts of the country.

28. Author's interviews with seven Surya Foundation volunteers working in the Gujarat state elections in 2017.

29. https://www.indiatoday.in/magazine/the-big-story/story/20150406-rss-bjp-modi-ministers-saffron-school-hindu-nationalist-817887-2015-03-26 (accessed on 13 May 2019).

30. Author's interview with Santosh Taneja in January 2019.

31. https://aajtak.intoday.in/story/rss-coaching-institution-samkalp-claims-tina-dabi-qualified-upsc-because-of-their-coaching-1-872214.html (accessed on 12 February 2019).

32. Author's conversation with a former pracharak and senior BJP leader in November 2013.

33. https://www.indiatoday.in/magazine/nation/story/20051003-leadership-crisis-deepens-in-bjp-as-lk-advani-prepares-to-step-down-786801-2005-10-03 (accessed on 29 July 2019).

34. Discussion paper, 'Tasks Ahead: Immediate and Long-Term', Bharatiya Janata Party Publication no. E/7/2004 (Central Office).

35. Dinesh Narayanan, 'RSS 3.0'.

36. https://www.frontline.in/static/html/fl2223/stories/20051118003603300.htm (accessed on 26 November 2018).

37. http://www.india-seminar.com/2010/605/605_swapan_dasgupta.htm (accessed on 13 May 2019).

38. Ibid.

39. Walk the Talk with Shekhar Gupta aired on NDTV on 17 April 2005 https://www.ndtv.com/video/shows/walk-the-talk/k-s-sudarshan-part-i-7080 (accessed on 13 May 2019).

40. http://www.milligazette.com/Archives/2004/16-30Nov04-Print-Edition/163011200483.htm (accessed on 13 July 2018).

41. https://www.thehindu.com/todays-paper/tp-opinion/the-many-myths-of-jhandewalan/article3181124.ece (accessed on 13 July 2018).

42. https://www.organiser.org/archives/dynamic/modulesfc04.html?name=Content&pa=showpage&pid=116&page=7 (accessed on 29 January 2020).

43. https://www.organiser.org/archives/dynamic/modulesb689.html?name=Content&pa=showpage&pid=117&page=4 (accessed on 29 January 2020).

44. https://www.thehindu.com/todays-paper/tp-opinion/the-manymyths-of-jhandewalan/article3181124.ece (accessed on 13 July 2018).

45. http://www.thehindu.com/2001/10/08/stories/02080001.htm (accessed on 5 November 2018).

46. Nilanjan Mukhopadhyay, *Narendra Modi: The Man, the Times*, p. 248.

47. Report by the Commission of Inquiry consisting of Justice G.T. Nanavati and Justice Akshay M. Mehta into the facts, circumstances and all the course of events of the incidents that led to setting on fire some coaches of the Sabarmati Express Train on 27 February 2002 near Godhra Railway Station and the subsequent incidents of violence in the State in the aftermath of the Godhra incident. Part-I (Sabarmati Express Train Incident at Godhra), Chapter 1, para 1, p. 1.

48. Author's conversation with the person in 2015.

49. Nilanjan Mukhopadhyay, *Narendra Modi: The Man, the Times*, p. 260.

50. https://www.indiatoday.in/magazine/states/story/20040209-gujarat-farmers-reposes-faith-in-keshubhai-patel-over-modi-790933-2004-02-09 (accessed on 5 November 2018).

51. https://timesofindia.indiatimes.com/india/VHPs-Singhal-Modi-meet-on-Gujarat-temple-demolitions/articleshow/3741417.cms (accessed on 5 November 2018).

52. M.V. Kamath, Kalindi Randeri, *Narendra Modi: The Architect of a Modern State* (Rupa and Co, New Delhi, 2009), pp. 188–89.

53. http://www.forbesindia.com/article/boardroom/narendra-modi-role-model-of-governance/33783/1 (accessed on 5 November 2018).

54. http://www.caravanmagazine.in/reportage/emperor-uncrowned-narendra-modi-profile (accessed on 8 September 2018).

55. Author's conversations with several leaders in the RSS and BJP, including persons close to Modi and the RSS leadership of the time.

56. Dinesh Narayanan, 'RSS 3.0'.

57. http://www.caravanmagazine.in/reportage/son-of-the-sangh (accessed on 13 July 2018).

58. Ibid.

59. Author's interview with R.H. Tupkary in March 2018. Also mentioned in R.H. Tupkary, *To Rajhans Ek (Ek Atmakathan)* (Shri Mangesh Prakashan, Nagpur, 2016), p. 245.

60. https://www.indiatoday.in/magazine/profile/story/20110425-bjp-president-nitin-gadkari-rs-500-crore-purti-group-produces-36-mw-of-power-energy-every-month-745665-2011-04-21 (accessed on 13 July 2018).

61. http://www.caravanmagazine.in/reportage/son-of-the-sangh (accessed on 13 July 2018).

62. https://economictimes.indiatimes.com/opinion/interviews/bjp-should-get-younger-leaders-says-rss-chief/articleshow/4909051.cms (accessed on 3 December 2018).

63. https://timesofindia.indiatimes.com/city/nagpur/RSS-on-backfootover-new-BJP-chief/articleshow/5245624.cms (accessed on 15 July 2018).

64. Author's interview with the friend of Narendra Modi in 2018.

65. http://www.dnaindia.com/india/report-advani-is-old-rancid-pickle-says-manohar-parrikar-1292201 (accessed on 15 July 2018).

66. https://www.hindustantimes.com/india/rss-chief-upset-over-joshi-ouster-modi-spared/story-u0q3Fm9NmiEBX01iOups0J.html (accessed on 15 July 2018).

67. https://www.indiatoday.in/magazine/cover-story/story/20140203-india-today-mood-of-the-nation-opinion-poll-bjp-congress-modi-kejriwal-799923 2014 01 24 (accessed on 29 July 2019).

68.   Dinesh Narayanan, 'RSS 3.0'.
69.   Author's conversations with a person close to Modi and Bhagwat.
70.   Ibid.
71.   https://economictimes.indiatimes.com/news/politics-and-nation/
      assembly-elections-2012-bjp-wins-gujarat-polls-congress-himachal/
      articleshow/17699417.cms (accessed on 15 July 2018).
72.   Dinesh Narayanan, 'RSS 3.0'.

Chapter 5: Hindu Economics: The Third Way

1.   Amal Sanyal, 'The Curious Case of the Bombay Plan', *Contemporary
      Issues and Ideas in Social Sciences*, 2010. http://journal.ciiss.in/index.
      php/ciiss/article/view/78 (accessed on 13 May 2019).
2.   https://archive.org/stream/gandhianplan033211mbp/
      gandhianplan033211mbp_djvu.txt (accessed on 19 November 2018).
3.   Amal Sanyal, 'The Curious Case of the Bombay Plan'.
4.   Ibid.
5.   https://heinonline.org/HOL/LandingPage?handle=hein.journals/
      fora23&div=66&id=&page= (accessed on 19 November 2018).
6.   Amal Sanyal, 'The Curious Case of the Bombay Plan'.
7.   https://archive.org/stream/gandhianplan033211mbp/
      gandhianplan033211mbp_djvu.txt (accessed on 19 November 2018).
8.   https://www.thehindubusinessline.com/2004/09/07/
      stories/2004090700010800.htm (accessed on 21 August 2018).
9.   Amal Sanyal, 'The Curious Case of the Bombay Plan'.
10.   Jawaharlal Nehru quoted by P.V. Narasimha Rao at the Tirupati
      AICC Plenary in 1992.
11.   http://pib.nic.in/newsite/mbErel.aspx?relid=111476   (accessed   on
      29 July 2019).
12.   Amal Sanyal, 'The Curious Case of the Bombay Plan'.
13.   Note of dissent on the memorandum of the panel of economists,
      B.R. Shenoy.
14.   Deendayal Upadhyaya, *The Two Plans: Promises, Performance,
      Prospects* (Prabhat Prakashan, New Delhi, 2015), p. 8.
15.   Tathagata Roy, *Syama Prasad Mookerjee: Life and Times*, pp. 288–89,
      310.
16.   Deendayal Uapadhyaya, *Bharatiya Arth Niti: Vikas ki ek Disha*
      (Rashtradharm Pustak Prakashan, Lucknow), p. 13.
17.   Deendayal Upadhayaya, *Political Diary* (Suruchi Prakashan, New
      Delhi, 2014), p. 17.
18.   https://ccs.in/masani-and-swatantra-party (accessed on 3 December
      2018).
19.   Deendayal Upadhayaya, *Political Diary*, p. 49.

20. Deendayal Uapadhyaya, *Bharatiya Arth Niti: Vikas ki ek Disha*, p. 57.

21. H.L. Erdman, *The Swatantra Party and Indian Conservatism* (Cambridge University Press, New York, 1967), p. 218.

22. Deendayal Upadhayaya, *Political Diary*, p. 179.

23. Bruce Graham, 'The Leadership and Organization of the Jana Sangh 1951 to 1967', in Christophe Jaffrelot (ed.), *The Sangh Parivar: A Reader*, (Oxford University Press, New Delhi, 2005), p. 227.

24. Industrial Policy Resolution of 6 April 1948. https://dipp.gov.in/sites/default/files/chap001_0_0.pdf (accessed on 29 July 2019).

25. Industrial Policy Resolution of 30 April 1956 https://dipp.gov.in/sites/default/files/chap001_0_0.pdf (accessed on 29 July 2019).

26. Shankkar Aiyar, *Accidental India: A History of the Nation's Passage through Crisis and Change* (Aleph Book Company, New Delhi, 2012), p. 145.

27. https://data.worldbank.org/indicator/NY.GDP.MKTP.KD.ZG?end=1975&locations=IN&start=1961 (accessed on 14 May 2019).

28. Bipan Chandra, *In the Name of Democracy* (Penguin Books India, New Delhi, 2003), pp. 16, 18–19.

29. Bimal Jalan, *The Future of India: Politics, Economics and Governance* (Penguin Books, New Delhi, 2006), pp. 74–75.

30. https://www.indiatoday.in/india/story/full-text-of-rajiv-gandhis-famous-1985-speech-152145-2013-01-21 (accessed on 21 August 2018).

31. https://www.hindustantimes.com/india-news/only-15-paise-reaches-the-needy-sc-quotes-rajiv-gandhi-in-its-aadhaar-verdict/story-I8dniDGXF6ksulggTDgb9L.html (accessed on 21 August 2018).

32. Yashwant Sinha, *Confessions of a Swadeshi Reformer* (Penguin Viking, New Delhi, 2007), p. xii.

33. Vinod K. Jose, 'Falling Man', *The Caravan*, October 2011.

34. Dinesh Narayanan, 'In Search of the Holy Grail', *Forbes India*, 14 July 2009.

35. Manmohan Singh, *Budget Speech 1991–92, Changing India, Volume IV, Economic Reforms 1991 and Beyond* (Oxford University Press, New Delhi, 2018), pp. 89.

36. Ibid., p. 129.

37. http://www.forbesindia.com/printcontent/2192 (accessed on 3 June 2018).

38. P.V. Narasimha Rao, 'Tasks Ahead', presidential address delivered at the Tirupati session of the AICC held between 14 and 16 April 1992.

39. Ibid.

40. https://www.wto.org/english/news_e/pres05_e/pr409_e.htm (accessed on 2 June 2019).

41. JM, *EPW*, Vol. 27, Issue No. 4, 25 Januart 1992, https://www. epw.in/journal/1992/4/policy-watch-specials/gatt-dunkel-draft-and-india.html (accessed on 30 July 2019).

42. Dattopant Thengadi, *Third Way* (Sahitya Sindhu Prakashana, Bangalore, 2017), p. 203.

43. Deoras on 16 December 1973; *Onward March*, a booklet based on Deoras's interaction with journalists in Bangalore (Prakashan Vibhag, Rashtriya Swayamsevak Sangh, 1974), p. 38.

44. Balasaheb Deoras with Delhi newsmen in the Press Club of India, 12 March 1979.

45. M.G. Bokare, *Hindu Economics (Eternal Economic Order)* (Janaki Prakashan, New Delhi, 1993), pp. xviii, xxxi–xxxiii, xlvi, il, 129, 132, 139, 249. Elements of this economic thought are discernible in the Modi government's initiatives such as the Micro Units Development and Refinance Agency or MUDRA scheme; https://www. narendramodi.in/text-of-pms-address-at-the-launch-of-pradhan-mantri-mudra-yojana-2971 (accessed on 6 September 2019).

46. Ibid., pp. 146–47, xxxi–xxxiii.

47. https://www.organiser.org/archives/dynamic/modulese967. html?name=Content&pa=showpage&pid=115&page=2 (accessed on 29 January 2020).

48. *RSS Resolves 1950–2007* (Suruchi Prakashan, New Delhi, 2007), p. 204.

49. Ibid.

50. M.G. Bokare, *Hindu Economics*, p. 54.

51. Ibid., pp. 134–35.

52. Raghuram Rajan, *Fault Lines: How Hidden Fractures Still Threaten the World Economy* (Collins Business, Noida, India, 2010), p. 238.

53. Author's interview with Ravindra Mahajan in March 2018.

54. Author's interview with Surendra Thatte in 2013.

55. Author's interviews in March 2018 with a former kshetra pracharak present at the Vrindavan meeting and with Surendra Thatte in 2013.

56. 'Fact sheet for Minority Staff Committee on Government Reform', US House of Representatives, 22 February 2002, Background on Enron's Dabhol Power Project.

57. Ibid.

58. https://www.indiatoday.in/magazine/special-report/story/19950831-shiv-sena-bjp-alliance-scraps-enron-power-project-at-dabhol-congress-plays-safe-807699-1995-08-31 (accessed on 30 July 2019).

59. https://www.indiatoday.in/magazine/special-report/
     story/19950831-shiv-sena-bjp-alliance-scraps-enron-power-project-
     at-dabhol-congress-plays-safe-807699-1995-08-31   (accessed   on
     3 June 2019).

60. Ibid.

61. 'Fact sheet for Minority Staff Committee on Government Reform',
     US House of Representatives, 22 February 2002, Background on
     Enron's Dabhol Power Project.

62. https://www.indiatoday.in/magazine/special-report/story/19950831-
     shiv-sena-bjp-alliance-scraps-enron-power-project-at-dabhol-
     congress-plays-safe-807699-1995-08-31 (accessed on 3 June 2018).

63. https://www.indiatoday.in/magazine/special-report/story/19951215-
     remote-control-must-be-there-because-it-is-a-shiv-sena-and-bjp-
     government-bal-thackeray-808098-1995-12-15 (accessed on 3 June
     2018).

64. 'Fact sheet for Minority Staff Committee on Government Reform',
     US House of Representatives, 22 February 2002, Background on
     Enron's Dabhol Power Project.

65. Rajesh Ramachandran, 'Enron Saga: Powered by Government
     Generosity', 14 February 2001. https://timesofindia.indiatimes.com/
     Enron-saga-Powered-by-govt-generosity/articleshow/20945448.cms

66. Author's interviews with several Sangh and BJP leaders.

67. Author's interview with Ravindra Mahajan in March 2018.

68. Author's interview with Surendra Thatte in 2013.

69. https://samvada.org/2012/news/full-text-of-rss-sarasanghachalak-
     mohan-bhagwats-the-idea-exchange-interaction/ (accessed on 14 May
     2019).

70. http://www.keshavbank.com/ (accessed on 13 July 2018).

71. Author's interview with a former kshetra pracharak in March 2018.

72. Interview with Mahesh Sharma, member of the action group that
     drafted the plan.

73. National Action Group on Development, Swadeshi Jagran Manch,
     'Rebuilding the Nation: A Swadeshi Outline', pp. 5–7, 16–17.

74. Christophe Jaffrelot, 'The BJP at the Centre: A Central and Centrist
     Party', *The Sangh Parivar: A Reader* (Oxford University Press,
     New Delhi, 2005), p. 290.

75. Interview with Mahesh Sharma, member of the action group that
     drafted the plan.

76. https://archivepmo.nic.in/abv/speech-details.php?nodeid=9238

77. Interview with Mahesh Sharma.

78. Venkitesh Ramakrishnan, *Frontline*, 2–15 January 1999 http://www.frontline.in/static/html/fl1601/16010300.htm

79. NationAL Action Group on Development, Swadeshi Jagran Manch, 'Rebuilding the Nation: A Swadeshi Outline', p. 27.

80. https://www.moneycontrol.com/news/business/economy/throwback-to-budget-2002-when-yashwant-sinha-earned-the-nickname-rollback-sinha-2495145.html (accessed on 19 November 2018).

81. http://www.thehindu.com/2001/04/17/stories/02170003.htm

82. https://www.rediff.com/news/1999/feb/16bjp.htm

83. https://m.rediff.com/business/1998/jun/27mitra.htm (accessed on 30 July 2019).

84. K.S. Sudarshan, *Sameeksha* (RSS provincial camp, Kerala, January 2004), p 38–39.

85. http://www.caravanmagazine.in/reportage/rss-30 (accessed on 9 October 2018).

86. Vinay Sitapati, *Half Lion: How P.V. Narasimha Rao Transformed India* (Penguin Viking, New Delhi, 2016), p. 290.

87. Author's interview in 2018 with a top RBI official present at the meeting.

88. Author's interview in 2018 with a top RBI official closely involved with the decision making.

89. http://www.frontline.in/static/html/fl1512/15120180.htm

90. Shaji Vikraman, 'PM's economic advisory body returns—at a time of both continuity and change', *Indian Express*, 27 September 2017 http://indianexpress.com/article/explained/pms-economic-advisory-body-returns-at-a-time-of-both-continuity-and-change-4862770/

91. https://www.nytimes.com/2005/12/04/world/asia/mile-by-mile-india-paves-a-smoother-road-to-its-future.html (accessed on 30 June 2018).

92. Deendayal Uapadhyaya, *Bharatiya Arth Niti: Vikas ki ek Disha*, pp. 132–33.

93. https://www.nytimes.com/2005/12/04/world/asia/mile-by-mile-india-paves-a-smoother-road-to-its-future.html (accessed on 30 June 2018).

94. https://www.outlookindia.com/magazine/story/rigging-the-pmo-south-bloc/210992 (accessed on 8 November 2018).

95. Nilanjan Mukhopadhyay, *Narendra Modi: The Man, the Times*, p. 242.

96. https://www.youtube.com/watch?v=TlndRGCHn8k (accessed on 6 February 2019).

97. https://data.worldbank.org/indicator/NY.GDP.MKTP.
     KD.ZG?locations=IN (accessed on 3 June 2018).

98. Deendayal Uapadhyaya, *Bharatiya Arth Niti: Vikas ki ek Disha*
     (Rashtradharm Pustak Prakashan, Lucknow), pp. 27, 70.

99. Author's interview with Sharad Gupta in 2018.

100. Karan Thapar, *Devil's Advocate: The Untold Story*, excerpted in the
     Wire.in,   https://thewire.in/books/narendra-modi-karan-thapar-
     interview (accessed on 2 June 2019).

101. http://www.caravanmagazine.in/reportage/emperor-uncrowned-
     narendra-modi-profile/2 (accessed on 5 November 2018).

102. http://www.rediff.com/money/2003/sep/27gujarat.htm (accessed on
     5 November 2018).

103. https://scroll.in/article/690280/billion-dollar-loan-to-adani-cements-
     modis-friendship-with-corporate-india (accessed on 5 November
     2018).

104. http://www.forbesindia.com/article/boardroom/narendra-modi-role-
     model-of-governance/33783/1 (accessed on 5 November 2018).

105. https://scroll.in/article/690280/billion-dollar-loan-to-adani-cements-
     modis-friendship-with-corporate-india (accessed on 5 November
     2018).

106. Author's conversation with the person who attended the meeting.

107. Author's conversation with a senior Sangh leader.

108. Lucas Chancel and Thomas Piketty, 'Indian Income Inequality,
     1922–2014: From British Raj to Billionaire Raj?' https://papers.ssrn.
     com/sol3/papers.cfm?abstract_id=3066021 (accessed on 31 August
     2019).

109. http://www.thehindu.com/news/national/Text-of-Narendra-
     Modi%E2%80%99s-speech-at-Central-Hall-of-Parliament/
     article11624655.ece (accessed on 3 June 2018).

110. https://economictimes.indiatimes.com/tech/ites/25-years-of-reforms-
     when-narayana-murthy-took-3-years-and-50-trips-to-delhi-to-
     import-one-computer/articleshow/53308935.cms   (accessed   on
     3 June 2018).

111. https://data.worldbank.org/indicator/NY.GDP.MKTP.
     KD.ZG?locations=IN (accessed on 3 June 2018).

112. https://www.mckinsey.com/featured-insights/asia-pacific/the-bird-
     of-gold

113. https://economictimes.indiatimes.com/news/economy/agriculture/
     government-must-look-at-policy-options-that-go-beyond-loan-
     write-offs-to-address-farmers-woes/articleshow/59149257.cms
     (accessed on 3 June 2018).

114. https://timesofindia.indiatimes.com/india/When-Manmohan-Singh-speaks-world-listens-Obama/articleshow/6102950.cms (accessed on 3 December 2018).
115. https://indianexpress.com/article/business/market/bse-sensex-soars-1000-pts-as-lok-sabha-election-results-pour-in/ (accessed on 21 August 2018).
116. https://www.narendramodi.in/prime-minister-s-speech-at-inauguration-of-make-in-india-week-mumbai-413789 (accessed on 23 August 2018).
117. https://www.businesstoday.in/current/corporate/india-inc-on-modi-economic-revival-wef-economic-summit-2014/story/212083.html (accessed on 3 December 2018).
118. https://economictimes.indiatimes.com/news/economy/policy/uday-kotak-anand-mahindra-lash-out-at-proliferation-of-regulations/articleshow/66864030.cms (accessed on 3 December 2018).
119. Author's interview with leaders of these organizations in May 2015.
120. http://samvada.org/2014/news/full-text-of-speech-by-rss-sarasanghchalak-mohan-bhagwat-on-vijaya-dashmi-2014-nagpur/ (accessed on 23 August 2018).
121. http://www.prsindia.org/uploads/media/Ordinances/RTFCTLARR%20Ordinance%202014.pdf (accessed on 23 August 2018).
122. https://timesofindia.indiatimes.com/india/Rahul-Gandhi-tears-into-Modis-suit-boot-ki-sarkar/articleshow/46993611.cms (accessed on 24 August 2018).
123. Author's interview with a top leader of the BMS.
124. https://blogs.economictimes.indiatimes.com/it-doesnt-add-up/dattapant-thengadi-may-spoil-pm-modis-first-anniversary-after-coming-to-power/ (accessed on 24 August 2018).
125. Ibid.
126. https://www.thehindu.com/news/national/threeday-rss-coordination-meeting-modi-other-leaders-attend/article7616091.ece (accessed on 24 August 2018).
127. From a document published by the Kerala RSS.
128. https://www.news18.com/news/india/modi-govt-has-failed-farmers-says-leader-of-rss-affiliated-farmer-union-1427389.html (accessed on 8 November 2018).
129. https://www.thehindubusinessline.com/economy/agri-business/what-right-does-jaitley-have-to-deny-loan-waivers-to-farmers-bks-leader-kelkar/article9730641.ece (accessed on 8 November 2018).

130. https://www.pmindia.gov.in/en/news_updates/prime-ministers-address-to-the-nation/ (accessed on 30 July 2019).

131. https://www.cmie.com/kommon/bin/sr.php?kall=warticle&dt=2017-07-11%2011:07:31&msec=463 (accessed on 8 November 2018).

132. https://www.businesstoday.in/current/economy-politics/pm-modis-demonetisation-brings-gdp-down-to-61-per-cent-top-economists-stand-vindicated/story/253436.html (accessed on 8 November 2018).

133. https://economictimes.indiatimes.com/news/company/corporate-trends/rahul-bajaj-questions-amit-shah-responds-at-the-et-awards-2019/videoshow/72315646.cms (accessed on 29 January 2020).

134. https://www.indiatoday.in/business/story/india-unemployment-rate-6-1-per-cent-45-year-high-nsso-report-1539580-2019-05-31 (accessed on 29 January 2020).

135. https://www.indiatoday.in/business/story/after-imf-another-ratings-agency-places-india-s-gdp-growth-in-5-bracket-1639055-2020-01-22 (accessed on 20 January 2020).

136. https://economictimes.indiatimes.com/news/economy/indicators/cag-demonstrates-how-govt-relies-on-off-budget-resources-to-fund-deficit/articleshow/70360281.cms?from=mdr (accessed on 29 January 2020).

137. https://economictimes.indiatimes.com/news/defence/nk-singh-headed-finance-commission-working-on-proposal-cabinet-cleared-enabling-approvals-on-july-17/articleshow/70384389.cms (accessed on 29 January 2020).

138. https://economictimes.indiatimes.com/news/economy/finance/the-centre-vs-states-fiscal-fight-/primeshow/72816022.cms (accessed on 29 January 2020).

139. https://economictimes.indiatimes.com/magazines/panache/india-slips-5-spots-on-henley-passport-index-heres-how-it-affects-the-economy/articleshow/70766432.cms?from=mdr (accessed on 29 January 2020).

140. https://economictimes.indiatimes.com/news/economy/indicators/india-slips-10-places-on-global-competitiveness-index-singapore-on-top/articleshow/71498559.cms?from=mdr (accessed on 29 January 2020).

141. http://rss.org/vijayadashmi-2019-english-speech.pdf (accessed on 29 January 2020).

Chapter 6: Alien Nation

1. Mohan Bhagwat's speech at Vigyan Bhavan, New Delhi, 18 September 2018, http://rss.org//Encyc/2018/9/18/Bharat-of-Future-An-RSS-perspective.html (accessed on 15 May 2019).

2. Walter K. Andersen and Shridhar D. Damle, *The RSS: A View to the Inside* (Penguin Viking, New Delhi, 2018), p. 329.

3. Conversations with a pracharak present at the general body meeting.

4. Author's private conversation with the director of the think tank in 2018.

5. M.K. Gandhi's letter of 22 June 1920 to Viceroy Chemsford, National Archives of India HOME_POLITICAL_A_1920_NOV_19-31 http://www.abhilekh-patal.in/jspui/handle/123456789/2723340?-searchWord=golwalkar&backquery=[query=golwalkar&originalquery=&sort_by=dc.date.accessioned_dt&order=desc& rpp=20&etal=0&start=40] (accessed on 22 July 2019).

6. https://www.indiatoday.in/india/story/-read-here-the-full-text-of-pranab-mukherjee-s-speech-at-rss-event-1254156-2018-06-07 (accessed on 1 September 2019)

7. Joseph Baptista's letter of 27 May 1920, National Archives of India HOME_POLITICAL_A_1920_NOV_19-31 http://www.abhilekh-patal.in/jspui/handle/123456789/2723340?searchWord=golwalkar&backquery=[query=golwalkar&originalquery=&sort_by=dc.date.accessioned_dt&order=desc&rpp=20&etal=0&start=40] (accessed on 22 July 2019).

8. Dattopant Thengadi, *Nationalist Pursuit: Lectures by Dattopant Thengadi*, tr. by M.K. (Bhausaheb) Paranjpe and Sudhakar Raje (Sahitya Sindhu Prakashan, Bangalore, 1992), p. 46.

9. Manifesto issued by the Central Khilafat Committee of India. National Archives of India HOME_POLITICAL_A_1920_NOV_19-31 http://www.abhilekh-patal.in/jspui/handle/123456789/2723340?search-Word=golwalkar&backquery=[query=golwalkar&originalquery=&sort_by=dc.date.accessioned_dt&order=desc&rpp=20&etal=0&start=40] (accessed 22 July 2019).

10. https://indianexpress.com/article/research/fact-checking-bjps-kummanam-rajasekharan-was-the-malabar-rebellion-a-case-of-jihad-4886275/ (accessed on 1 September 2019).

11. Walter K. Andersen and Shridhar D. Damle, *The Brotherhood in Saffron*, p. 28.

12. Dinesh Narayanan, 'RSS 3.0', *The Caravan*, May 2014.

13. https://www.scribd.com/doc/61469863/How-to-Wipe-Out-Islamic-Terror-Article-by-Dr-Subramaniam-in-DNA (accessed on 7 July 2018).

14. Author's interview in 2018 with a person who was part of the group that visited Vajpayee.

15. K.R. Malkani, 'One Country, One People, Secret of BJP's Success', Sita Ram Goel (ed), *Time for Stock Taking: Whither Sangh Parivar*, http://voiceofdharma.org/books/tfst/intro.htm.

16. Sita Ram Goel (ed), *Time for Stock Taking: Whither Sangh Parivar*, http://voiceofdharma.org/books/tfst/intro.htm.

17. Ibid.

18. Shreerang Godbole made the paper available to the author by email on 15 December 2017.

19. V.D. Savarkar, *Essentials of Hindutva*, downloaded from savarkar.org.

20. M.S. Golwalkar's 'Hindus must wake up' speech delivered at VHP conference of 2 October 1966; extracted from World Hindu Conference 1979. See also: Manjari Katju, *Vishva Hindu Parishad and Indian Politics* (Orient Longman, New Delhi, 2003), p. 29.

21. M.S. Golwalkar, *Rashtra* (Hindi), Foreword by Dattopant Thengadi (Janki Prakashan, New Delhi, 1991), p. 82.

22. Ibid., p. 83

23. Ibid., p. 85.

24. Ibid., p. 104.

25. http://archiv.ub.uni-heidelberg.de/volltextserver/9086/1/HPSACP_NANDY.pdf

26. A booklet published by the BJP's publication division after the Census 2001 was released, p. 1, 22–23, 25 (soft copy in author's possession).

27. Author's interview with Sharad Dhole, national chief of RSS wing Dharam Jagran in 2018.

28. A.P. Joshi, M.D. Srinivas and J.K. Bajaj, *Religious Demography of India* (Centre for Policy Studies, Chennai, 2005), p. xvii.

29. http://rss.org//Encyc/2018/9/20/Bharat-of-Future-An-RSS-Perspective-Day-3.html (accessed on 1 December 2018).

30. Author's interview with Sharad Dhole in 2018. Dhole, however, said it was retold to him and he himself was not present when Sheshadri related the story.

31. https://www.indiatoday.in/magazine/religion/story/19860630-vhp-launches-massive-drive-to-reconvert-muslim-meherat-rajputs-to-hindu-fold-800987-1986-06-30 (accessed on 11 August 2018).

32. K.S. Singh, *People of India: Introduction,* (Oxford University Press, New Delhi, 2002), p. xxii.

33. https://www.indiatoday.in/magazine/special-report/ story/19930415-survey-discovers-astonishing-facts-about-people-of-india-810925-1993-04-15 (accessed on 11 August 2018).

34. https://www.frontline.in/static/html/fl2312/ stories/20060630006312500.htm (accessed on 11 August 2018).

35. https://www.indiatoday.in/magazine/special-report/ story/19930415-survey-discovers-astonishing-facts-about-people-of-india-810925-1993-04-15 (accessed on 11 August 2018).

36. An example of data analytics for a Christian missionary project based on 'People of India' data https://joshuaproject.net/people_ groups/17643/IN (accessed on 1 September 2019).

37. https://www.frontierventures.org/about (accessed on 12 August 2018).

38. https://joshuaproject.net/people_groups/16871/IN (accessed on 1 September 2019); https://joshuaproject.net/about/details (accessed on 12 August 2018).

39. The Manila meeting was a conclave in 1989 that brought together global church leaders and partnered them with US churches. Luis Bush, head of the AD 2000 and Beyond movement, offered a concept for the new evangelism called 10/40.

40. https://frontline.thehindu.com/static/html/fl2204/ stories/20050225000506400.htm (accessed on 8 February 2019).

41. Ashis Nandy, *Time Warps The Insistent Politics of Silent and Evasive Pasts* (Permanent Black, New Delhi, 2002), p. 133.

42. https://www.census2011.co.in/religion.php (accessed on 12 August 2018).

43. http://johndayal.com/2014/08/24/thomas-christians-crypto-christians/ (accessed on 12 August 2018).

44. Author's interview with Sharad Dhole in 2018.

45. Shripaty Sastry, A Retrospect Christianity in India (An exposition of the RSS view of Christianity in India today) (Bharatiya Vichar Sadhana, Pune, 1983), p. 9.

46. Author's interview with Sharad Dhole in 2018.

47. https://www.indiatoday.in/magazine/religion/story/19860630-vhp-launches-massive-drive-to-reconvert-muslim-meherat-rajputs-to-hindu-fold-800987-1986-06-30 (accessed on 13 August 2018).

48. Ashis Nandy, *Time Warps The Insistent Politics of Silent and Evasive Pasts* (Permanent Black, New Delhi, 2002), pp. 124-125.

49. http://www.rediff.com/news/report/rss-angrily-denies-it-organised-iftar/20150708.htm (accessed on 8 July 2018).

50. http://www.vsktamilnadu.org/2016/06/rss-clarifies-reports-on-mrms-iftar.html (accessed on 8 July 2018).

51. https://indianexpress.com/article/india/rss-muslim-wing-iftar-party-nagpur-smruti-mandir-maharashtra-5204905/ (accessed on 8 July 2018).

52. https://www.youtube.com/watch?v=Q6MXvONgjM0&t=10s (accessed on 8 July 2018).

53. https://www.Indiatoday.in/india/north/story/ex-rss-chief-sudarshan-goes-missing-in-mysore-found-after-5-hours-112218-2012-08-03 (accessed on 1 September 2019)

54. https://web.archive.org/web/20120929225926/http://www.hindustantimes.com/India-news/Bhopal/RSS-stumped-Jamaat-hails-Sudarshan/Article1-936870.aspx (accessed on 15 May 2019).

55. Author's interview in 2018 with Dinesh Tyagi former VHP pracharak and Hindu Mahasabha president.

56. https://indianexpress.com/article/india/rss-chief-mohan-bhagwat-reads-out-sister-nivedita-to-speak-about-bhartiyata-and-why-he-is-opposed-to-sachar-committee-4872981/ (accessed on 13 August 2018).

57. Shreerang Godbole emailed his views on MRM to the author on 30 January 2018.

58. Narayan Hari Palkar, *Dr Hedgewar (Charitra)* published by Dr Surendranath Mittal (Prayag Varsh pratipada Vikram Year 2019 (1962), p. 310.

59. Shreerang Godbole emailed his views on MRM to the author on 30 January 2018.

60. https://indianexpress.com/article/india/india-news-india/muslims-vote-bank-modi-bjp-pandit-deendayal-upadhyaya/ (accessed on 31 July 2019).

61. https://www.news18.com/news/india/for-sale-sign-comes-up-on-houses-of-muslims-in-up-village-after-alleged-police-harassment-1794271.html (accessed on 09 July 2018).

62. Author's interview with Sharad Dhole in 2018.

63. Author's interviews with Durga Nand Jha in 2018.

64. Author's interview with Mahesh Chandra Sharma in 2018.

65. Durga Nand Jha, *India Minority Report: An Enquiry into India's Minority Policy and Analysis of Socio-economic Status of Muslim Community of India'* (Centre for Policy Analysis, Patna, 2018), pp., 8, 16, 18, 27–28.

66. https://indianexpress.com/article/india/politics/bjps-muslim-score-7-of-482-fielded-no-winners/ (accessed on 19 December 2019).

67. RSS booklet based on a senior leader speaking to RSS Kerala office-bearers during 5, 6, 7 December 2008. Privately circulated document reviewed by author.

68. http://specials.rediff.com/news/2009/jan/07slide2-a-account-from-nariman-house.htm (accessed on 2 December 2018).

69. Hanif Khan was a local boy who had rescued four Sindhi and Gujarati families stuck in the building next to Nariman House.

70. https://indianexpress.com/article/opinion/columns/heroes-of-nariman-house/ (accessed on 2 December 2018).

Chapter 7: War of Ideologies

1.   https://www.hindustantimes.com/india/what-really-happened-on-the-night-of-feb-9-a-jnu-student-recounts/story-Hz3USZC3NwntZFwKpF2g1M.html (accessed on 16 September 2018).

2.   https://indianexpress.com/article/india/india-news-india/dalit-student-suicide-full-text-of-suicide-letter-hyderabad/ (accessed on 15 May 2018).

3.   Author's conversations with the chief of a Sangh division in 2017.

4.   https://timesofindia.indiatimes.com/india/RSS-Anna-links-go-back-a-long-way-says-RSS-chief-Mohanrao-Bhagwat/articleshow/10669172.cms (accessed on 15 May 2018).

5.   Author's interview with R.H. Tupkary in November 2013.

6.   Walter K. Andersen and Shridhar D. Damle, *The Brotherhood in Saffron*, p. 115–16.

7.   Author's interview with a person who was a 'tick' scribe.

8.   Author's interview with Manmohan Vaidya in 2018.

9.   https://www.indiatoday.in/india/story/with-eye-on-2019-polls-rss-flexes-muscle-to-change-niche-1177411-2018-02-25 (accessed on 5 August 2019).

10. Author's conversation with a senior prachar vibhag official in 2018.

11. Author's conversations with multiple RSS volunteers who lead such groups.

12. Author's conversation with the swayamsevak journalist in 2014.

13. Dinesh Narayanan, 'RSS 3.0', *The Caravan*, May 2014.

14. Ibid.

15. Author's interview with Manmohan Vaidya in 2018.

16. https://samvada.org/2016/news/research-for-resurgence/ (accessed on 6 February 2019).

17. https://economictimes.indiatimes.com/industry/services/education/bharatiya-shikshan-mandal-an-offshoot-of-rss-vows-to-recast-

framework-for-research-education-in-india/articleshow/54705249.
cms (accessed on 6 February 2019).

18.   http://rfrfoundation.org/ (accessed on 5 August 2019).

19.   http://rfrfoundation.org/honorable-prime-minister-inaugurates-the-conference/ (accessed on 5 August 2019).

20.   Author's interview with BSM organising secretary Mukul Kanitkar in May 2019.

21.   http://rfrfoundation.org/honorable-prime-minister-inaugurates-the-conference/ (accessed on 5 August 2019).

22.   https://samvada.org/2016/news/lokmanthan/ (accessed on 6 February 2019).

23.   http://rss.org//Encyc/2016/3/11/rss-annual-report-2016.html (accessed on 5 August 2019).

24.   *Deendayal Upadhyaya to Janasangh workers of Kerala* (Bharatiya Janasangh, Kerala Pradesh, 1968), p. 3–4; also, https://samvada.org/2016/news/lokmanthan/ (accessed on 6 February 2019).

25.   https://economictimes.indiatimes.com/news/elections/lok-sabha/india/how-faith-and-enterprise-take-centre-stage-in-ls-polls-in-kerala/articleshow/68755865.cms (accessed on 1 September 2019).

26.   https://www.thenewsminute.com/article/kerala-rss-plans-expand-across-state-end-2019-104901 (accessed on 1 September 2019).

27.   RSS ideologue and former national chief of intellectual training, R. Hari's booklet on history of RSS in Kerala, *Sangh Charitravali-1*, p. 2.

28.   N.P. Ullekh, *Kannur: Inside India's Bloodiest Revenge Politics* (Penguin Random House, Delhi, 2018), p. 18.

29.   http://www.newindianexpress.com/states/kerala/2017/sep/01/kathiroor-manoj-murder-cbi-chargesheets-6-including-kannur-cpm-leader-jayarajan-1650904.html (accessed on 21 May 2019).

30.   N.P. Ullekh, *Kannur: Inside India's Bloodiest Revenge Politics* (Penguin Random House, Delhi, 2018) pp. 53–54.

31.   Author's interview with P. Jayarajan at CPI(M) district office in March 2018.

32.   https://samvada.org/2016/news/redtrocity-untold-story-of-communist-violence-in-kerala/ (accessed on 5 August 2019).

33.   R. Hari, *Sangh Charitravali-1*, p. 3.

34.   Author's interview with Choorayi Chandran in March 2018.

35.   http://samvada.org/2016/news/redtrocity-untold-story-of-communist-violence-in-kerala/ (accessed on 21 May 2019).

36.   Author's interview with Choorayi Chandran in March 2018.

37. Ram Bahadur Rai, in Ram Bahadur Rai and Rajiv Gupta (eds), *Hamare Balasaheb Deoras* (Prabhat Paperbacks, New Delhi, 2017), p. 204.

38. Author's interview with Choorayi Chandran in March 2018.

39. Author's conversation with Nandakumar in 2017.

40. https://wikileaks.org/plusd/cables/08NEWDELHI795_a.html (accessed on 31 August 2018).

41. https://www.outlookindia.com/magazine/story/red-earth-tales/296927 (accessed on 15 May 2019).

42. Author was present at the event.

43. https://www.thehindu.com/news/cities/kozhikode/grave-for-principal-kicks-up-a-controversy/article8444183.ece (accessed on 15 May 2019).

44. K.S. Sudarshan in *Walk the Talk* with Shekhar Gupta aired on NDTV on 17 April 2005 https://www.youtube.com/watch?v=TlndRGCHn8k (accessed on 21 May 2019).

45. Author's interview with K.C. Kannan in January 2018.

46. http://www.openthemagazine.com/article/living/guru-m (accessed on 21 May 2019).

47. Author's interview with Sri M in 2017.

48. Author's interview with Sri M in 2017 and P. Jayarajan in 2018.

49. Author's interviews with Sri M, Pinarayi Vijayan and P. Gopalan Kutty in 2017 and 2018.

50. Author's interview with Sri M in 2017.

51. Events reconstructed from author's conversations with Sri M, Pinarayi Vijayan, P. Gopalan Kutty, M. Radhakrishnan, Valsan Thillenkeri in 2017 and 2018.

52. Author's interview with Sri M in 2017.

53. Events reconstructed from author's conversations with Sri M, Pinarayi Vijayan, P. Gopalan Kutty, M. Radhakrishnan, Valsan Thillenkeri in 2017 and 2018.

54. https://timesofindia.indiatimes.com/city/thiruvananthapuram/Sanghis-force-Pinarayi-to-skip-Bhopal-event/articleshow/55916716.cms (accessed on 21 May 2019).

55. Author's interview with Pinarayi Vijayan in 2018.

56. https://factchecker.in/in-north-kerala-hotbed-of-bjprss-cpm-clashes-roughly-equal-deaths/ (accessed on 21 May 2019).

57. Author's interview with Pinarayi Vijayan in 2018.

58. Author's interview with RSS Kannur district chief of publicity, Valsan Thillenkeri, in March 2018.

59. https://economictimes.indiatimes.com/opinion/interviews/people-of-kerala-have-seen-through-cpms-deceit-kummanam-rajasekharan-bjps-state-president/articleshow/51474502.cms (accessed on 2 June 2019).

60. https://economictimes.indiatimes.com/news/politics-and-nation/supreme-court-allows-women-to-enter-sabarimala-temple/articleshow/65989807.cms (accessed on 8 February 2019),

61   http://rss.org//Encyc/2016/3/11/rss-annual-report-2016.html (accessed on 8 February 2019).

62. https://www.youtube.com/watch?v=NtkJ567VP-g (accessed on 8 February 2019).

63. R. Hari, *Mattuvin Chattangale* (Malayalam) (Kurukshetra Prakashan, Kochi, 2017), p. 9.

64. https://www.janmabhumidaily.com/news836513 (accessed on 8 February 2019).

65. http://rss.org//Encyc/2018/10/3/Statement-on-Sabarimala-Devasthanam-Judgement.html (accessed on 8 February 2019).

66. https://www.youtube.com/watch?v=tdBDJZxy_8U (accessed on 8 February 2019).

67. https://eci.gov.in/files/file/3472-tripura-general-legislative-election-2018/ (accessed on 8 February 2019).

68. https://economictimes.indiatimes.com/news/politics-and-nation/lenins-statue-pulled-down-in-tripura/articleshow/63184144.cms (accessed on 4 September 2018).

69. https://www.news18.com/news/politics/left-icons-marx-and-engels-make-way-for-syama-prasad-mookerjee-on-agartalas-roads-1715619.html (accessed on 4 September 2018).

Chapter 8: A Nation Within

1. https://wikileaks.org/plusd/cables/05NEWDELHI4761_a.html (accessed on 22 May 2019).

2. https://www.ndtv.com/india-news/dalit-man-killed-in-gujarat-for-riding-horse-says-police-1830867 (accessed on 22 May 2019).

3. https://timesofindia.indiatimes.com/city/meerut/dalit-man-thrashed-mercilessly-forced-to-chant-jai-shri-ram/articleshow/62529138.cms (accessed on 22 May 2019).

4. http://www.business-standard.com/multimedia/video-gallery/general/dalit-youth-abused-thrashed-for-sporting-moustache-53753.htm (accessed on 22 May 2019).

5. Author's conversation with a senior Sangh leader in August 2017.

6. *Athatho Sanghajigyasa*, booklet compiled from a question-and-answer session with Mohan Bhagwat in Kerala in 2014. RSS publication.

7. https://timesofindia.indiatimes.com/edit-page/Bihar-formula/articleshowprint/1651685.cms (accessed on 22 May 2019).

8. http://www.bjp.org/index.php?option=com_content&view=article&id=298:resolution-on-the-issue-of-shri-ram-janmabhoomi-at-national-executive-meeting-raipur-july-18-20-2003&catid=87&Itemid=503?option=com_content&view=article&id=298:resolution-on-the-issue-of-shri-ram-janmabhoomi-at-national-executive-meeting-raipur-july-18-20-2003&catid=87&Itemid=503 (accessed on 22 May, 2019)

9. https://www.indiatoday.in/magazine/cover-story/story/19901015-storm-created-by-mandal-commission-poses-serious-threat-to-v.p.-singh-political-survival-813100-1990-10-15 (accessed on 22 May 2019); see also, L.K. Advani, *My Country My Life* (Rupa and Co, New Delhi, 2008), p. 379.

10. Author's conversations in 2018 with two participants in the conference.

11. http://www.business-standard.com/article/news-ians/jignesh-mevani-s-dalit-muslim-ekta-manch-begins-outreach-programme-118031800585_1.html (accessed on 22 May 2019).

12. Order of Justice Adarsh Kumar Goel in *Dr Subhash Kashinath Mahajan* vs *The State of Maharashtra* on 20 March 2018, https://indiankanoon.org/doc/108728085/ (accessed on 22 May 2019).

13. https://www.thehindu.com/news/national/many-dead-as-dalit-protests-over-sc-st-act-rock-north-india/article23418008.ece (accessed on 22 May 2019).

14. Author's conversation in 2017 with the former RSS leader of Gujarat.

15. https://economictimes.indiatimes.com/news/politics-and-nation/what-bjp-should-do-to-win-back-uttar-pradesh-in-upcoming-lok-sabha-polls/articleshow/65018058.cms?from=mdr (accessed on 22 May 2019).

16. https://timesofindia.indiatimes.com/india/manmohan-vaidya-stirs-quota-pot-ahead-of-polls/articleshow/56691197.cms (accessed on 5 August 2018).

17. https://indianexpress.com/article/india/rss-chief-mohan-bhagwat-caste-in-politics-because-voting-is-on-caste-5039615/ (accessed on 22 May 2019).

18. Author's conversation with the former pracharak in 2018.

19. http://www.archivesofrss.org/Speeches-and-articles.aspx (accessed on 22 May 2019).

20. Balasaheb Deoras, 'Social Equality and Hindu Consolidation', Vasant Vyakhyanmala speech delivered in Pune on 8 May 1974 http://www.archivesofrss.org/Speeches-and-articles.aspx (accessed on 22 May 2019).

21. Sanjeev Kelkar, *Lost Years of the RSS* (Sage Publications, New Delhi, 2011), p. 112.

22. Ramesh Patange, *Manu, Sangh and I*, digital version of English translation of the Marathi original *Me, Manu ani Sangh* available at http://www.hvk.org/specialreports/mms/ch2.html (accessed on 22 May 2019).

23. Ibid. All preceding discussion on Ramesh Patange quoted from and based on Ramesh Patange, *Manu, Sangh and I*.

24. I.P. Desai, *EPW*, http://www.epw.in/system/files/pdf/1981_16/18/special_articles_anti_reservation_agitation_and_structure.pdf (accessed on 22 May 2019).

25. Mohan Bhagwat press conference, Chandigarh, 5 December 2009 https://www.youtube.com/watch?v=-PjnpskOYXo (accessed on 13 July 2018).

26. https://samvada.org/2015/articles/bhagwat-interview-organiser/ (accessed on 2 June 2019).

27. https://www.news18.com/news/opinion/opinion-by-kn-govindacharya-why-ambedkar-came-very-close-to-rss-1716853.html (accessed on 15 September 2018).

28. Ramesh Patange, *Manu, Sangh and I*, digital version of English translation of the Marathi original *Me, Manu ani Sangh* available at http://www.hvk.org/specialreports/mms/ch3.html (accessed on 22 May 2019).

29. Author's conversation with the senior leader in 2018.

30. Ramesh Patange, *Manu, Sangh and I* digital version of English translation of the Marathi original *Me, Manu ani Sangh* available at http://www.hvk.org/specialreports/mms/ch4.html (accessed on 22 May 2019).

31. Ibid.

32. Ibid.

33. Ibid.

34. C.P. Bhishikar, *Shri Guruji: Pioneer of a New Era*, translated by Sudhakar Raje (Sahitya Sindhu Prakashana, Bangalore, 1999), p. 123.

35. *Dr Babasaheb Ambedkar: Speeches and Writings*, vol. 3, p. 38, https://www.mea.gov.in/books-writings-of-ambedkar.htm (accessed on 22 May 2019).

36. Valerian Rodrigues (ed.), *The Essential Writings of B.R. Ambedkar* ((Oxford University Press, Place, 2002), p. 228.

37. Ashis Nandy, *Time Warps: The Insistent Politics of Silent and Evasive Pasts* (Permanent Black, New Delhi, 2002), p. 143.

38. Arun Shourie, *Worshipping False Gods: Ambedkar, and the Facts which Have Been Erased* (HarperCollins *Publishers* India, Noida, 2012), p. 13.

39. Durga Nand Jha, *India Minority Report: An enquiry into India's minority policy and analysis of socio-economic status of Muslim community of India.* (Centre for Policy Analysis, Patna, 2018). P. 16

40. https://samvada.org/2017/news/drbhagwat-interview-organiser/ (accessed on 24 February 2019).

41. Note. https://main.sci.gov.in/judgments.

Chapter 9: Ashwamedha: Final Mile on the Political Horse

1. https://www.orwellfoundation.com/the-orwell-foundation/orwell/essays-and-other-works/notes-on-nationalism/

2. Author's conversations with a person who was present at the meeting.

3. http://rashtrasevikasamiti.org/encyc/2013/1/2/336826.aspx (Accessed on 11 June 2019).

4. Dr P.K. Jayasree in preface to *Women: The Champions of Change* (Bharatiya Stree Shakti National Conference, Nagpur, 2018), p. 7.

5. National seminar on Stree Shakti in Bhartiya Thought and Practice: Interrogating Epistemic Dichotomies, Socio-political Dialogues and Media Discourses by Group of Intellectuals and Academicians at Indian Institute of Mass Communications, organized by Prajna Pravah, 27–28 January 2018, New Delhi.

6. Author's interview with a senior Stree Shakti leader in 2018.

7. Author's conversation with a Delhi-based RSS insider.

8. http://rss.org//Encyc/2019/3/10/ABPS-resolution-2.html (Accessed on 13 June 2019).

9. R.Hari, *Mattuvin Chattangale* (Malayalam) (Kurukshetra Prakashan, Kochi, 2017), p. 9.

10. Author's visit to constituencies where pracharaks were in charge of election campaigns.

11. https://www.news18.com/news/politics/how-rss-is-running-a-silent-social-media-campaign-to-give-heft-to-bjp-in-rajasthan-2123669.html (accessed on 13 June 2019).

12. https://economictimes.indiatimes.com/news/politics-and-nation/rss-will-give-constructive-advice-to-govt-whenever-it-falters-mohan-

bhagwat/articleshow/69623929.cms?from=mdr (accessed on 13 June 2019).

13. http://www.india-seminar.com/2010/605/605_swapan_dasgupta. htm (accessed on 28 July 2019).

14. https://timesofindia.indiatimes.com/india/ram-mandir-should-be-built-at-the-earliest-mohan-bhagwat/articleshow/65875558.cms (accessed on 28 July 2019).

15. https://www.firstpost.com/politics/mohan-bhagwat-vijayadashami-2018-speech-full-text-rss-chief-discusses-2019-elections-ramjanmabhoomi-and-urban-naxals-5401441.html (accessed on 28 July 2019).

16. https://economictimes.indiatimes.com/news/politics-and-nation/revised-swayamsevak-sangh-hindu-consolidation-and-image-makeover-at-the-same-time/articleshow/66156987.cms (accessed on 28 July 2019).

17. https://economictimes.indiatimes.com/news/politics-and-nation/shiv-sena-vhp-intensify-call-for-ram-temple/articleshow/66788056. cms?from=mdr (accessed on 28 July 2019).

18. https://www.firstpost.com/india/vhp-organises-dharma-sabha-at-delhis-ramlila-maidan-in-second-major-agitation-for-ram-temple-in-recent-weeks-5700401.html (accessed on 28 July 2019).

19. Author's informal conversations with BJP leaders.

20. https://timesofindia.indiatimes.com/india/37-crpf-jawans-martyred-in-ied-blast-in-jks-pulwama/articleshow/67992189.cms (accessed on 29 July 2019).

21. https://www.reuters.com/article/us-india-kashmir/pakistan-releases-captured-indian-pilot-confrontation-cools-idUSKCN1QI40J (Accessed on 3 August 2019).

22. Based on author's conversations with RSS leaders.

A Note on Sources and References

The author has relied on information available in published books, papers, journals and newspaper articles for this book. These have been clearly identified. Some documents and internal publications of the Sangh Parivar have been exclusively accessed by the author and are not publicly available. Wherever the reference is available on the Internet, it has been preferred over print to provide the reader with easy access. For example, the works of Mahatma Gandhi, Vivekananda and Rabindranath Tagore are available in several Internet archives as well as books. The author has preferred to give the Internet link wherever it is readily available. It is likely that some links may have moved or got corrupted after the author had accessed them. Wherever possible, the last accessed date is given. Apart from published material, the author has also relied extensively on sources within the Sangh Parivar for information and perspectives. Some have spoken on record, but many have chosen to remain anonymous. They include high-ranking current and former office-bearers of the RSS, its affiliates as well as some organizations that are not recognized officially as affiliates (for example, the Muslim Rashtriya Manch) but are closely monitored by senior RSS officials. Occasionally, some have chosen to speak both on and off record. The author has known several people for a long time and has had multiple conversations with them. Hence there is no specific date or time that can be attributed to perspectives and information shared by them.

Acknowledgements

This book would not have seen the light of the day without scores of people who went out of their way to spare time and effort to help me. Several RSS leaders as well as others from parivar organizations helped with perspective, information and contacts. I won't be able to individually name all of them not only because they are quite a few in number but also because many of them prefer to remain anonymous. I'm deeply indebted to each one of them.

My sincere thanks to RSS sarsanghchalak Mohan Bhagwat; Kerala chief minister and CPI(M) leader Pinarayi Vijayan; spiritual guru Sri M; senior lawyer Chinmay Khaladkar, former editor of *Tarun Bharat*, Sudhir Pathak; former editor of Malayalam daily *Janmabhoomi*, P. Narayanan (he is also my uncle); senior journalist and IGNCA president Ram Bahadur Rai; ideologue K.N. Govindacharya; former ABVP leader and Khadi Board chairman, Mahesh Sharma; director of Deendayal Research Institute, Atul Jain; and the journalist (late) T.V.R. Shenoy.

Author of *Lost Years of the RSS*, Dr Sanjeev Kelkar, and former bhag sanghchalak and Savarkar devotee Dr Shreerang Godbole not only shared their experiences but also helped me find rare and often out-of-print books. They have my gratitude.

Nagpur-based businessman and self-styled spokesperson for the RSS, Dilip Deodhar, dug out for me fascinating nuggets about the organization's prominent personalities stored away in his elephantine memory. Journalists Abhishek Chaudhary, Anu Narayanan, Sharad Gupta and Sandeep Somanathan too helped me procure books, documents and information. I'll always remain in their debt.

My sincere thanks to Rajiv Tuli and Arun Anand for helping me with meetings and information.

I'm deeply indebted to Niranjan Rajadhyaksha, professor Prateek Raj, Jeanette Rodrigues, Indrajit Gupta, T.K. Arun, Ullekh N.P., Praveen Thampi, Amrith Lal, R. Prasad, Asif Anis Khan, Anilkumar, Ajoy V., Anil Nair, Ajay Chaudhary, Arun Ghosh and Sumedh Rajendran for reading my drafts and offering valuable suggestions and critical opinion.

I'm grateful to Bodhisatva Ganguli, editor of the *Economic Times*, for allowing me time off to write this book.

This book would be impossible without Premanka Goswami, commissioning editor at Penguin, Shantanu Ray Chaudhuri, and Parag Chitale, who designed the flaming hot cover. Thank you. A big thank you to Dinesh Krishnan for the author photo.

I'm thankful to my son Agastya whose persistent query 'how long is this book going to take?' kept me on the keyboard. The most important person I need to thank, however, is my wife Archana who not only gave me the confidence that I could write this book but also pulled me out of frequent writing lows. She not only offered constant encouragement but also translated Marathi texts, provided critical insights and read the drafts with a sharp eye.

Index

Scan QR code to access the
Penguin Random House India website